THE OLD FARMER'S ALMANAC

CALCULATED ON A NEW AND IMPROVED PLAN FOR THE YEAR OF OUR LORD

Being the 1st after Leap Year and (until July 4) 249th year of American Independence

FITTED FOR BOSTON AND THE NEW ENGLAND STATES, WITH SPECIAL CORRECTIONS AND CALCULATIONS TO ANSWER FOR ALL THE UNITED STATES.

Containing, besides the large number of Astronomical Calculations and the Farmer's Calendar for every month in the year, a variety of NEW, USEFUL, & ENTERTAINING MATTER.

ESTABLISHED IN 1792
BY ROBERT B. THOMAS (1766–1846)

Time is what keeps everything from happening at once.
–Ray Cummings, American writer (1887–1957), in *The Girl in the Golden Atom*

Cover design registered U.S. Trademark Office

Copyright © 2024 by Yankee Publishing Incorporated, a 100% Employee-Owned Company

ISSN 0078-4516

Library of Congress Card No. 56-29681

Cover illustration by Steven Noble • Original wood engraving (above) by Randy Miller

The Old Farmer's Almanac • Almanac.com
P.O. Box 520, Dublin, NH 03444 • 603-563-8111

CONTENTS

7

12

14

2025 TRENDS
Fun facts and forecasts defining today and describing tomorrow 6

56

74

28

78

TO THE LETTER

For 233 years, patrons of this trusted annual have let us know what's on their minds. When this publication began, feedback came by post—including over the fence post. Now we receive your emails, phone calls, and other "posts" (via Almanac.com and social media), as well as letters delivered to our post office box.

A secret to our continued success is listening to you. We know that you count on *this* Almanac to provide "correct, amusing, and useful" material, as founder Robert B. Thomas described our mission 200 years ago. We were just 33 years old back then—a mere seedling compared to the sprawling mother tree that we have since become.

As centuries pass, we note the steadfastness of readers' interests. Articles in 1825 concerned raising calves, growing asparagus, and keeping a kitchen garden ("highly important to a farmer, vegetables save meat and promote health"). A century later, we described the hazards of rearing chicks, how to thwart houseflies, and the seven best woods for fence posts. Our 2025 offerings seem reassuringly familiar: how to raise backyard chickens, grow plants from outside your hardiness zone, and garden in sync with the Moon.

We appreciate feedback and are delighted to hear from friends—4Hers, birders, gardeners, prisoners, Rotarians, and Scouts—to name just a few. Like Tom M. phoning from Asheville, North Carolina, searching for gas plant seeds; Bill M. from Dayton, Ohio, needing to know the best days to make sauerkraut; and fan Mary Frances G. from Culpeper, Virginia, who got her first Almanac upon joining NASA's Moon-mapping project in 1966. Thanks go to poet Heather S. from Saugus, Massachusetts, for reminding us to "Consider the Bees" and to Gordon S. from Calgary for his clever amusements.

Finally, a debt of gratitude goes to retiring managing editor Jack Burnett, who—for two decades—has worked to uphold the legacy of this publication. His writing, editing, and project management expertise will be missed, as will his wealth of knowledge about all things Almanac.

–C. C., June 2024

In hope that this year's Almanac is worthy of its predecessors, we close with the words of its founder . . .

It is by our works and not our words that we would be judged. These, we hope, will sustain us in the humble though proud station we have so long held in the name of

Your obedient servant,

celebrating
100 YEARS
OF LAND & LIFESTYLE
REAL ESTATE EXPERTISE

Since 1925, United Country has led the way in country and lifestyle real estate, specializing in land, farms, ranches, horse properties, certified organic properties, recreational land, country homes and the most sought-after lifestyle real estate across the nation.

DISCOVER WHAT A CENTURY'S WORTH OF EXPERTISE & KNOWLEDGE CAN DO FOR YOU

UnitedCountry.com | 800.999.1020

ON THE FARM

A new wave of young agriculture specialists will have a keen understanding of AI. An engineering degree may be just as relevant as a traditional degree from an agricultural college.

–Jo-Ann McArthur, president, Nourish Food Marketing, Toronto

ROBO-FARMS ON THE RISE

■ **Solar-powered robots** are now able to spray weeds with precision.

■ **$13.5 billion:** estimated value of the global agricultural robotics market

THE CHANGING FARMSCAPE
According to Bryce Berglund, content marketing specialist, National Land Realty, Greenville, S.C., farmland is . . .

■ **In transition.** "We're currently at the onset of one of the largest wealth transfers in the history of the U.S., with approximately $24 trillion in real estate assets slated to transfer over the next 20 years

or so," he states. "As the current population of farmland owners continues to age, it may be possible for aspiring landowners to acquire land in the coming years—assuming that they have the means to capitalize on these opportunities."

■ **Costing more.** Prices have increased across many parts of the country, especially in the Midwest.

FOLLOW US:

"LAND, OH!"

■ Average cost of an acre of Iowa farmland—low-quality: **$7,664;** medium-quality: **$11,075;** high-quality: **$14,296.**
–Iowa State University Land Value Survey

■ **58%** of Iowa farmland is rented.
–Center for Agricultural and Rural Development, Iowa State University

■ **$486:** average cost, per acre, to rent irrigated cropland in California; in Wyoming, **$86.50**

■ **$17,962:** average price per acre of Ontario farmland

BEE MY HONEY!
In the U.S. . . .
■ **2.67 million** domestic bee colonies are making honey.

■ **125 million** pounds of honey are produced annually.
–National Agricultural Statistics Service

In Alberta . . .
■ The number of

beekeepers (1,950) is increasing; some are sending bees to pollinate blueberries in British Columbia.

■ **$105.6 million:** annual value of Albertan honey

■ Scientists are using "bee vectoring" with specially designed hives to allow bees to transport trace amounts of naturally derived pest control powders to flowers (blueberries, apples, tomatoes).

FARMERS ARE . . .
■ adding hedgerows with native plants along field edges and roadways to attract beneficial insects.

■ controlling pests naturally by installing structures like songbird and barn owl nest boxes and raptor perches.
–Ashley Chesser, communications director, Wild Farm Alliance

(continued)

BY THE NUMBERS

1.9 million: farms and ranches in the U.S.

153,101: farms and ranches using renewable energy (e.g., solar panels)

116,617: farms selling directly to consumers

296,480: producers under the age of 35

58% of farms have at least one female decision-maker.

463: average acreage of farms and ranches
–USDA 2022 Census of Agriculture

- **making home deliveries.** Dairy farmers are delivering milk to homes and collecting glass bottles for reuse—with online ordering and flexible delivery times.

- **using "floatovoltaics"** (solar panels floating on water) in hydroponics.

- **teaming up with restaurants.** In Toronto, farmers are growing heirloom

crops for sale to local chefs, who then create dishes featuring them.

- **repairing their own tractors.** Policymakers are introducing legislation requiring manufacturers to make available necessary parts and software.

CALL ME . . . "FARMER"!

By far, most people in the U.S. who farm want to be described as a "farmer," with much smaller percentages preferring the terms "farm operator," "producer," or "grower."

–Iowa Farm and Rural Life Poll

IN THE GARDEN

Many people are looking for vegetables and herbs that they can grow in smaller spaces. There is a significant increase in the popularity of dwarf plants.

–Dave Whitinger, executive director,
National Gardening Association

BUZZWORD
Edimentals: plants that are both edible and ornamental

WHERE DO OUR GARDENERS GROW?

75%: in yard
30%: on balcony
21%: indoors
2%: in community garden
–Statistics Canada

WHAT DO OUR GARDENS GROW?

76%: flowers
55%: vegetables
50%: houseplants
30%: fruit trees
–Axiom Gardening Survey

(continued)

WORKING HERBS

Gardeners are interested in growing an assortment of herbs that have culinary, medicinal, and decorative uses.

–Ashleigh Smith, managing editor, True Leaf Market

LEMON BALM

■ **In-demand herbs:** calendula, chamomile, holy basil, lemon balm, yarrow

TINY AND TASTY

There is increased demand for microgreens, as people embrace a lifestyle that values freshness, nutrition, and culinary delight.

–Carrie Spoonemore, Park Seed

■ 'Calabrese' broccoli is easy to grow in soil or hydroponically.

■ 'Spicy Salad Mix' microgreens are a visual stunner, with green hues and purple/red highlights.

New on the scene:
■ 'Gondwana Moon' dwarf tomato, with dark skin that produces high levels of antioxidants

NEW BITES

In development . . .
■ Calabaza pumpkin varieties to grow in the southeastern U.S.

■ strawberries with a vanilla flavor

Available now . . .
■ 'Yellow Submarine', a small, oblong, yellow-flesh tomato that resists cracking on the vine

'YELLOW SUBMARINE'

ON-TREND PLANTS ARE . . .

■ **heat-tolerant.** 'Bronze Beauty' cleyera offers multihue foliage.

■ **water-thrifty.** "Gardeners are embracing aesthetically pleasing, low-water plants in cool hues of purples and blues," reports Kenny Silveira, West

Conservatory manager at Pennsylvania's Longwood Gardens.

Some appealing examples: echeveria; euphorbia; lavender; sedum; ZZ plant *(Zamioculcas zamiifolia)*; 'Platinum Beauty' lomandra, with draping, grasslike foliage that sways in the breeze

BOOMING BLOOMING

Gardeners are opting for a mix of perennials and annuals to have flowers blooming at any given time in early spring and late fall.

–Miles Dakin, director, Bee Friendly Farming, Pollinator Partnership

■ **For early flowers:** 'Caliburst Yellow' is a bright yellow petchoa that is great for mixed containers, with a 9-hour day length response for flowering; blooms in early spring in cold-growing conditions. *(continued)*

BUZZWORD
Interiorscaping: designing our homes to include houseplants and/or edible indoor gardens

HOW DOES YOUR GARDEN GROW?

VISIT SIMPLYGRO.COM FOR THE BEST IN GARDENING

'SILVER SWIRL' CENTAUREA

■ **For a moonlight garden:** 'Silver Swirl' centaurea is drought-tolerant, with wavy leaf edges on silver-white foliage to brighten up front-of-the-border plantings even at nighttime.

'PASSIONFRUIT' LANTANA

■ **For flowers until frost:** 'Passionfruit' trailing lantana produces a huge number of multicolor blooms and never cycles out of flower.

■ **To provide food and shelter for pollinators** when they need it most (not just in the peak season), we're planting snowdrops, hellebores, and crocuses for the early season and turtlehead, asters, and coreopsis for the late one.
–Julie Weisenhorn, educator, University of Minnesota Extension Horticulture

CITY SMARTS

■ Urban gardeners are minimizing tilling, not leaving bare soil, using plant diversity to build resilience, creating microclimates, managing stormwater runoff, and conserving water.
–Michael Levenston, City Farmer Society, Vancouver

TREE SIZE MATTERS

■ Gardeners are choosing shorter, columnar trees to better fit smaller properties, to frame an entrance, or to add vertical interest.

■ First Edition series 'Standing Ovation' serviceberry offers showy white flowers and edible fruit in early summer.

STANDING OVATION SERVICEBERRY

■ 'Kindred Spirit' and 'Regal Prince' are hybrid oaks with compact foliage that are suitable for sites with space constraints.
–Spencer Campbell, plant clinic manager, The Morton Arboretum, Lisle, Ill.

FAST FOOD

■ New gardeners are starting quick-maturing plants from seed in order to harvest homegrown vegetables within a month or two.
–Campbell

'QUICK SNACK' CUCUMBER

■ **Indoors:** 'Quick Snack' cucumber produces handfuls of small, crisp, sweet cucumbers over a few weeks; it can be grown inside near a sunny window for handy, healthy addition to a sandwich or a salad.

■ **In containers:** Sweet, early-maturing, and highly productive,

FOLLOW US: 🅿 f 📷

'Pepper Prism' is perfect for salads or being stuffed.

SHARING IS CARING

■ To reduce food waste—as well as to meet the neighbors—folks are placing excess homegrown produce in front of their home, posting their location on a digital map, and waiting for people to come to pick it up.

PRETTY GOOD EATING

■ 'Candle Fire' okra,

'ANTARES' FENNEL

'Warrior' onion, and 'Antares' fennel, along with herbs like purple basil and culinary sage, are beautiful as well as consumable.
–Jason Reeves, research horticulturist and curator of UT Gardens, Jackson, Tenn.

Vegetable bed hero:
■ 'Love Gourmansun Sunrise' beefsteak

tomato, in red/orange/yellow—a feast for the eyes as well as the palate.

HOUSEPLANTS ARE THRIVING . . .

■ **in low light:** "There are more and more low-light plants on the market today, and at affordable prices."
–Weisenhorn

■ **as partitions,** with a strategic row of hanging plants of varying lengths creating a living curtain effect.
–Weisenhorn

GOOD EATS

Instead of traditional menus, holographic images of food items will be projected onto tables, allowing diners to view 3-D representations of a dish before ordering.
–Sylvain Charlebois, Ph.D., director, Agri-Food Analytics Lab, Dalhousie University, Halifax, N.S.

DATA-DRIVEN DINING

■ Health food stores will offer genetic testing, uploaded to a wearable device, so that shoppers can be guided to foods best suited to their genetic makeup.

■ Drive-throughs will have voice recognition that triggers suggestions based on previous orders, time of day, and weather.

■ Grocery stores are using AI to determine the risk of an item

expiring before being sold, marking down items accordingly, and alerting people, via apps, about food that's about to expire. Bargain-shoppers can then pick it up in-store at a discount.

–Nourish: The 2024 Trend Report

PEOPLE ARE TALKING ABOUT . . .

■ virtual-reality dining experiences, with digitally crafted meals to stimulate taste buds.

■ vacations centered on food, with chefs serving as tour guides.

BY THE NUMBERS

6:19 P.M.: most popular dinnertime in the U.S.

68% of discarded food is still edible.

21% of restaurant diners admit to splitting entrées to save money.

COMING SOON

■ Restaurants and food companies will offer ant-infused chocolates, cricket flour, and grasshopper burgers.

■ Algae will be used in pasta and spirulina-infused beverages (expect to see green-color dishes on menus).

–Charlebois

OUR ANIMAL FRIENDS

The French bulldog has been steadily rising in popularity— and has finally eclipsed the Labrador retriever. The love for Frenchies shows no signs of stopping, as their adaptability, portability, and friendly disposition make them irresistible.

–Brandi Munden, vice president, public relations & communications, American Kennel Club

(continued)

FOLLOW US: 🅟 f 📷

BY THE NUMBERS

50% of pet owners prefer in-person shopping for pet supplies.

31% of pet owners plan to curtail purchases to save money.

12.7 million: small pets living in U.S. households (including 6 million reptiles)
–American Pet Products Association National Pet Owners Survey

62% of Americans own a pet.

35% own multiple pets.

51% of pet owners say that pets are as much a part of the family as a human member.
–Pew Research Center

4,849,540: cats and dogs with health insurance in the U.S.; in Canada, **508,730**
–North American Pet Health Insurance Association's State of the Industry Report, 2023

38% of pet owners check on pets with a camera or device when away.

SMALL PETS, BIG LUXURIES

- Bearded dragons are reclining on faux leather couches.

- Guinea pigs are being carried about in slings and sleeping in bunk beds.

PETS' NO. 1 OFFENSES

By dogs: Got into the trash!

By cats: Scratched the furniture!
–Ring Pet Behavior Survey

PEOPLE ARE BARKING ABOUT . . .

- birthday or adoption anniversary parties for dogs, with other animals in attendance

- pet psychics to tell us if our pets are happy

- closets or the empty space underneath staircases converted into nooks for dogs

- showers for dogs in laundry rooms

BUZZWORD
Cat-ios: screened-in outdoor spaces that enable indoor cats to go outside

TOP TECH FOR PETS

AI will continue to grow and become a fixture in pet care.
–Chris Nash, executive director, Pet Food Association of Canada

- **AI-powered robots** are now able to learn an animal's behavior and try to calm it down if necessary, as well as dispense treats.

- **Smart dog collars** can track movements, sleep, heart rate, appetite, and bark.

- **Pet doors** are being programmed to open only for specific pets (linked to a chip on the animal's collar).

FANCY FEASTS

- More and more consumers will be buying freeze-dried and raw pet food products. Cultivated meat will continue to grow as a sustainable

FOLLOW US: 🅿 f 📷

Here's WHY Normal Septic Bacteria & Enzyme Additives Don't Work to Clean Your Septic System

You already know that your septic system needs bacteria to work BUT...

There's a darn good chance...

...that the septic additive you've been flushing into your septic tank doesn't have *nearly enough* bacteria to make a difference in cleaning your system (not even close). Sure, the package says there are billions of bacteria in each packet or scoop but there are *trillions* (with a "t") of bacteria in your system. **That packet is a drop in the proverbial bucket -- like spitting on a fire.** It doesn't hurt anything but it doesn't *help* either.

"The Gallon Analogy": Imagine you filter all the bacteria out of your system and you get one gallon of pure bacteria -- a milk jug of bacteria.

Now imagine that packet or scoop of bacteria additive next to that jug. It's a *tiny fraction* of that gallon. It's not enough to make a difference but it's what the septic industry has always said to do.

Fortunately for you, Accelerator by Dr. Pooper® solves this issue! It's a "bio-accelerator" that was developed for cleaning municipal wastewater. It works by multiplying the reproduction of bacteria by up to 40 times! **So that 1-gallon jug becomes 40 gallons of bacteria -- plenty to eat organic solids fast and clean your system.** This innovation is changing the industry and can save you big money. Plus, it's easy. Just flush a tablet.

Clears Clogs, Sludge, and Scum in Your Septic Tank & Drain Field to Get it Flowing & Flushing Smoothly!

Accelerator
Drain Field Cleaner
by Dr. Pooper

Commercial-Strength Septic System Cleaner

Easy to Use! Just Flush a Tablet!

- Clears Tanks & Drain Fields
- Cleans Tough Organic Clogs
- Eliminates Odors
- Gets Your Tank & Drain Field Flowing Smoothly Again
- Amazing Stay-Clean Maintenance

It's **NOT** just another bacteria or enzyme. It's a **BIO-ACCELERATOR**, based on our commercial products for clearing organic sludge, clogs, and odors in municipal wastewater treatment and livestock lagoons. Discover how it works at DoctorPooper.com.

✔ Totally Safe & Non-toxic
✔ Safe For Old Systems
✔ Aerobic & Anaerobic Systems
✔ Easy to Use: Just Flush a Tablet!
✔ Rejuvenates Failing Drain Fields

⭐⭐⭐⭐⭐ *Real Customer Testimonials*

"Our septic system is 27 years old, and had not been pumped in many, many, many years. We were amazed by these Dr. Pooper products! Oh my...NO PUMPING WAS NECESSARY, and the flushing capability, in both of our toilets, has increased by 75%. Thank you, Dr. Pooper!!!" -- Bill Bennet, Homeowner

"I can complete laundry & take showers on the same day now. No water in yard. YEAH!" -- Jessica Bowen, Homeowner

"Was skeptical at first as our septic system is 53 years old, has a huge 1500 gallon tank and 4 leech lines, drains very slowly, not now, drains good, and still have some more to add, highly recommended." -- Steven Williams

"I can't believe it. We were about to order the $468 pump service and canceled it. It was full of built-up [stuff]. We poured the Accelerator in the toilet and BOOM! A week later no more problems. Flowin' smooth! This stuff is crazy." -- Robert Voss

100% Money-Back Guarantee
No Risk. Accelerator by Dr Pooper® is Guaranteed to Work or Your Money Back.

Buy today at DoctorPooper.com

Save 10% with coupon code ALMANAC

ingredient source, and product lines using this will increase.
–Nash

THE VET IS IN

■ Periodontal disease—which is common in pets (especially smaller ones)—can now be detected earlier. A new 10-second test administered to awake dogs and cats determines the best timing for a dental cleaning.

■ Until recently, the treatment of feline diabetes required daily insulin injections. Fortunately, new drugs in the form of daily pills or liquid can now be used to manage blood sugar levels.
–Kristen Levine, publisher, Pet Living

BUZZWORDS
Yappy hours: social events for dogs (with treats, sprinklers or small pools, etc.)

AROUND THE HOUSE

Our homes are becoming personal sanctuaries that also reflect our commitment to the environment.
–Carolyn Wilbrink, designer, HGTV Canada

COLORING LOOK

■ **Interiors:** warm neutrals (e.g., beiges, creamy off-whites, rich browns) throughout the home.
–Houzz

■ **Exteriors:** darker neutral colors (e.g., midnight blue, charcoal gray); nature-inspired hues (greens, taupe, browns, creams)

■ People are painting an entire room (ceiling, trim, walls) one color.

BUYERS' RECOURSE

■ Home buyers, particularly first-time purchasers, are actively exploring alternative forms of housing and financing, in response to the persistent challenge of affordability.
–Nick Bailey, president & CEO, RE/MAX

Buyers are considering:
■ nontraditional financing options (borrowing from friends and family, purchasing with a

FOLLOW US:

down payment of less than 20%, paying with all cash).

- co-ownership with friends or family
- fixer-uppers, foreclosures, and tiny homes
- a "super commute" (buying homes 2 or more hours from where they work)

–RE/MAX Consumer Pulse Survey, 2024

- **14%** of home buyers purchased a multi-generational home in 2023.

–National Association of Realtors 2023 Home Buyers and Sellers Generational Trends Report

BY THE NUMBERS

66% of U.S. adults are homeowners.

27% of homeowners live in a community governed by a homeowners' association

28% of households are single-person.

2,374: average square footage of a new single-family home

HOME ON THE CHANGE

Look for . . .

- **"zero waste" décor** (e.g., wall coverings and tiles made from corncobs)
- **3-D–printed furniture**—lamps, tables, chairs

- **augmented-reality walls** (e.g., wallpaper that changes color; walls that show the occupant's favorite images or artwork)

–Ana Cummings, president, Alberta chapter, Decorators and Designers Association of Canada

- **"snug rooms"**—small sitting areas specifically for reading or conversation that have hidden or no screens.

ECO CHAMBERS

- We're choosing classic leather sofas; durable wood pieces made of oak, walnut, or mahogany; and

sofas and chairs made of high-performance, stain-resistant fabrics.

–Kerrie Kelly, fellow, American Society of Interior Designers

- People are moving away from "fast furniture" and prioritizing items that promise longevity, in terms of both style and durability.

AMENITIES IN DEMAND

- pickleball courts
- saunas in basements
- boxing gyms

TOP-RETURNING REMODELING INVESTMENTS

1. HVAC conversion
2. garage door replacement
3. manufactured stone veneer
4. entry-door replacement
5. vinyl siding replacement

–Remodeling Magazine's 2023 Cost vs. Value Report

(continued)

CULTURE

Shared "neighborhood" space—gardens, pools, and work spaces—is becoming more popular.

–Kelly DeVore, professor, interior architecture and design, Columbus (OH) College of Art & Design

TECH-ING ACCOUNT

- **24:** electronic products in the average home

- **$382:** amount families could save annually by repairing electronic products instead of buying new ones

–"Repair Saves Families Big," U.S. PIRG Education Fund 2023 report

- Device that makes us the most happy: **game console**

- Device that makes us least happy: **smart refrigerator**

KEEPING UP APPEARANCES

People are getting . . .

- casual clothing (T-shirts, shorts, jeans, swim trunks) professionally tailored.

- tattoos of bar codes that play songs when scanned.

KINDNESS PAYS

- **17%** of respondents have paid someone else's bill.

- **19%** of American flyers have given up their seat to someone else during the previous 3 months.

- Top places where U.S. adults see acts of kindness:
1. grocery stores
2. places of worship
3. at home
4. in their neighborhood

–American Psychiatric Association's Healthy Minds Poll

PEOPLE ARE TALKING ABOUT . . .

- couples paying for hawks or falcons to deliver their rings at wedding ceremonies.

- repurposing historic metal truss bridges as pedestrian or bike bridges or relocating them to private residences for preservation.

(continued)

BY THE NUMBERS

48% of Americans have a passport.

66% of U.S. consumers don't consider themselves tech-savvy.

43% of people surveyed said that middle-seat passengers are entitled to both armrests.

FOLLOW US:

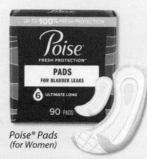

21

MONEY MATTERS

Consumers are buying experiences instead of more stuff—and are buying less stuff overall—reflecting an emerging minimalist mindset.

–Michael Norton, Harvard Business School, coauthor,
Happy Money: The Science of Smarter Spending
(Simon & Schuster, 2013)

MONEY MOVES
■ Folks are taking concrete steps to meet financial goals. "People are budgeting for travel, using their tax-sheltered accounts, moving to more affordable communities, looking at variable mortgage rates, focusing on job security, and comparison-shopping for financial products," says Lisa Hannam, executive editor, *MoneySense*.

PEOPLE ARE TALKING ABOUT . . .
■ **"no spend" months,** when they spend only on essentials and cut out all luxuries.

■ **the top states in which to retire** (based on affordability, well-being, health care, weather, low crime):
1. Iowa
2. Delaware
3. West Virginia
4. Missouri
5. Mississippi
–Bankrate

(continued)

BY THE NUMBERS
81% of U.S. workers think that a 4-day workweek would be more productive.

$187: average value of unused gift cards, vouchers, or store credit held by an American

18% of U.S. adults tip less than the suggested amount or not at all when presented with a pre-entered tip screen.

$810: average monthly earnings from a "side hustle"
–Bankrate

13 hours: average time a U.S. adult spends doing taxes

$1,967: median monthly rent paid in the U.S.

$731: average annual amount that U.S. families spend per child for after-school activities

Train at home to

Work at Home

Be a Medical Coding & Billing Specialist

WORK AT HOME!

✓ Be home for your family
✓ Be your own boss
✓ Choose your own hours

SAVE MONEY!

✓ No day care, commute, or office wardrobe/lunches
✓ Possible tax breaks
✓ Tuition discount for eligible military and their spouses
✓ Military education benefits & MyCAA approved

Train at home in as little as 5 months to earn up to $48,780 a year!*

Now you can train in the comfort of your own home to work in a medical office, or from home as your experience and skills increase.

Make great money...up to $48,780 a year with experience! It's no secret, healthcare providers need Medical Coding & Billing Specialists. In fact, the U.S. Department of Labor projects 8% growth by 2032, for specialists doing coding and billing.

10 Years	
5 Years	**8%**
	Increase
	In
Now	**Demand!'**

No previous medical experience required. Compare the money you can make!

Coders earn great money because they make a lot of money for the people they work for. Entering the correct codes on medical claims can mean the difference in thousands of dollars in profits for doctors, hospitals and clinics. Since each and every medical procedure must be coded and billed, there's plenty of work available for well-trained Medical Coding & Billing Specialists.

Get FREE Facts. Contact Us Today!

U.S. Career Institute®
2001 Lowe St., Dept. FMAB2A94
Fort Collins, CO 80525

1-800-388-8765
Dept. FMAB2A94
www.uscieducation.com/FMA94

SENT FREE!

YES! Rush me my free Medical Coding & Billing information package.

Name _____ Age _____

Address _____ Apt _____

City, State, Zip _____

E-mail _____ Phone _____

✳DEAC
DISTANCE EDUCATION ACCREDITING COMMISSION

DEAC Accredited • Affordable • Approved
Celebrating over 40 years of education excellence!

CB010

BBB
ACCREDITED BUSINESS
A+ Rating

*W/experience, https://www.bls.gov/ooh/healthcare/medical-records-and-health-information-technicians.htm, 4/25/24

COMING SOON

- We'll be paying more often through our watches, devices, and even voices.

- Full-time workers will increasingly have side hustles, as technology will enable them to manage these gigs more seamlessly.

- As many services become digitized and AI-powered, working with a human will be marketed as premium—like "hand-crafted" products are today.

–Jason Feifer, editor in chief, Entrepreneur *magazine*

BETTER TO GIVE

- **Consumers experience less "pain of payment"** (a negative psychological feeling that stems from spending money) when buying gifts for others vs. products for themselves.

–Julian Givi, Ph.D., John Chambers College of Business and Economics, West Virginia University, Morgantown, W.Va.

TO OUR HEALTH

From habit-tracking to the real-time monitoring of our blood sugars and vital signs, health tech will be in the palm of our hands—or even affixed to our skin.

–Uma Naidoo, M.D., author, Calm Your Mind With Food
(Little, Brown Spark, 2023)

HEALTHCARE HELPERS

- **smart garments** that measure the wearer's blood sugar levels through sweat and produce their own electricity from the wearer's walking motion

- **robotic boots** to help improve balance

- **toilet attachments** to monitor our vitamin C levels

- **backpacks** containing portable systems that can produce and read X-rays

BRAIN GAINS

- Fragrant essential oils (e.g., rose, orange, lemon, peppermint) diffused while older adults sleep have been shown to boost cognitive performance.

–University of California–Irvine

- Older adults who read stories for 90 minutes a day over 8 weeks were found to have stronger memory skills than older volunteers who had just done puzzles.

–Beckman Institute

(continued)

■Older adult volunteers (average age: 74) had better cognitive function, and those who volunteered several times a week had the highest levels of executive functioning.
–University of California–Davis

■Men who regularly participate in recreational angling have better mental health—and the more often they fished, the better became their well-being.
–Anglia Ruskin University, UK

BEHAVE YOURSELF!

■People increasingly recognize that most chronic diseases are driven by lifestyle behaviors, not genetics, and are committed to replacing unhealthy behaviors with healthy ones.
–Beth Frates, M.D., Harvard Medical School, Boston, Mass.

BY THE NUMBERS

1,000: additional steps taken by people on days when they drank coffee

30 minutes: extra sleep for folks after days when they didn't drink coffee (vs. drank as much as desired)

10 minutes: extra time spent as a family at the dinner table that results in kids eating another serving of vegetables or fruit

2.5 years: average difference in biological age between people who live near green spaces and those who don't.
–Northwestern University Feinberg School of Medicine

GUT FEELINGS

■There is growing awareness that the health of our gut and that of our body and mind are inextricably intertwined. As the role of the gut microbiome in physical and mental health is better understood, we will see reduced stigma attached to mental illness.
–Naidoo

SWEETER DREAMS

■**snore score: 45%** of adults snore occasionally; **25%**, regularly.

■**in development:** mattresses that sense trouble in falling asleep and then send a signal to external speakers to play soothing sounds (e.g., rain or crashing waves) coordinated with massage motors

■Hotels are offering soundproof walls, mattresses that regulate temperature, and totally dark rooms.

■Wearing socks to bed helps to more quickly lower core body temperature, resulting in falling asleep faster and staying asleep longer.

FOLLOW US: 🅿 f 📷

BUZZWORD
Feedforward: employer comments to workers focused on their potential

AT WORK

The outdoor boom will extend all the way to the outdoor home office. People will work from balconies, in gardens—or even in the woods.
–WGSN

HOT JOBS

■ **"Empty-nest coaches"** are giving advice to parents whose offspring have left for college.

■ **Urban farmers** are transforming unused spaces into farms, maintaining hydroponic indoor farms, and installing farms on city rooftops.

■ **Botanists** are giving lectures on how to combat "plant blindness" (the inability to notice plants in our everyday lives).

■ **"Farm-sitters"** care for animals, machinery, and crops when the owner of a small or hobby farm (any farm without full-time staff) is away or working off-farm.

JOB GROWTH

■ Skills-based hiring is doing away with the "paper ceiling" requiring a college degree for many jobs.

■ Personalized benefit plans allow employees to pick and choose from an array of benefits.

■ "Grandternity leave" serves as a way to retain older workers who want to spend time with newborn grandchildren. ■

A GARDENER'S GUIDE TO
CLIMATE TRICKERY

BY TOVAH MARTIN

Admit it. You lust after edible figs. Although you live in a northern clime—where a fig's hardiness is iffy (at best)—in your heart, you want to savor a sweet, chewy fruit harvested from a tree in your backyard. Or maybe you live in the South and hanker to grow daffodils—even though they need 12 to 16 weeks of temperatures in the lower 40s. Whether you are coveting a palm in New Hampshire or jonesing in Georgia for a lilac, you may find the suggestions here helpful in turning a fleeting, cheating thought into a full-fledged con job. These solutions aren't bulletproof, but they're worth a try when you're surrounded by 3 feet of snow and dreaming of palms. *(continued)*

NORTHERN CHEATERS: SOME LIKE IT WARM

WITH SOME SAVVY TRICKS, YOU CAN PUSH *CAMELLIA JAPONICA* TO FLOURISH OUTDOORS.

CAMELLIAS

It's possible to host camellias in Connecticut—or equally chilly states. Shiny green–leaf camellia trees (which are normally goners when the thermometer drops below 10°F) and their divine, frilly, rose-impersonating flowers can survive in the North, no greenhouse needed. With some savvy tricks and careful siting, you can push *Camellia japonica,* with its ginormous blossoms, to flourish outdoors.

The trick is to shelter your coveted camellia from light. When the winter sun hits its leaves (and, yes, the foliage holds on to camellia branches throughout the year), they think that they're getting warm because toasty rays are beating down, they open their pores, and they get thirsty—but, meanwhile, the ground is frozen. No drinks are possible, the leaves wither, and it's curtains for your camellia. Give them winter shade and protection from brutal winds, and you stand a chance of success. (This is also a good trick for other questionably hardy broadleaf evergreens, such as *Aucuba japonica.*)

(continued)

IF YOU WANT YOUR FIG TO SURVIVE AND BEAR ITS GOODIES, IT SHOULD BE WINTERED INDOORS.

'CHICAGO HARDY'

EDIBLE FIGS

The fact that figs are not reliably hardy in below-freezing temps frustrates many wishful gardeners. Sharing secrets for success has reached almost cultlike proliferation. Although no two gardeners can agree on the hardiest figs, they do agree that if you want your fig to survive and bear its goodies, it should be wintered indoors. Their broad, glovelike leaves of Eden fame drop, leaving the stems naked over winter—so pulling a potted plant into the garage is a viable solution.

We recommend starting with a *Ficus carica* that can take some freezing: 'Chicago Hardy' is readily available, followed by 'Brown Turkey'. Other contenders include the more obscure 'Saint Martin', 'Little Ruby', and 'Ronde de Bordeaux'. Most experts agree that 10°F is about as low as an unprotected hardy fig can safely withstand. They have the best chance of squeaking through winter if close to the foundation of a heated building.

Fig afficionados in colder regions are willing to go into contortions.Well, actually, it's the fig that gets twisted when landscape, or earth, staples (long, narrow, C-shape, metal clips) are used to pin bent over branches along the ground, after which they are covered with a generous layer of wood chips. Encircle larger, more mature figs in chicken wire, insulating the inside with shredded leaves and wrapping the whole shebang in layers of tarps or tar paper. Then pray.

(continued)

Photo: Brandon Friend-Solis/Monrovia

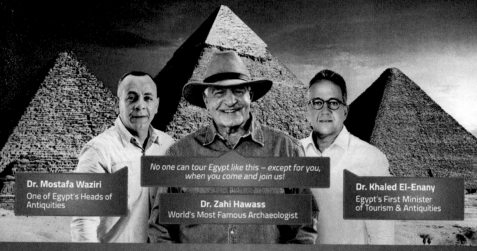

PALMS

If causing double takes is your goal, flaunting a palm tree in a cold region is going to cause lots of driversby to slam on the brakes. Your little secret (we won't tell a soul!) is that the needle palm *(Rhapidophyllum hystrix)* is hardy to Zone 6. In fact, this evergreen has been known to survive unprotected as far north as parts of New York. The rest of the palms—think the saw palmetto, windmill, sago—can barely eke by in Zone 7. The needle palm has the signature fanlike leaves that we love in a palm, but it never boasts those towering naked trunks that tropical palms develop. However, it is salt-tolerant for coastal regions and happy in shade or sun.

A few caveats should help you to fool the neighborhood into thinking that they're in the tropics: When your needle palm is a toddler, grow it as a potted plant, bringing it indoors during the winter. Its defense against cold is the fiber on its mature stems, so let your plant age enough to develop this fiber before putting it through the freeze cycle. Mulch it generously when you plant it outside . . . and then have fun watching the rubberneckers.

(continued)

THE NEEDLE PALM HAS BEEN KNOWN TO SURVIVE UNPROTECTED AS FAR NORTH AS PARTS OF NEW YORK.

Photo: Brookgreen Gardens

SOUTHERN CHEATERS:
SPRING FLOWERS WITHOUT THE CHILL CYCLE

When you flew south, nobody told you that your favorite spring performers—
long-awaited daffodils and lilacs—need a certain number of subfreezing
days to burst into blossom. The good news is that you can have your spring
magic, but you'll need to search out the right performers.

YOU DON'T HAVE TO FORFEIT NARCISSUSES TO DWELL WHERE SNOW IS NOT A CONSTANT THREAT.

'BABY BOOMER'

DAFFODILS

Who can blame you for missing daffodils? You don't have to forfeit narcissuses to dwell where snow is not a constant threat. Most narcissuses (aka daffodils) need the cold spells that northern climates deliver, but a few varieties are willing to perform without chilling out. Select jonquils *(Narcissus jonquilla),* and you'll get your shot of cheerful yellow blossoms plus a generous dose of heavenly perfume. Southern Florida might be iffy, but this is worth a try from Zone 8b north. You can also try the *N. tazetta* group, which boasts many blooms of open-face flowers in nosegay-like clusters in the full range of colors with fragrances that will make you swoon. Want the best of all worlds? Plant *N.* 'Baby Boomer'. This bright yellow sweetie is what happened when a tazetta married a jonquil. Incidentally, you can always stash a few pots of planted daffodils in the refrigerator for 13 to 15 weeks to imitate a real winter.

Photo: John Scheepers, Inc.

LILACS

Beyond those big, fat, cotton candy–like bunches of blossoms that have launched lilacs into the stratosphere of fame, their swoon-worthy scent is the stuff of dreams. The whole package is so seductive that lilacs are the primary reason that transplanted northerners have second thoughts after heading south to make their homes. Sweet, ethereal, with a hint of baby powder, this fragrance is all things heady. And the colors! Lavender, creamy white, pink, blue, and every hue in between.

Prompting this nirvana for your senses requires some cold winter weather. Although lilacs probably aren't in your cards in southern California and the Deep South, *Syringa vulgaris* 'Lavender Lady' has been lauded as a warm weather solution in Zone 9. In addition, hybrids of the Manchurian lilac, *S. pubescens* ssp. *patula* (e.g., 'Miss Kim') are rumored to flower in southern gardens, although they're rated as Zones 3 to 8. But the trick to making lilacs sublime has to do not only with temperature. They also prefer alkaline soil, and they're not drought-resistant. Don't try the shade trick to keep them cool, as they are unapologetic Sun worshippers.

(continued)

LILACS' SWOON-WORTHY SCENT IS THE STUFF OF DREAMS.

'MISS KIM'

Photo: Doreen Wynja/Monrovia

RUMOR HAS IT THAT TREE PEONIES WILL PERFORM AS FAR SOUTH AS NORTHERN FLORIDA!

PEONIES

Sometimes getting what you want is just a matter of tweaking your needs. Those herbaceous peonies that you remember from the North are probably beyond your grasp in the South, as you just can't furnish the 6 weeks below 40° to 45°F that they demand in order to perform. Big, flouncy, tree peonies *(Paeonia suffruticosa),* with their hubba-hubba oversize flowers, are a definite option that should even overcompensate for any lingering peony lust that you brought south with you. Rumor has it that tree peonies will perform as far south as northern Florida! Like their name suggests, tree peonies grow on deciduous woody stems that don't disappear in the North or South. In spring, they pop into Frisbee-size flowers in a glorious array of colors. Give them partial shade rather than baking sun, especially in the South; well-draining soil is a must.

So, zonal deniers . . . take heart! Or better yet, take your cheatin' heart! As some gutsy gardeners know, cheating is what it's all about. ∎

Connecticut-based **Tovah Martin** is a frequent gardening contributor to Almanac publications. To learn more and check out her books, go to TovahMartin.com.

The
TORTOISE
and the
TOMATO

... plus other little-known
tales from your favorite veggie's
surprising past

BY WILLIAM ALEXANDER
ILLUSTRATIONS BY TIM ROBINSON

During its short history in
North America, no vegetable
has been more vilified, prized,
or mythologized than the tomato,
which—if truth be told—got off to
a pretty shaky start.

Although tomatoes had been
eaten in a few Southern households
(Thomas Jefferson served them at
Monticello), they were generally
despised north of the Mason–Dixon
Line (and even thought poisonous by
some folks). *The Horticulturalist* dis-
missed them as "odious and repelling-
smelling berries." In 1834, the *Boston
Courier* called them "the mere fungus
of an offensive plant."

Yet, somewhat miraculously, by
1840 many people had become abso-
lutely mad about tomatoes. A London
journalist staying at a Madison, Wisconsin, hotel complained that "tomato
was the word—the theme—the song
from morning till night," including

IN THIS WORLD OF UNCERTAINTY AND WOE, ONE THING REMAINS
UNCHANGED: FRESH, CANNED, PURÉED, DRIED, SALTED,
SLICED, AND SERVED WITH SUGAR AND CREAM, OR PRESSED
INTO JUICE, THE TOMATO IS RELIABLE, FRIENDLY, AND
DELICIOUS. WE WOULD BE NOTHING WITHOUT IT.
—LAURIE COLWIN, AMERICAN FOOD WRITER (1944-92)

breakfast, when his fellow diners dressed them with sugar, molasses, or mustard. "I essayed to follow suit," the newspaperman wrote, "and was very near refunding the rest of my breakfast upon the table." So, how did the tomato go from reviled to revered in just a decade?

The tomato's fortunes began to rise in 1834 when an itinerant Ohio physician named John Cook Bennett brought the vegetable to national prominence in the United States after publishing a lecture given to his medical students that had made wild health claims for the tomato, including that it could prevent cholera, which had arrived in America just 2 years earlier. Reprinted in hundreds of newspapers, Bennett's assurances were an irresistible balm for anxious and newly health-conscious Americans, who were already enthusiastic consumers of the various cure-all patent medicines whose advertisements filled the back pages of newspapers (and almanacs).

THE TOMATO PILL WARS

One of these often questionable products was American Hygiene Pills, which were peddled by a Brunswick, Ohio, patent medicine salesman named Archibald Miles. *(continued)*

SOMETHING A-MYTH?

We can almost certainly dismiss as myth the widely circulated legend (reenacted in 1949 on the CBS Radio program *You Are There*) that on September 26, 1820, Col. Robert Gibbon Johnson ate an entire bucket of tomatoes on the steps of the Salem, New Jersey, courthouse to prove to a fainting (some accounts say cheering) crowd that tomatoes were safe to eat.

In 1837, Miles had had a chance encounter with a physician—likely Bennett—who suggested a strategic name change for Miles's pills. Miles consequently awarded himself a

dice, Bilious Diseases, Gravel, Rheumatism, Coughs, Colds, Influenza, Catarrh, Nervous Diseases, Acid Stomachs, Glandular Swellings of all kinds, Costiveness, Colic,

is, the liver. In truth, i "peculiar effect" kicked in a little lower: The pill was essentially a laxative. The product sold so successfully that Miles soon found himself fighting off a bushelful of imitators, including, most notably, Dr. Phelps' Compound Tomato Pills. Indeed, Guy Phelps was actually a real physician, having graduated from Harvard Medical School.

THE PRODUCT SOLD SO SUCCESSFULLY THAT MILES SOON FOUND HIMSELF FIGHTING OFF A BUSHELFUL OF IMITATORS.

medical degree—or perhaps bought one from Bennett, who was reputed to sell them for $10—and Dr. Miles' Compound Extract of Tomato was born. Advertisements claimed that the pills cured "Dyspepsia, Jaun-

Headache, &c." Not to mention cholera and syphilis.

The magical ingredient was, Miles claimed, a concentrated extract "from the tomato, which [has] its peculiar effect upon the hepatic or biliary organs"—that

If the pills' name sounded familiar to Miles, it was because his New York distributor was the pharmaceutical firm Hoadley, Phelps, and Co., the "Phelps" being Guy's brother, George— which explained why Miles had not sold a single box of his pills in the largest market in the country. The feud between Miles and Phelps soon grew uglier than a tomato hornworm, with each side accusing the other of cheating, lying, patent infringement, and endangering the public by producing pills containing calomel or

other forms of mercury.

The *Hartford Courant,* examining Guy Phelps's invoices in 1839, found orders for licorice, aloe, gum arabic, cinnamon, alcohol, and green and yellow pigments, but hardly any for tomatoes. Phelps, in turn, had Miles's pills analyzed and reported that they contained only "aloe, rhubarb, pepper, colocynth [a plant from the gourd family with a robust purgative effect], and some essential oil."

The mudslinging continued, benefiting competitors such as Hallock's Tomato Panacea and Dr. Payne's Compound Tomato Pills, until the tomato pill market collapsed in 1840, having fallen victim to the mistrust sowed by the Miles–Phelps feud, the tapering of the cholera epidemic, and the Panic of 1837, a lingering financial crisis that made health elixirs a luxury that few could afford.

By then, the tomato had firmly taken root in America's diet. Recipes were abundant; breeders were developing new, tastier varieties; and the nascent canning industry was about to make tomatoes available year-round.

CLEANING UP THE JOINT

However, even as late as the 1960s, all tomatoes— even those packed into cans—had to be painstakingly harvested by hand because a tomato mechanically removed from the vine would usually separate not at the fruit but at a weaker "joint" an inch or so up the vine, leaving a small piece of stem attached. During processing, this sharp stub in a bin of tomatoes would be akin to a drunken pirate waving a cutlass on a crowded ship.

All known tomatoes had this weak joint except one, which had been discovered some years earlier in the Galápagos Islands by UC–Davis tomato researcher Charles Rick. He had brought home seeds of the Galápagos "jointless" tomato, whose stem detached cleanly at the fruit, knowing that if he could breed this property into canning tomatoes, the industry dream of

---

TIMELESS TIPS FOR GROWING TOMATOES

- Basil is said to improve the flavor and vigor of tomatoes and to deter insects such as whiteflies; plant close by.
- Lay red plastic mulch around tomato plants to hold in the soil's heat and increase productivity.
- Pinching off the suckers from tomato plants will delay the first yield and result in slightly fewer fruit. However, the size of the tomatoes will be larger and the overall weight of fruit per plant will be greater.
- For delicious tomatoes, pour a cup of beer around the roots after the plant blossoms. Repeat once a week until fruit are ripe.
- For better flavor, withhold water from tomatoes for 3 days before harvesting.

–Almanac editors

OVER 8 MILLION SOLD!

7-Day Knit Pant

WAS ~~$36.99~~

NOW **$9.99**

USE CODE **WWC4M1**

Raspberry

Deep Claret

Sage

Pine

Turq Blue

French Blue

Navy

Royal Navy

Deep Cobalt

Radiant Purple

Soft Iris

White

New Khaki

Chocolate

Medium Heather Grey

Heather Charcoal

Black

All-around ELASTIC WAISTBAND

Comfortable fits in sizes S-6X

Also in PETITE & TALL!

Petite & Tall Navy

Save 72%

THE 7-DAY KNIT STRAIGHT-LEG PANT. Full elastic waist. Side pockets. Cotton/poly knit. Machine wash.
Average: 26-12849-1160 30" inseam.
Petite: 26-42688-1160 28" inseam.
Tall: 26-50851-1160 33" inseam.
Sizes S-6X WAS ~~36.99~~
NOW 9.99

S-6X SIZING:
S(12), M(14-16), L(18-20), 1X(22-24), 2X(26-28), 3X(30-32), 4X(34-36), 5X(38-40), 6X(42-44)

FREE SHIPPING

USE CODE **WWC4M1** SEE DETAILS BELOW

Woman Within The TRUSTED EXPERTS in SIZES 12W TO 44W

Item #	Color	Item name	Size	Qty	Price	Total
26-12849-1160		7-Day Knit Pant				

Use code WWC4M1 to get items 26-12849-1160, 26-42688-1160, 26-50851-1160 for $9.99 and get free shipping on your order. Free shipping applies to standard shipping only, not including any additional shipping surcharges. Shipping upgrades additional. Does not apply to clearance. Discount is priced as marked in checkout. Not applicable to gift cards or prior purchases. May not be redeemed for cash or combined with other offers. Returns credited at discounted price. Only applies to in-stock merchandise. Expires 10/24/2024. Order by mail: Woman Within, 500 S. Mesa Hills Drive, El Paso, TX 79912

Merchandise total	
Shipping & handling	**FREE**
☐ For express delivery add $11.99	
Sales Tax: We collect sales tax where legally required. These states include: CA, FL, IN, KY, NY, RI, TX, and WA, but are subject to change at any time.	
Total	
Your satisfaction is guaranteed!	

Charge my (circle one):

Card# _____
Signature _____
Card expires (month/year) _____
Name _____
Address _____
City/State/Zip _____
Phone _____
Email _____

READY TO SAVE? HERE'S HOW TO SHOP ONLINE!

1 Go to: WOMANWITHIN.COM

2 Find at the top of the page CLICK CATALOG TO ORDER FROM CATALOG

SEARCH CATALOG CARD ACCOUNT MY BAG

3 Type in your item number

ORDER FROM CATALOG

4 Hit SEARCH

SEARCH

Call 1.800.248.2000 Now... or go to WOMANWITHIN.COM

RICK COULDN'T GET HIS SEEDS TO GERMINATE—UNTIL HE THOUGHT TO TRY FEEDING THEM TO A GALÁPAGOS GIANT TORTOISE.

creating a mechanical harvester—which could yank plants out of the ground and then shake their tomatoes loose—could be realized.

The problem, though, was that Rick couldn't get his seeds to germinate—until he thought to try feeding them to a Galápagos giant tortoise, knowing that a journey through a local fauna's digestive tract was sometimes required for seed viability in the wild. Rick mailed the seeds to a colleague who kept a pair of Galápagos tortoises in his backyard. When he received the scat back a month later (true to their reputation, tortoises are slow in every regard!), Eureka! Here were seeds that would germinate! The jointless trait was subsequently bred into commercial varieties, and today almost all American canned tomatoes have been harvested by machine.

Is there another vegetable that has as many stories to tell? Or—wait!—is America's favorite vegetable actually a fruit? In 1893, the tomato stood trial as the U.S. Supreme Court deliberated this very question. By decree of the Hon. Justice Horace Gray, for tariff purposes, the tomato would legally be considered a vegetable—although, the opinion added, botanically speaking, it's technically a fruit. ∎

William Alexander is the author of *Ten Tomatoes That Changed the World: A History* (Grand Central Publishing, 2022).

YOU'RE NOT CHICKEN,
RIGHT?

THEN WHY HAVEN'T YOU
STARTED A BACKYARD FLOCK?

BY CHRIS LESLEY

IN RECENT YEARS, the bohemian suburban family with a chicken coop has gone from being rare to being everywhere—for good reason. While chicken-keeping has its challenges, it comes with many practical and emotional benefits: I haven't bought a carton of eggs at the market since my first flock came of age in 2018, and, given the superior flavor and nutritional value of backyard eggs, I don't miss the store-bought ones.

These days, more and more people are coming around to this way of thinking. Back in 2010, the U.S. Department of Agriculture declared urban chicken-keeping to be "a growing phenomenon," and all indications are that it has continued

WHILE CHICKEN-KEEPING HAS ITS CHALLENGES, IT COMES WITH MANY PRACTICAL AND EMOTIONAL BENEFITS.

REASONS TO NOT LET US EGG YOU ON?

As much as we love chickens, we're not in the habit of disguising the challenges of keeping them. While some of the downsides (lots of poop!) can easily become upsides (lots of fertilizer!), there's no denying that some chicken-keeping peck-adillos can be as challenging and frustrating as the pastime itself is rewarding. *(continued)*

to grow. Many hatcheries report unprecedented interest, selling out of eggs and chicks in the spring of 2020 and again during the egg-price boom in 2022. Read on to find out why you should have started a brood—yesterday!

THE EGG COMES FIRST

It's no secret that the egg industry is vulnerable to disruptions, which for most people means high prices and empty shelves. When this happens, chicken owners can be generous to friends and neighbors, or, depending on their situation, they can raise their prices at farmers' markets. This is arguably truer now than at any time in the past 30 years, as annual egg consumption in the United States has been steadily increasing from a 100-year low in 1991 of 229 eggs per capita to almost 300 at the onset of the 2020s. Keeping your own chickens frees you from the anxiety of wondering whether there will be any eggs left at the store.

GARDEN HELPER

Chickens love gardens, and gardeners love chickens. The poultry are happy to eat any and all ugly, overripe veggies and greens, as well as many pests—insects and other bugs are a chicken's favorite source of protein! This means that letting your flock roam your rows throughout the spring and fall—before and after the most active time for your garden—can be a great way to rid your patch of all sorts of nemeses.

THE SCOOP ON POOP

Because of its high nitrogen content, chicken poop is an especially good fertilizer once it's composted. Nitrogen is one of the most important nutrients for a healthy garden, and lots of common plants strip it from the soil. Chicken fertilizer restores this balance and acts like rocket fuel for high-nitrogen–loving plants like rosebushes, tomatoes, and fruit trees. Just be sure to age your poop—let the manure mature for a few months before using it, or it could burn your plants. *(continued)*

AN EGG-SPENSIVE START-UP

Whenever egg prices skyrocket, people begin considering backyard chicken coops as a way to save money. These bargain-hunters are in for a surprise, as the upfront costs of establishing a coop are extensive. Moreover, it often takes years for a keeper to break even—if they ever do—in comparison to what they would have shelled out for supermarket eggs.

In an age of (usually) readily available eggs, a chicken coop is not primarily an economic venture: Instead, it is a labor of love. Although there are plenty of measures that you can take to significantly reduce the costs of keeping a flock—for instance, coops can be built from scrap wood for next to nothing—you should prepare to lay out more financially than you'll get in return. *(continued)*

DAILY GRIND

Speaking of putting in more than you get out: Unless you walk 5 miles uphill both ways to the grocery store, chicken-keeping is going to be more of a workout for you than you get in acquiring store-bought eggs. There's a reason that most people buy eggs instead of raising them. You will be outside every day of the year feeding and watering your chickens, as well as occasionally patching fences and regularly shoveling poop. If you're not able to perform some degree of physical labor—or don't expect to be able to 5 years down the line—a chicken coop is probably not a wise choice.

(continued)

WASTE NOT

While the main source of nutrients in a flock's diet should always be chicken feed (along with a calcium supplement for egg-layers), these birds are natural omnivores—and for chickens, "omni" really does mean "all." There are a few exceptions to this, of course—highly processed foods and most seasonings are a no-go—but your flock will be more than happy to help you to dispose of your kitchen scraps, from fruit rinds to overripe vegetables to fish guts.

YOUR FLOCK WILL BE MORE THAN HAPPY TO HELP YOU TO DISPOSE OF YOUR KITCHEN SCRAPS.

Photos, from top: MauleDesignCo/Getty Images; Alina Rosanova/Getty Images

WE HAVE GOTTEN THROUGH SOME LOW MOMENTS BY CUDDLING AND CARING FOR OUR HENS.

MOOD BOOST FROM THE ROOST

Articles advocating for chicken-keeping often focus on practical concerns, but if you talk to folks with flocks, what's more likely to come through is the joy that chickens bring to their lives. Whether they're watching their birds boss each other around the yard or they're cuddling up with a Cochin at the end of a long day, many people consider their flocks to be members of the family that can always provide a daily bright spot. I know that at my own home we have gotten through some low moments by cuddling and caring for our seven lively hens. And although research supports this therapeutic potential and suggests that interacting with animals can provide a significant boost to people's mental and even physical health, the bottom line is even simpler: Chickens are a lot of fun. ■

Chris Lesley, a fourth-generation chicken farmer, has been raising backyard birds for more than 20 years.

THERE GOES THE NEIGHBORHOOD

Chickens are always smelly and often loud—even if you don't have a rooster crowing at all hours of the day. (Roosters don't crow only at dawn. They vocalize mainly to warn their hens of potential threats or to mark their territory—and also sometimes just because they want to.) Depending on where you live, your coop might fall "afowl" of noise, building, or livestock ordinances. You might be able to avoid some of this by choosing to keep smaller or quieter chickens—and if the problem isn't an ordinance but an unhappy neighbor, a well-intended gift of a few eggs every now and then typically works wonders.

PADDLING IN THE PAST

Exploring history in the remote wilderness of the Boundary Waters

BY PORTER FOX

CANOER ON KEKEKABIC
LAKE IN MINNESOTA'S
BOUNDARY WATERS

**AT TIMES ON QUIET WATERS, ONE DOES NOT SPEAK
ALOUD BUT ONLY IN WHISPERS, FOR THEN ALL NOISE IS SACRILEGE.**

–Sigurd F. Olson, American writer and environmentalist (1899–1982)

The official line that marks the lowermost border between Canada and the United States is nowhere more remote than in the Boundary Waters Canoe Area of Minnesota, a vast wilderness almost smack dab in the middle of North America. Author Porter Fox paddled these waters while tracing the westward history of settlement and industry, as he would later recount in *Northland: A 4,000-mile Journey Along America's Forgotten Border* (W. W. Norton & Company, 2018), which is excerpted here and has been edited for space.

Minnesota's Boundary Waters are primitive, carved by nature and untouched by humans. This landscape west of the Great Lakes predates Paleo Indigenous Peoples and the local Ojibwe (Chippewa) tribe. It does not reference human presence in any way. There are no roads. No towns or airports. There are no people, gas stations, businesses, cars, or airplanes—not to mention any electricity or phone service. There is water. If you are not on it, you are in the woods. Looking down from an airplane, you see a land marbled blue and green, water and trees.

A FLAWED MAP

It took surveyors 150 years to mark the Canada–U.S. border that runs through this region (and 45 to lay out our 1,538-mile-long other border, which runs between B.C./Yukon and Alaska). In some places, crews had to wait for winter to freeze the ground before they could walk over previously impassable wetlands. A flawed map and ambiguous language in the 1783 Treaty of Paris both created and confused the Canada–U.S. border here. Boundary Commission surveyors searched for months for fictitious islands and lakes and drew three possible lines through the Boundary Waters—along the St. Louis, Pigeon, and Kaministiquia rivers. The middle boundary, the Pigeon, was eventually chosen.

Most of the line was left unmarked until 1908, when an American surveying team arrived at the mouth of the Pigeon River on Lake Superior, near Grand Portage, Minnesota. It took this group 3 years, traveling by canoe and on foot, to reach Gneiss Lake, about a fifth of the way across the Boundary Waters. Proper geolocation at the time required triangulation, meaning that stargazing surveyors had to scramble up vertical gorge walls and ferry across dangerous whitewater rapids to fix a position. Three additional teams, one Canadian, sped up the process 5 years later when they started surveying eastward from the Rainy River toward Lac La Croix.

(continued)

THE MYTHIC THUNDERBIRD'S VIEW

My guide, Paul Schurke, had lived in Ely for 30 years, much of which he had spent exploring the Boundary Waters. Moonlighting as a summer canoe guide today, he is best known for co-leading the historic International Polar Expedition with Will Steger in 1986. His wife, Sue, often helps to lead trips.

They showed the way along the border: lake after lake, with subtle changes in weather, depth, geology, topography, plants, and sky distinguishing each scene. If you could fly a few thousand feet above the canopy like the Ojibwe's mythic thunderbird, what you would see is Lake Superior 70 miles to the east; Grand Forks, North Dakota, 200 miles west; Lake Winnipeg 250 miles northwest; and Chicago 400 miles southeast.

Paul led us to a small island, where we crossed into Canada. Two border guards wearing navy blue uniforms, flat-brim campaign hats, and sneakers waited for us behind a makeshift pine podium.

TALES OF THE VOYAGEURS

Paul began to tell us stories of the French-Canadian voyageurs who had transported goods in canoes (bateaux) to remote trading points and brought furs back. They knew more about the North American West at the time than anyone except western indigenous peoples. The millions of pounds of furs that they carried financed British and French colonies. When delegates sat down to draw the Canada–U.S. border for the Treaty of Paris, they charted it along the voyageurs' route, so that the fur trade in both countries could continue uninterrupted.

Voyageurs were expected to paddle 14 to 18 hours a day. Most came from farms around Montréal and were accustomed to hard work. There were hundreds of portages on the route. They usually carried two bales of furs totalling 180 pounds. The more they carried, the more money they made, so some loaded up four or five. The average life span of a voyageur lasted until age 32.

We beached on a wooded island and shuttled gear to a campsite on the point. The site was atop a granite bluff. It came with a cast iron grill set over the fire pit and a Dutch oven. It was the most perfect campsite I had ever seen. I asked Paul how many of them there were in the Boundary Waters. "Around 2,000," he replied.

THE "PATH OF SOULS"

I stayed up to watch the Ojibwe's "Path of Souls"—what we call the Milky Way—march overhead and disappear into the shadowy canopy. The fire crackled and the lake moved through shades of blue and gray. A small rise called Warrior Hill lifted off the opposite shore. Ojibwe warriors had run up it to test their strength before going into battle.

The next morning we followed the border south and east to Bottle Lake. Paul dug his paddle deep into the water and pulled it back with his entire upper body. His pace was close to that of the voyageurs, who were expected to paddle at 55 strokes a minute. Their day typically began at 2:00 A.M., with a break at

LOOKING DOWN FROM AN AIRPLANE, YOU SEE A LAND MARBLED BLUE AND GREEN, WATER AND TREES.

8:00 A.M. to eat breakfast. Lunch was dried buffalo meat mixed with fat—a concoction called pemmican.

Pale corydalis and harebell grew near the shore of Iron Lake. Sphagnum, leatherleaf, and Labrador tea spread across the swampy sections of the hike. There was a small gravel beach on one side of the first portage, a flat rock for launching canoes on the other. We paddled hard for an hour through Iron Lake before stopping at Rebecca Falls to snack and rest.

SILVER WATER SPILLS

We paddled another 40 minutes to Curtain Falls and hiked to Crooked Lake. I tried to match Paul's stride and pace, but I couldn't keep up. It was hard to imagine how the voyageurs had hauled hundreds of pounds of pelts over portages—plus guns, ammo, flour, and kegs of liquor.

Around midnight, a thunderstorm hit the lake with lightning, hail, and heavy winds. I watched the tent poles bend under the force of the gale. Another storm blew through at dawn, with raindrops the size of nickels. I looked outside in the middle of it and saw Paul in his raincoat, crouched over a pile of sopping wet wood. It was 5:00 A.M. Fifteen minutes later, he had a fire going and coffee on.

A SLAM IN THE MIST

It rained on and off all the next day. It was almost dark by the time we made it to Mudro Lake—and raining harder. We paddled southwest along the lake and entered an inlet framed by tall reeds. A thick mist settled, and I almost fell out of the canoe when a beaver 5 feet away slammed its tail.

We had traveled 17 miles, and it was almost dark. I spotted a white sand beach ahead but wasn't sure if it was real. I heard a car door slam and realized that it was. This was a strange sound. After a few days in the Boundary Waters, everything other than water, stone, and wood seemed unnatural. Just like that, we slipped back into the modern world. ∎

Porter Fox lives, writes, and edits in upstate New York. His most recent book is *Category Five: Superstorms and the Warming Oceans That Feed Them* (Little, Brown and Company, 2024).

FARMING SMARTER,

TULLICHEWAN RANCH
Black Diamond, Alberta

Some 25 miles southwest of Calgary, rancher Ben Campbell has one eye on his 270 yearling cattle grazing in the foothills of the Rockies and one on the planet.

Although he sometimes trades his ballcap for a Stetson, Campbell is the opposite of the stereotypical Marlboro Man of old. Early on—such was the magnetic pull of his Scottish grandfather's ranch—he found himself abandoning a promising engineering career in favor of being in closer touch with the land.

"A lot of our grassland ecosystem has been converted to crops," observes Campbell. "I enjoy the bread from the wheat that's grown, but I also realize that we're losing an ecosystem that supports birds and wildlife."

Since 2013, he and his wife, Stephanie, have made the Tullichewan Ranch (pronounced tell-a-HEW-an) a model of rotational grazing. They stock about 50,000 pounds of animals per acre, moving them every day from one electric-fenced area to the next. The result is that cattle gain weight on the tenderest grasses while trampling their nitrogen-rich manure into the soil. Their hooves also puncture the soil to allow moisture to penetrate. This scenario mimics the practices of the bison that once roamed a native prairie hosting sage grouse and burrowing owls—species that are in now steep decline in Alberta.

The intensive grazing of cattle encourages the grass to put down deep roots, which keeps carbon in the soil. Meanwhile, the bovines convert the roughage into high-quality protein that is direct-marketed as grass-fed beef to consumers in the Calgary area. The enterprise is called Grazed Right.

The family narrative is not without struggles, as the 2023 drought necessitated lower stocking rates, for example. But the Campbells' commitment to the land is unwavering: They are stewards—not miners.

"You can be a rancher and an environmentalist at the same time," Campbell proudly declares. ■ *(continued)*

Photo: Stephanie Campbell

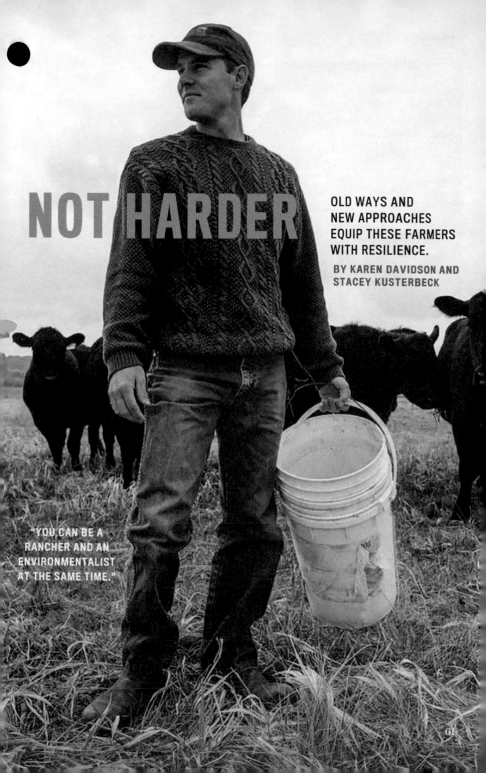

NOT HARDER

OLD WAYS AND
NEW APPROACHES
EQUIP THESE FARMERS
WITH RESILIENCE.

BY KAREN DAVIDSON AND
STACEY KUSTERBECK

"YOU CAN BE A
RANCHER AND AN
ENVIRONMENTALIST
AT THE SAME TIME."

61

"THE PURPOSE [OF THE PROJECT] WAS GETTING FOLKS TALKING TO EACH OTHER—AND, BOY, HAVE WE DONE THAT!"

WE SOW WE GROW
Chicago, Illinois

Natasha Nicholes fondly recalls her grandmother tending a kitchen garden during hot summer days, just as she remembers marveling at a great-aunt getting meat and eggs from a small family farm instead of the grocery store. Many years later, when Nicholes moved to Chicago with her husband, she observed right away that neighbors didn't speak to one another. She also noticed an unused empty lot, which she was then able to obtain through a land trust grant from the city.

With hard work and determination, Nicholes and her family fostered community through growing food. In 2016, the tiny farm started out with four 4x4-foot raised beds with the purpose of getting folks talking to each other—"And, boy, have we done that!," she explains.

The fledgling urban farmers obtained two more parcels of land on the same street. The unlikely sight of a farm in the urban neighborhood drew curious passersby. A small army of volunteers materialized to clear the land, build raised beds, and spread mulch.

Today, about 175 families get food at the farm. Tomatoes, cabbages, collard, cucumbers, kale, mustard greens, and turnips are sold on-site (only garlic is shipped, with about 150 pounds harvested annually).

The farm has generated connections of all kinds. One customer posts pictures of meals on social media and tags the local farms that grew the ingredients. "It's been amazing to see her tag us each time that she's used our garlic," says Nicholes. The farmers keep 53 chickens and sell the eggs. We Sow We Grow is determined to expand, with plans to obtain additional parcels of land to establish an orchard, sell community-supported agriculture (CSA) shares, and renovate a local building for seed-starting and cold storage. "We're just getting started," Nicholes proclaims. ■ *(continued)*

CREEKSIDE CHEESE + CREAMERY
Agassiz, British Columbia

For Julaine and Johannes Treur, the wheel of fortune is turning, as it should. On the 200 acres near Agassiz, British Columbia, that they farm organically, their 100 Brown Swiss cows produce milk for Vancouver dairies—and their on-farm Creekside Cheese + Creamery.

About one-quarter—14,500 liters or 31,967 pounds—of the milk produced each month is used in cheese-making. Their ambition is to make more value-added dairy products at home.

March 2020—when the pandemic shut down most commerce—happened to be when the Treurs somewhat fortuitously bought used equipment from a retiring cheese-maker. They brought his mobile cheese-making trailer to their farm and—with no small amount of gusto—started making Gouda, the iconic cheese from Johannes's homeland of the Netherlands.

"The local demand for our first products was so overwhelming that we decided to build an on-farm store with a basement that acts as an aging cave," explains Julaine; the shop opened in August 2021.

In the interim, Julaine and Johannes tinkered in their kitchen to develop three flavors of Gouda, plus their own Gruyère, raclette, Reblochon-style (soft washed-rind), and Morbier (semisoft).

"Different stirring and heating techniques result in a different feel in the cheese," reports Julaine. "We want to make cheeses that we can call our own."

The Brown Swiss cows are key to the success story because they produce milk that contains a butterfat content of 4.3 percent. This figure is much higher than the average 3.5 percent produced by the more common Holstein breed. Butterfat is at the heart of cheese, adding flavor and texture.

The days are long, 12 hours and more, but Julaine vows that her reward is always simple: "Give me a piece of stinky cheese." ■ *(continued)*

"WE WANT TO MAKE CHEESES THAT WE CAN CALL OUR OWN."

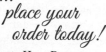

"DATES ARE CLIMATE CHANGE PLANTS. THEY LIKE HEAT AND TOLERATE DROUGHT."

SAM COBB FARMS
Desert Hot Springs, California

As a young boy growing up in California, Sam Cobb waved to farmers driving tractors past his front porch. Decades later, he finds that what he calls the "farm feeling" has never left him. As a teen, Cobb became active in Future Farmers of America; subsequently, he worked multiple farm jobs and obtained degrees in agronomy and agricultural education.

After graduation, Cobb took a job with the USDA's Natural Resources Conservation Service, helping farmers to make long-term plans; at the same time, he was plotting his own, saving money and buying equipment and land. What he would grow was still a question.

While working in the Coachella Valley, he got his answer after unexpectedly falling in love with date palms. The trees go through three distinct 7-year periods on their way to fully maturing at 21, and Cobb appreciated their complexity and tenacity: "Dates are climate change plants. They like heat and tolerate drought." He was soon planting 100 Medjool date palm offshoots—along with an unidentified one that he had spotted on the side of a road—on a 5-acre plot of land.

Years later, when harvested, the mystery dates were found to be particularly tasty. Cobb trademarked the variety, naming it Black Gold. "The flavor is a little chocolate, a little caramel, and something that no one can really describe," he reports. "I call it 'indescribably good.'"

By the time he retired in 2019, Cobb had planted more than 2,000 trees across 65 of his 115 acres—and was ready to live his dream: "I walked out of the USDA and into Sam Cobb Farms," he recalls.

On weekends, he and his wife sell dates at their farm stand, and they also ship directly to consumers—with the farm's mission statement, "We Grow Good Dates," printed on every package. Date-farming is a labor of love for him. It's also profitable—and soon to become even more so with an investment in a processing facility: "Things are about to happen in a big way." ■ *(continued)*

Photo: Amey Matthews

FINALLY ... LIFE INSURANCE YOU CAN AFFORD

PENDRAGON FARMS
Cambridge, Ontario

Goats are browsers, not grazers. Unlike other ruminants, they would rather nibble on tree leaves than forage with their heads down.

This preference is a tendency that third-generation farmer Brianna Miller uses to her advantage when she lets her Pendragon Farms herd of 100 Kiko goats loose to browse on a variety of plant species. On her 10 acres near Cambridge, Ontario, she's witnessed her goats "obliterate" common motherwort, buckthorn, and creeping bellflower, to name just a few invasive species.

"These Kiko goats have grit in their personality," says Miller. "They're not afraid to go after feed, and they're very protective of their kids."

Known for their hardiness, New Zealand–origin Kiko goats first appeared in Canada as recently as 1998. They thrive in an outdoor environment year-round, as long as shelter is provided during harsh winters and muddy springs.

Since her first purchase of Kiko goats more than a decade ago, Miller has been perfecting her rotational grazing program. For one thing, she has planted little bluestem, a native grass species that forms dense mounds 18 to 24 inches tall—an attribute attractive to browsers. Every 3 to 5 years, in the fall, she broadcasts nitrogen-fixing clover seed to rejuvenate the pasture. In 2022, she installed high-tensile-strength fencing so that she could divide her acreage into strips and rotate the herd to a fresh pasture every day or so. "These pastures have come back to life with rotational grazing," Miller points out.

The system has worked so well that she's introduced cross-species grazing, with goats first to munch, then horses, then ducks. The preferred diets of the animal species are mutually exclusive, which means that each pasture species ends up being totally utilized.

Miller sells her pasture-raised goat meat to the halal market in southern Ontario. With more pasture fine-tuning, she aims to enable the doubling of her herd. ∎ *(continued)*

"THESE KIKO GOATS HAVE GRIT IN THEIR PERSONALITY."

REINFORD FARMS
Mifflintown, Pennsylvania

I n the eyes of many, cow manure and food waste are worthless—or, worse yet, something to get rid of. At Reinford Farms, they're a source of revenue and vehicles for good environmental stewardship.

Brett Reinford grew up on the dairy farm that his parents purchased in 1991 and ran for 30 years. Now, he and his brothers are in charge of the 1,300-acre operation. "Dairy farming is rapidly changing," observes Reinford, and technology is the driving force behind many of the shifts: Farmers use GPS to precisely apply seed and fertilizer, and,

in Reinford's case, his farm's 750 cows wear activity monitors (like bovine Fitbits) that track their sleep and diet. The cows produce about 6,000 gallons of milk each day, which is sold to Land O'Lakes for butter. "Right now, milk prices are low, so it is hard to make a living from just selling milk, so you need to be diversified," says Reinford.

By investing in an anaerobic digester, the brothers found a way to profit from the 12,000 to 15,000 gallons of cow manure produced each day. The system filters and cleans the manure, which is then used as compost bedding for cows

Photo: Reinford Farms

"OUR GOAL IS TO ASK, 'HOW DO WE MAKE THIS A BETTER PLACE FOR THE NEXT GENERATION?'"

and fertilizer for crops. At the same time, the digester provides for the capture of methane gas, which powers and heats the farm.

When a local supermarket called to ask if the technology could be used to recycle food waste, the Reinfords figured out a way to do it. For the market, using this outlet was cheaper than sending it to a landfill; for the farm, the partnership was a way to earn some money and save some, too, by converting the combined manure and food waste into energy.

Today, more than 50 food manufac-turers, warehouse distributors, and supermarkets pay the farm to process food waste, the methane from which produces enough electricity to enable the brothers to sell the excess back to the grid. The next step was investing in a depacking facility to remove from food waste the boxes, cans, and plastic wrap in which it is packaged—all of which are recycled.

Reinford takes a long-term view of things: "Our goal is to make our farm more efficient and more profitable and to ask, 'How do we make this a better place for the next generation?'" ■

Canadian profiles are by **Karen Davidson,** editor of *The Grower,* a leading Canadian horticultural magazine, and frequent contributor to the Almanac. U.S. profiles are by **Stacey Kusterbeck,** also a regular contributor to the Almanac.

Choose Life
Grow Young with HGH

From the landmark book Grow Young with HGH comes the most powerful, over-the-counter health supplement in the history of man. Human growth hormone was first discovered in 1920 and has long been thought by the medical community to be necessary only to stimulate the body to full adult size and therefore unnecessary past the age of 20. Recent studies, however, have overturned this notion completely, discovering instead that the natural decline of Human Growth Hormone (HGH), from ages 21 to 61 (the average age at which there is only a trace left in the body) and is the main reason why the body ages and fails to regenerate itself to its 25 year-old biological age.

Like a picked flower cut from the source,

we gradually wilt physically and mentally and become vulnerable to a host of degenerative diseases, that we simply weren't susceptible to in our early adult years.

Modern medical science now regards aging as a disease that is treatable and preventable and that "aging", the disease, is actually a compilation of various diseases and pathologies, from everything, like a rise in blood glucose and pressure to diabetes, skin wrinkling and so on. All of these aging symptoms can be stopped and rolled back by maintaining Growth Hormone levels in the blood at the same levels HGH existed in the blood when we were 25 years old.

There is a receptor site in almost every

ll in the human body for HGH, so its regenerative and healing effects are very comprehensive.

Growth Hormone, first synthesized in 1985 under the Reagan Orphan drug act, to treat dwarfism, was quickly recognized to stop aging in its tracks and reverse it to a remarkable degree. Since then, only the lucky and the rich have had access to it at the cost of $10,000 US per year.

The next big breakthrough was to come in 1997 when a group of doctors and scientists, developed an all-natural source product which would cause your own natural HGH to be released again and do all the remarkable things it did for you in your 20's. Now available to every adult for about the price of a coffee and donut a day.

GHR is now available in America, just in time for the aging Baby Boomers and everyone else from age 30 to 90 who doesn't want to age rapidly but would rather stay young, beautiful and healthy all of the time.

The new HGH releasers are winning converts from the synthetic HGH users as well, since GHR is just as effective, is oral instead of self-injectable and is very affordable.

GHR is a natural releaser, has no known side effects, unlike the synthetic version and has no known drug interactions. Progressive doctors admit that this is the direction medicine is seeking to go, to get the body to heal itself instead of employing drugs. GHR is truly a revolutionary paradigm shift in medicine and, like any modern leap frog advance, many others will be left in the dust holding their limited, or useless drugs and remedies.

It is now thought that HGH is so comprehensive in its healing and regenerative powers that it is today, where the computer industry was twenty years ago, that it will displace so many prescription and non-prescription drugs and health remedies that it is staggering to think of.

The president of BIE Health Products stated in a recent interview, "I've been waiting for these products since the 70's. We knew they would come, if only we could stay healthy and live long enough to see them! If you want to stay on top of your game, physically and mentally as you age, this product is a boon, especially for the highly skilled professionals who have made large investments in their education, and experience. Also with the failure of Congress to honor our seniors with pharmaceutical coverage policy, it's more important than ever to take pro-active steps to safeguard your health. Continued use of GHR will make a radical difference in your health, HGH is particularly helpful to the elderly who, given a choice, would rather stay independent in their own home, strong, healthy and alert enough to manage their own affairs, exercise and stay involved in their communities. Frank, age 85, walks two miles a day, plays golf, belongs to a dance club for seniors, had a girl friend again and doesn't need Viagra, passed his driver's test and is hardly ever home when we call - GHR delivers."

HGH is known to relieve symptoms of Asthma, Angina, Chronic Fatigue, Constipation, Lower back pain and Sciatica, Cataracts and Macular Degeneration, Menopause, Fibromyalgia, Regular and Diabetic Neuropathy, Hepatitis, helps Kidney Dialysis and Heart and Stroke recovery.

For more information or to order call
877-849-4777
www.biehealth.us

These statements have not been evaluated by the FDA. Copyright © 2000. Code OFA.

2024 RECIPE CONTEST WINNERS

After we asked you to share your best holiday recipes, we received many tempting entries for celebrating Valentine's Day, St. Patrick's Day, Thanksgiving, and so many other special days. Sincere thanks go out to all of you who took the time to share your recipes!

Styling and photography: Samantha Jones/Vaughan Communications

FIRST PRIZE: $300
RED, WHITE, AND BLUEBERRY CHEESECAKE BARS
(recipe on page 174)

SECOND PRIZE: $200
**MAPLE-ROASTED BUTTERNUT
SQUASH PUDDING CAKES**
(recipe on page 174)

(continued)

THIRD PRIZE: $100
**NEW YEAR'S DAY
SAUERKRAUT**
(recipe on page 175)

ENTER THE 2025 RECIPE CONTEST: TOMATOES

Got a great recipe using tomatoes that is
loved by family and friends? Send it in and it could win!
See contest rules on page 251.

HONORABLE MENTION
**MOM'S CHRISTMAS
CARAMEL CORN**
(recipe on page 175)

(continued on page 174)

SECRETS

AVALANCHE NEAR
TELLURIDE, COLORADO

OF THE
SNOWPACK

IS CLIMATE CHANGE CAUSING AVALANCHE SAFETY TO GO DOWNHILL?

BY BENJAMIN HATCHETT, PH.D.

A snow avalanche— sometimes called a "white dragon"—is a common natural hazard in mountain environments. Make no mistake: Even if you are nowhere near a mountain, the white dragon is a force of nature to be respected.

Avalanches are deadly and uncontrollable, in addition to being notoriously difficult to forecast. However, decades of observation and study indicate that they occur most frequently during snowstorms, within 24 hours of a heavy snowfall, or when winds load slopes with snow. They can also occur days or even months after a snowfall if conditions are favorable.

WHAT GIVES?

An avalanche will occur when the weight of snow on a slope exceeds its ability to remain stationary. Most avalanches occur on slopes of between 30 and 45 degrees, although in springtime, wet avalanches can occur on 20-degree inclines. Some or all of the snowpack collapses, fractures (or breaks), and flows downhill—with dry avalanches reaching speeds of 60 to 80 miles per hour within 5 seconds. During the cascade, the avalanche gathers additional snow as well as objects in its path—rocks, trees, and, potentially, people (e.g., skiers) and vehicles (e.g., snowmobiles).

The scale of an avalanche can range from small, such as snow sliding off a rooftop, to enormous, such as snow cascading down a mountain slope or ridgeline—but the damage can be catastrophic no matter the size. A rooftop avalanche can easily bury workers, children, or animals,

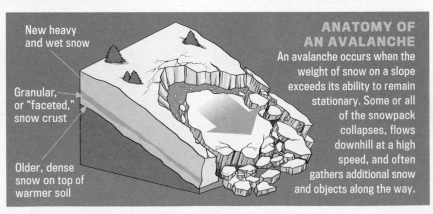

New heavy and wet snow

Granular, or "faceted," snow crust

Older, dense snow on top of warmer soil

ANATOMY OF AN AVALANCHE
An avalanche occurs when the weight of snow on a slope exceeds its ability to remain stationary. Some or all of the snowpack collapses, flows downhill at a high speed, and often gathers additional snow and objects along the way.

A weakened snowpack begins to cave under the pressure of newly fallen snow.

More melt days make existing snowpacks shallower than they would typically be during the middle of winter.

while a mountain avalanche can eliminate roads or entire towns several miles downslope from its point of origin.

WARM WEATHER MATTERS

A warming climate makes avalanche prediction more difficult and avalanche events potentially more dangerous. Projected changes in climate (e.g., warmer temperatures, on average) will affect both individual weather events and the long-term expectations of avalanche activity.

Warming temperatures tend to slow the jet stream, the air currents that flow approximately 35,000 feet above Earth's surface and largely control weather patterns. As the jet stream slows, it becomes wavier, dipping farther south and rising farther north.

We expect a slower, wavier jet stream to generate more frequent extended dry periods (days without precipitation) during which the warm air and sunshine act together to accelerate snowmelt (assuming, of course, that snow has fallen). Increased snowmelt during winter months influences avalanche size and frequency. The jet stream will also generate more frequent heavy precipitation periods, too.

GETTING GRANULAR

More melt days make existing snowpacks shallower, or less deep, than they would typically be during the middle of winter. Shallow snowpacks are weaker due to the dramatic temperature differences between the warm soil below the snow and the cold air in the

An avalanche preparedness sign in British Columbia

AVALANCHE SAFETY

UNDERSTAND: Find out where and why avalanches occur so that you can avoid them when you are in avalanche country. Ninety percent of avalanche accidents are triggered by the victims or someone in their party.

CHECK: A network of avalanche centers in the U.S. provides daily forecasts with detailed information about conditions to help you prepare.

CARRY: Travel in groups with rescue gear—a beacon for yourself, a probe for locating a person buried in an avalanche, and a shovel to dig them out.

OBSERVE: Learn to recognize key signs of an unstable snowpack: recent avalanches in the area, the cracking or collapsing of snow, wind-loading (i.e., snowdrifts), recent heavy snowfall, and rapid warming.

atmosphere. This temperature difference promotes the development of granular snow, called "faceted" snow. (If you have ever plunged thigh-deep into sugary snow, you've met a weak, faceted snowpack!)

When a faceted snowpack becomes loaded with new heavy and wet snow, it gives way or collapses (think of pouring granulated sugar). This creates a large and potentially deadly avalanche. These kinds of snowpacks are most common in cold, high-elevation mountains such as in the interior Canadian Rockies of British Columbia and Alberta as well as Montana, Wyoming, Colorado, and Utah. Although rare, they also can occur in the Northeast.

In addition, surface snow that melts on warm days and/or during periods of plentiful sunshine often refreezes at night into a crust layer. Frozen crusts form a slick, less stable surface on which new-fallen or wind-deposited snow will slide. Once buried, crusts act as a moisture source or barrier within the snowpack.

This can lead to weak layer formation that can persist throughout the snow season, prolonging the risk of an avalanche. These slick layers can form again and again on top of each other, especially in sunny places like California, potentially increasing the avalanche risk for every subsequent snowfall event after a crust forms. *(continued)*

GROW YOUR KNOWLEDGE—
AND YOUR BEST GARDENS!

Never touched a trowel in your life? Been gardening at home for decades? Gardeners of every skill level always benefit from having trusted knowledge at their fingertips.

The Old Farmer's Almanac's Gardener's Handbooks are loaded with advice and inspiration to guarantee success for every gardener.

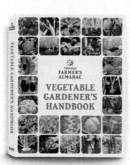

EACH HANDBOOK INCLUDES . . .

- step-by-step guidance on growing more than 30 vegetables or flowering plants
- advice to minimize maintenance and maximize harvests, color, and fragrance
- pages for notes and records

- tips for seed-starting
- the lowdown on disease and pest prevention
- charts and tables for ready reference
- and much more to help you achieve the gardens of your dreams!

COLLECT THEM ALL! GET YOUR COPIES TODAY!
GO TO ALMANAC.COM/SHOP OR AMAZON

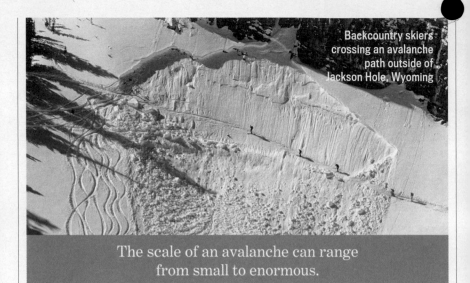

Backcountry skiers crossing an avalanche path outside of Jackson Hole, Wyoming

The scale of an avalanche can range from small to enormous.

WHAT'S RAIN GOT TO DO WITH IT?

A warming climate means that precipitation will increasingly fall as rain, rather than snow. Rain falling on a cold snowpack can refreeze upon hitting it, forming a layer that—just like the melt-freeze crust—can create a later avalanche hazard when more snowfall is added.

This can also lead to weak layers by changing how moisture and energy flow through the snowpack. Heavy rainfall can saturate the snowpack, increasing its mass and therefore the risk of an avalanche. This is a big problem not only in spring but also during warm winter storms.

In extreme cases, rainfall flowing through the snowpack or snowmelt following days of extremely warm and sunny conditions saturates the soil beneath it. Melt water can lubricate the area where the snow meets the soil, leading to reduced soil and snowpack strength. When this happens, landslides that mix soil with snow to create dangerous debris flows can be triggered.

Such an event happened on Slide Mountain, Nevada, during a heat wave in the spring of 1983 that followed an extremely snowy winter. Beginning near 9,000 feet, this debris flow traveled 4,000 vertical feet and over 3 miles down a canyon, where it moved houses off their foundations and damaged a highway as it spilled into Washoe Valley. Unfortunately, one life was also lost, and a number of injuries were reported.

WETTER, WHITER WINTERS

Predictive tools such as Earth-system models help us to

CELEBRATE YOUR LOVE OF GARDENING!

iPad not included

THE OLD FARMER'S ALMANAC
GARDENING CLUB

Your membership has privileges and benefits that are reserved exclusively for *you*—just look at what it includes!

IN PRINT . . .

THE 2025 OLD FARMER'S ALMANAC: The newest edition includes everything that you've come to expect from the world's premier Almanac! You'll also have access to the 2025 digital edition.

THE 2025 GARDENING CALENDAR: Enjoy beautiful botanical illustrations, useful gardening tips, inspirational quotes, and folklore.

THE 2024 *GARDEN GUIDE:* Your ultimate companion for growing herbs, vegetables, flowers, and houseplants. *Plus, you'll automatically receive the 2025 edition when it's ready,* ensuring that you stay ahead with the latest tips and trends in gardening.

ONLINE . . .

You can begin to benefit from the following digital resources as soon as you activate your membership!

THE *GARDEN GUIDE* ONLINE LIBRARY: You'll find our complete collection of *Garden Guides* packed with no-nonsense tips, tricks, and inspiration!

DIGITAL BACK ISSUES: As part of your membership, you can read, download, or print past editions of *The Old Farmer's Almanac* going back to 2010!

EXTRA! Our monthly digital magazine features articles on topics such as gardening, food, weather, and more!

Go to Almanac.com/Garden2025
or call 1-800-Almanac (800-256-2622) and select option 2.

U.S. Shipping Only

understand the effects of changes in the atmosphere, including to jet streams. For example, these tools are predicting stronger winter snow and rain storms in a warmer climate, due to, for example, atmospheric rivers (long, narrow corridors of water vapor steered by the jet stream's fast-moving winds). More moisture means more fuel for precipitation, while stronger winds lift moisture over mountains

frequent, widespread, and large.

A slower, wavier jet stream will also cause occasional extreme cold outbreaks, bringing heavy snow to places that rarely experience it. In these cases, the potential for rooftop avalanches increases. Extreme cold makes shallow snowpacks weaker by helping to create noncohesive, sugary, faceted snow grains rather than promoting bonds to form between snow grains that

> Heavy snowfalls onto shallower and weaker snowpacks suggest that avalanches could become more frequent, widespread, and large.

and more effectively wring out this wetness as precipitation. The end result? Heavier, longer-lasting precipitation in the form of rain at increasingly higher elevations and snow in the highest mountains.

Within warmer, windier winter storms, which may last longer than we are used to—in the same way that recent heat waves or dry spells have been growing longer—we expect higher precipitation rates and larger multiday precipitation totals. Both increase the chances of low-elevation flooding and higher-elevation heavy snow accumulation.

Heavy snowfalls onto shallower and weaker snowpacks—those more likely to have melt-freeze or rain crusts or sugary, faceted snow—suggest that avalanches on mountains and rooftops could become more

strengthen the snowpack. After extreme cold periods—especially those that occur in early winter—subsequent storms load the weakened snowpack and increase the chances of an avalanche.

As extended periods of extreme weather become more common, warmer, sunnier, and rainier conditions will reduce overall chances of avalanche formation at lower elevations. At higher elevations, however, the risks are likely to magnify with increasingly variable and changing weather. The white dragon will continue to lurk in snowscapes—and can awaken when we least expect it. ■

Benjamin Hatchett, Ph.D., is a meteorologist at the Cooperative Institute for Research in the Atmosphere at Colorado State University.

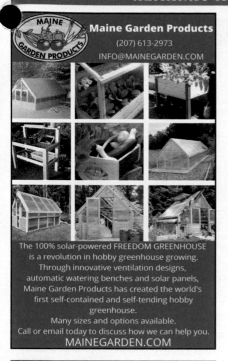

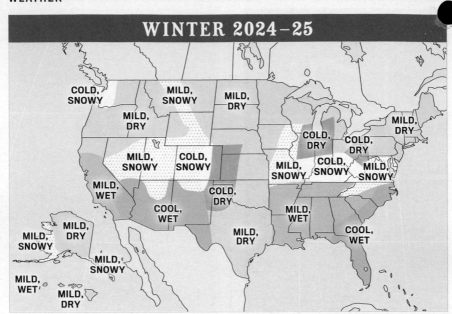

WINTER 2024–25

These weather maps correspond to the winter and summer predictions in the General Weather Forecast (opposite) and on the regional forecast pages, 206–223. To learn more about how we make our forecasts, turn to page 202.

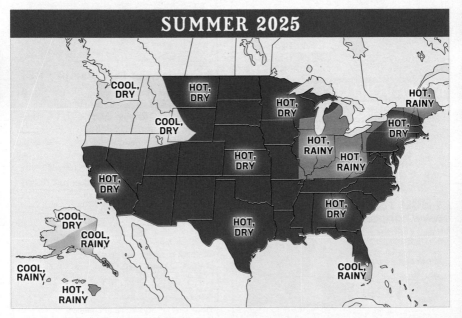

SUMMER 2025

Maps: AccuWeather, Inc.

THE GENERAL WEATHER REPORT AND FORECAST

FOR REGIONAL FORECASTS, SEE PAGES 206-223.

We are currently moving deeper into Solar Cycle 25, which is expected to reach its maximum around July 2025. High solar activity levels have historically been linked to warmer temperatures, on average, across Earth, although this relationship has become weaker in recent decades. Meanwhile, Solar Cycle 25 has been steadily increasing in intensity and has already exceeded the peak of Solar Cycle 24.

"Oscillations" are ocean–atmosphere weather patterns recurring over long periods. In addition to expecting a neutral ENSO (El Niño Southern Oscillation) or even a La Niña, a warm Atlantic Multidecadal Oscillation (AMO), and a cool Pacific Decadal Oscillation (PDO), we're also watching solar activity and equatorial stratospheric winds known as the Quasi-Biennial Oscillation (QBO). Some or all of these factors may cause the polar vortex to displace southward this winter, releasing added cold shots into North America.

WINTER temperatures will be above normal except for along the Southeast coast; in much of Florida, the Ohio Valley, and western Great Lakes; from the southern High Plains into the Desert Southwest; and in western Washington. Precipitation will be near to below normal everywhere but in the Southeast, Florida, Deep South, High Plains, Desert Southwest, much of the Rockies, most of California, western Washington, and central and western Hawaii. Snowfall will be near to below normal everywhere that normally receives snow except for from the Delmarva into the central and southern Appalachians, in the Southeast and western Ohio Valley, from the western High Plains into the Rockies and Great Basin, in the Desert Southwest and mountains of the Pacific Southwest, and in western Washington and southern and western Alaska.

SPRING temperatures will be above normal from the Atlantic coast and northern Florida up into the Appalachians, eastern Great Lakes, and eastern Ohio Valley; from the Deep South and Texas–Oklahoma up into the Heartland and Upper Midwest; from the High Plains and Intermountain West into the Pacific Northwest; and in Alaska and eastern Hawaii. They will be near to below normal elsewhere. Skies will be drier than normal in New England and southern Florida, from the western Ohio Valley and Lower Great Lakes into the northern Upper Midwest, from the southern Plains into the Heartland and northern High Plains, and along much of the Pacific coast and near to wetter than normal elsewhere.

SUMMER will be hotter than normal, except for near- to below-normal temps in southern Florida, from the northern Rockies into the Pacific Northwest, and in Alaska and western Hawaii. Rainfall will be above normal in central and northern New England, southern Florida, the Lower Great Lakes, the Ohio Valley, Hawaii, and southern Alaska and near to below normal elsewhere.

Watch for **TROPICAL STORMS** from Florida through southern Virginia and from the central Gulf Coast into Texas in mid-July, in Florida and Texas in late August, and in Hawaii in late September. The best chances for **HURRICANES** will occur in Texas in early August and Louisiana in late August.

AUTUMN temps will be above normal from Delmarva down into the Southeast and Florida; in the Deep South, southern Plains, Heartland, High Plains, and Intermountain West; from Arizona to the West Coast (except for the southern Pacific Southwest); and in Alaska. They will be near to below normal elsewhere. Precipitation will be below normal, except for near- to above-normal amounts across the central Gulf Coast, the northern High Plains, the Pacific Northwest, southern Alaska, and eastern and western Hawaii.

WEATHER

TO GET A SUMMARY OF THE RESULTS OF OUR FORECAST FOR LAST WINTER, TURN TO PAGE 204.

THE OLD
FARMER'S ALMANAC

Established in 1792 and published every year thereafter
ROBERT B. THOMAS, *founder* (1766–1846)

YANKEE PUBLISHING INC.
EDITORIAL AND PUBLISHING OFFICES
P.O. Box 520, 1121 Main Street, Dublin, NH 03444
Phone: 603-563-8111 • Fax: 603-563-8252

EDITOR *(14th since 1792):* Carol Connare
CREATIVE DIRECTOR: Colleen Quinnell
MANAGING EDITOR: Jack Burnett
SENIOR EDITORS: Sarah Perreault, Heidi Stonehill
ASSOCIATE EDITOR: Tim Goodwin
WEATHER GRAPHICS AND CONSULTATION:
AccuWeather, Inc.

V.P., NEW MEDIA AND PRODUCTION:
Paul Belliveau
PRODUCTION DIRECTOR: David Ziarnowski
PRODUCTION MANAGER: Brian Johnson
SENIOR PRODUCTION ARTISTS:
Jennifer Freeman, Rachel Kipka, Janet Selle

WEB SITE: ALMANAC.COM
SENIOR DIGITAL EDITOR: Catherine Boeckmann
ASSOCIATE DIGITAL EDITOR: Jennifer Keating
SENIOR WEB DESIGNER: Amy O'Brien
DIGITAL MARKETING SPECIALISTS:
Jessica Garcia, Holly Sanderson
E-MAIL MARKETING SPECIALIST: Eric Bailey
E-COMMERCE DIRECTOR: Alan Henning
SENIOR DRUPAL DEVELOPER: Mark Gordon

CONTACT US
We welcome your questions and comments about articles in and topics for this Almanac. Mail all editorial correspondence to Editor, The Old Farmer's Almanac, P.O. Box 520, Dublin, NH 03444-0520; fax us at 603-563-8252; or contact us through Almanac.com/Contact. *The Old Farmer's Almanac* can not accept responsibility for unsolicited manuscripts and will not acknowledge any hard-copy queries or manuscripts that do not include a stamped and addressed return envelope.

OUR CONTRIBUTORS

DAVID BARTONE writes the Farmer's Calendars from his multi-acre permaculture homestead in the western Massachusetts foothills. A faculty member at UMass Amherst's University Without Walls, he teaches courses in writing, sustainability, and other subjects. His poetry books include *Spring Logic* (H_NGM_N, 2010) and *Practice on Mountains* (Ahsahta Press, 2014).

BOB BERMAN, our astronomy editor, leads annual tours to Chilean observatories as well as to view solar eclipses and the northern lights. He is the author of 12 books, including *Zoom* (2015) and *Earth-Shattering: Violent Supernovas, Galactic Explosions, Biological Mayhem, Nuclear Meltdowns, and Other Hazards to Life in Our Universe* (2019), both published by Little, Brown and Company.

DAN CLARK writes the weather doggerel verse that runs down the center of the Right-Hand Calendar Pages. His late father, Tim Clark, wrote the weather doggerel for more than 40 years.

BETHANY E. COBB, our astronomer, is an Associate Professor of Honors and Physics at George Washington University. In addition to conducting research on gamma-ray bursts and teaching astronomy and physics courses to non–science majors, she enjoys rock climbing, figure skating, and reading science fiction.

CELESTE LONGACRE, our astrologer, often refers to astrology as "a study of timing, and timing is everything." A New Hampshire native, she has been a practicing astrologer for more than 40 years. Her book, *Celeste's Garden Delights* (2015), is available on her Web site, CelesteLongacre.com.

BOB SMERBECK and **BRIAN THOMPSON,** our meteorologists, bring more than 50 years of forecasting expertise to the task, as well as some unique early accomplishments: a portable, wood-and-PVC-pipe tornado machine built by Bob and prescient 5-day forecasts made by Brian—in fourth grade.

●opular CoQ10 Pills Leave Millions Suffering

Could this newly-discovered brain fuel solve America's worsening memory crisis?

PALM BEACH, FLORIDA — Millions of Americans take the supplement known as CoQ10. It's the coenzyme that supercharges the "energy factories" in your cells known as *mitochondria*. But there's a serious flaw that's leaving millions unsatisfied.

As you age, your mitochondria break down and fail to produce energy. In a revealing study, a team of researchers showed that 95 percent of the mitochondria in a 90-year-old man were damaged, compared to almost no damage in the mitochondria of a 5-year-old.

Taking CoQ10 alone is not enough to solve this problem. Because as powerful as CoQ10 is, there's one critical thing it fails to do: it can't create new mitochondria to replace the ones you lost.

And that's bad news for Americans all over the country. The loss of cellular energy is a problem for the memory concerns people face as they get older.

"We had no way of replacing lost mitochondria until a recent discovery changed everything," says Dr. Al Sears, founder and medical director of the Sears Institute for Anti-Aging Medicine in Palm Beach, Florida. "Researchers discovered the only nutrient known to modern science that has the power to trigger the growth of new mitochondria."

Why Taking CoQ10 is Not Enough

Dr. Sears explains, "This new discovery is so powerful, it can multiply your mitochondria by 55 percent in just a few weeks. That's the equivalent of restoring decades of lost brain power."

This exciting nutrient — called PQQ *(pyrroloquinoline quinone)* — is the driving force behind a revolution in aging. When paired with CoQ10, this dynamic duo has the power to reverse the age-related memory losses you may have thought were beyond your control.

Dr. Sears pioneered a new formula — called **Ultra Accel Q** — that combines both CoQ10 and PQQ to support maximum cellular energy and the normal growth of new mitochondria. **Ultra Accel Q** is the first of its kind to address both problems and is already creating huge demand.

In fact, demand has been so overwhelming that inventories repeatedly sell out. But a closer look at **Ultra Accel Q** reveals there are good reasons why sales are booming.

Science Confirms the Many Benefits of PQQ

The medical journal *Biochemical Pharmacology* reports that PQQ is up to 5,000 times more efficient in sustaining energy production than common antioxidants. With the ability to keep every cell in your body operating at full strength, **Ultra Accel Q** delivers more than just added brain power and a faster memory.

People feel more energetic, more alert, and don't need naps in the afternoon. The boost in cellular energy generates more power to your heart, lungs, muscles, and more.

"With the PQQ in Ultra Accel, I have energy I never thought possible at my age," says Colleen R., one of Dr. Sears's patients. "I'm in my 70s but feel 40 again. I think clearly, move with real energy and sleep like a baby."

The response has been overwhelmingly positive, and Dr. Sears receives countless emails from his patients and readers. "My patients tell me they feel better than they have in years. This is ideal for people who are feeling old and run down, or for those who feel more forgetful. It surprises many that you can add healthy and productive years to your life simply by taking **Ultra Accel Q** every day."

You may have seen Dr. Sears on television or read one of his 12 best-selling books. Or you may have seen him speak at the 2016 WPBF 25 Health and Wellness Festival in South Florida, featuring Dr. Oz and special guest Suzanne Somers. Thousands of people attended Dr. Sears's lecture on anti-aging breakthroughs and waited in line for hours during his book signing at the event.

Will Ultra Accel Q Multiply Your Energy?

Ultra Accel Q is turning everything we thought we knew about youthful energy on its head. Especially for people over age 50. In less than 30 seconds every morning, you can harness the power of this breakthrough discovery to restore peak energy and your "spark for life."

So, if you've noticed less energy as you've gotten older, and you want an easy way to reclaim your youthful edge, this new opportunity will feel like blessed relief.

The secret is the "energy multiplying" molecule that activates a dormant gene in your body that declines with age, which then instructs your cells to pump out fresh energy from the in-

MEMORY-BUILDING SENSATION: Top doctors are now recommending new *Ultra Accel Q* because it restores decades of lost brain power without a doctor's visit.

side-out. This growth of new "energy factories" in your cells is called mitochondrial biogenesis.

Instead of falling victim to that afternoon slump, you enjoy sharp-as-a-tack focus, memory, and concentration from sunup to sundown. And you get more done in a day than most do in a week. Regardless of how exhausting the world is now.

Dr. Sears reports, "The most rewarding aspect of practicing medicine is watching my patients get the joy back in their lives. **Ultra Accel Q** sends a wake-up call to every cell in their bodies... And they actually feel young again."

And his patients agree. "I noticed a difference within a few days," says Jerry from Ft. Pierce, Florida. "My endurance has almost doubled, and I feel it mentally, too. There's a clarity and sense of well-being in my life that I've never experienced before."

How To Get Ultra Accel Q

This is the official nationwide release of **Ultra Accel Q** in the United States. And so, the company is offering a special discount supply to anyone who calls during the official launch.

An Order Hotline has been set up for local readers to call. This gives everyone an equal chance to try **Ultra Accel Q**. And your order is backed up by a no-hassle, 90-day money back guarantee. No questions asked.

Starting at 7:00 AM today, the discount offer will be available for a limited time only. All you have to do is call TOLL FREE 1-800-997-7461 right now and use promo code OFAUAQ0824 to secure your own supply.

Important: Due to **Ultra Accel Q**'s recent media exposure, phone lines are often busy. If you call and do not immediately get through, please be patient and call back.

THE OLD
FARMER'S ALMANAC

Established in 1792 and published every year thereafter
ROBERT B. THOMAS, *founder* (1766–1846)

YANKEE PUBLISHING INC.
P.O. Box 520, 1121 Main Street, Dublin, NH 03444
Phone: 603-563-8111 • Fax: 603-563-8252
PUBLISHER *(23rd since 1792)*: Sherin Pierce

FOR DISPLAY ADVERTISING RATES
Go to Almanac.com/AdvertisingInfo or call 800-895-9265, ext. 109

Stephanie Bernbach-Crowe • 914-827-0015
Steve Hall • 800-736-1100, ext. 320

FOR CLASSIFIED ADVERTISING
Cindy Levine, RJ Media • 212-986-0016

SENIOR AD PRODUCTION COORDINATOR:
Janet Selle • 800-895-9265, ext. 168

PUBLIC RELATIONS
Vaughan Communications • 360-620-9107
Ginger Vaughan • ginger@vaughancomm.com

CONSUMER ORDERS & INFO
Call 800-ALMANAC (800-256-2622), ext. 1
or go to Almanac.com/Shop

RETAIL SALES
Stacey Korpi • 800-895-9265, ext. 160
Janice Edson, ext. 126

DISTRIBUTORS
NATIONAL: Comag Marketing Group
Smyrna, GA
BOOKSTORE: HarperCollins Publishers
New York, NY
NEWSSTAND CONSULTANT: PSCS Consulting
Linda Ruth • 603-924-4407

Old Farmer's Almanac publications are available for sales promotions or premiums. Contact Beacon Promotions, info@beaconpromotions.com.

YANKEE PUBLISHING INCORPORATED
A 100% EMPLOYEE-OWNED COMPANY

Jamie Trowbridge, *President*
Paul Belliveau, Ernesto Burden, Judson D. Hale Jr., Brook Holmberg, Jennie Meister, Sherin Pierce, *Vice Presidents*
Judson D. Hale Sr., *Editor Emeritus*

2025

ECLIPSES

There will be four eclipses in 2025, two of the Sun and two of the Moon. Solar eclipses are visible only in certain areas and require eye protection to be viewed safely. Lunar eclipses are technically visible from the entire night side of Earth, but during a penumbral eclipse, the dimming of the Moon's illumination is slight. See the **Astronomical Glossary, page 110,** for explanations of the different types of eclipses.

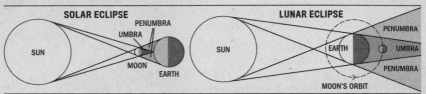

MARCH 13-14: TOTAL ECLIPSE OF THE MOON. This eclipse is visible from North America. The Moon will enter the penumbra at 11:56 P.M. EDT (8:56 P.M. PDT) on March 13 and umbra at 1:09 A.M. EDT on March 14 (10:09 P.M. PDT, March 13). It will leave the umbra at 4:48 A.M. EDT (1:48 A.M. PDT) on March 14 and penumbra at 6:02 A.M. EDT (3:02 A.M. PDT).

MARCH 29: PARTIAL ECLIPSE OF THE SUN. This eclipse is visible from northeastern North America, although it will be difficult to observe in the U.S. without an unobstructed view of the horizon. The Sun will rise at 6:31 A.M. EDT in Boston, but when the eclipse ends at 7:07 A.M. EDT, it will be only about 6 degrees above the horizon. Observers in some areas of eastern Canada, including Newfoundland and Labrador, will have a better view of the eclipse. As with all partial eclipses, this event is safe to observe only when using proper eye protection, such as "eclipse glasses."

SEPTEMBER 7: TOTAL ECLIPSE OF THE MOON. This eclipse is not visible from North America, although a brief period of the penumbral eclipse will be visible from Hawaii and very western Alaska before the Moon sets. Since the Moon will be very low on the horizon, this portion of the eclipse may not be visible from these areas if the Moon is obscured by local terrain. The Moon will enter the penumbra at 5:27 A.M. HAT and set just after 6:00 A.M. HAT.

SEPTEMBER 21: PARTIAL ECLIPSE OF THE SUN. This eclipse is not visible from North America. (It is visible only from the South Pacific, New Zealand, and parts of Antarctica.)

THE MOON'S PATH

The Moon's path across the sky changes with the seasons. Full Moons are very high in the sky (at midnight) between November and February and very low in the sky between May and July.

FULL-MOON DATES (ET)

	2025	2026	2027	2028	2029
JAN.	13	3	22	11	30
FEB.	12	1	20	10	28
MAR.	14	3	22	10	29
APR.	12	1	20	9	28
MAY	12	1 & 31	20	8	27
JUNE	11	29	18	7	25
JULY	10	29	18	6	25
AUG.	9	28	17	5	23
SEPT.	7	26	15	3	22
OCT.	6	26	15	3	22
NOV.	5	24	13	2	20
DEC.	4	23	13	1 & 31	20

New Blood Flow Breakthrough Helps Men Enjoy Strong, Long-Lasting Intimacy – At Any Age

Men across America are raving about a newly enhanced potency supplement that helps achieve healthy blood flow on demand

After age 40, it's common knowledge that performance begins to decline in many men. However, a new, performance empowering pill is showing that any relatively healthy man can now enjoy long-lasting, and frequent intimacy – at any age.

This doctor-designed formula, created by leading anti-aging expert Dr. Al Sears, has already helped men overcome low and sinking libido -- and has recently undergone a potency-enhancing update – with remarkable new results.

When the first pill -- **Primal Max Black** -- was first released, it quickly became a top-selling men's performance helper, promoting intimacy across America.

It worked by supporting healthy testosterone levels. However, Dr. Sears soon realized that this isn't the only challenge men face with performance. That's when he turned his attention to blood flow.

And this became **Primal Max Red**.

THIS PROVEN SOLUTION IS MORE MECHANICAL THAN HORMONAL

Truth is, once blood flow slows down for men, no matter how exciting it is, it won't be enough without the necessary amount...

So enjoying intimacy without healthy blood flow becomes difficult for most men.

Luckily, a Nobel prize-winning scientist discovered the simple answer to help support performance strength and confidence -- by boosting vital blood flow -- and enhancing this essential performance function.

Using this landmark Nobel Prize as its basis, **Primal Max Red** enhanced healthy blood flow for untold millions of men around the world with the use of strong nitric oxide boosters.

While **Primal Max Black** helped maintain optimal testosterone, **Primal Max Red** tackles a lesser-known challenge.

Director, Al Sears MD, who has authored over 500 scientific papers and has appeared on more than 50 media outlets including ABC News, CNN, ESPN, Discovery, Lifetime, and many more say, *"Less than optimal blood flow can be part of a huge problem that affects a lot of men. And it needed to be addressed once and for all, so men would not dwell on it. Then, once we optimized it and had a great deal of success, we set out to see if we could do even better."*

The former formula had excellent results. However, new research showed that for even faster, anytime, anywhere results, increasing the dose of a key compound was needed.

So, one of the three nitric oxide boosters in the new **Primal Max Red**, L-Citrulline, was clinically boosted to 9000 mg, and the results were astounding. Which is no surprise considering that 5000 mg is considered a "normal amount" -- giving the new version nearly doubled the blood flow boosting power.

Men who had previously been unsure about their

A new discovery that increases nitric oxide availability was recently proven to boost blood flow 275% - resulting in improved performance.

power and stamina were overjoyed to be back to their old selves and to get and maintain a healthy bloodflow when they needed it.

BETTER BLOOD FLOW, STRONGER RESULTS

The best way to promote healthy blood flow throughout the body is with the use of **Primal Max Red**. By using it, when exciting signals leave the brain, blood flows much faster like it used to.

This critical action is how men across the country are enjoying full and satisfying performance at any age. No need to bother with testosterone-boosting shots, blue pills, or shady capsules that have no effect.

Primal Max Red can effectively promote healthy blood flow that most men can use for maximum intimacy. This is leading to more greater capacity and satisfaction, coupled with long-lasting performance.

"There was a time when men had little control when it came to boosting their blood flow," Dr. Sears said. "But science has come a long way in recent years. And now, with the creation of nitric oxide-boosting **Primal Max Red**, men can perform better than ever, and enjoy intimacy at any age."

Now for men across America, it's much easier to stay at their performance peak as they get older.

HOW TO GET PRIMAL MAX RED (AND FREE PRIMAL MAX BLACK):

To secure free bottles of **Primal Max Black** and get the hot, new **Primal Max Red** formula, buyers should contact the Sears Health Hotline at **1-800-908-1498** TODAY. "It's not available in retail stores yet," says Dr. Sears. "The Hotline allows us to ship directly to the customer." Dr. Sears feels so strongly about **Primal Max**, all orders are backed by a 100% money-back guarantee. "Just send me back the bottle and any unused product within 90 days from purchase date, and I'll send you all your money back."

Call NOW at **1-800-908-1498** to secure your supply of **Primal Max Red** and free bottles of **Primal Max Black**. Use Promo Code **OFAPMAX0824** when you call. Lines are frequently busy, but all calls will be answered!

BRIGHT STARS

TRANSIT TIMES

This table shows the time (ET) and altitude of a star as it transits the meridian (i.e., reaches its highest elevation while passing over the horizon's south point) at Boston on the dates shown. The transit time on any other date differs from that of the nearest date listed by approximately 4 minutes per day. To find the time of a star's transit for your location, convert its time at Boston using Key Letter C **(see Time Corrections, page 238).**

STAR	CONSTELLATION	MAGNITUDE	TIME OF TRANSIT (ET) BOLD = P.M. LIGHT = A.M.						ALTITUDE (DEGREES)
			JAN. 1	**MAR. 1**	**MAY 1**	**JULY 1**	**SEPT. 1**	**NOV. 1**	
Altair	Aquila	0.8	**12:50**	8:58	5:58	1:58	**9:50**	**5:50**	56.3
Deneb	Cygnus	1.3	**1:40**	9:48	6:48	2:48	**10:41**	**6:41**	92.8
Fomalhaut	Psc. Aus.	1.2	**3:56**	**12:04**	9:04	5:05	1:01	**8:57**	17.8
Algol	Perseus	2.2	**8:06**	**4:14**	**1:14**	9:15	5:11	1:11	88.5
Aldebaran	Taurus	0.9	**9:34**	**5:42**	**2:42**	10:42	6:38	2:38	64.1
Rigel	Orion	0.1	**10:12**	**6:20**	**3:20**	11:20	7:16	3:17	39.4
Capella	Auriga	0.1	**10:15**	**6:23**	**3:23**	11:23	7:19	3:19	93.6
Bellatrix	Orion	1.6	**10:23**	**6:31**	**3:31**	11:31	7:27	3:27	54.0
Betelgeuse	Orion	var. 0.4	**10:53**	**7:01**	**4:01**	**12:01**	7:57	3:57	55.0
Sirius	Can. Maj.	-1.4	**11:42**	**7:50**	**4:50**	**12:51**	8:47	4:47	31.0
Procyon	Can. Min.	0.4	12:40	**8:44**	**5:45**	**1:45**	9:41	5:41	52.9
Pollux	Gemini	1.2	12:47	**8:51**	**5:51**	**1:51**	9:47	5:47	75.7
Regulus	Leo	1.4	3:09	**11:13**	**8:13**	**4:13**	**12:10**	8:10	59.7
Spica	Virgo	var. 1.0	6:25	2:33	**11:30**	**7:30**	**3:26**	11:26	36.6
Arcturus	Boötes	-0.1	7:15	3:23	12:24	**8:20**	**4:16**	**12:16**	66.9
Antares	Scorpius	var. 0.9	9:29	5:37	2:37	**10:34**	**6:30**	**2:30**	21.3
Vega	Lyra	0	11:36	7:44	4:44	12:44	**8:36**	**4:36**	86.4

RISE AND SET TIMES

To find the time of a star's rising at Boston on any date, subtract the interval shown at right from the star's transit time on that date; add the interval to find the star's setting time. To find the rising and setting times for your city, convert the Boston transit times above using the Key Letter shown at right before applying the interval **(see Time Corrections, page 238).** Deneb, Algol, Capella, and Vega are circumpolar stars—they never set but appear to circle the celestial north pole.

STAR	INTERVAL (H.M.)	RISING KEY	DIR.*	SETTING KEY	DIR.*
Altair	6 36	B	EbN	E	WbN
Fomalhaut	3 59	E	SE	D	SW
Aldebaran	7 06	B	ENE	D	WNW
Rigel	5 33	D	EbS	B	WbS
Bellatrix	6 27	B	EbN	D	WbN
Betelgeuse	6 31	B	EbN	D	WbN
Sirius	5 00	D	ESE	B	WSW
Procyon	6 23	B	EbN	D	WbN
Pollux	8 01	A	NE	E	NW
Regulus	6 49	B	EbN	D	WbN
Spica	5 23	D	EbS	B	WbS
Arcturus	7 19	A	ENE	E	WNW
Antares	4 17	E	SEbE	A	SWbW

*b = "by"

THE TWILIGHT ZONE/METEOR SHOWERS

Twilight is the time when the sky is partially illuminated preceding sunrise and again following sunset. The ranges of twilight are defined according to the Sun's position below the horizon. **Civil twilight** occurs when the Sun's center is between the horizon and 6 degrees below the horizon (visually, the horizon is clearly defined). **Nautical twilight** occurs when the center is between 6 and 12 degrees below the horizon (the horizon is distinct). **Astronomical twilight** occurs when the center is between 12 and 18 degrees below the horizon (sky illumination is imperceptible). When the center is at 18 degrees (**dawn** or **dark**) or below, there is no illumination.

LENGTH OF ASTRONOMICAL TWILIGHT (HOURS AND MINUTES)

LATITUDE	JAN. 1– APR. 10	APR. 11– MAY 2	MAY 3– MAY 14	MAY 15– MAY 25	MAY 26– JULY 22	JULY 23– AUG. 3	AUG. 4– AUG. 14	AUG. 15– SEPT. 5	SEPT. 6– DEC. 31
25°N to 30°N	1 20	1 23	1 26	1 29	1 32	1 29	1 26	1 23	1 20
31°N to 36°N	1 26	1 28	1 34	1 38	1 43	1 38	1 34	1 28	1 26
37°N to 42°N	1 33	1 39	1 47	1 52	1 59	1 52	1 47	1 39	1 33
43°N to 47°N	1 42	1 51	2 02	2 13	2 27	2 13	2 02	1 51	1 42
48°N to 49°N	1 50	2 04	2 22	2 42	–	2 42	2 22	2 04	1 50

TO DETERMINE THE LENGTH OF TWILIGHT: The length of twilight changes with latitude and the time of year. See the **Time Corrections, page 238,** to find the latitude of your city or the city nearest you. Use that figure in the chart above with the appropriate date to calculate the length of twilight in your area.

TO DETERMINE ARRIVAL OF DAWN OR DARK: Calculate the sunrise/sunset times for your locality using the instructions in **How to Use This Almanac, page 116.**

Subtract the length of twilight from the time of sunrise to determine when dawn breaks. Add the length of twilight to the time of sunset to determine when dark descends.

EXAMPLE:
BOSTON, MASS. (LATITUDE 42°22')

Sunrise, August 1	5:37 A.M. ET
Length of twilight	– 1 52
Dawn breaks	3:45 A.M.
Sunset, August 1	8:03 P.M. ET
Length of twilight	+1 52
Dark descends	9:55 P.M.

PRINCIPAL METEOR SHOWERS

SHOWER	BEST VIEWING	POINT OF ORIGIN	DATE OF MAXIMUM*	NO. PER HOUR**	ASSOCIATED COMET
Quadrantid	**Predawn**	N	Jan. 4	25	–
Lyrid	Predawn	S	Apr. 22	10	Thatcher
Eta Aquarid	Predawn	SE	May 4	10	Halley
Delta Aquarid	Predawn	S	July 30	10	–
Perseid	**Predawn**	**NE**	**Aug. 11–13**	**50**	**Swift-Tuttle**
Draconid	Late evening	NW	Oct. 9	6	Giacobini-Zinner
Orionid	Predawn	S	Oct. 21–22	15	Halley
Northern Taurid	Late evening	S	Nov. 9	3	Encke
Leonid	Predawn	S	Nov. 17–18	10	Tempel-Tuttle
Andromedid	Late evening	S	Nov. 25–27	5	Biela
Geminid	**All night**	**NE**	**Dec. 13–14**	**75**	**–**
Ursid	Predawn	N	Dec. 22	5	Tuttle

*May vary by 1 or 2 days   **In a moonless, rural sky   **Bold** = most prominent

THE VISIBLE PLANETS

Listed here for Boston are viewing suggestions for and the rise and set times (ET) of Venus, Mars, Jupiter, and Saturn on specific days each month, as well as when it is best to view Mercury. Approximate rise and set times for other days can be found by interpolation. Use the Key Letters at the right of each listing to convert the times for other localities **(see pages 116 and 238).**

GET ALL PLANET RISE AND SET TIMES BY ZIP CODE VIA ALMANAC.COM/2025.

VENUS

Venus has been beloved by civilizations for centuries. In reality, though, space probes report woodstove-like surface temperatures of 850°F and an atmosphere made up of thick carbon dioxide laced with sulfuric acid droplets. Still, Earth's "sister planet" and closest neighbor has a dazzling brilliance that keeps our eyes glued its way. Venus starts off the year brilliant after sunset and remains a riveting evening star until descending into dusk's twilight on March 9. After an inferior conjunction on March 22, the planet quickly shifts to being a morning star that endures until mid-November. Its 2025 highlights include an extremely close predawn meeting with Jupiter on August 12 and a three-way conjunction with the Moon and Leo's bright star, Regulus, on September 19 at 6:00 A.M.

Jan. 1	set	**8:16**	B	Apr. 1	rise	5:20	C	July 1	rise	2:37	B	Oct. 1	rise	4:38	C
Jan. 11	set	**8:33**	B	Apr. 11	rise	4:45	C	July 11	rise	2:33	B	Oct. 11	rise	5:02	C
Jan. 21	set	**8:45**	C	Apr. 21	rise	4:19	C	July 21	rise	2:33	A	Oct. 21	rise	5:26	C
Feb. 1	set	**8:52**	C	May 1	rise	3:59	C	Aug. 1	rise	2:40	A	Nov. 1	rise	5:53	D
Feb. 11	set	**8:51**	D	May 11	rise	3:41	C	Aug. 11	rise	2:51	A	Nov. 11	rise	5:18	D
Feb. 21	set	**8:38**	D	May 21	rise	3:25	C	Aug. 21	rise	3:07	A	Nov. 21	rise	5:44	E
Mar. 1	set	**8:15**	D	June 1	rise	3:09	B	Sept. 1	rise	3:29	B	Dec. 1	rise	6:10	E
Mar. 11	set	**8:28**	D	June 11	rise	2:56	B	Sept. 11	rise	3:51	B	Dec. 11	rise	6:34	E
Mar. 21	rise	6:10	B	June 21	rise	2:45	B	Sept. 21	rise	4:14	B	Dec. 21	rise	6:55	E
												Dec. 31	rise	7:12	E

MARS

The Red Planet spectacularly brightens every 26 months—and its appearance in early January will have been worth the wait. Its greatest display arrives on January 13, just as it reaches its brightest presence until 2031. On this night at around 8:00 P.M., Mars becomes totally eclipsed by the Moon in a rare event called an "occultation." Fortunately, this occurrence is visible from nearly all of mainland North America and lasts for an hour. Mars comes to opposition on January 15. After January, Mars gradually fades and sinks until it vanishes into the evening twilight in late August—but not before gliding near the "Beehive" star cluster, a true spectacle seen best through binoculars from May 1 to 6.

Jan. 1	**rise**	**5:38**	A	Apr. 1	set	3:28	E	July 1	set	**11:22**	D	Oct. 1	set	**7:29**	B
Jan. 11	**rise**	**4:38**	A	Apr. 11	set	3:00	E	July 11	set	**10:55**	D	Oct. 11	set	**7:07**	B
Jan. 21	set	7:14	E	Apr. 21	set	2:32	E	July 21	set	**10:29**	C	Oct. 21	set	**6:47**	B
Feb. 1	set	6:17	E	May 1	set	2:05	E	Aug. 1	set	**10:00**	C	Nov. 1	set	**6:27**	A
Feb. 11	set	5:28	E	May 11	set	1:39	E	Aug. 11	set	**9:34**	C	Nov. 11	set	**5:11**	A
Feb. 21	set	4:44	E	May 21	set	1:13	E	Aug. 21	set	**9:08**	C	Nov. 21	set	**4:57**	A
Mar. 1	set	4:12	E	June 1	set	12:44	E	Sept. 1	set	**8:40**	C	Dec. 1	set	**4:45**	A
Mar. 11	set	4:35	E	June 11	set	12:17	E	Sept. 11	set	**8:15**	B	Dec. 11	set	**4:37**	A
Mar. 21	set	4:02	E	June 21	set	**11:48**	D	Sept. 21	set	**7:51**	B	Dec. 21	set	**4:30**	A
												Dec. 31	set	**4:26**	A

BOLD = P.M. LIGHT = A.M.

JUPITER

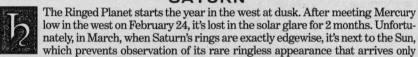

Earth's much faster orbital speed causes rare odd years with no Jovian opposition at all—2025 being one of them. Jupiter begins the year as a brilliant "star" in the south after nightfall. By April, it occupies the western sky after nightfall. The gas giant gets lower in the western sky in May before vanishing behind the Sun in June. Jupiter reappears in the east before dawn in early July. It meets Venus from August 11 to 13, then rises earlier until it's visible all night in December. By year's end, Jupiter is at its brightest as it approaches its opposition on January 9, 2026.

Jan. 1	set	5:15	E	Apr. 1	set	12:36	E	July 1	rise	4:51	A	Oct. 1	rise	12:13	A
Jan. 11	set	4:32	E	Apr. 11	set	12:05	E	July 11	rise	4:22	A	Oct. 11	**rise**	**11:35**	A

Jan. 1	set	5:15	E	Apr. 1	set	12:36	E	July 1	rise	4:51	A	Oct. 1	rise	12:13	A
Jan. 11	set	4:32	E	Apr. 11	set	12:05	E	July 11	rise	4:22	A	Oct. 11	**rise**	**11:35**	A
Jan. 21	set	3:49	E	Apr. 21	**set**	**11:31**	E	July 21	rise	3:53	A	Oct. 21	**rise**	**11:00**	A
Feb. 1	set	3:05	E	May 1	**set**	**11:01**	E	Aug. 1	rise	3:21	A	Nov. 1	**rise**	**10:19**	A
Feb. 11	set	2:26	E	May 11	**set**	**10:31**	E	Aug. 11	rise	2:51	A	Nov. 11	**rise**	**8:40**	A
Feb. 21	set	1:49	E	May 21	**set**	**10:02**	E	Aug. 21	rise	2:22	A	Nov. 21	**rise**	**8:00**	A
Mar. 1	set	1:20	E	June 1	**set**	**9:29**	E	Sept. 1	rise	1:48	A	Dec. 1	**rise**	**7:18**	A
Mar. 11	set	1:45	E	June 11	**set**	**9:00**	E	Sept. 11	rise	1:17	A	Dec. 11	**rise**	**6:35**	A
Mar. 21	set	1:12	E	June 21	**set**	**8:30**	E	Sept. 21	rise	12:45	A	Dec. 21	**rise**	**5:50**	A
												Dec. 31	**rise**	**5:04**	A

SATURN

The Ringed Planet starts the year in the west at dusk. After meeting Mercury low in the west on February 24, it's lost in the solar glare for 2 months. Unfortunately, in March, when Saturn's rings are exactly edgewise, it's next to the Sun, which prevents observation of its rare ringless appearance that arrives only once every 15 years. Saturn returns as a morning star and gradually rises earlier until it's visible in August. Its opposition and closest approach occur on September 21, when its rings will still be nearly edgewise to our view and its southern hemisphere will be tilted our way. For the rest of the year, Saturn remains visible most of the night. It meets the Moon on October 6 and is the nearest "star" to the Moon on November 28 and 29.

Jan. 1	**set**	**9:37**	B	Apr. 1	rise	5:59	C	July 1	rise	12:18	C	Oct. 1	set	5:50	C
Jan. 11	**set**	**9:02**	B	Apr. 11	rise	5:22	C	July 11	**rise**	**11:36**	C	Oct. 11	set	5:07	C
Jan. 21	**set**	**8:27**	C	Apr. 21	rise	4:45	C	July 21	**rise**	**10:56**	C	Oct. 21	set	4:24	C
Feb. 1	**set**	**7:50**	C	May 1	rise	4:08	C	Aug. 1	**rise**	**10:13**	C	Nov. 1	set	3:38	C
Feb. 11	**set**	**7:16**	C	May 11	rise	3:31	C	Aug. 11	**rise**	**9:33**	C	Nov. 11	set	1:57	C
Feb. 21	**set**	**6:43**	C	May 21	rise	2:54	C	Aug. 21	**rise**	**8:52**	C	Nov. 21	set	1:16	C
Mar. 1	**set**	**6:17**	C	June 1	rise	2:13	C	Sept. 1	**rise**	**8:08**	C	Dec. 1	set	12:37	C
Mar. 11	**set**	**6:44**	C	June 11	rise	1:35	C	Sept. 11	**rise**	**7:27**	C	Dec. 11	set	11:55	C
Mar. 21	rise	6:39	C	June 21	rise	1:01	C	Sept. 21	**rise**	**6:46**	C	Dec. 21	set	11:17	C
												Dec. 31	set	10:40	C

MERCURY

Mercury visually dashes from one side of the Sun to the other, spending about 2 months visible before dawn before later becoming an evening star low in the west after sunset. Between these brief observation windows, the innermost planet is positioned in front of or behind the Sun, lost in its glare. This year, its most favorable evening star conditions occur from February 22 to March 15 and June 12 to July 8. In the predawn eastern sky, Mercury is best seen from August 12 to September 3 and November 27 to December 25.

DO NOT CONFUSE: *Saturn with Mercury, very low in the west on February 24. Mercury is orange and brighter. • Jupiter with Venus from August 11 to 13 before dawn. While the two planets seemingly almost touch, Venus is dramatically brighter. • Uranus during its opposition on November 21 with the many faint stars in Taurus. Seen through binoculars, Uranus is the only green "star" below the famous Pleiades star cluster.*

APHELION (APH.): The point in a planet's orbit that is farthest from the Sun.

APOGEE (APO.): The point in the Moon's orbit that is farthest from Earth.

CELESTIAL EQUATOR (EQ.): The imaginary circle around the celestial sphere that can be thought of as the plane of Earth's equator projected out onto the sphere.

CELESTIAL SPHERE: An imaginary sphere projected into space that represents the entire sky, with an observer on Earth at its center. All celestial bodies other than Earth are imagined as being on its inside surface.

CIRCUMPOLAR: Always visible above the horizon, such as a circumpolar star.

CONJUNCTION: The time at which two or more celestial bodies appear closest in the sky. **Inferior (Inf.):** Mercury or Venus is between the Sun and Earth. **Superior (Sup.):** The Sun is between a planet and Earth. Actual dates for conjunctions are given on the **Right-Hand Calendar Pages, 121–147**; the best times for viewing the closely aligned bodies are given in **Sky Watch** on the **Left-Hand Calendar Pages, 120–146.**

DECLINATION: The celestial latitude of an object in the sky, measured in degrees north or south of the celestial equator; comparable to latitude on Earth. This Almanac gives the Sun's declination at noon.

ECLIPSE, LUNAR: The full Moon enters the shadow of Earth, which cuts off all or part of the sunlight reflected off the Moon. **Total:** The Moon passes completely through the umbra (central dark part) of Earth's shadow. **Partial:** Only part of the Moon passes through the umbra. **Penumbral:** The Moon passes through only the penumbra (area of partial darkness surrounding the umbra). See **page 102** for more information about eclipses.

ECLIPSE, SOLAR: Earth enters the shadow of the new Moon, which cuts off all or part of the Sun's light. **Total:** Earth passes through the umbra (central dark part) of the Moon's shadow, resulting in totality for observers within a narrow band on Earth. **Annular:** The Moon appears silhouetted against the Sun, with a ring of sunlight showing around it. **Partial:** The Moon blocks only part of the Sun.

ECLIPTIC: The apparent annual path of the Sun around the celestial sphere. The plane of the ecliptic is tipped 23½° from the celestial equator.

ELONGATION: The difference in degrees between the celestial longitudes of a planet and the Sun. **Greatest Elongation (Gr. Elong.):** The greatest apparent distance of a planet from the Sun, as seen from Earth.

EPACT: A number from 1 to 30 that indicates the Moon's age on January 1 at Greenwich, England; used in determining the date of Easter.

EQUINOX: When the Sun crosses the celestial equator. This event occurs two times each year: **Vernal** is around March 20 and **Autumnal** is around September 22.

EVENING STAR: A planet that is above the western horizon at sunset and less than 180° east of the Sun in right ascension.

GOLDEN NUMBER: A number in the 19-year Metonic cycle of the Moon, used in determining the date of Easter. See **page 149** for this year's Golden Number.

MAGNITUDE: A measure of a celestial object's brightness. **Apparent magnitude** measures the brightness of an object as seen from Earth. Objects with an apparent magnitude of 6 or less are observable to the naked eye. The lower the magnitude, the greater the brightness; an object with a magnitude of –1, e.g., is brighter than one with a magnitude of +1.

MIDNIGHT: Astronomically, the time when the Sun is opposite its highest point in the sky. Both 12 hours before and after noon (so, technically, both A.M. and P.M.), midnight in civil time is usually treated as the beginning of the day. It is displayed as 12:00 A.M. on 12-hour digital clocks. On a 24-hour cycle, 00:00, not 24:00, usually indicates midnight.

MOON ON EQUATOR: The Moon is on the celestial equator.

MOON RIDES HIGH/RUNS LOW: The Moon is highest above or farthest below the celestial equator.

MOONRISE/MOONSET: When the Moon rises above or sets below the horizon.

MOON'S PHASES: The changing appearance of the Moon, caused by the different angles at which it is illuminated by the Sun. **First Quarter:** Right half of the Moon is illuminated. **Full:** The Sun and the Moon are in opposition; the entire disk of the Moon is illuminated. **Last Quarter:** Left half of the Moon is illuminated. **New:** The Sun and the Moon are in conjunction; the Moon is darkened because it lines up between Earth and the Sun.

MOON'S PLACE, Astronomical: The position of the Moon within the constellations on the celestial sphere at midnight. **Astrological:** The position of the Moon within the tropical zodiac, whose twelve 30° segments (signs) along the ecliptic were named more than 2,000 years ago after constellations within each area. Because of precession and other factors, the zodiac signs no longer match actual constellation positions.

MORNING STAR: A planet that is above the eastern horizon at sunrise and less than 180° west of the Sun in right ascension.

NODE: Either of the two points where a celestial body's orbit intersects the ecliptic. **Ascending:** When the body is moving from south to north of the ecliptic. **Descending:** When the body is moving from north to south of the ecliptic.

OCCULTATION (OCCN.): When the Moon or a planet eclipses a star or planet.

OPPOSITION: The Moon or a planet appears on the opposite side of the sky from the Sun (elongation 180°).

PERIGEE (PERIG.): The point in the Moon's orbit that is closest to Earth.

PERIHELION (PERIH.): The point in a planet's orbit that is closest to the Sun.

PRECESSION: The slowly changing position of the stars and equinoxes in the sky caused by a slight wobble as Earth rotates around its axis.

RIGHT ASCENSION (R.A.): The celestial longitude of an object in the sky, measured eastward along the celestial equator in hours of time from the vernal equinox; comparable to longitude on Earth.

SOLSTICE, Summer: When the Sun reaches its greatest declination (23½°) north of the celestial equator, around June 21. **Winter:** When the Sun reaches its greatest declination (23½°) south of the celestial equator, around December 21.

STATIONARY (STAT.): The brief period of apparent halted movement of a planet against the background of the stars shortly before it appears to move backward/westward (retrograde motion) or forward/eastward (direct motion).

SUN FAST/SLOW: When a sundial is ahead of (fast) or behind (slow) clock time.

SUNRISE/SUNSET: The visible rising/setting of the upper edge of the Sun's disk across the unobstructed horizon of an observer whose eyes are 15 feet above ground level.

TWILIGHT: See **page 106.** ∎

Note: These definitions apply to the Northern Hemisphere; some do not hold true for locations in the Southern Hemisphere.

THE PLANETS OF THE SOLAR SYSTEM

–ChrisGorgio/Getty Images

Our solar system is made up of eight planets (including Earth), each unique in its own way. Five of these—Mercury, Venus, Mars, Jupiter, and Saturn—are visible with the naked eye, but to truly see all of the planets and their remarkable features, you should use a telescope if you can. (In 2006, the International Astronomical Union reclassified Pluto—once considered our solar system's ninth planet—as a dwarf planet.)

The best times to view each planet, including its conjunctions and brightest moments, can be found in **Visible Planets (pages 108–109)** and **Sky Watch (pages 120–146).** (Note: Only objects farther from Earth than the Sun can be in opposition—when the Moon or a planet is at its brightest and appears on the opposite side of the sky from the Sun.)

How do planets in our solar system compare? Read on to learn more.

MERCURY
Facts: smallest planet and closest to the Sun; temperature can go to as low as –290°F at night; second densest planet
Mean temperature: 333°F
Radius: 1,516 miles
Distance from Sun (avg.): 36 million miles
Closest distance to Earth: 48 million miles
Length of day: 59 Earth days
Structure: solid, metallic inner core with molten outer core; rocky mantle; solid crust
Length of year: 88 Earth days
Moons: None

VENUS
Facts: 1 day on Venus is longer than 1 Venus year; 36,000-foot-tall Maxwell Montes (mountain) is taller than Mount Everest; thousands of volcanoes
Mean temperature: 867°F
Radius: 3,760 miles
Distance from Sun (avg.): 67 million miles
Closest distance to Earth: 24 million miles
Length of day: 243 Earth days
Structure: iron core (similar to Earth's) enveloped by a hot rock mantle; rocky, exterior crust
Length of year: 224.7 Earth days
Moons: None

EARTH
Facts: 70 percent ocean; surface includes volcanoes, mountains, valleys, rivers, lakes, trees, plants; densest planet in solar system; only planet to sustain life
Mean temperature: 59°F
Radius: 3,963 miles
Distance from Sun (avg.): 93 million miles
Length of Day: 23.9 hours
Structure: iron and nickel metals (core), iron and nickel fluids; molten rock; oceanic and continental crust
Length of year: 365.25 days
Moons: 1

MARS

Facts: reddish surface due to oxidation; Valles Marineris canyon system is 10 times the size of Grand Canyon; Olympus Mons is largest volcano in solar system
Mean temperature: –85°F
Radius: 2,106 miles
Distance from Sun (avg.): 142 million miles
Closest distance to Earth: 34.6 million miles
Length of day: 24.6 hours
Structure: core made of iron, nickel, and sulfur; rocky mantle; crust made of iron, magnesium, aluminum, calcium, and potassium
Length of year: 687 Earth days
Opposition: every 26 months—next: January 15, 2025
Moons: 2—Phobos and Deimos

JUPITER

Facts: largest planet in solar system; four rings; largest ocean in solar system—made of hydrogen
Mean temperature: –166°F
Radius: 43,441 miles
Distance from Sun (avg.): 484 million miles
Closest distance to Earth: 367 million miles
Length of day: 10 hours
Structure: hydrogen and helium
Length of year: 4,333 Earth days (about 12 Earth years)
Opposition: every 13 months—next: December 7, 2024; January 9, 2026
Moons: 95, including Callisto and Ganymede (largest in solar system)

SATURN

Facts: rings composed of ice, dust, and rock; winds in upper atmosphere reach 1,090 mph—more than four times faster than the strongest hurricane-force winds on Earth
Mean temperature: –220°F
Radius: 36,183 miles
Distance from Sun (avg.): 886 million miles
Closest distance to Earth: 746 million miles
Length of day: 10.7 hours
Structure: core of iron and nickel; hydrogen and helium

Length of year: 10,756 Earth days (about 29.4 Earth years)
Opposition: every 378 days—next: September 8, 2024; September 21, 2025
Moons: 146, including Titan—second largest in solar system

URANUS

Facts: two sets of rings (13 total); blue-green color comes from methane gas in atmosphere; near core, temperature can reach 9,000°F
Mean temperature: –320°F
Radius: 15,759 miles
Distance from Sun (avg.): 1.8 billion miles
Closest distance to Earth: 1.6 billion miles
Length of day: 17.4 hours
Structure: small, rocky core; one of two ice giants in solar system; most of mass made up of swirling fluids—water, methane, and ammonia
Length of year: 30,687 Earth days (about 84 Earth years)
Opposition: every 369 days—next: November 16, 2024; November 21, 2025
Moons: 28—named for characters in works by William Shakespeare and Alexander Pope

NEPTUNE

Facts: has the only large moon (Triton) in the solar system that orbits in the opposite direction of its planet's rotation; 5 rings, 4 ring arcs; windiest planet with surface speeds of more than 1,200 mph
Mean temperature: –330°F
Radius: 15,299 miles
Distance from Sun (avg.): 2.8 billion miles
Closest distance to Earth: 2.7 billion miles
Length of day: 16 hours
Structure: small, rocky core; one of two ice giants in solar system; most of mass made up of swirling fluids—water, methane, and ammonia
Length of year: 60,190 Earth days (about 165 Earth years)
Opposition: every 367 days—next: September 20, 2024; September 23, 2025
Moons: 16, including Triton

2024

JANUARY
S	M	T	W	T	F	S
	1	2	3	4	5	6
7	8	9	10	11	12	13
14	15	16	17	18	19	20
21	22	23	24	25	26	27
28	29	30	31			

FEBRUARY
S	M	T	W	T	F	S
				1	2	3
4	5	6	7	8	9	10
11	12	13	14	15	16	17
18	19	20	21	22	23	24
25	26	27	28	29		

MARCH
S	M	T	W	T	F	S
					1	2
3	4	5	6	7	8	9
10	11	12	13	14	15	16
17	18	19	20	21	22	23
24	25	26	27	28	29	30
31						

APRIL
S	M	T	W	T	F	S
	1	2	3	4	5	6
7	8	9	10	11	12	13
14	15	16	17	18	19	20
21	22	23	24	25	26	27
28	29	30				

MAY
S	M	T	W	T	F	S
			1	2	3	4
5	6	7	8	9	10	11
12	13	14	15	16	17	18
19	20	21	22	23	24	25
26	27	28	29	30	31	

JUNE
S	M	T	W	T	F	S
						1
2	3	4	5	6	7	8
9	10	11	12	13	14	15
16	17	18	19	20	21	22
23	24	25	26	27	28	29
30						

JULY
S	M	T	W	T	F	S
	1	2	3	4	5	6
7	8	9	10	11	12	13
14	15	16	17	18	19	20
21	22	23	24	25	26	27
28	29	30	31			

AUGUST
S	M	T	W	T	F	S
				1	2	3
4	5	6	7	8	9	10
11	12	13	14	15	16	17
18	19	20	21	22	23	24
25	26	27	28	29	30	31

SEPTEMBER
S	M	T	W	T	F	S
1	2	3	4	5	6	7
8	9	10	11	12	13	14
15	16	17	18	19	20	21
22	23	24	25	26	27	28
29	30					

OCTOBER
S	M	T	W	T	F	S
		1	2	3	4	5
6	7	8	9	10	11	12
13	14	15	16	17	18	19
20	21	22	23	24	25	26
27	28	29	30	31		

NOVEMBER
S	M	T	W	T	F	S
					1	2
3	4	5	6	7	8	9
10	11	12	13	14	15	16
17	18	19	20	21	22	23
24	25	26	27	28	29	30

DECEMBER
S	M	T	W	T	F	S
1	2	3	4	5	6	7
8	9	10	11	12	13	14
15	16	17	18	19	20	21
22	23	24	25	26	27	28
29	30	31				

2025

JANUARY
S	M	T	W	T	F	S
			1	2	3	4
5	6	7	8	9	10	11
12	13	14	15	16	17	18
19	20	21	22	23	24	25
26	27	28	29	30	31	

FEBRUARY
S	M	T	W	T	F	S
						1
2	3	4	5	6	7	8
9	10	11	12	13	14	15
16	17	18	19	20	21	22
23	24	25	26	27	28	

MARCH
S	M	T	W	T	F	S
						1
2	3	4	5	6	7	8
9	10	11	12	13	14	15
16	17	18	19	20	21	22
23	24	25	26	27	28	29
30	31					

APRIL
S	M	T	W	T	F	S
		1	2	3	4	5
6	7	8	9	10	11	12
13	14	15	16	17	18	19
20	21	22	23	24	25	26
27	28	29	30			

MAY
S	M	T	W	T	F	S
				1	2	3
4	5	6	7	8	9	10
11	12	13	14	15	16	17
18	19	20	21	22	23	24
25	26	27	28	29	30	31

JUNE
S	M	T	W	T	F	S
1	2	3	4	5	6	7
8	9	10	11	12	13	14
15	16	17	18	19	20	21
22	23	24	25	26	27	28
29	30					

JULY
S	M	T	W	T	F	S
		1	2	3	4	5
6	7	8	9	10	11	12
13	14	15	16	17	18	19
20	21	22	23	24	25	26
27	28	29	30	31		

AUGUST
S	M	T	W	T	F	S
					1	2
3	4	5	6	7	8	9
10	11	12	13	14	15	16
17	18	19	20	21	22	23
24	25	26	27	28	29	30
31						

SEPTEMBER
S	M	T	W	T	F	S
	1	2	3	4	5	6
7	8	9	10	11	12	13
14	15	16	17	18	19	20
21	22	23	24	25	26	27
28	29	30				

OCTOBER
S	M	T	W	T	F	S
			1	2	3	4
5	6	7	8	9	10	11
12	13	14	15	16	17	18
19	20	21	22	23	24	25
26	27	28	29	30	31	

NOVEMBER
S	M	T	W	T	F	S
						1
2	3	4	5	6	7	8
9	10	11	12	13	14	15
16	17	18	19	20	21	22
23	24	25	26	27	28	29
30						

DECEMBER
S	M	T	W	T	F	S
	1	2	3	4	5	6
7	8	9	10	11	12	13
14	15	16	17	18	19	20
21	22	23	24	25	26	27
28	29	30	31			

2026

JANUARY
S	M	T	W	T	F	S
				1	2	3
4	5	6	7	8	9	10
11	12	13	14	15	16	17
18	19	20	21	22	23	24
25	26	27	28	29	30	31

FEBRUARY
S	M	T	W	T	F	S
1	2	3	4	5	6	7
8	9	10	11	12	13	14
15	16	17	18	19	20	21
22	23	24	25	26	27	28

MARCH
S	M	T	W	T	F	S
1	2	3	4	5	6	7
8	9	10	11	12	13	14
15	16	17	18	19	20	21
22	23	24	25	26	27	28
29	30	31				

APRIL
S	M	T	W	T	F	S
			1	2	3	4
5	6	7	8	9	10	11
12	13	14	15	16	17	18
19	20	21	22	23	24	25
26	27	28	29	30		

MAY
S	M	T	W	T	F	S
					1	2
3	4	5	6	7	8	9
10	11	12	13	14	15	16
17	18	19	20	21	22	23
24	25	26	27	28	29	30
31						

JUNE
S	M	T	W	T	F	S
	1	2	3	4	5	6
7	8	9	10	11	12	13
14	15	16	17	18	19	20
21	22	23	24	25	26	27
28	29	30				

JULY
S	M	T	W	T	F	S
			1	2	3	4
5	6	7	8	9	10	11
12	13	14	15	16	17	18
19	20	21	22	23	24	25
26	27	28	29	30	31	

AUGUST
S	M	T	W	T	F	S
						1
2	3	4	5	6	7	8
9	10	11	12	13	14	15
16	17	18	19	20	21	22
23	24	25	26	27	28	29
30	31					

SEPTEMBER
S	M	T	W	T	F	S
		1	2	3	4	5
6	7	8	9	10	11	12
13	14	15	16	17	18	19
20	21	22	23	24	25	26
27	28	29	30			

OCTOBER
S	M	T	W	T	F	S
				1	2	3
4	5	6	7	8	9	10
11	12	13	14	15	16	17
18	19	20	21	22	23	24
25	26	27	28	29	30	31

NOVEMBER
S	M	T	W	T	F	S
1	2	3	4	5	6	7
8	9	10	11	12	13	14
15	16	17	18	19	20	21
22	23	24	25	26	27	28
29	30					

DECEMBER
S	M	T	W	T	F	S
		1	2	3	4	5
6	7	8	9	10	11	12
13	14	15	16	17	18	19
20	21	22	23	24	25	26
27	28	29	30	31		

Love calendar lore? Find more via Almanac.com/2025.

A CALENDAR OF THE HEAVENS FOR 2025

–Beth Krommes

The Calendar Pages (120–147) are the heart of *The Old Farmer's Almanac*. They present sky sightings and astronomical data for the entire year and are what make this book a true almanac, a "calendar of the heavens." In essence, these pages are unchanged since 1792, when Robert B. Thomas published his first edition. The long columns of numbers and symbols reveal all of nature's precision, rhythm, and glory, providing an astronomical look at the year 2025.

HOW TO USE THE CALENDAR PAGES

The astronomical data on the **Calendar Pages (120–147)** are calculated for Boston (where Robert B. Thomas learned to calculate the data for his first Almanac). Guidance for calculating the times of these events for your locale appears on **pages 116–117**. Note that the results will be *approximate*. Find the *exact* time of any astronomical event at your locale via **Almanac.com/2025**. You can also go to **Almanac.com/SkyMap** to print each month's "Sky Map," which may be useful for viewing with "Sky Watch" in the Calendar Pages.

For a list of 2025 holidays and observances, see **pages 148–149**. Also check out the **Glossary of Almanac Oddities** on **pages 150–151**, which describes some of the more obscure entries traditionally found on the **Right-Hand Calendar Pages (121–147)**.

ABOUT THE TIMES: All times are given in ET (Eastern Time), except where otherwise noted as AT (Atlantic Time, +1 hour), CT (Central Time, –1), MT (Mountain Time, –2), PT (Pacific Time, –3), AKT (Alaska Time, –4), or HAT (Hawaii-Aleutian Time, –5). Between 2:00 A.M., March 9, and 2:00 A.M., November 2, Daylight Saving Time is assumed in those locales where it is observed.

ABOUT THE TIDES: Tide times for Boston appear on **pages 120–146**; for Boston tide heights, see **pages 121–147**. Tide Corrections for East Coast locations appear on **pages 236–237**. Tide heights and times for locations across the United States and Canada are available via **Almanac.com/2025**.

The Left-Hand Calendar Pages, 120 to 146

On these pages are the year's astronomical predictions for Boston (42°22' N, 71°3' W). Learn how to calculate the times of these events for your locale here or via **Almanac.com/2025**.

A SAMPLE MONTH

SKY WATCH: The paragraph at the top of each Left-Hand Calendar Page describes the best times to view conjunctions, meteor showers, planets, and more. (Also see **How to Use the Right-Hand Calendar Pages, page 118.**)

			1		2		3	4	5		6			7	8
DAY OF YEAR	DAY OF MONTH	DAY OF WEEK	☼ RISES H. M.	RISE KEY	☼ SETS H. M.	SET KEY	LENGTH OF DAY H. M.	SUN FAST M.	SUN DECLINATION ° '	HIGH TIDE TIMES BOSTON	☾ RISES H. M.	RISE KEY	☾ SETS H. M.	SET KEY	☾ ASTRON. PLACE	☾ AGE
60	1	Fr.	6:20	D	5:34	C	11 14	4	7 s. 30	7¼ 8	3:30	E	12:58	B	SAG	25
61	2	Sa.	6:18	D	5:35	C	11 17	4	7 s. 07	8¼ 9	4:16	E	1:51	B	SAG	26
62	3	F	6:17	D	5:36	C	11 19	4	6 s. 44	9¼ 9¾	4:56	E	2:47	B	CAP	27
63	4	M.	6:15	D	5:37	C	11 22	4	6 s. 21	10 10½	5:31	E	3:45	C	CAP	28

1. To calculate the sunrise time in your locale: Choose a day. Note its Sun Rise Key Letter. Find your (nearest) city on **page 238**. Add or subtract the minutes that correspond to the Sun Rise Key Letter to/from the sunrise time for Boston.[†]

EXAMPLE:

To calculate the sunrise time in Denver, Colorado, on day 1:

Sunrise, Boston, with Key Letter D (above)	6:20 A.M. ET
Value of Key Letter D for Denver (p. 238)	+ 11 minutes
Sunrise, Denver	6:31 A.M. MT

To calculate your sunset time, repeat, using Boston's sunset time and its Sun Set Key Letter value.

2. To calculate the length of day: Choose a day. Note the Sun Rise and Sun Set Key Letters. Find your (nearest) city on **page 238**. Add or subtract the minutes that correspond to the Sun Set Key Letter to/from Boston's length of day. *Reverse* the sign (e.g., minus to plus) of the Sun Rise Key Letter minutes. Add or subtract it to/from the first result.

EXAMPLE:

To calculate the length of day in Richmond, Virginia, on day 1:

Length of day, Boston (above)	11h.14m.
Sunset Key Letter C for Richmond (p. 242)	+ 25m.
	11h.39m.
Reverse sunrise Key Letter D for Richmond (p. 242, +17 to -17)	- 17m.
Length of day, Richmond	11h.22m.

3. Use Sun Fast to change sundial time to clock time. A sundial reads natural (Sun) time, which is neither Standard nor Daylight time. To calculate clock time on a sundial in Boston, subtract the minutes given in this column; add the minutes when preceded by an asterisk [*].

[†]For locations where Daylight Saving Time is never observed, subtract 1 hour from results between the second Sunday of March and first Sunday of November.

–Beth Krommes

To convert the time to your (nearest) city, use Key Letter C on **page 238.**

EXAMPLE:

To change sundial to clock time in Boston or Salem, Oregon, on day 1:

Sundial reading (Boston or Salem)	12:00 noon
Subtract Sun Fast (p. 116)	- 4 minutes
Clock time, Boston	11:56 A.M. ET**
Use Key Letter C for Salem (p. 241)	+ 27 minutes
Clock time, Salem	12:23 P.M. PT**

**Note: Add 1 hour to the results in locations where Daylight Saving Time is currently observed.

4. This column gives the degrees and minutes of the Sun from the celestial equator at noon ET.

5. This column gives the approximate times of high tide in Boston. For example, the first high tide occurs at 7:15 A.M. and the second occurs at 8:00 P.M. the same day. (A dash indicates that high tide occurs on or after midnight and is recorded on the next day.) Figures for calculating approximate high tide times for localities other than Boston are given in the **Tide Corrections** table on **page 236.**

6. To calculate the moonrise time in your locale: Choose a day. Note the Moon Rise Key Letter. Find your (nearest) city on **page 238.** Add or subtract the minutes that correspond to the Moon Rise Key Letter to/from the moonrise time given for Boston.

LONGITUDE OF CITY	CORRECTION MINUTES	LONGITUDE OF CITY	CORRECTION MINUTES
58°–76°	0	116°–127°	+4
77°–89°	+1	128°–141°	+5
90°–102°	+2	142°–155°	+6
103°–115°	+3		

(A dash indicates that the moonrise occurs on/after midnight and is recorded on the next day.) Find the longitude of your (nearest) city on **page 238.** Add a correction in minutes for your city's longitude (see table, bottom left). Use the same procedure with Boston's moonset time and the Moon Set Key Letter value to calculate the time of moonset in your locale.[†]

EXAMPLE:

To calculate the time of moonset in Lansing, Michigan, on day 1:

Moonset, Boston, with Key Letter B (p. 116)	12:58 P.M. ET
Value of Key Letter B for Lansing (p. 240)	+ 53 minutes
Correction for Lansing longitude, 84°33'	+ 1 minute
Moonset, Lansing	1:52 P.M. ET

7. This column gives the Moon's *astronomical* position among the constellations (not zodiac) at midnight. For *astrological* data, see **pages 224–227.**

Constellations have irregular borders; on successive nights, the midnight Moon may enter one, cross into another, and then move to a new area of the previous. It visits the 12 zodiacal constellations, as well as Auriga **(AUR),** a northern constellation between Perseus and Gemini; Cetus **(CET),** which lies south of the zodiac, just south of Pisces and Aries; Ophiuchus **(OPH),** primarily north of the zodiac but with a small corner between Scorpius and Sagittarius; Orion **(ORI),** whose northern limit first reaches the zodiac between Taurus and Gemini; and Sextans **(SEX),** which lies south of the zodiac except for a corner that just touches it near Leo.

8. This column gives the Moon's age: the number of days since the previous new Moon. (The average length of the lunar month is 29.53 days.) *(cont.)*

The Right-Hand Calendar Pages, 121 to 147

The Right-Hand Calendar Pages contain celestial events; religious observances; proverbs and poems; civil holidays; historical events; folklore; tide heights; weather prediction rhymes; Farmer's Calendar essays; and more.

A SAMPLE MONTH

	1	**2**	**3**	**4**	**5**	**6**	**7**	**8**	**9**	**10**
1	Fr.	ALL FOOLS' •				*If you want to make a fool of yourself, you'll find a lot of people ready to help you.*			*Flakes*	an inch long, who v
2	Sa.	Tap dancer Charles "Honi" Coles born, 1911 •					Tides {9.5 / 9.0		*alive!*	in fresh water, pro pond across the
3	**B**	2nd ☉. of Easter •				Writer F. Scott Fitzgerald married Zelda Sayre, 1920			*Spring's*	emerged a month of to spend the next 3
4	M.	AnnunciationᵀT • ♂♆☾ •				*Ben Hur* won 11 Academy Awards, 1960			*arrived!*	on land before ret their wet world.
5	Tu.	☾ AT ☋ •				Blizzard left 27.2" snow, St. John's, Nfld., 1999	• Tides {10.8 / 10.8		*Or is this*	
6	W.	☾ ON EQ. • ♂♀☾ •				Twin mongoose lemurs born, Busch Gardens, Tampa, Fla., 2012			*warmth*	You can't mis

1. The bold letter is the Dominical Letter (from A to G), a traditional ecclesiastical designation for Sunday determined by the date on which the year's first Sunday falls. For 2025, the Dominical Letter is **E**.

2. Civil holidays and astronomical events.

3. Religious feasts: A ᵀ indicates a major feast that the church has this year temporarily transferred to a date other than its usual one.

4. Sundays and special holy days.

5. Symbols for notable celestial events. For example, ♂♆☾ on the 4th day means that a conjunction (♂) of Neptune (♆) and the Moon (☾) occurs.

6. Proverbs, poems, and adages.

7. Noteworthy historical events, folklore, and legends.

8. High tide heights, in feet, Boston, Massachusetts.

9. Weather prediction rhyme.

10. Farmer's Calendar essay.

Celestial Symbols

☉ Sun	⊕ Earth	♅ Uranus	♂ Conjunction (on the same celestial longitude)	☊ Descending node
○ ● ☾ Moon	♂ Mars	♆ Neptune		☍ Opposition (180 degrees from Sun)
☿ Mercury	♃ Jupiter	♇ Pluto	☋ Ascending node	
♀ Venus	♄ Saturn			

PREDICTING EARTHQUAKES

Note the dates in the Right-Hand Calendar Pages when the Moon rides high or runs low. The date of the high begins the most likely 5-day period of earthquakes in the Northern Hemisphere; the date of the low indicates a similar 5-day period in the Southern Hemisphere. Also noted are the 2 days each month when the Moon is on the celestial equator, indicating the most likely time for earthquakes in either hemisphere.

EARTH AT PERIHELION AND APHELION

Perihelion: January 4, 2025 (EST). Earth will be 91,405,993 miles from the Sun. **Aphelion:** July 3, 2025 (EDT). Earth will be 94,502,939 miles from the Sun.

CALENDAR

Why We Have Seasons

The seasons occur because as Earth revolves around the Sun, its axis remains tilted at 23.5 degrees from the perpendicular. This tilt causes different latitudes on Earth to receive varying amounts of sunlight throughout the year.

In the Northern Hemisphere, the summer solstice marks the beginning of summer and occurs when the North Pole is tilted toward the Sun. The winter solstice marks the beginning of winter and occurs when the North Pole is tilted away from the Sun.

The equinoxes occur when the hemispheres equally face the Sun. At this time, the Sun rises due east and sets due west. The vernal equinox marks the beginning of spring; the autumnal equinox marks the beginning of autumn.

In the Southern Hemisphere, the seasons are the reverse of those in the Northern Hemisphere.

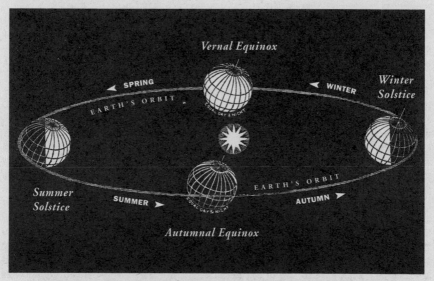

THE FIRST DAYS OF THE 2025 SEASONS

VERNAL (SPRING) EQUINOX: March 20, 5:01 A.M. EDT

SUMMER SOLSTICE: June 20, 10:42 P.M. EDT

AUTUMNAL (FALL) EQUINOX: Sept. 22, 2:19 P.M. EDT

WINTER SOLSTICE: Dec. 21, 10:03 A.M. EST

NOVEMBER 2024

SKY WATCH: On the 1st, Mars, now a brilliant magnitude 0, rises at midnight just below the Gemini twins, Castor and Pollux, with dazzling Jupiter high above them. On the 10th, don't miss the very close conjunction of the Moon and Saturn, with the best viewing between 9:30 and 10:00 P.M. Jupiter, now rising at around 6:30 P.M., hangs just below the Moon on the 16th. On this same night, Uranus comes to opposition, at its closest and brightest appearance of the year. Just to the right of the famous Pleiades star cluster, Uranus's magnitude of 5.6 means that it can be seen as a faint star from dark rural sites, although binoculars make for easier viewing of its green color. On the 20th, Mars rises around 8:45 P.M. and hovers next to the Moon.

● NEW MOON	1st day 8:47 A.M.	○ FULL MOON	15th day 4:29 P.M.
☽ FIRST QUARTER	9th day 12:55 A.M.	☾ LAST QUARTER	22nd day 8:28 P.M.

After 2:00 A.M. on November 3, Eastern Standard Time is given.

GET THESE PAGES WITH TIMES SET TO YOUR ZIP CODE VIA ALMANAC.COM/2025.

DAY OF YEAR	DAY OF MONTH	DAY OF WEEK	☼ RISES H. M.	RISE KEY	☼ SETS H. M.	SET KEY	LENGTH OF DAY H. M.	SUN FAST M.	SUN DECLINATION ° '	HIGH TIDE TIMES BOSTON		☾ RISES H. M.	RISE KEY	☾ SETS H. M.	SET KEY	ASTRON. PLACE	☾ AGE
306	1	Fr.	7:18	D	5:37	B	10 19	32	14 s. 44	11¾	—	7:27	E	5:25	B	VIR	0
307	2	Sa.	7:19	D	5:36	B	10 17	32	15 s. 03	12¼	12½	8:33	E	5:53	A	LIB	1
308	3	F	6:21	D	4:34	B	10 13	32	15 s. 21	1	12	8:39	E	5:27	A	SCO	2
309	4	M.	6:22	D	4:33	B	10 11	32	15 s. 40	12½	12½	9:44	E	6:10	A	SCO	3
310	5	Tu.	6:23	E	4:32	B	10 09	32	15 s. 58	1¼	1¼	10:44	E	7:03	A	OPH	4
311	6	W.	6:24	E	4:31	B	10 07	32	16 s. 16	2	2	11:36	E	8:06	A	SAG	5
312	7	Th.	6:26	E	4:30	B	10 04	32	16 s. 33	2¾	2¾	12:18	E	9:16	B	SAG	6
313	8	Fr.	6:27	E	4:29	B	10 02	32	16 s. 51	3¾	3¾	12:53	E	10:30	B	CAP	7
314	9	Sa.	6:28	E	4:27	B	9 59	32	17 s. 08	4½	4¾	1:22	E	11:45	C	CAP	8
315	10	F	6:29	E	4:26	B	9 57	32	17 s. 24	5½	5¾	1:47	D	—	-	AQU	9
316	11	M.	6:31	E	4:25	B	9 54	32	17 s. 41	6½	7	2:10	D	1:01	D	AQU	10
317	12	Tu.	6:32	E	4:24	B	9 52	32	17 s. 57	7½	7¾	2:32	C	2:18	D	PSC	11
318	13	W.	6:33	E	4:24	B	9 51	31	18 s. 13	8¼	8¾	2:56	C	3:36	E	PSC	12
319	14	Th.	6:34	E	4:23	B	9 49	31	18 s. 28	9¼	9¾	3:23	B	4:56	E	PSC	13
320	15	Fr.	6:36	E	4:22	B	9 46	31	18 s. 43	10	10¾	3:56	B	6:19	E	ARI	14
321	16	Sa.	6:37	E	4:21	B	9 44	31	18 s. 58	10¾	11½	4:38	A	7:42	E	TAU	15
322	17	F	6:38	E	4:20	B	9 42	31	19 s. 12	11¾	—	5:30	A	8:59	E	TAU	16
323	18	M.	6:39	E	4:19	B	9 40	30	19 s. 27	12½	12½	6:32	A	10:06	E	TAU	17
324	19	Tu.	6:40	E	4:19	B	9 39	30	19 s. 40	1¼	1½	7:41	B	10:59	E	GEM	18
325	20	W.	6:42	E	4:18	B	9 36	30	19 s. 54	2¼	2¼	8:52	B	11:39	E	GEM	19
326	21	Th.	6:43	E	4:17	B	9 34	30	20 s. 07	3	3¼	10:01	C	12:11	E	CAN	20
327	22	Fr.	6:44	E	4:16	B	9 32	29	20 s. 20	4	4¼	11:07	C	12:35	E	LEO	21
328	23	Sa.	6:45	E	4:16	A	9 31	29	20 s. 32	5	5¼	—	-	12:56	D	LEO	22
329	24	F	6:46	E	4:15	A	9 29	29	20 s. 44	6	6¼	12:11	C	1:14	D	LEO	23
330	25	M.	6:48	E	4:15	A	9 27	29	20 s. 55	6¾	7	1:12	D	1:31	C	VIR	24
331	26	Tu.	6:49	E	4:14	A	9 25	28	21 s. 07	7½	8	2:12	D	1:49	C	VIR	25
332	27	W.	6:50	E	4:14	A	9 24	28	21 s. 17	8¼	8¾	3:14	E	2:08	B	VIR	26
333	28	Th.	6:51	E	4:13	A	9 22	28	21 s. 28	9	9½	4:17	E	2:29	B	VIR	27
334	29	Fr.	6:52	E	4:13	A	9 21	27	21 s. 38	9½	10¼	5:22	E	2:55	B	LIB	28
335	30	Sa.	6:53	E	4:13	A	9 20	27	21 s. 47	10¼	11	6:29	E	3:27	A	LIB	29

NOVEMBER

But the dinner—ah! the dinner—words are feeble to portray
What a culinary triumph is achieved Thanksgiving Day!
–**Horatio Alger Jr.**

DAY OF MONTH	DAY OF WEEK	DATES, FEASTS, FASTS, ASPECTS, TIDE HEIGHTS, AND WEATHER	
1	Fr.	All Saints' • NEW ● • Baseball player Fernando Valenzuela born, 1960	*Snowflakes*
2	Sa.	All Souls' • Sadie Hawkins Day • N.Dak. and S.Dak. statehood, 1889 • Tides {9.2/10.1	*fall*
3	F	24th S. af. P. • Daylight Saving Time ends, 2:00 A.M. • ☌☿☾ • {9.1/10.1	*on*
4	M.	☌♀☾ • Humorist Will Rogers born, 1879 • Tides {8.9/10.0	*people*
5	Tu.	Election Day • ☾ runs low • "Cotton candy" lobster caught, Casco Bay, Maine, 2021	*voting*
6	W.	*Sleep is the equalizer of all.* • Tides {8.5/9.8	*(for those*
7	Th.	☌♇☾ • 1st robot-assisted human hip replacement, 1992 • Tides {8.4/9.7	*up*
8	Fr.	Poet John Milton likely died, 1674 • Mont. statehood, 1889 • Tides {8.4/9.6	*north,*
9	Sa.	Canada joined the United Nations, 1945 • Tides {8.6/9.6	*a*
10	F	25th S. af. P. • ☌♄☾ • "Charmed quark" discovered, 1974 • {9.0/9.7	*decent*
11	M.	St. Martin of Tours • Veterans Day • ☌♆☾ • Wash. statehood, 1889	*coating).*
12	Tu.	Indian Summer (aka Second Summer) • ☾ on Eq. • ☾ at ☊ • {10.3/10.2	*Chills*
13	W.	1st modern-day cloud-seeding experiment, Mt. Greylock, Mass., 1946 • Tides {10.9/10.4	*retreat*
14	Th.	☾ at perig. • Home improvement expert Chip Gaines born, 1974 • USS *Nimitz* "Tic Tac" UFO incident, off Calif., 2004	
15	Fr.	Full Beaver ○ • ☌♅☾ • 1st U.S. poultry show began, Boston, Mass., 1849	*from sun*
16	Sa.	♄ stat. • ♅ at ☍ • ☿ gr. elong. (23° east) • Tides {12.1/10.5	*serene,*
17	F	26th S. af. P. • ☌♃☾ • Sculptor Auguste Rodin died, 1917 • {12.0/—	*then*
18	M.	St. Hilda of Whitby • ☾ rides high • Ballerina Evelyn Cisneros-Legate born, 1958	*rain*
19	Tu.	World's first surviving septuplets born, Des Moines, Iowa, 1997 • Tides {9.8/11.1	*and heat*
20	W.	☌♂☾ • *What has been, may be.* • Tides {9.4/10.5	*go to*
21	Th.	World Hello Day • N.C. statehood, 1789 • {9.0/9.9	*extremes!*
22	Fr.	Humane Society of the United States founded, 1954 • 15 tornadoes hit Ind., 1992 • {8.7/9.4	*Prepare*
23	Sa.	St. Clement • 1st smartphone (IBM Simon) introduced, COMDEX show, Las Vegas, Nev., 1992	*a feast,*
24	F	27th S. af. P. • Artist Henri de Toulouse-Lautrec born, 1864	*and as*
25	M.	☾ on Eq. • ☾ at ☋ • ☿ stat. • Tides {8.8/8.6	*ice*
26	Tu.	☾ at apo. • *Evening red and morning gray Help the traveler on his way.* • {9.0/8.6	*melts,*
27	W.	Mauna Loa eruption began, Hawaii, 2022 • {9.3/8.7	*do give*
28	Th.	Thanksgiving Day • Basketball game inventor James Naismith died, 1939 • {9.6/8.7	*thanks for*
29	Fr.	Entertainer Garry Shandling born, 1949 • Tides {9.8/8.8	*loosened*
30	Sa.	St. Andrew • Writer Lucy Maud Montgomery born, 1874 • {10.0/8.8	*belts!*

Farmer's Calendar

Most "traditional food" that we enjoy on Thanksgiving wasn't consumed by the Pilgrims. Turkey is a notable exception. The wild turkeys around Plimoth were the likely quarry of the "fowling" party dispatched in 1621 by Governor William Bradford in preparation for the 3-day (first Thanksgiving) event. The Pilgrims couldn't have eaten mashed potatoes because potatoes weren't cultivated in North America until the 1700s, and cranberry sauce and pumpkin pie wouldn't have been on the menu because sugar, flour, and butter were in short supply. Seafood was probably part of the feast. As colonist Edward Winslow reported, "In September, we can take a hogshead of eels in a night.... We have mussels . . . at our doors." Recently harvested corn, onions, beans, lettuce, spinach, cabbage, and carrots were probably served. Wampanoag guests contributed five deer.

In 1939, Franklin Roosevelt attempted to boost retail sales by moving Thanksgiving up a week. Such was the opposition to "Franksgiving" that in 1941 he reluctantly signed a bill codifying Thanksgiving on November's fourth Thursday instead. –*Ted Williams*

DECEMBER 2024

SKY WATCH: Venus, now a bright magnitude –4.2, is an evening star in the west from 5:00 to 6:30 P.M. On the 6th, look for Mercury low in the southeast at dawn, after which it remains visible until the 15th. Jupiter floats below the Moon on the 6th and is in opposition on the morning of the 7th, creating a conjunction with the Moon. Now at its brightest of the year, Jupiter rises at around 9:30 P.M. before hovering close to the Moon on the 14th. The Geminid meteor shower arrives on the 13th and is best seen before the Moon rises at around 1:00 A.M. On the 28th, Mercury hovers to the left of the crescent Moon in dawn's twilight. Winter in the Northern Hemisphere begins with the solstice on the 21st at 4:21 A.M. EST.

● NEW MOON	1st day 1:21 A.M.	◐ LAST QUARTER	22nd day 5:18 P.M.
◑ FIRST QUARTER	8th day 10:27 A.M.	● NEW MOON	30th day 5:27 P.M.
○ FULL MOON	15th day 4:02 A.M.		

All times are given in Eastern Standard Time.

GET THESE PAGES WITH TIMES SET TO YOUR ZIP CODE VIA ALMANAC.COM/2025.

DAY OF YEAR	DAY OF MONTH	DAY OF WEEK	☼ RISES H. M.	RISE KEY	☼ SETS H. M.	SET KEY	LENGTH OF DAY H. M.	SUN FAST M.	SUN DECLINATION ° '	HIGH TIDE TIMES BOSTON		☾ RISES H. M.	RISE KEY	☾ SETS H. M.	SET KEY	ASTRON. PLACE	☾ AGE
336	1	**F**	6:54	E	**4:12**	A	9 18	26	21 s. 56	11	11½	7:35	E	**4:07**	A	SCO	0
337	2	M.	6:55	E	**4:12**	A	9 17	26	22 s. 05	11½	—	8:37	E	**4:58**	A	OPH	1
338	3	Tu.	6:56	E	**4:12**	A	9 16	26	22 s. 13	12¼	12¼	9:32	E	**5:59**	A	SAG	2
339	4	W.	6:57	E	**4:12**	A	9 15	25	22 s. 21	1	1	10:18	E	**7:08**	B	SAG	3
340	5	Th.	6:58	E	**4:12**	A	9 14	25	22 s. 29	1¾	1¾	10:55	E	**8:21**	B	CAP	4
341	6	Fr.	6:59	E	**4:12**	A	9 13	24	22 s. 36	2½	2½	11:25	E	**9:35**	C	CAP	5
342	7	Sa.	7:00	E	**4:11**	A	9 11	24	22 s. 42	3¼	3½	11:51	D	**10:49**	C	AQU	6
343	8	**F**	7:01	E	**4:11**	A	9 10	24	22 s. 48	4¼	4½	**12:13**	D	—	-	AQU	7
344	9	M.	7:02	E	**4:11**	A	9 09	23	22 s. 54	5¼	5½	**12:35**	C	12:03	D	PSC	8
345	10	Tu.	7:03	E	**4:12**	A	9 09	23	22 s. 59	6	6½	**12:57**	C	1:17	E	PSC	9
346	11	W.	7:04	E	**4:12**	A	9 08	22	23 s. 04	7	7½	**1:22**	B	2:33	E	PSC	10
347	12	Th.	7:04	E	**4:12**	A	9 08	22	23 s. 08	8	8½	**1:51**	B	3:52	E	ARI	11
348	13	Fr.	7:05	E	**4:12**	A	9 07	21	23 s. 12	8¾	9½	**2:27**	B	5:13	E	ARI	12
349	14	Sa.	7:06	E	**4:12**	A	9 06	21	23 s. 15	9¾	10½	**3:14**	A	6:33	E	TAU	13
350	15	**F**	7:07	E	**4:13**	A	9 06	20	23 s. 18	10½	11¼	**4:12**	A	7:45	E	TAU	14
351	16	M.	7:07	E	**4:13**	A	9 06	20	23 s. 21	11½	—	**5:19**	A	8:45	E	AUR	15
352	17	Tu.	7:08	E	**4:13**	A	9 05	19	23 s. 23	12¼	12¼	**6:31**	B	9:32	E	GEM	16
353	18	W.	7:09	E	**4:14**	A	9 05	19	23 s. 24	1	1	**7:43**	B	10:08	E	CAN	17
354	19	Th.	7:09	E	**4:14**	A	9 05	18	23 s. 25	1¾	1¾	**8:52**	C	10:36	E	CAN	18
355	20	Fr.	7:10	E	**4:15**	A	9 05	18	23 s. 26	2½	2¾	**9:57**	C	10:58	E	LEO	19
356	21	Sa.	7:10	E	**4:15**	A	9 05	17	23 s. 26	3½	3½	**11:00**	D	11:18	D	LEO	20
357	22	**F**	7:11	E	**4:16**	A	9 05	17	23 s. 25	4¼	4½	—	-	11:36	C	VIR	21
358	23	M.	7:11	E	**4:16**	A	9 05	16	23 s. 25	5	5¼	12:01	D	11:53	C	VIR	22
359	24	Tu.	7:12	E	**4:17**	A	9 05	16	23 s. 23	5¾	6¼	1:02	E	**12:11**	C	VIR	23
360	25	W.	7:12	E	**4:17**	A	9 05	15	23 s. 21	6¾	7¼	2:04	E	**12:31**	B	VIR	24
361	26	Th.	7:12	E	**4:18**	A	9 06	15	23 s. 19	7½	8	3:08	E	**12:55**	B	LIB	25
362	27	Fr.	7:13	E	**4:19**	A	9 06	14	23 s. 16	8¼	9	4:14	E	**1:25**	A	LIB	26
363	28	Sa.	7:13	E	**4:19**	A	9 06	14	23 s. 13	9	9¾	5:21	E	**2:02**	A	SCO	27
364	29	**F**	7:13	E	**4:20**	A	9 07	13	23 s. 10	9¾	10½	6:26	E	**2:49**	A	OPH	28
365	30	M.	7:13	E	**4:21**	A	9 08	13	23 s. 05	10½	11¼	7:24	E	**3:48**	A	SAG	0
366	31	Tu.	7:13	E	**4:22**	A	9 09	13	23 s. 01	11¼	11¾	8:14	E	**4:56**	B	SAG	1

To use this page, see p. 116; for Key Letters, see p. 238. LIGHT = A.M. BOLD = P.M.

DECEMBER

Welcome all and make good cheer,
Welcome all another year.
–**Anonymous**

DAY OF MONTH	DAY OF WEEK	DATES, FEASTS, FASTS, ASPECTS, TIDE HEIGHTS, AND WEATHER	
1	**F**	**1st S. of Advent** • NEW ● • ☌☿☾ • {10.1 / 8.8	*Mulled*
2	M.	St. Viviana • ☾ RUNS LOW • Major League Baseball agreed to accept cowhide baseballs, 1974	*wine or*
3	Tu.	John Backus, who led team that designed FORTRAN programming language, born, 1924 • {8.8 / 10.3	*ciders*
4	W.	☌♀☾ • ☌♇☾ • Montreal Canadiens founded, 1909 • Tides {8.7 / 10.2	*warm*
5	Th.	☿ IN INF. ☌ • Chemist Hazel Bishop died, 1998 • Tides {8.7 / 10.2	*snowboard*
6	Fr.	St. Nicholas • *Joy that we can not share with others is only half enjoyed.* • {8.8 / 10.1	*riders,*
7	Sa.	St. Ambrose • NAT'L PEARL HARBOR REMEMBRANCE DAY • ☌♀♇ • ♂ STAT. • ♃ AT ☍	
8	**F**	**2nd S. of Advent** • ☌♄☾ • ♆ STAT.	*alpine sliders,*
9	M.	☾ ON EQ. • ☾ AT ☊ • ☌♆☾ • {9.6 / 9.6	*and cross-country*
10	Tu.	St. Eulalia • Colonel John P. Stapp attained 632 mph on rocket sled, 1954 • {10.0 / 9.6	*gliders.*
11	W.	Actress Rita Moreno born, 1931 • Statute of Westminster passed, 1931 • {10.5 / 9.6	*They're*
12	Th.	OUR LADY OF GUADALUPE • ☾ AT PERIG. • F3 waterspout-turned-tornado, Des Moines to Kent, Wash., 1969	*all*
13	Fr.	St. Lucia • ☌♅☾ • Royal charter for Dartmouth College (Hanover, N.H.) granted, 1769	*out in*
14	Sa.	Halcyon Days begin. • ☌♃☾ • U.S. president George Washington died, 1799 • {11.6 / 9.8	*frigid*
15	**F**	**3rd S. of Advent** • FULL COLD ○ • ☾ RIDES HIGH • ☿ STAT.	*air,*
16	M.	Discovery of 1st millipede species having more than 1,000 legs (1,306) announced, 2021 • {11.5 / —	*while*
17	Tu.	105.6°F national average set record for hottest day, Australia, 2019 • Tides {9.7 / 11.3	*others*
18	W.	Ember Day • ☌♂☾ • *How the Grinch Stole Christmas!* TV special 1st aired, 1966	*hibernate*
19	Th.	Beware the Pogonip. • Gustl, a terrier mix, undid 10 knots in 1 minute, setting record, 2012	*like*
20	Fr.	Ember Day • *When the night's darkest, the dawn is nearest.* • {9.0 / 9.8	*bears.*
21	Sa.	St. Thomas • Ember Day • WINTER SOLSTICE • Tides {8.9 / 9.3	*Raise*
22	**F**	**4th S. of Advent** • ☾ ON EQ. • ☾ AT ☋ • Tides {8.7 / 8.8	*a toast,*
23	M.	20-lb. 9-oz. southern flounder caught, Nassau Sound, Fla., 1983 • Tides {8.7 / 8.4	*give*
24	Tu.	☾ AT APO. • ☿ GR. ELONG. (22° WEST) • –57°F (–82°F old formula) windchill, Chicago, Ill., 1983	*a cheer,*
25	W.	**Christmas** • Chanukah begins at sundown • Actor Humphrey Bogart born, 1899	*here's*
26	Th.	St. Stephen • BOXING DAY (CANADA) • FIRST DAY OF KWANZAA • {9.1 / 8.1	*wishing*
27	Fr.	St. John • Radio City Music Hall opened, N.Y.C., 1932 • Tides {9.3 / 8.2	*all*
28	Sa.	Holy Innocents • National Call a Friend Day (U.S.) • ☌☿☾ • Tides {9.6 / 8.3	*a*
29	**F**	**1st S. af. Ch.** • *Be it dry or be it wet, The weather'll always pay its debt.*	*grand*
30	M.	NEW ● • ☾ RUNS LOW • Musician Artie Shaw died, 2004 • Tides {10.2 / 8.7	*New*
31	Tu.	St. Sylvester • Educator Jaime Escalante born, 1930 • Tides {10.4 / 9.0	*Year!*

Farmer's Calendar

If you stand under wild American mistletoe, which grows from New Jersey to Florida and west through Texas, you may get something less welcome than a kiss. This is because the juicy white berries, now ripe, are relished by birds. The plant's seeds pass through avian digestive tracts, germinate on the bark of trees, and then send roots into sap-conducting tissues. But most mistletoe species are only partially parasitic; their evergreen leaves contain chlorophyll, which enables them to manufacture their own food once they have purloined water and nutrients from their host trees. In some of the range, foresters consider American mistletoe a pest because it can retard tree growth and break branches. However, ecologists recognize it as a keystone species because not only do many forest creatures forage on its leaves and shoots but also its berries help to sustain birds.

Ancient Europeans reasoned that because mistletoe stayed green in the dead of winter, it must provide shelter for woodland spirits—hence its use in rituals for fertility, health, peace, safety, and good luck. –*Ted Williams*

CALENDAR

SKY WATCH: The year begins with celestial fireworks leaping from dusk's twilight on the 1st, as the crescent Moon hovers low with dazzling Venus to its upper left and Saturn between them. On the 10th, the Moon forms a striking conjunction with brilliant Jupiter. The greatest headliner arrives on the 13th, when the Moon not only meets but eclipses Mars, with the Red Planet just days from opposition on the 15th. This rare event appears halfway up the eastern sky from most locations, with Mars now at its brightest until 2031. The occultation is visible throughout the mainland U.S. and nearly all of Canada, beginning between 7:30 and 8:00 P.M. local time, depending on location. Mars reappears about an hour later.

◑ FIRST QUARTER	6th day 6:56 P.M.	◐ LAST QUARTER	21st day 3:31 P.M.
○ FULL MOON	13th day 5:27 P.M.	● NEW MOON	29th day 7:36 A.M.

All times are given in Eastern Standard Time.

GET THESE PAGES WITH TIMES SET TO YOUR ZIP CODE VIA ALMANAC.COM/2025.

DAY OF YEAR	DAY OF MONTH	DAY OF WEEK	☼ RISES H. M.	RISE KEY	☼ SETS H. M.	SET KEY	LENGTH OF DAY H. M.	SUN FAST M.	SUN DECLINATION ° '	HIGH TIDE TIMES BOSTON		☾ RISES H. M.	RISE KEY	☾ SETS H. M.	SET KEY	ASTRON. PLACE	☾ AGE
1	1	W.	7:13	E	4:23	A	9 10	12	22 s. 56	12	—	8:55	E	6:09	B	SAG	2
2	2	Th.	7:13	E	4:24	A	9 11	12	22 s. 50	12½	12¾	9:28	E	7:25	C	CAP	3
3	3	Fr.	7:13	E	4:24	A	9 11	11	22 s. 44	1¼	1½	9:55	E	8:40	C	CAP	4
4	4	Sa.	7:13	E	4:25	A	9 12	11	22 s. 38	2	2¼	10:18	D	9:54	D	AQU	5
5	5	E	7:13	E	4:26	A	9 13	10	22 s. 31	2¾	3	10:40	C	11:07	E	AQU	6
6	6	M.	7:13	E	4:27	A	9 14	10	22 s. 24	3¾	4	11:01	C	—	-	PSC	7
7	7	Tu.	7:13	E	4:28	A	9 15	9	22 s. 16	4½	5	11:24	B	12:22	E	PSC	8
8	8	W.	7:13	E	4:29	A	9 16	9	22 s. 08	5½	6	11:51	B	1:38	E	ARI	9
9	9	Th.	7:13	E	4:30	A	9 17	9	21 s. 59	6½	7¼	12:23	A	2:56	E	ARI	10
10	10	Fr.	7:12	E	4:32	A	9 20	8	21 s. 50	7½	8¼	1:04	A	4:14	E	TAU	11
11	11	Sa.	7:12	E	4:33	A	9 21	8	21 s. 41	8½	9¼	1:56	A	5:27	E	TAU	12
12	12	E	7:12	E	4:34	A	9 22	7	21 s. 31	9½	10¼	2:59	A	6:31	E	AUR	13
13	13	M.	7:11	E	4:35	A	9 24	7	21 s. 20	10¼	11	4:09	B	7:23	E	GEM	14
14	14	Tu.	7:11	E	4:36	A	9 25	7	21 s. 10	11¼	11¾	5:21	B	8:03	E	CAN	15
15	15	W.	7:11	E	4:37	B	9 26	6	20 s. 59	12	—	6:33	C	8:34	E	CAN	16
16	16	Th.	7:10	E	4:38	B	9 28	6	20 s. 47	12½	12¾	7:40	C	8:59	E	LEO	17
17	17	Fr.	7:10	E	4:40	B	9 30	6	20 s. 35	1¼	1½	8:45	D	9:20	D	LEO	18
18	18	Sa.	7:09	E	4:41	B	9 32	5	20 s. 23	2	2¼	9:48	D	9:39	D	LEO	19
19	19	E	7:08	E	4:42	B	9 34	5	20 s. 10	2¾	3	10:49	E	9:56	C	VIR	20
20	20	M.	7:08	E	4:43	B	9 35	5	19 s. 57	3½	3¾	11:51	E	10:14	C	VIR	21
21	21	Tu.	7:07	E	4:45	B	9 38	4	19 s. 44	4¼	4½	—	-	10:33	B	VIR	22
22	22	W.	7:06	E	4:46	B	9 40	4	19 s. 30	5	5½	12:54	E	10:55	B	VIR	23
23	23	Th.	7:06	E	4:47	B	9 41	4	19 s. 16	5¾	6½	1:59	E	11:22	A	LIB	24
24	24	Fr.	7:05	E	4:48	B	9 43	4	19 s. 01	6¾	7½	3:05	E	11:55	A	SCO	25
25	25	Sa.	7:04	E	4:50	B	9 46	3	18 s. 46	7½	8¼	4:10	E	12:38	A	SCO	26
26	26	E	7:03	E	4:51	B	9 48	3	18 s. 31	8½	9¼	5:11	E	1:31	A	OPH	27
27	27	M.	7:02	E	4:52	B	9 50	3	18 s. 15	9¼	10	6:05	E	2:36	A	SAG	28
28	28	Tu.	7:01	E	4:54	B	9 53	3	17 s. 59	10	10¾	6:50	E	3:49	B	SAG	29
29	29	W.	7:00	E	4:55	B	9 55	3	17 s. 43	10¾	11½	7:26	E	5:06	B	CAP	0
30	30	Th.	6:59	E	4:56	B	9 57	3	17 s. 27	11½	—	7:56	E	6:24	C	CAP	1
31	31	Fr.	6:58	E	4:57	B	9 59	2	17 s. 10	12¼	12¼	8:21	D	7:40	D	AQU	2

To use this page, see p. 116; for Key Letters, see p. 238. LIGHT = A.M. BOLD = P.M.   **2025**

THE FIRST MONTH • 2025

JANUARY

JANUARY HATH 31 DAYS

O January, month of joy! we hear / On every side thy voice;
It fills our spirits with its life and cheer.
–**Ernest Warburton Shurtleff**

DAY OF MONTH	DAY OF WEEK	DATES, FEASTS, FASTS, ASPECTS, TIDE HEIGHTS, AND WEATHER	
1	W.	Holy Name • **New Year's Day** • ☌♇☾ • Tides 10.7 / —	*First*
2	Th.	1st winter refuge of monarch butterflies discovered, Mexico, 1975 • Tides 9.2 / 10.8	*sunrise*
3	Fr.	☌♀☾ • *By the hands of many, a great work is made light.* • Tides 9.4 / 10.7	*vermilion,*
4	Sa.	St. Elizabeth Ann Seton • ☌♄☾ • ⊕ AT PERIHELION	*it's perihelion!*
5	E	**2nd S. af. Ch.** • Twelfth Night • ☾ ON EQ. • ☾ AT ☊ • ☌♆☾	*Typical*
6	M.	**Epiphany** • "Wheel of Fortune" game show debuted on TV, 1975 • Actor Sidney Poitier died, 2022	
7	Tu.	Orthodox Christmas (Julian) • Distaff Day • ☾ AT PERIG. • 10.1 / 9.3	*warming,*
8	W.	Inventor Eli Whitney died, 1825 • Entertainer Elvis Presley born, 1935 • 10.3 / 9.0	*fog is*
9	Th.	☌♅☾ • Evidence of accelerating universe expansion announced, 1998 • 10.4 / 8.9	*forming.*
10	Fr.	☌♃☾ • ♀ GR. ELONG. (47° EAST) • Houseplant Appreciation Day • 10.6 / 8.9	*Who*
11	Sa.	☾ RIDES HIGH • Suffragette Alice Paul born, 1885 • 10.7 / 9.0	*can*
12	E	**1st S. af. Ep.** • 196-lb. 9-oz. bluefin tuna caught, Morehead City, N.C., 2001 • 10.9 / 9.1	*say*
13	M.	St. Hilary • Plough Monday • FULL WOLF ○ • OCCN. ♂☾ • 10.9 / 9.3	*the*
14	Tu.	Children's writer Thornton Burgess born, 1874 • Physician Albert Schweitzer born, 1875	*mist's*
15	W.	♂ AT ☍ • Warmest January on record at time, Conn., Maine, Mass., N.H., N.J., R.I., Vt., 2023	*duration?*
16	Th.	47.5" snow fell, Valdez, Alaska, 1990 • Tides 9.4 / 10.5	*Perhaps*
17	Fr.	U.S. statesman Benjamin Franklin born, 1706 • Tides 9.3 / 10.1	*it'll lift*
18	Sa.	☾ ON EQ. • ☾ AT ☋ • Willie O'Ree's (NHL Boston Bruins) no. 22 retired, 2022	*for MLK's*
19	E	**2nd S. af. Ep.** • *A wet January, a wet spring.* • Tides 9.1 / 9.1	*celebration—*
20	M.	**Martin Luther King Jr.'s Birthday, observed** • **Inauguration Day** • ☾ AT APO. • ☌♀♄	
21	Tu.	☌♇☉ • The Wilderness Society founded, 1935 • Tides 8.9 / 8.1	*he turned*
22	W.	St. Vincent • Lottie Williams likely 1st to be hit by manmade space debris, Tulsa, Okla., 1997	*wrongs*
23	Th.	Fact-finder Joseph Nathan Kane born, 1899 • 8.7 / 7.6	*into*
24	Fr.	Moving picture of solar eclipse taken from dirigible, Long Island, N.Y., 1925 • Tides 8.8 / 7.6	*rights.*
25	Sa.	Conversion of Paul • January thaw traditionally begins about now. • Tides 9.1 / 7.8	*Turn*
26	E	**3rd S. af. Ep.** • ☾ RUNS LOW • Actor Paul Newman born, 1925 • 9.5 / 8.1	*up*
27	M.	U.S. admiral Hyman George Rickover born, 1900 • 9.9 / 8.5	*your*
28	Tu.	St. Thomas Aquinas • ☌☿☾ • ☌♇☾ • Tides 10.4 / 9.0	*heaters*
29	W.	**Lunar New Year (China)** • NEW ● • ☌☿♇ • Tides 10.8 / 9.5	*for cold*
30	Th.	♅ STAT. • Raccoons mate now. • Tides 11.1 / —	*winter*
31	Fr.	☌♄☾ • *A fair exchange brings no quarrel.* • 9.9 / 11.2	*nights.*

Farmer's Calendar

Enough soup! Back to the wood. Light begins to make sense of the forest. A fern pattern in the ice indicates that frost has formed slowly, deeply. A quilt of stillness surrounds the steaming thermos left open on an icy round of oak for splitting wood. I hate to waste hot coffee on the toe of my ax to dislodge it from the stump, but that's what it takes. Working a few stubborn lengths of hickory into meaningful size for the stove, a familiar sentiment of cold-weather gratitude gets unknotted in me. You see, I belong to a patchwork of farmers, gardeners, and homesteaders who wake early every January 15 for the ritual of wood-splitting. We're making good on wisdom that we picked up from Beattie, the orchardist up on Windchime Mountain. She may have retired from her farmcraft, but we still feed on her hard-toothed charms, her georgic acumen. Adages rattle off her tongue in perfect time with the season, be it green-up, high-heat, or leaf-turn. "If ash is out before the oak, prepare your land for a good soak." "Happy is the wound hose." And many mid-Januaries, she warns, "Sleep good tonight, so long as you have half your winter's wood left."

FEBRUARY

SKY WATCH: Venus continues its January prominence on the 1st, growing more brilliant to magnitude –4.8, enough to cast shadows. In the opposite part of the sky, extraordinary celestial brightness fills the east at nightfall. While Betelgeuse, Castor, Pollux, and Aldebaran shine at magnitude 1, the stars Procyon, Rigel, and Capella—surrounding Orion—boast a magnitude 0. Even brighter, Mars blazes at –1 and Sirius and Jupiter dazzle at –2. This celestial eye candy continues all month, while Mars slightly fades to magnitude 0 as it stands stationary in Gemini. On the 24th, Mercury and Saturn meet very low in the west in the bright evening twilight—a treat for those with an unobstructed view of the horizon.

◐ FIRST QUARTER	5th day 3:02 A.M.	◑ LAST QUARTER	20th day 12:32 P.M.
○ FULL MOON	12th day 8:53 A.M.	● NEW MOON	27th day 7:45 P.M.

All times are given in Eastern Standard Time.

GET THESE PAGES WITH TIMES SET TO YOUR ZIP CODE VIA ALMANAC.COM/2025.

DAY OF YEAR	DAY OF MONTH	DAY OF WEEK	☀ RISES H.M.	RISE KEY	☀ SETS H.M.	SET KEY	LENGTH OF DAY H.M.	SUN FAST M.	SUN DECLINATION ° '	HIGH TIDE TIMES BOSTON		☽ RISES H.M.	RISE KEY	☽ SETS H.M.	SET KEY	☽ ASTRON. PLACE	☽ AGE
32	1	Sa.	6:57	E	4:59	B	10 02	2	16 s. 53	12¾	1	8:44	D	8:56	D	AQU	3
33	2	**E**	6:56	E	5:00	B	10 04	2	16 s. 35	1½	2	9:06	C	10:12	E	PSC	4
34	3	M.	6:55	E	5:01	B	10 06	2	16 s. 18	2½	2¾	9:29	B	11:28	E	PSC	5
35	4	Tu.	6:54	E	5:03	B	10 09	2	16 s. 00	3¼	3¾	9:54	B	—	-	ARI	6
36	5	W.	6:53	D	5:04	B	10 11	2	15 s. 41	4¼	4¾	10:24	B	12:46	E	ARI	7
37	6	Th.	6:52	D	5:05	B	10 13	2	15 s. 23	5¼	5¾	11:02	A	2:03	E	TAU	8
38	7	Fr.	6:51	D	5:07	B	10 16	2	15 s. 04	6¼	7	11:49	A	3:17	E	TAU	9
39	8	Sa.	6:49	D	5:08	D	10 19	2	14 s. 45	7¼	8¼	12:47	A	4:23	E	TAU	10
40	9	**E**	6:48	D	5:09	B	10 21	2	14 s. 25	8¼	9¼	1:53	A	5:18	E	GEM	11
41	10	M.	6:47	D	5:10	B	10 23	2	14 s. 06	9¼	10	3:04	B	6:01	E	GEM	12
42	11	Tu.	6:46	D	5:12	B	10 26	2	13 s. 46	10¼	10¾	4:16	B	6:35	E	CAN	13
43	12	W.	6:44	D	5:13	B	10 29	2	13 s. 26	11	11½	5:25	C	7:01	E	LEO	14
44	13	Th.	6:43	D	5:14	B	10 31	2	13 s. 06	11¾	—	6:31	C	7:23	D	LEO	15
45	14	Fr.	6:42	D	5:16	B	10 34	2	12 s. 45	12¼	12¼	7:34	D	7:43	D	LEO	16
46	15	Sa.	6:40	D	5:17	B	10 37	2	12 s. 25	12¾	1	8:36	E	8:01	C	VIR	17
47	16	**E**	6:39	D	5:18	B	10 39	2	12 s. 04	1½	1¾	9:38	E	8:18	C	VIR	18
48	17	M.	6:37	D	5:19	B	10 42	2	11 s. 43	2	2¼	10:41	E	8:37	B	VIR	19
49	18	Tu.	6:36	D	5:21	B	10 45	2	11 s. 22	2¾	3	11:45	E	8:57	B	VIR	20
50	19	W.	6:34	D	5:22	B	10 48	2	11 s. 00	3¼	4	—	-	9:21	B	LIB	21
51	20	Th.	6:33	D	5:23	B	10 50	2	10 s. 39	4¼	4¾	12:50	E	9:51	A	LIB	22
52	21	Fr.	6:31	D	5:25	B	10 54	2	10 s. 17	5	5¾	1:55	E	10:29	A	SCO	23
53	22	Sa.	6:30	D	5:26	B	10 56	3	9 s. 55	6	6¾	2:57	E	11:16	A	OPH	24
54	23	**E**	6:28	D	5:27	B	10 59	3	9 s. 33	7	7¾	3:54	E	12:15	A	SAG	25
55	24	M.	6:27	D	5:28	B	11 01	3	9 s. 11	8	8½	4:42	E	1:24	B	SAG	26
56	25	Tu.	6:25	D	5:30	B	11 05	3	8 s. 48	8¾	9½	5:22	E	2:39	B	CAP	27
57	26	W.	6:24	D	5:31	B	11 07	3	8 s. 26	9½	10¼	5:54	E	3:57	C	CAP	28
58	27	Th.	6:22	D	5:32	C	11 10	3	8 s. 03	10½	11	6:21	E	5:16	C	AQU	0
59	28	Fr.	6:21	D	5:33	C	11 12	3	7 s. 41	11¼	11¾	6:45	D	6:34	D	AQU	1

To use this page, see p. 116; for Key Letters, see p. 238. LIGHT = A.M. **BOLD** = P.M.

Far, far above the ebon clouds
Thy splendours sweep the blue profound.
—**J. Fellowes, of the Sun**

DAY OF MONTH	DAY OF WEEK	DATES, FEASTS, FASTS, ASPECTS, TIDE HEIGHTS, AND WEATHER	
1	Sa.	☾ ON EQ. • ☾ AT ☊ • ☾ AT PERIG. • ☌♀☾ • ☌♆☾	*Groundhogs*
2	**E**	4th S. af. Ep. • Candlemas • Groundhog Day • Dogs delivered serum, Nome, Alaska, 1925	*stand*
3	M.	☌♀♆ • Writer Gertrude Stein born, 1874 • Tides {10.6 / 10.3}	*tall by*
4	Tu.	♃ STAT. • Museum of Fine Arts, Boston, founded, 1870 • Tides {10.6 / 9.7}	*shallow*
5	W.	St. Agatha • ☌♅☾ • *A work well begun is half ended.* –Plato • {10.5 / 9.1}	*burrows,*
6	Th.	☌♃☾ • Singer Natalie Cole born, 1950 • {10.3 / 8.6}	*no shadows*
7	Fr.	13 tackles by Gary Brackett (Colts) set Super Bowl world record, 2010 • Tides {10.1 / 8.4}	*fall on*
8	Sa.	☾ RIDES HIGH • Naturalist Henry Walter Bates born, 1825 • {10.1 / 8.4}	*fallow*
9	**E**	**5th S. af. Ep.** • ☌♂☾ • ☿ IN SUP. ☌ • {10.2 / 8.7}	*furrows.*
10	M.	Olympic champion swimmer Mark Spitz born, 1950 • Tides {10.3 / 8.9}	*Eros's*
11	Tu.	Lord Durham's Report submitted to British Parliament, 1839 • Tides {10.4 / 9.2}	*arrow*
12	W.	FULL SNOW ○ • U.S. president Abraham Lincoln born, 1809 • {10.5 / 9.4}	*zeros in*
13	Th.	1st well-documented birth of U.S. quintuplets, Watertown, Wis., 1875 • Tides {10.4 / —}	*for love's*
14	Fr.	Sts. Cyril & Methodius • VALENTINE'S DAY • *On St. Valentine's day, the ice will only bear a finch.*	*sake,*
15	Sa.	NATIONAL FLAG OF CANADA DAY • ☾ ON EQ. • ☾ AT ☋ • {9.6 / 9.9}	*as snowflakes*
16	**E**	**Septuagesima** • Winter's back breaks. • {9.5 / 9.5}	*decorate the*
17	M.	PRESIDENTS' DAY • ☾ AT APO. • Tides {9.4 / 9.1}	*presidents'*
18	Tu.	M. Twain's *Adventures of Huckleberry Finn* published in U.S., 1885 • Pluto discovered, 1930	*cake.*
19	W.	*One of these days is none of these days.* • Tides {9.1 / 8.1}	*An arctic*
20	Th.	12-lb. 13-oz. red hake caught, Mudhole Wreck, N.J., 2010 • Tides {8.9 / 7.7}	*blast brings*
21	Fr.	International Mother Language Day • Agriculturist Jethro Tull died, 1741	*a freeze to the*
22	Sa.	☾ RUNS LOW • U.S. president George Washington born, 1732 • Actress Drew Barrymore born, 1975	*aether!*
23	**E**	**Sexagesima** • Mathematician Carl Friedrich Gauss died, 1855 • {9.0 / 7.8}	*At last,*
24	M.	St. Matthias • ♂ STAT. • Brown snow fell (due to dust from Great Plains), N.H., Vt., 1936	*a warm*
25	Tu.	☌☿♄ • ☌♇☾ • Chicago OK'd lights at Wrigley Field for limited night games, Ill., 1988	*breeze*
26	W.	Skunks mate now. • 18,853-ft. line of toothbrushes set record, Loveland, Colo., 2019 • {10.5 / 9.5}	*gives*
27	Th.	NEW ● • ♀ STAT. • Writer Laura Elizabeth Richards born, 1850 • {11.0 / 10.2}	*us a*
28	Fr.	St. Romanus • Ramadan begins at sundown • ☌☿☾ • ☌♄☾ • {11.3 / 10.8}	*breather.*

Q: What did the baby corn say to the mama corn?
A: Where's popcorn?

Farmer's Calendar

Chookie: "Buk buk, b-gwak!"

No joke, it really is my favorite time of year in the garden. When people ask what we farm, a good answer is "piles, mostly." Any organic matter. The cold compost is no doubt locked frozen, the leaf mold is under a boot of snowpack, and the coop waste is deep-littered until the crocuses come up. Yet, a chimney of steam puffing from the decomposing wood chip pile allows me and my wheelbarrow to stay in business. Our village tree doctor sends us the chips that his customers don't want, saving gas money and driving time to offload them at our lot, and we're happy to keep him rich in fresh eggs. Win-win. The trick is keeping our aging flock in laying condition. My wife doesn't take to forcing production with light and heat lamps—honoring the birds' natural cycles. The mercury-in-glass drives our nightly panic for their well-being, which prompts some ingenuity. An experiment seems to be working: We've put about 4 yards of fresh chips under the raised coop, with some PVC through the middle of the heap, to transfer a couple of much needed degrees to the roosting loft. Okay, perhaps you could say that our farm is a plot of experiments, mostly.

MARCH

SKY WATCH: On the 1st at around 6:15 P.M., Mercury, at magnitude –1, is the only "star" low in the west below the Moon and dazzling Venus. Mercury rises a bit higher during the next few evenings and approaches Venus from the 8th to the 10th, when it's easy to spot to the lower left of the gleaming evening star. In the south, the Moon meets Jupiter on the 5th, with Taurus's famous orange star Aldebaran below them. The Moon sits extremely close to fading Mars on the 8th, with Gemini's Castor and Pollux to the left. After Daylight Saving Time begins on the 9th, hunt for Mercury from 7:15 to 7:30 P.M. Positioned between Earth and the Sun, Venus reaches inferior conjunction on the 22nd and moves into the morning sky. Spring begins with the vernal equinox on the 20th at 5:01 A.M. EDT.

◑ **FIRST QUARTER** 6th day 11:31 A.M.   ◐ **LAST QUARTER** 22nd day 7:29 A.M.
○ **FULL MOON** 14th day 2:55 A.M.   ● **NEW MOON** 29th day 6:58 A.M.

After 2:00 A.M. on March 9, Eastern Daylight Time is given.

GET THESE PAGES WITH TIMES SET TO YOUR ZIP CODE VIA ALMANAC.COM/2025.

DAY OF YEAR	DAY OF MONTH	DAY OF WEEK	☀ RISES H. M.	RISE KEY	☀ SETS H. M.	SET KEY	LENGTH OF DAY H. M.	SUN FAST M.	SUN DECLINATION ° ′	HIGH TIDE TIMES BOSTON	☾ RISES H. M.	RISE KEY	☾ SETS H. M.	SET KEY	☾ ASTRON. PLACE	☾ AGE
60	1	Sa.	6:19	D	5:34	C	11 15	4	7 s. 18	12 —	7:08	C	7:52	E	PSC	2
61	2	E	6:17	D	5:36	C	11 19	4	6 s. 55	12½ 12¾	7:31	C	9:12	E	PSC	3
62	3	M.	6:16	D	5:37	C	11 21	4	6 s. 32	1¼ 1¾	7:56	B	10:32	E	PSC	4
63	4	Tu.	6:14	D	5:38	C	11 24	4	6 s. 09	2 2½	8:25	B	11:52	E	ARI	5
64	5	W.	6:12	D	5:39	C	11 27	5	5 s. 45	2¾ 3½	9:01	A	—	-	TAU	6
65	6	Th.	6:11	D	5:40	C	11 29	5	5 s. 22	3¾ 4½	9:46	A	1:09	E	TAU	7
66	7	Fr.	6:09	D	5:42	C	11 33	5	4 s. 59	4¾ 5¾	10:41	A	2:18	E	TAU	8
67	8	Sa.	6:07	C	5:43	C	11 36	5	4 s. 35	6 6¾	11:45	A	3:16	E	AUR	9
68	9	E	7:06	C	6:44	C	11 38	6	4 s. 12	8 9	1:54	B	5:02	E	GEM	10
69	10	M.	7:04	C	6:45	C	11 41	6	3 s. 48	9¼ 10	3:04	B	5:37	E	CAN	11
70	11	Tu.	7:02	C	6:46	C	11 44	6	3 s. 25	10¼ 10¾	4:13	C	6:06	E	CAN	12
71	12	W.	7:01	C	6:48	C	11 47	6	3 s. 01	11 11½	5:19	C	6:28	E	LEO	13
72	13	Th.	6:59	C	6:49	C	11 50	7	2 s. 38	11¾ —	6:23	D	6:48	D	LEO	14
73	14	Fr.	6:57	C	6:50	C	11 53	7	2 s. 14	12 12¼	7:25	D	7:06	D	LEO	15
74	15	Sa.	6:56	C	6:51	C	11 55	7	1 s. 50	12¾ 1	8:27	E	7:24	C	VIR	16
75	16	E	6:54	C	6:52	C	11 58	7	1 s. 26	1¼ 1½	9:30	E	7:42	B	VIR	17
76	17	M.	6:52	C	6:53	C	12 01	8	1 s. 03	1¾ 2¼	10:33	E	8:01	B	VIR	18
77	18	Tu.	6:50	C	6:55	C	12 05	8	0 s. 39	2½ 2¾	11:38	E	8:24	B	LIB	19
78	19	W.	6:49	C	6:56	C	12 07	8	0 s. 15	3 3½	—	-	8:51	A	LIB	20
79	20	Th.	6:47	C	6:57	C	12 10	9	0 N. 07	3¾ 4¼	12:42	E	9:25	A	SCO	21
80	21	Fr.	6:45	C	6:58	C	12 13	9	0 N. 31	4½ 5¼	1:45	E	10:08	A	OPH	22
81	22	Sa.	6:43	C	6:59	C	12 16	9	0 N. 55	5¼ 6	2:43	E	11:00	A	SAG	23
82	23	E	6:42	C	7:00	C	12 18	9	1 N. 18	6¼ 7	3:34	E	12:03	A	SAG	24
83	24	M.	6:40	C	7:01	C	12 21	10	1 N. 42	7¼ 8	4:16	E	1:14	B	SAG	25
84	25	Tu.	6:38	C	7:03	C	12 25	10	2 N. 06	8¼ 9	4:51	E	2:29	B	CAP	26
85	26	W.	6:36	C	7:04	C	12 28	10	2 N. 29	9¼ 9¾	5:20	E	3:46	C	CAP	27
86	27	Th.	6:35	C	7:05	C	12 30	11	2 N. 53	10¼ 10¾	5:45	D	5:04	D	AQU	28
87	28	Fr.	6:33	C	7:06	C	12 33	11	3 N. 16	11 11½	6:08	D	6:23	E	AQU	29
88	29	Sa.	6:31	C	7:07	D	12 36	11	3 N. 39	11¾ —	6:31	C	7:44	E	PSC	0
89	30	E	6:30	C	7:08	D	12 38	12	4 N. 03	12¼ 12¾	6:55	B	9:06	E	PSC	1
90	31	M.	6:28	C	7:09	D	12 41	12	4 N. 26	1 1½	7:23	B	10:29	E	ARI	2

CALENDAR

THE THIRD MONTH • 2025 **MARCH** MARCH HATH 31 DAYS

The stormy March is come at last,
With wind, and cloud, and changing skies.
–William Cullen Bryant

DAY OF MONTH	DAY OF WEEK	DATES, FEASTS, FASTS, ASPECTS, TIDE HEIGHTS, AND WEATHER	
1	Sa.	St. David • ☾ ON EQ. • ☾ AT ☊ • ☾ AT PERIG. • ☌♀☾ • ☌♆☾	*Clouds*
2	E	**Quinquagesima** • Curler Sandra Marie Schmirler died, 2000 • {11.2 / 11.2}	*form*
3	M.	**Orthodox Lent begins** • ☌☿♆ • Florida statehood, 1845	*a late*
4	Tu.	Shrove Tuesday • ☌♅☾ • Avalanche disaster, Rogers Pass, B.C., 1910	*snowstorm—*
5	W.	**Ash Wednesday** • Calculations for 1st computerized (ENIAC) weather forecast began, 1950	*Stop*
6	Th.	☌♃☾ • Artist Michelangelo born, 1475 • {10.6 / 8.9}	*what*
7	Fr.	St. Perpetua • ☾ RIDES HIGH • 1st photos of Pluto's surface released, 1996 • {10.1 / 8.5}	*you're*
8	Sa.	☌♂☾ • ☿ GR. ELONG. (18° EAST) • *Time is the herald of truth.* • Tides {9.8 / 8.3}	*doing,*
9	E	**1st S. in Lent** • DAYLIGHT SAVING TIME BEGINS, 2:00 A.M. • ☌☿♀	*time to go*
10	M.	Alexandra Trusova 1st female to land quadruple toe loop in figure skating competition, 2018	*snowshoeing!*
11	Tu.	World Health Organization declared COVID-19 outbreak a pandemic, 2020 • {9.9 / 9.1}	*Too*
12	W.	Ember Day • ☌♄☉ • Hummingbirds migrate north now. • Tides {10.0 / 9.4}	*late,*
13	Th.	National K9 Veterans Day (U.S.) • Chicken nugget innovator Robert Carl Baker died, 2006	*it's*
14	Fr.	Ember Day • FULL WORM ○ • ECLIPSE ☾ • ☾ ON EQ. • ☾ AT ☋ • ☿ STAT.	
15	Sa.	Ember Day • Beware the ides of March. • John McCloskey became 1st U.S. Cardinal, 1875 • {9.8 / 9.9}	*gone!*
16	E	**2nd S. in Lent** • Nathaniel Hawthorne's *The Scarlet Letter* 1st published, 1850 •	*Mercury's*
17	M.	ST. PATRICK'S DAY • ☾ AT APO. • Children's librarian Lillian H. Smith born, 1887	*rising.*
18	Tu.	Deadly Tri-State Tornado event hit Ind., Ill., Mo., 1925 • Tides {9.7 / 9.0}	*We're*
19	W.	St. Joseph • ☌♆☉ • 31-lb. 2-oz. longnose gar caught, Coosa River, Ga., 2022	*surmising*
20	Th.	VERNAL EQUINOX • ☌♀♆ • Birthday of *Sesame Street*'s Big Bird • {9.3 / 8.2}	*a spring*
21	Fr.	*A March Sun sticks like a lock of wool.* • Tides {9.1 / 7.9}	*surprising!*
22	Sa.	☾ RUNS LOW • ♀ IN INF. ☌ • Singer Stephanie Mills born, 1957 • {8.9 / 7.7}	*Flowing*
23	E	**3rd S. in Lent** • Patrick Henry delivered "Give me liberty, or give me death" speech, Richmond, Va., 1775	
24	M.	☌♇☾ • ☿ IN INF. ☌ • Ground-breaking for N.Y.C. subway system, 1900	*creeks,*
25	Tu.	**Annunciation** • 3.2" snow, Baltimore, Md., 2013 • {9.5 / 8.7}	*new buds*
26	W.	U.S. Supreme Court Justice Sandra Day O'Connor born, 1930 • Tides {10.1 / 9.5}	*grow,*
27	Th.	☌☿♆ • Astronomer Wilhelm Beer died, 1850 • {10.6 / 10.3}	*a crocus*
28	Fr.	☾ ON EQ. • ☾ AT ☊ • ☌☿☾ • ☌♀☾ • ☌♄☾ • ☌♆☾	*peeks*
29	Sa.	NEW ● • ECLIPSE ☉ • *A word once out flies everywhere.* • {11.3 / —}	*through*
30	E	**4th S. in Lent** • ☾ AT PERIG. • ☌♀♄ • Tides {11.6 / 11.3}	*melting*
31	M.	Chipmunks emerge from hibernation now. • {11.9 / 11.1}	*snow.*

CALENDAR

Farmer's Calendar

In like a who? *Out like* a what? It requires some optimism. We tend a little farm, snugly tucked into a pocket of old-growth forest, where we are called to pay a certain reverence fee for the charms of this living. The winter cost comes in downed limbs, at the least. Each day finds some wild new weather. Soon spring levies a heavy tax in the form of allergies. Some farmsteader friends are prone to grumbling: *Is it even worth it?*

If you know where to look, you can find the stitches of hope and dream for the growing years ahead. Today, I'm lending a hand at the garden club in my daughter's school. A row of fourth graders is broken by a harsh line of wind. The boy in an oversized trapper hat asks if there isn't any gardening we can do indoors. "Sure," Ms. Teacher concedes, "but if March has to be all the seasons scrambled together, shouldn't we see what today's got on offer?" She starts the old proverb to assure him of forgiving weather on the horizon. The trapper hat interrupts with wordplay, "In like a *liar,* out like *ka-blam.*" A gust of laughter meets the full force of the actual wind. Suddenly, the kid has learned one way to defeat the weather.

APRIL

SKY WATCH: On the 1st at nightfall, the crescent Moon hovers just above the famous Pleiades star cluster, a major treat visible through binoculars. On the 2nd, the Moon meets Jupiter before moving on to meet Mars on the 5th. The Red Planet, still very bright at magnitude 0.5, resumes its direct eastward (leftward) motion, leaving the area occupied by Castor and Pollux. In the east at dawn, Venus moves higher each morning, shining at a maximum brilliance of magnitude –4.8. At around 5:30 A.M. from the 19th to the 30th, very low Mercury and Saturn are seen below blazing Venus. The waning crescent Moon joins the trio of planets on the 25th to the left of Saturn, above Mercury—with Venus higher than them all.

◐ **FIRST QUARTER** 4th day 10:15 P.M.　　◑ **LAST QUARTER** 20th day 9:35 P.M.
○ **FULL MOON** 12th day 8:22 P.M.　　● **NEW MOON** 27th day 3:31 P.M.

All times are given in Eastern Daylight Time.

GET THESE PAGES WITH TIMES SET TO YOUR ZIP CODE VIA ALMANAC.COM/2025.

DAY OF YEAR	DAY OF MONTH	DAY OF WEEK	☼ RISES H.M.	RISE KEY	☼ SETS H.M.	SET KEY	LENGTH OF DAY H.M.	SUN FAST M.	SUN DECLINATION ° '	HIGH TIDE TIMES BOSTON	☽ RISES H.M.	RISE KEY	☽ SETS H.M.	SET KEY	☽ ASTRON. PLACE	☽ AGE
91	1	Tu.	6:26	C	7:10	D	12 44	12	4 N. 49	1¾ 2¼	7:57	A	11:51	E	ARI	3
92	2	W.	6:24	C	7:12	D	12 48	12	5 N. 12	2½ 3¼	8:40	A	—	-	TAU	4
93	3	Th.	6:23	C	7:13	D	12 50	13	5 N. 35	3½ 4¼	9:33	A	1:07	E	TAU	5
94	4	Fr.	6:21	C	7:14	D	12 53	13	5 N. 58	4½ 5¼	10:36	A	2:10	E	AUR	6
95	5	Sa.	6:19	C	7:15	D	12 56	13	6 N. 21	5½ 6½	11:45	B	3:01	E	GEM	7
96	6	E	6:18	B	7:16	D	12 58	14	6 N. 43	6¾ 7½	12:55	B	3:40	E	CAN	8
97	7	M.	6:16	B	7:17	D	13 01	14	7 N. 06	7¾ 8¾	2:05	B	4:10	E	CAN	9
98	8	Tu.	6:14	B	7:18	D	13 04	14	7 N. 28	9 9½	3:11	C	4:34	E	LEO	10
99	9	W.	6:13	B	7:19	D	13 06	14	7 N. 51	9¾ 10¼	4:15	D	4:55	D	LEO	11
100	10	Th.	6:11	B	7:21	D	13 10	15	8 N. 13	10½ 11	5:17	D	5:13	D	LEO	12
101	11	Fr.	6:09	B	7:22	D	13 13	15	8 N. 35	11¼ 11½	6:19	E	5:30	C	VIR	13
102	12	Sa.	6:08	B	7:23	D	13 15	15	8 N. 57	12 —	7:21	E	5:48	C	VIR	14
103	13	E	6:06	B	7:24	D	13 18	15	9 N. 18	12¼ 12½	8:24	E	6:07	B	VIR	15
104	14	M.	6:04	B	7:25	D	13 21	16	9 N. 40	12¾ 1¼	9:28	E	6:29	B	VIR	16
105	15	Tu.	6:03	B	7:26	D	13 23	16	10 N. 01	1¼ 1¾	10:33	E	6:54	B	LIB	17
106	16	W.	6:01	B	7:27	D	13 26	16	10 N. 23	1¾ 2½	11:36	E	7:26	A	SCO	18
107	17	Th.	6:00	B	7:28	D	13 28	16	10 N. 44	2½ 3¼	—	-	8:05	A	SCO	19
108	18	Fr.	5:58	B	7:30	D	13 32	17	11 N. 05	3¼ 4	12:35	A	8:53	A	OPH	20
109	19	Sa.	5:56	B	7:31	D	13 35	17	11 N. 25	4 4¾	1:28	A	9:52	A	SAG	21
110	20	E	5:55	B	7:32	D	13 37	17	11 N. 46	4¾ 5½	2:12	E	10:58	B	SAG	22
111	21	M.	5:53	B	7:33	D	13 40	17	12 N. 06	5¾ 6½	2:49	E	12:09	B	CAP	23
112	22	Tu.	5:52	B	7:34	D	13 42	17	12 N. 26	6¾ 7½	3:19	E	1:23	C	CAP	24
113	23	W.	5:50	B	7:35	D	13 45	18	12 N. 46	7¾ 8½	3:45	E	2:38	C	AQU	25
114	24	Th.	5:49	B	7:36	D	13 47	18	13 N. 06	8¾ 9¼	4:08	D	3:54	D	AQU	26
115	25	Fr.	5:47	B	7:37	D	13 50	18	13 N. 25	9¾ 10	4:30	C	5:12	E	PSC	27
116	26	Sa.	5:46	B	7:39	D	13 53	18	13 N. 45	10½ 11	4:54	C	6:33	E	PSC	28
117	27	E	5:44	B	7:40	D	13 56	18	14 N. 04	11½ 11¾	5:20	B	7:57	E	PSC	0
118	28	M.	5:43	B	7:41	D	13 58	18	14 N. 23	12¼ —	5:51	B	9:22	E	ARI	1
119	29	Tu.	5:42	B	7:42	E	14 00	18	14 N. 41	12½ 1¼	6:30	A	10:44	E	TAU	2
120	30	W.	5:40	B	7:43	E	14 03	19	15 N. 00	1½ 2	7:20	A	11:56	E	TAU	3

　To use this page, see p. 116; for Key Letters, see p. 238. LIGHT = A.M. BOLD = P.M.　

CALENDAR

APRIL

Great, wide, beautiful, wonderful World,
With the wonderful water round you curled.
–William Brighty Rands

DAY OF MONTH	DAY OF WEEK	DATES, FEASTS, FASTS, ASPECTS, TIDE HEIGHTS, AND WEATHER	
1	Tu.	ALL FOOLS' • ☌♅☾ • *Fools grow without watering.* • Tides {11.9/10.7	*No fools,*
2	W.	☌♃☾ • CN tower completed, Toronto, Ont., 1975 • Cat Merlin purred at 67.8 decibels, 2015	*they,*
3	Th.	St. Richard of Chichester • ☾ RIDES HIGH • Pony Express began postal service, 1860	*farmers*
4	Fr.	Film critic Roger Ebert died, 2013 • Tides {10.6/8.9	*use every*
5	Sa.	☌♂☾ • John Winthrop, founder of Mass. Bay Colony, died, 1649 • Singer Agnetha Åse Fältskog born, 1950	*day*
6	E	5th S. in Lent • ☿ STAT. • James Dewar invented Twinkies, 1930	*of the*
7	M.	International Beaver Day • Grand Trunk Pacific Railway completed near Fort Fraser, B.C., 1914	*season.*
8	Tu.	Supreme Court of Canada established, 1875 • {9.4/9.0	*They*
9	W.	1st baseball game in indoor stadium (Astrodome), Houston, Tex., 1965 • Tides {9.5/9.3	*know*
10	Th.	☾ ON EQ. • ☾ AT ☋ • ♀ STAT. • Tides {9.6/9.6	*what*
11	Fr.	Astronomer Samuel Schwabe died, 1875 • {9.6/9.8	*they*
12	Sa.	Passover begins at sundown • FULL PINK ○ • 231-mph wind gust, Mt. Washington, N.H., 1934	*grow,*
13	E	Palm Sunday • ☾ AT APO. • U.S. president Thomas Jefferson born, 1743	*and*
14	M.	"Black Sunday" dust storm hit Great Plains, 1935	*this*
15	Tu.	U.S. pres. Abraham Lincoln died, 1865 • Tides {10.0/9.1	*rain is*
16	W.	☌☿♆ • *April weather, Rain and sunshine, both together.* • {9.9/8.9	*quite*
17	Th.	Maundy Thursday • Canada's Constitution Act took effect, 1982	*pleasin'!*
18	Fr.	Good Friday • ☾ RUNS LOW • Paul Revere's ride began, 1775 • {9.5/8.3	*They*
19	Sa.	Football player Chase Winovich born, 1995 • {9.4/8.2	*always*
20	E	Easter • Orthodox Easter • Activist Dorothy Height died, 2010	*treasure*
21	M.	Easter Monday • ☌♇☾ • ☿ GR. ELONG. (27° WEST) • {9.3/8.4	*Planet*
22	Tu.	EARTH DAY • *What much is worth comes from the earth.* • Tides {9.4/8.8	*Earth,*
23	W.	Poplars leaf out about now. • Poet William Wordsworth died, 1850 • {9.7/9.5	*our home*
24	Th.	☾ AT ☊ • ☌♀☾ • *The Old Farmer's Almanac* founder Robert B. Thomas born, 1766	*sweet*
25	Fr.	☾ ON EQ. • ☌☿☾ • ☌♄☾ • ☌♆☾ • Tides {10.5/11.0	*terrarium,*
26	Sa.	Likely earliest photo of tornado taken, by A. A. Adams, Garnett, Kans., 1884 • {10.8/11.6	*and think*
27	E	2nd S. of Easter • NEW ● • ☾ AT PERIG. • {11.0/12.0	*about seeds,*
28	M.	St. George[T] • ☌♀♄ • ☌♅☾ • Tides {10.9/—	*like just*
29	Tu.	St. Mark[T] • Lightning bolt stretched 477.2 miles, Tex., La., Miss., 2020 • {12.2/10.8	*when to*
30	W.	☌♃☾ • Discovery of mendelevium (element 101) announced, 1955 • {12.1/10.4	*bury 'em.*

Farmer's Calendar

A fool's month for plowing

The soil is a sop-shop—this is the kind of thing that Gretchen says. She has hoed herself into the soggy center of her potato patch. She spins in the mud, slowed by her sodden galoshes. The wind is at my back, and I holler a good old *next-time-you-oughta.* She seems to hear, but maybe not. She takes a filthy seat in the muck, fatigued as a first-calf heifer in the calving, and shakes her hands in the air. Later, I bring a loaf of sourdough to dry up the day's remains, and she digs into me for teasing her. There's a debate: Is it worse to be worn out by mud or outwitted by it?

There's something like a wink in our way. We both know that soon she'll be upwind, romping her own nagging advice around my garden gate, some well-soaked knowledge about properly skinned seed tubers and what I should have done with the cornstalks from last fall—and I'll be cursing the split handle on my digging fork. "There's a poem in here," I say. "Ah! But you would need a gentleman to write it," she returns. She leaves her porch light on, until I've slopped my way home. Then I light mine, like a hug goodnight.

CALENDAR

MAY

SKY WATCH: From the 1st to the 6th, Mars approaches and passes the gorgeous but faint star cluster M44, which is known as "The Beehive." Use binoculars for a celestial thrill. On the 3rd, the Moon closely meets Mars in the dim constellation of Cancer the Crab. Remember that actual constellations do not match up with tropical zodiacal signs, which is why the descriptions of the astronomical and astrological locations of the planets may differ. Throughout the month, brilliant Jupiter sinks lower into the western dusk twilight. On the 15th at 5:45 A.M., Saturn returns as a morning star to hover at the right of Venus, low in the east. Stunning Venus appears noticeably higher each morning. Back in the west at nightfall, Mars in Leo, fading to magnitude 1.3, stands just above the crescent Moon on the 31st.

◐ FIRST QUARTER	4th day	9:52 A.M.	☾ LAST QUARTER	20th day	7:59 A.M.
○ FULL MOON	12th day	12:56 P.M.	● NEW MOON	26th day	11:02 P.M.

All times are given in Eastern Daylight Time.

GET THESE PAGES WITH TIMES SET TO YOUR ZIP CODE VIA ALMANAC.COM/2025.

DAY OF YEAR	DAY OF MONTH	DAY OF WEEK	☼ RISES H. M.	RISE KEY	☼ SETS H. M.	SET KEY	LENGTH OF DAY H. M.	SUN FAST M.	SUN DECLINATION ° '	HIGH TIDE TIMES BOSTON		☾ RISES H. M.	RISE KEY	☾ SETS H. M.	SET KEY	☾ ASTRON. PLACE	☾ AGE
121	1	Th.	5:39	B	7:44	E	14 05	19	15 N. 18	2¼	3	8:21	A	—	-	AUR	4
122	2	Fr.	5:38	B	7:45	E	14 07	19	15 N. 36	3¼	4	9:30	A	12:54	E	GEM	5
123	3	Sa.	5:36	B	7:46	E	14 10	19	15 N. 53	4¼	5	10:43	B	1:38	E	GEM	6
124	4	E	5:35	B	7:48	E	14 13	19	16 N. 10	5¼	6	11:54	B	2:12	E	CAN	7
125	5	M.	5:34	B	7:49	E	14 15	19	16 N. 27	6¼	7	1:03	C	2:39	E	LEO	8
126	6	Tu.	5:32	B	7:50	E	14 18	19	16 N. 44	7½	8	2:08	C	3:00	D	LEO	9
127	7	W.	5:31	B	7:51	E	14 20	19	17 N. 01	8½	9	3:10	D	3:19	D	LEO	10
128	8	Th.	5:30	B	7:52	E	14 22	19	17 N. 17	9¼	9¾	4:12	D	3:37	C	VIR	11
129	9	Fr.	5:29	B	7:53	E	14 24	19	17 N. 33	10	10¼	5:13	E	3:55	C	VIR	12
130	10	Sa.	5:28	B	7:54	E	14 26	19	17 N. 48	10¾	11	6:16	E	4:13	B	VIR	13
131	11	E	5:27	B	7:55	E	14 28	19	18 N. 04	11½	11½	7:19	E	4:34	B	VIR	14
132	12	M.	5:26	B	7:56	E	14 30	19	18 N. 19	12¼	—	8:24	E	4:58	B	LIB	15
133	13	Tu.	5:24	B	7:57	E	14 33	19	18 N. 34	12¼	12¾	9:28	E	5:28	A	LIB	16
134	14	W.	5:23	B	7:58	E	14 35	19	18 N. 48	12¾	1½	10:29	E	6:05	A	SCO	17
135	15	Th.	5:22	B	7:59	E	14 37	19	19 N. 02	1½	2	11:24	E	6:50	A	OPH	18
136	16	Fr.	5:21	B	8:00	E	14 39	19	19 N. 16	2	2¾	—	-	7:46	A	SAG	19
137	17	Sa.	5:20	B	8:01	E	14 41	19	19 N. 29	2¾	3½	12:10	E	8:49	B	SAG	20
138	18	E	5:19	A	8:02	E	14 43	19	19 N. 42	3½	4¼	12:49	E	9:58	B	CAP	21
139	19	M.	5:19	A	8:03	E	14 44	19	19 N. 55	4½	5¼	1:20	E	11:10	B	CAP	22
140	20	Tu.	5:18	A	8:04	E	14 46	19	20 N. 07	5¼	6	1:47	E	12:22	C	CAP	23
141	21	W.	5:17	A	8:05	E	14 48	19	20 N. 20	6¼	7	2:10	D	1:35	D	AQU	24
142	22	Th.	5:16	A	8:06	E	14 50	19	20 N. 31	7¼	7¾	2:32	D	2:49	D	PSC	25
143	23	Fr.	5:15	A	8:07	E	14 52	19	20 N. 43	8¼	8¾	2:54	C	4:06	E	PSC	26
144	24	Sa.	5:15	A	8:08	E	14 53	19	20 N. 54	9¼	9½	3:18	B	5:26	E	PSC	27
145	25	E	5:14	A	8:09	E	14 55	19	21 N. 04	10¼	10½	3:46	B	6:49	E	ARI	28
146	26	M.	5:13	A	8:10	E	14 57	19	21 N. 15	11	11¼	4:20	B	8:13	E	ARI	0
147	27	Tu.	5:12	A	8:11	E	14 59	18	21 N. 25	12	—	5:05	A	9:32	E	TAU	1
148	28	W.	5:12	A	8:12	E	15 00	18	21 N. 34	12¼	1	6:01	A	10:38	E	TAU	2
149	29	Th.	5:11	A	8:12	E	15 01	18	21 N. 43	1	1¾	7:09	A	11:30	E	AUR	3
150	30	Fr.	5:11	A	8:13	E	15 02	18	21 N. 52	2	2¾	8:23	B	—	-	GEM	4
151	31	Sa.	5:10	A	8:14	E	15 04	18	22 N. 01	3	3¾	9:38	B	12:09	E	CAN	5

THE FIFTH MONTH • 2025 **MAY** MAY HATH 31 DAYS

There's beauty in the break of day; / There's glory in the noon-tide ray;
There's sweetness in the twilight shades; / Magnificence in night.
–John Bowring

DAY OF MONTH	DAY OF WEEK	DATES, FEASTS, FASTS, ASPECTS, TIDE HEIGHTS, AND WEATHER	
1	Th.	Sts. Philip & James • MAY DAY • ☾ RIDES HIGH • Gwendolyn Brooks won Pulitzer Prize, 1950	*Gentle*
2	Fr.	St. Athanasius • *A contented mind is a great gift.* • Tides {11.2 9.5	*raindrops,*
3	Sa.	☌♀♆ • ☌♂☾ • Old Man of the Mountain rock face fell, Franconia Notch, N.H., 2003	*morning*
4	**E**	**3rd S. of Easter** • Misspelled Hollywood Walk of Fame star unveiled for actress Julia Louis-Dreyfus, 2010	
5	M.	Amy Johnson began 1st solo flight by woman from England to Australia, 1930 • Tides {9.5 8.9	*dew,*
6	Tu.	♇ STAT. • Coronation of Britain's King Charles III and Queen Camilla, 2023	*flowers*
7	W.	☾ AT ☋ • *Water in May is bread all the year.* • {9.1 9.2	*bloom for*
8	Th.	St. Julian of Norwich • ☾ ON EQ. • World Health Assembly declared global eradication of smallpox, 1980	*you-*
9	Fr.	St. Gregory of Nazianzus • Singer Lena Horne died, 2010 • Tides {9.1 9.7	*know-*
10	Sa.	☾ AT APO. • Dancer Fred Astaire born, 1899 • Astronaut Ellen Ochoa born, 1958	*who!*
11	**E**	Three • **4th S. of Easter** • MOTHER'S DAY • {9.1 10.0	*Mothers,*
12	M.	Chilly • Vesak • FULL FLOWER ○ • Baseball player Yogi Berra born, 1925	*to be*
13	Tu.	Saints • Cranberries in bud now. • Musician Stevie Wonder born, 1950 • {10.1 9.0	*quite*
14	W.	Carlsbad Caverns National Park established, N.Mex., 1930 • Tides {10.1 8.9	*specific,*
15	Th.	☾ RUNS LOW • Maurice and Richard McDonald opened precursor restaurant to McDonald's, San Bernadino, Calif., 1940	
16	Fr.	Marie Antoinette (age 14) married future King Louis XVI of France (age 15), 1770 • Tides {9.9 8.6	*all*
17	Sa.	☌♅☉ • 1st Kentucky Derby held, 1875 • Tides {9.8 8.6	*deserve an*
18	**E**	**5th S. of Easter** • ☌♇☾ • Major eruption of Mt. St. Helens, Wash., 1980	*honorific.*
19	M.	St. Dunstan • VICTORIA DAY (CANADA) • Tides {9.7 8.8	*Sunshine's*
20	Tu.	*LightSail-A* spacecraft launched, 2015 • {9.6 9.1	*divine*
21	W.	"Gustnado" whirlwind struck Sayler Park, Cincinnati, Ohio, 2022 • Tides {9.7 9.6	*for yards*
22	Th.	☾ ON EQ. • ☾ AT ☊ • ☌♄☾ • ☌♆☾ • 29.5" Pacific cod caught, Seward, Alaska, 2022	
23	Fr.	☌♀☾ • 16-year-old Temba Tsheri became youngest person at time to summit Mount Everest, 2001	*and*
24	Sa.	☌☿♅ • 1st flight of Goodyear B-class blimp (B-1), 1917 • Tides {10.1 11.4	*crops,*
25	**E**	Rogation Sunday • ☾ AT PERIG. • G. Lockhart 1st woman in British Emp. to earn bachelor's degree, N.B., 1875	*like*
26	M.	MEMORIAL DAY, OBSERVED • NEW ● • ☌☿☾ • ☌♅☾	*string*
27	Tu.	Chef Jamie Oliver born, 1975 • Olympic gymnast Jade Carey born, 2000 • {10.4 —	*beans,*
28	W.	☾ RIDES HIGH • ☌♃☾ • Wildfire near Halifax led to evacuations, N.S., 2023	*chard,*
29	Th.	**Ascension** • **Orthodox Ascension** • R.I. statehood, 1790	*and*
30	Fr.	☿ IN SUP. ☌ • European Space Agency established, 1975 • {11.6 9.8	*carrot*
31	Sa.	Visit. of Mary • National Smile Day (U.S.) • ♀ GR. ELONG. (46° WEST) • {11.1 9.5	*tops!*

Farmer's Calendar

Council is in session.

(Warning: contains nudity. The views expressed herein do not necessarily reflect the views or positions of *The Old Farmer's Almanac.*) To be clear, there isn't any actual nudity to speak of—just that of a newly proposed city resolution. Our city councilor is a bit of a local celebrity, and not just for founding our chapter of the pollinator's society. He's fantastic with bringing people together and can navigate a budget pretty well, too, but that's a different story. Everyone knows that the cost of his leadership means a couple of nutty ideas each year, usually aimed to promote our little hamlet as a regional destination. This time, his goal for the town is to stake claim as the unofficial capital of "World Naked Gardening Day," the first Saturday of every May. Imagine: a home garden tour in the stark. Will the Chamber host some sort of no-rag-shag parade down Main? Listen, I'm not here to be at odds with anybody's gardening aesthetics—my food forest may not meet the tidy standards of some neighbors—but isn't this the same town that debated the width of our bike path for 20 years? Well, alrighty, Mr. Councilor. If you say so!

CALENDAR

JUNE

SKY WATCH: On the 1st, the crescent Moon floats just above Leo's blue star Regulus and just below fading orange Mars. Jupiter's final weeks of visibility find it very low in the evening twilight at 9:15 P.M. From the 12th to the 30th, Mercury offers its finest showing of 2025, low in the WNW from 9:00 to 9:15 P.M.—its brightest magnitude, –0.8, occurs during the early part of the period. Look for Mercury low to the left of the crescent Moon on the 26th, before it achieves a more comfortable 8-degree elevation from the 29th to the 30th. On the 29th, Mars hovers just above the crescent Moon, seeming to observers in the eastern U.S. and Canada to almost touch it. Summer begins with the solstice on the 20th at 10:42 P.M. EDT.

◑ **FIRST QUARTER** 2nd day 11:41 P.M.   ◐ **LAST QUARTER** 18th day 3:19 P.M.
○ **FULL MOON** 11th day 3:44 A.M.   ● **NEW MOON** 25th day 6:31 A.M.

All times are given in Eastern Daylight Time.

GET THESE PAGES WITH TIMES SET TO YOUR ZIP CODE VIA ALMANAC.COM/2025.

DAY OF YEAR	DAY OF MONTH	DAY OF WEEK	☼ RISES H.M.	RISE KEY	☼ SETS H.M.	SET KEY	LENGTH OF DAY H.M.	SUN FAST M.	SUN DECLINATION ° ′	HIGH TIDE TIMES BOSTON		☾ RISES H.M.	RISE KEY	☾ SETS H.M.	SET KEY	☾ ASTRON. PLACE	☾ AGE
152	1	E	5:10	A	8:15	E	15 05	18	22 N. 09	3¾	4½	10:49	C	12:40	E	LEO	6
153	2	M.	5:09	A	8:16	E	15 07	18	22 N. 16	4¾	5½	11:57	C	1:04	D	LEO	7
154	3	Tu.	5:09	A	8:16	E	15 07	17	22 N. 24	5¾	6½	1:01	D	1:24	D	LEO	8
155	4	W.	5:09	A	8:17	E	15 08	17	22 N. 31	6¾	7¼	2:03	D	1:42	D	VIR	9
156	5	Th.	5:08	A	8:18	E	15 10	17	22 N. 37	7¾	8¼	3:05	E	2:00	C	VIR	10
157	6	Fr.	5:08	A	8:18	E	15 10	17	22 N. 43	8¾	9	4:07	E	2:18	C	VIR	11
158	7	Sa.	5:08	A	8:19	E	15 11	17	22 N. 49	9½	9¾	5:10	E	2:38	B	VIR	12
159	8	E	5:07	A	8:20	E	15 13	16	22 N. 54	10¼	10¼	6:15	E	3:01	B	LIB	13
160	9	M.	5:07	A	8:20	E	15 13	16	22 N. 59	11	11	7:19	E	3:29	A	LIB	14
161	10	Tu.	5:07	A	8:21	E	15 14	16	23 N. 03	11¾	11¾	8:22	E	4:04	A	SCO	15
162	11	W.	5:07	A	8:21	E	15 14	16	23 N. 08	12½	—	9:19	E	4:47	A	OPH	16
163	12	Th.	5:07	A	8:22	E	15 15	16	23 N. 11	12¼	1	10:09	E	5:40	A	SAG	17
164	13	Fr.	5:07	A	8:22	E	15 15	15	23 N. 14	1	1¾	10:49	E	6:42	A	SAG	18
165	14	Sa.	5:07	A	8:23	E	15 16	15	23 N. 17	1¾	2½	11:23	E	7:50	B	SAG	19
166	15	E	5:07	A	8:23	E	15 16	15	23 N. 20	2½	3¼	11:50	E	9:01	B	CAP	20
167	16	M.	5:07	A	8:23	E	15 16	15	23 N. 22	3¼	4	—	-	10:13	C	CAP	21
168	17	Tu.	5:07	A	8:24	E	15 17	15	23 N. 23	4	4¾	12:14	D	11:24	D	AQU	22
169	18	W.	5:07	A	8:24	E	15 17	14	23 N. 25	5	5½	12:36	D	12:36	D	AQU	23
170	19	Th.	5:07	A	8:24	E	15 17	14	23 N. 25	5¾	6½	12:57	C	1:49	E	PSC	24
171	20	Fr.	5:07	A	8:25	E	15 18	14	23 N. 26	6¾	7¼	1:19	C	3:05	E	PSC	25
172	21	Sa.	5:07	A	8:25	E	15 18	14	23 N. 26	7¾	8¼	1:44	B	4:25	E	ARI	26
173	22	E	5:08	A	8:25	E	15 17	14	23 N. 25	9	9¼	2:15	B	5:47	E	ARI	27
174	23	M.	5:08	A	8:25	E	15 17	13	23 N. 24	10	10	2:54	A	7:06	E	TAU	28
175	24	Tu.	5:08	A	8:25	E	15 17	13	23 N. 23	10¾	11	3:44	A	8:18	E	TAU	29
176	25	W.	5:09	A	8:25	E	15 16	13	23 N. 21	11¾	—	4:46	A	9:17	E	AUR	0
177	26	Th.	5:09	A	8:25	E	15 16	13	23 N. 19	12	12¾	5:59	B	10:03	E	GEM	1
178	27	Fr.	5:09	A	8:25	E	15 16	13	23 N. 17	12¾	1½	7:15	B	10:37	E	CAN	2
179	28	Sa.	5:10	A	8:25	E	15 15	12	23 N. 14	1¾	2½	8:30	B	11:04	E	CAN	3
180	29	E	5:10	A	8:25	E	15 15	12	23 N. 11	2½	3¼	9:41	C	11:27	E	LEO	4
181	30	M.	5:11	A	8:25	E	15 14	12	23 N. 07	3½	4	10:48	D	11:46	E	LEO	5

To use this page, see p. 116; for Key Letters, see p. 238. LIGHT = A.M. **BOLD = P.M.**   2025

Hail Summer! glory of the year,
And bright perfection of the Spring!
–**J. Dodds**

DAY OF MONTH	DAY OF WEEK	DATES, FEASTS, FASTS, ASPECTS, TIDE HEIGHTS, AND WEATHER	
1	**E**	**1st S. af. Asc.** • Shavuot begins at sundown • ☌♂☾ • {10.5 / 9.3	*Rain*
2	M.	Naturalist Edwin Way Teale born, 1899 • Tornado struck Three Hills, Alta., 2017 • {9.9 / 9.2	*is*
3	Tu.	☾ AT ☋ • John Adams became 1st U.S. president to live in D.C., 1800 • Tides {9.4 / 9.1	*still*
4	W.	☾ ON EQ. • Actress/humanitarian Angelina Jolie born, 1975 • Tides {9.0 / 9.2	*flowing,*
5	Th.	St. Boniface • Writer O. Henry died, 1910 • Tides {8.7 / 9.3	*summer*
6	Fr.	Chrysler Corporation founded, 1925 • D-Day, 1944 • {8.6 / 9.4	*is*
7	Sa.	☾ AT APO. • 1st U.S. gov. solar power plant dedicated, Natural Bridges Nat'l Monument, Utah, 1980	*lagging,*
8	**E**	**Whit S. • Pentecost** • Orthodox Pentecost • ☌☿♃	*we*
9	M.	John Barry's *Philadelphia Spelling Book* 1st item registered for U.S. copyright, 1790 • {8.6 / 9.9	*must*
10	Tu.	Baseball player Pokey Reese born, 1973 • {8.7 / 10.0	*admit*
11	W.	St. Barnabas • Ember Day • **FULL STRAWBERRY** ○ • ☾ RUNS LOW	*that our*
12	Th.	Closest approach of a comet to Earth (1,115,466 miles), 1999 • Tides {10.1 / 8.7	*spirits*
13	Fr.	Ember Day • *June damp and warm / Does the farmer no harm.* • Tides {10.2 / 8.8	*are*
14	Sa.	St. Basil • Ember Day • **FLAG DAY** • ☌♇☾ • U.S. Army established, 1775	*flagging!*
15	**E**	**Trinity** • Orthodox All Saints' • **FATHER'S DAY** • {10.2 / 9.0	*Dads lounge*
16	M.	Tennis player Bianca Andreescu born, 2000 • Tides {10.2 / 9.2	*as thunder*
17	Tu.	Cornerstone for Bunker Hill Monument laid, Mass., 1825 • Tides {10.0 / 9.5	*sounds the*
18	W.	☾ ON EQ. • ☾ AT ☊ • ☌♄☾ • Tides {9.9 / 9.8	*freedom*
19	Th.	**JUNETEENTH NATIONAL INDEPENDENCE DAY** • ☌♆☾ • 1st Father's Day, Spokane, Wash., 1910	*bell.*
20	Fr.	**SUMMER SOLSTICE** • Columbia Records formally introduced LP record, 1948 • {9.6 / 10.6	*Sunshine*
21	Sa.	Cat Tigger chased black bear from yard, North Vancouver, B.C., 2022 • Tides {9.6 / 11.0	*abounds*
22	**E**	**Corpus Christi** • ☌♀☾ • ☌♅☾ • {9.6 / 11.3	*and*
23	M.	☾ AT PERIG. • Polio vaccine creator Jonas Salk died, 1995 • Tides {9.6 / 11.6	*hearts*
24	Tu.	Nativ. John the Baptist • **MIDSUMMER DAY** • ☾ RIDES HIGH • ☌♃☉	*will*
25	W.	**NEW** ● • ☌♃☾ • Kim Campbell became Canada's 1st female prime minister, 1993	*swell,*
26	Th.	First of Muharram begins at sundown • {9.9 / —	*but then*
27	Fr.	☌☿☾ • U.S. entered Korean War, 1950 • Actor Tobey Maguire born, 1975	*clouds will*
28	Sa.	St. Irenaeus • National Paul Bunyan Day (U.S.) • Tides {11.3 / 9.7	*cast a*
29	**E**	**3rd S. af. P.** • ☌♂☾ • ☌♄♆ • *A change is as good as a rest.*	*showery*
30	M.	Sts. Peter & Paul[T] • ☾ AT ☋ • Tides {10.3 / 9.5	*spell.*

Farmer's Calendar

When apples say "thump"

June drop: It's when an apple tree naturally sheds its surplus fruit. I remember the first time I heard the term. I didn't know what it meant, but the sound of the words alone sweetened me. *June drop.* They conjured something of a world so familiar, it was as if I had always known it. I came to my love of all things farming a bit late. My childhood imagination often cradled something bucolic, but it seemed so distant from a life that I thought I was meant to have. Ultimately, love of language gave way to love of land. I was writing poetry with the gangbuster gusto of pioneer weeds, when I moved into the in-law quarters of some old farmhouse in some old farm town. The man who ran the place took care of two things, primarily: a handful of retired Holsteins, kept with love for their legacy, and a vast vocabulary of the earth. Every evening, especially those long evenings when the garden has been planted and first cut hay has been put up, I'd collect some new term. *Late-boot stage:* when the grasses are about to concentrate on seed head development; very nutritious. *Fleshing ability:* Can the cattle fatten up? And, music to my ears: *June drop.*

CALENDAR

JULY

SKY WATCH: Beginning on the 1st, Saturn rises before 11:00 P.M., a time that shifts ever earlier until the Ringed Planet appears at 9:00 P.M. at month's end. Its rings are now a remarkably thin line after being perfectly edgewise in March, although during this time the planet was next to the Sun and lost in the solar glare. For the first time in 15 years, Saturn's southern side is visible. In the morning sky, Venus is dazzling from 4:00 A.M. onward, low in the east. On the 22nd, the crescent Moon forms a striking predawn triangle with Jupiter and Venus. In the evening sky at nightfall, fading Mars, now in Virgo, hovers to the right of the crescent Moon on the 28th. The Moon dangles below Virgo's Spica, the sky's bluest star, on the 30th.

◑ **FIRST QUARTER** 2nd day 3:30 P.M.   ◐ **LAST QUARTER** 17th day 8:38 P.M.
○ **FULL MOON** 10th day 4:37 P.M.   ● **NEW MOON** 24th day 3:11 P.M.

All times are given in Eastern Daylight Time.

GET THESE PAGES WITH TIMES SET TO YOUR ZIP CODE VIA ALMANAC.COM/2025.

DAY OF YEAR	DAY OF MONTH	DAY OF WEEK	☼ RISES H. M.	RISE KEY	☼ SETS H. M.	SET KEY	LENGTH OF DAY H. M.	SUN FAST M.	SUN DECLINATION ° '	HIGH TIDE TIMES BOSTON		☾ RISES H. M.	RISE KEY	☾ SETS H. M.	SET KEY	☾ ASTRON. PLACE	☾ AGE
182	1	Tu.	5:11	A	8:25	E	15 14	12	23 N. 03	4¼	5	11:52	D	—	–	LEO	6
183	2	W.	5:12	A	8:25	E	15 13	12	22 N. 58	5¼	5¾	12:54	E	12:04	C	VIR	7
184	3	Th.	5:12	A	8:24	E	15 12	11	22 N. 53	6	6½	1:56	E	12:22	C	VIR	8
185	4	Fr.	5:13	A	8:24	E	15 11	11	22 N. 48	7	7¼	2:59	E	12:42	B	VIR	9
186	5	Sa.	5:14	A	8:24	E	15 10	11	22 N. 42	8	8¼	4:03	E	1:03	B	LIB	10
187	6	**E**	5:14	A	8:24	E	15 10	11	22 N. 36	8¾	9	5:08	E	1:29	B	LIB	11
188	7	M.	5:15	A	8:23	E	15 08	11	22 N. 29	9¾	9¾	6:12	E	2:02	A	SCO	12
189	8	Tu.	5:16	A	8:23	E	15 07	11	22 N. 23	10½	10½	7:11	E	2:42	A	OPH	13
190	9	W.	5:16	A	8:22	E	15 06	10	22 N. 15	11¼	11¼	8:04	E	3:32	A	SAG	14
191	10	Th.	5:17	A	8:22	E	15 05	10	22 N. 08	12	—	8:48	E	4:32	A	SAG	15
192	11	Fr.	5:18	A	8:21	E	15 03	10	22 N. 00	12	12¾	9:24	E	5:39	B	SAG	16
193	12	Sa.	5:19	A	8:21	E	15 02	10	21 N. 51	12¾	1¼	9:54	E	6:51	B	CAP	17
194	13	**E**	5:19	A	8:20	E	15 01	10	21 N. 42	1½	2	10:19	E	8:03	C	CAP	18
195	14	M.	5:20	A	8:20	E	15 00	10	21 N. 33	2	2¾	10:41	D	9:16	C	AQU	19
196	15	Tu.	5:21	A	8:19	E	14 58	10	21 N. 24	3	3½	11:02	C	10:28	D	AQU	20
197	16	W.	5:22	A	8:18	E	14 56	10	21 N. 14	3¾	4¼	11:23	C	11:40	E	PSC	21
198	17	Th.	5:23	A	8:18	E	14 55	10	21 N. 03	4½	5	11:47	B	12:54	E	PSC	22
199	18	Fr.	5:24	A	8:17	E	14 53	9	20 N. 53	5½	6	—	–	2:11	E	PSC	23
200	19	Sa.	5:24	A	8:16	E	14 52	9	20 N. 42	6½	7	12:15	B	3:30	E	ARI	24
201	20	**E**	5:25	A	8:15	E	14 50	9	20 N. 30	7½	8	12:49	B	4:48	E	TAU	25
202	21	M.	5:26	A	8:15	E	14 49	9	20 N. 19	8¾	9	1:33	A	6:02	E	TAU	26
203	22	Tu.	5:27	A	8:14	E	14 47	9	20 N. 07	9¾	10	2:29	A	7:05	E	TAU	27
204	23	W.	5:28	A	8:13	E	14 45	9	19 N. 54	10¾	10¾	3:37	A	7:55	E	GEM	28
205	24	Th.	5:29	A	8:12	E	14 43	9	19 N. 42	11½	11¾	4:51	B	8:34	E	GEM	0
206	25	Fr.	5:30	B	8:11	E	14 41	9	19 N. 29	12½	—	6:07	B	9:04	E	CAN	1
207	26	Sa.	5:31	B	8:10	E	14 39	9	19 N. 15	12½	1¼	7:21	C	9:28	D	LEO	2
208	27	**E**	5:32	B	8:09	E	14 37	9	19 N. 02	1½	2	8:30	C	9:49	D	LEO	3
209	28	M.	5:33	B	8:08	E	14 35	9	18 N. 48	2¼	2¾	9:37	D	10:08	C	LEO	4
210	29	Tu.	5:34	B	8:07	E	14 33	9	18 N. 33	3	3½	10:41	D	10:26	C	VIR	5
211	30	W.	5:35	B	8:06	E	14 31	9	18 N. 19	3¾	4¼	11:44	E	10:45	B	VIR	6
212	31	Th.	5:36	B	8:05	E	14 29	9	18 N. 04	4½	5	12:47	E	11:05	B	VIR	7

Come where the brookside willows / Droop o'er the cooling stream;
Come to the oak's thick shelter / From noontide's glowing beam.
–John Askham

DAY OF MONTH	DAY OF WEEK	DATES, FEASTS, FASTS, ASPECTS, TIDE HEIGHTS, AND WEATHER	
1	Tu.	Canada Day • ☾ on Eq. • Actor Walter Matthau died, 2000 • {9.7 9.4	*Big*
2	W.	Civil rights activist Medgar Evers born, 1925 • {9.2 9.3	*displays*
3	Th.	Dog Days begin. • ⊕ at aphelion • ☌♀♅ • Idaho statehood, 1890	*are*
4	Fr.	Independence Day • ☾ at apo. • ☿ Gr. elong. (26° east) • {8.4 9.2	*pyrotechnic,*
5	Sa.	♆ stat. • Lightning caused fire at oil refinery, Bayonne, N.J., 1900 • Arthur Ashe won Wimbledon, 1975	*skies*
6	**E**	4th S. af. P. • *July 2023:* Hottest month in global temperature record • {8.1 9.4	*ablaze*
7	M.	Writer Sir Arthur Conan Doyle died, 1930 • Tides {8.2 9.6	*with*
8	Tu.	Armadillos mate now. • *He who comes after sees with more eyes than his own.* • {8.3 9.8	*bolts*
9	W.	☾ runs low • 1st commercial outdoor theater opened (Mount Vernon Gardens), N.Y.C., 1800	*electric!*
10	Th.	Full Buck ○ • Wyo. statehood, 1890 • {8.6 10.3	*Humidity's*
11	Fr.	☌♇☾ • G. d'Aboville began solo row from Choshi, Japan, to Ilwaco, Wash. (134 days, 12 hrs., 15 mins.), 1991	*high,*
12	Sa.	Cornscateous air is everywhere. • Tides {10.5 9.1	*why's*
13	**E**	5th S. af. P. • 8.5" rain in 24 hours, Dover, Del., 1975 • Tides {10.6 9.4	*this*
14	M.	Bastille Day • ♄ stat. • 1st ascent of Matterhorn ended, Alps, 1865	*happening?*
15	Tu.	St. Swithin • ☾ on Eq. • ☾ at ☊ • Man. entered Canadian Confederation, 1870	*Tents*
16	W.	☌♄☾ • ☌♆☾ • Ornithologist David Lack born, 1910 • {10.3 10.2	*and*
17	Th.	☿ stat. • Vega 1st star photographed other than Sun, 1850 • {10.0 10.4	*flies,*
18	Fr.	*If woolly fleeces spread the heavenly way, Be sure no rain disturbs the summer day.* • {9.6 10.6	*mosquito*
19	Sa.	Comic book artist Jim Aparo died, 2005 • Tides {9.3 10.7	*slappening.*
20	**E**	6th S. af. P. • ☾ at perig. • ☌♅☾ • Tides {9.1 10.9	*How*
21	M.	☌♀☾ • Violinist Isaac Stern born, 1920 • Tides {9.1 11.0	*much*
22	Tu.	St. Mary Magdalene • ☾ rides high • Engineer Sir Sandford Fleming died, 1915	*roasting*
23	W.	☌♃☾ • Alan Hale and Thomas Bopp discovered Comet Hale-Bopp, 1995 • {9.3 11.2	*can*
24	Th.	New ● • Black-eyed Susans in bloom now. • Tides {9.5 11.2	*we*
25	Fr.	Sts. James & Christopher • ☌☿☾ • ♇ at ☍ • Tides {9.7 —	*take?*
26	Sa.	St. Anne • Benjamin Franklin became 1st U.S. postmaster general, 1775 • Psychologist Carl Jung born, 1875	*Folks*
27	**E**	7th S. af. P. • *All the brains are not in one head.* • Tides {10.9 9.8	*are*
28	M.	☾ on Eq. • ☾ at ☋ • ☌♂☾ • Composer J. S. Bach died, 1750 • {10.5 9.7	*mostly*
29	Tu.	St. Martha • International Tiger Day • Mary Roebling, 1st woman to head major U.S. bank, born, 1905	*in*
30	W.	Oceanographic cartographer Marie Tharp born, 1920 • Actress Nichelle Nichols died, 2022	*the*
31	Th.	St. Ignatius of Loyola • ☿ in inf. ☌ • Rare spotless giraffe born, Brights Zoo, Limestone, Tenn., 2023	*lake!*

Farmer's Calendar

Puddle's looking awful good.

Water is the first obligation. We are lucky to have a good bit of it. The rain barrels have caught what we need to keep our late succession seeds in good spirits. There's a surplus barrel that the kids are allowed to mess with—on one condition. There's a creek out back that goes into the woods, and sometimes, in high heat, it stays there for days. *If it's up to your knees, you can draw from the play barrel.* We've put down a foot of wood chips in the driest acre to retain warm weather soaks. Come fall, we'll put in a row of trees here using the "trios" concept: nitrogen-fixer, apple, and pear/plum. But today, Louisa and her little cousin Sylvie, in polka-dot swimsuits and tie-dyed rain boots, set about making "mushroom mud soup." The girls' hand-dug "cauldron" prepares one of our fall planting holes (stacking functions!). The wood chips that they toss in are coated in white fungal hyphae (the "mushrooms"). The grown-ups are recruited to fill the cauldron with water, singing some bizarre song—an improvised two-part round that dissolves into tomfoolery. Some call it Thunder Moon; others, vacation time. Around here, summer is silly season.

AUGUST

SKY WATCH: On the 1st, embedded in dusk's twilight, Mars begins to sink ever lower throughout the month. Try observing it at 8:15 P.M., especially on the 26th, when the Red Planet hovers near the crescent Moon. Although the Perseid meteors are mostly washed out by a nearly full Moon on the 11th and 12th, a predawn spectacle can be beheld at 5:00 A.M.: From the 11th to the 13th—but especially on the morning of the 12th—the year's most glorious conjunction unfolds low in the east, with dazzling Venus and brilliant Jupiter closely huddled together. On the 20th, the crescent Moon forms a dramatic triangle with the two planets, best seen at 5:00 A.M.

◗ FIRST QUARTER	1st day 8:41 A.M.	● NEW MOON	23rd day 2:06 A.M.
○ FULL MOON	9th day 3:55 A.M.	◗ FIRST QUARTER	31st day 2:25 A.M.
◖ LAST QUARTER	16th day 1:12 A.M.		

All times are given in Eastern Daylight Time.

GET THESE PAGES WITH TIMES SET TO YOUR ZIP CODE VIA ALMANAC.COM/2025.

DAY OF YEAR	DAY OF MONTH	DAY OF WEEK	☼ RISES H. M.	RISE KEY	☼ SETS H. M.	SET KEY	LENGTH OF DAY H. M.	SUN FAST M.	SUN DECLINATION ° '	HIGH TIDE TIMES BOSTON	☽ RISES H. M.	RISE KEY	☽ SETS H. M.	SET KEY	☽ ASTRON. PLACE	☽ AGE
213	1	Fr.	5:37	B	8:03	E	14 26	9	17 N. 49	5¼ 5¾	1:50	E	11:30	B	VIR	8
214	2	Sa.	5:38	B	8:02	E	14 24	10	17 N. 33	6¼ 6½	2:55	E	11:59	A	LIB	9
215	3	E	5:39	B	8:01	E	14 22	10	17 N. 18	7¼ 7½	3:59	E	—	-	LIB	10
216	4	M.	5:40	B	8:00	E	14 20	10	17 N. 01	8¼ 8¼	5:00	E	12:36	A	SCO	11
217	5	Tu.	5:41	B	7:59	E	14 18	10	16 N. 45	9 9¼	5:56	E	1:22	A	OPH	12
218	6	W.	5:42	B	7:57	E	14 15	10	16 N. 29	10 10	6:44	E	2:18	A	SAG	13
219	7	Th.	5:43	B	7:56	E	14 13	10	16 N. 12	10¾ 10¾	7:23	E	3:23	B	SAG	14
220	8	Fr.	5:44	B	7:55	E	14 11	10	15 N. 55	11½ 11½	7:55	E	4:34	B	CAP	15
221	9	Sa.	5:45	B	7:53	E	14 08	10	15 N. 37	12¼ —	8:22	E	5:48	C	CAP	16
222	10	E	5:46	B	7:52	E	14 06	11	15 N. 20	12¼ 12¾	8:45	D	7:02	C	AQU	17
223	11	M.	5:47	B	7:51	D	14 04	11	15 N. 02	1 1½	9:07	D	8:16	D	AQU	18
224	12	Tu.	5:48	B	7:49	D	14 01	11	14 N. 44	1¾ 2¼	9:28	C	9:29	E	PSC	19
225	13	W.	5:50	B	7:48	D	13 58	11	14 N. 25	2½ 3	9:51	B	10:44	E	PSC	20
226	14	Th.	5:51	B	7:46	D	13 55	11	14 N. 07	3½ 3¾	10:18	B	12:01	E	PSC	21
227	15	Fr.	5:52	B	7:45	D	13 53	11	13 N. 48	4¼ 4¾	10:50	B	1:19	E	ARI	22
228	16	Sa.	5:53	B	7:43	D	13 50	12	13 N. 29	5¼ 5½	11:30	A	2:37	E	ARI	23
229	17	E	5:54	B	7:42	D	13 48	12	13 N. 10	6¼ 6½	—	-	3:52	E	TAU	24
230	18	M.	5:55	B	7:40	D	13 45	12	12 N. 51	7½ 7¾	12:21	A	4:57	E	TAU	25
231	19	Tu.	5:56	B	7:39	D	13 43	12	12 N. 31	8½ 8¾	1:23	A	5:51	E	AUR	26
232	20	W.	5:57	B	7:37	D	13 40	13	12 N. 11	9½ 9¾	2:34	B	6:32	E	GEM	27
233	21	Th.	5:58	B	7:36	D	13 38	13	11 N. 51	10½ 10¾	3:49	B	7:05	E	CAN	28
234	22	Fr.	5:59	B	7:34	D	13 35	13	11 N. 31	11¼ 11½	5:02	C	7:30	E	LEO	29
235	23	Sa.	6:00	B	7:33	D	13 33	13	11 N. 10	12 —	6:13	C	7:52	D	LEO	0
236	24	E	6:01	B	7:31	D	13 30	14	10 N. 50	12¼ 12¾	7:21	D	8:11	D	LEO	1
237	25	M.	6:02	B	7:29	D	13 27	14	10 N. 29	1 1½	8:26	D	8:30	C	VIR	2
238	26	Tu.	6:03	B	7:28	D	13 25	14	10 N. 08	1¾ 2	9:30	E	8:48	C	VIR	3
239	27	W.	6:04	B	7:26	D	13 22	14	9 N. 47	2½ 2¾	10:33	E	9:08	B	VIR	4
240	28	Th.	6:05	B	7:24	D	13 19	15	9 N. 26	3¼ 3½	11:37	E	9:31	B	VIR	5
241	29	Fr.	6:07	B	7:23	D	13 16	15	9 N. 05	4 4¼	12:41	E	9:58	A	LIB	6
242	30	Sa.	6:08	B	7:21	D	13 13	15	8 N. 43	4¾ 5	1:46	E	10:31	A	LIB	7
243	31	E	6:09	B	7:19	D	13 10	16	8 N. 21	5½ 5¾	2:48	E	11:12	A	SCO	8

AUGUST

Our little buff cow, Buttercup,
Has large eyes, dark and soft and meek.
–Anna Boynton Averill

DAY OF MONTH	DAY OF WEEK	DATES, FEASTS, FASTS, ASPECTS, TIDE HEIGHTS, AND WEATHER	
1	Fr.	Lammas Day • ☾ AT APO. • Britain's Slavery Abolition Act took effect, 1834 • {8.5 9.2	*In a*
2	Sa.	*When the glowworm lights her lamp, The air is always damp.* • Tides {8.1 9.1	*cloudy*
3	E	8th S. af. P. • 3 stranded Micronesian mariners rescued via "SOS" in island sand, 2020	*night*
4	M.	**Civic Holiday (Canada)** • Writer Hans Christian Andersen died, 1875 • Canada entered WWI, 1914	*sky,*
5	Tu.	☾ RUNS LOW • Ragweed in bloom. • Actor Sir Alec Guinness died, 2000 • {7.9 9.4	*do I*
6	W.	Transfiguration • ☌♄♆ • Tides {8.2 9.8	*spy the*
7	Th.	27-lb. 6-oz. tiger trout caught, Loon Lake, Wash., 2022 • Tides {8.5 10.1	*space*
8	Fr.	St. Dominic • Sneak Some Zucchini Onto Your Neighbor's Porch Day • ☌♇☾	*shuttle?*
9	Sa.	**FULL STURGEON** ○ • Betty Boop debuted in "Dizzy Dishes" animated cartoon, 1930 • {9.3 —	*No,*
10	E	9th S. af. P. • ☿ STAT. • U.S. president Herbert Hoover born, 1874	*it's*
11	M.	St. Clare • Dog Days end. • ☾ AT ☊ • Tides {10.9 10.2	*fragments*
12	Tu.	☾ ON EQ. • ☌♀♃ • ☌♄☾ • ☌♆☾ • Gray squirrels have second litters now.	*that*
13	W.	Clarinet inventor Johann Christoph Denner born, 1655 • Nurse Florence Nightingale died, 1910	*fly*
14	Th.	☾ AT PERIG. • Cartoonist Gary Larson born, 1950 • Tides {10.4 10.8	*from*
15	Fr.	Assumption • Jazz pianist Oscar Peterson born, 1925 • Tides {9.9 10.8	*Comet*
16	Sa.	☌⛢☾ • From altitude of 102,800 ft., Joe Kittinger free-fell for 4 mins., 36 secs., New Mex., 1960	*Swift-*
17	E	10th S. af. P. • Cat Nights commence. • *Few words, many deeds.* • {9.0 10.6	*Tuttle!*
18	M.	☾ RIDES HIGH • Hail destroyed corn crops, SE Iowa, 1925 • Plant patent #1 granted for climbing rose, 1931	*Clear*
19	Tu.	☌♃☾ • ☿ GR. ELONG. (19° WEST) • American Revolution began, 1775 • {8.8 10.5	*days*
20	W.	☌♀☾ • *Viking 1* space probe to Mars launched, 1975 • Tides {8.9 10.6	*chased*
21	Th.	☌☿☾ • Staff began moving into United Nations Secretariat Building, N.Y.C., 1950	*away by*
22	Fr.	1st U.S. patent for liquid soap granted to William Sheppard, 1865 • Tides {9.5 10.8	*a hazy*
23	Sa.	**NEW** ● • *Every tide hath its ebb.* • Tides {9.7 —	*hot*
24	E	11th S. af. P. • ☾ AT ☋ • Mt. Vesuvius erupted, destroying ancient Roman city of Pompeii, 79 A.D.	
25	M.	St. Bartholomew[T] • ☾ ON EQ. • Tides {10.5 9.9	*muddle.*
26	Tu.	☌♂☾ • Roald Amundsen sighted whaler, confirming existence of Northwest Passage, 1905	*Cut hay*
27	W.	Hummingbirds migrate south. • Maiden flight of 1st jet aircraft, Heinkel He 178, 1939 • {9.7 9.8	*while the*
28	Th.	St. Augustine of Hippo • Figure skater Todd Eldredge born, 1971 • {9.3 9.6	*Sun shines,*
29	Fr.	St. John the Baptist • ☾ AT APO. • After Fla. (Aug. 25), Hurricane Katrina made 2nd landfall in La., 2005	*no*
30	Sa.	17.4-pound "potato" named Doug dug from garden (later test found it to be gourd tuber), New Zealand, 2021	*time to*
31	E	12th S. af. P. • Honolulu officially declared capital of Hawaiian Islands, 1850 • {8.0 8.9	*scuttle.*

Farmer's Calendar

Honey, you have to let the whole house become part of the process.

Turn an eye to autumn, and it's canning season again. There had been no problem with the sowing, thinning, trellising, mulching, whatnot. But what's to be made of the strange algebra that says that the greener my thumb, the less I get around to preserving? Rot on the vine, mush in a bushel, mildew in the crisper. This failure to properly *put food by* is my Dog Days curse. My Aunt Dorothy taught me the term for this craft. I am grateful that my wife has picked up the penchant. The counter shines a rainbow of fresh picks from the plot. The dish rack guards the sterile jars. The banana basket has grape leaves—there's some enchanting thought that they keep the pickles crisp. The dining table is mostly pails of goopy tomato innards. The parlor is riddled with "popped" jars, out of the cooker. It's the soundscape of pressure canning that I appreciate, and I'm not alone. Today, we have a mason—some young start who works with pace and cheer—up on the roof, setting my lousy attempt at tuck-pointing straight. He hears the hissing suddenly stop and hollers, "Another batch coming!" Gotta love him.

SEPTEMBER

SKY WATCH: The predawn eastern sky offers very bright Mercury far below blazing Venus and brilliant Jupiter. Early risers will see the concentrated brilliance as Venus, Jupiter, and eight 0- and 1st-magnitude stars light up the eastern sky. On the 17th and 18th, the crescent Moon floats between Venus and Jupiter. Then comes a predawn conjunction on the 19th, when the Moon closely meets Venus and Leo's bright blue star, Regulus. The 21st brings Saturn's opposition and nearest 2025 approach to Earth. Through a telescope, Saturn's rings can be observed almost as a straight line, more edgewise than will be seen again until 2040. Neptune comes to opposition on the 23rd, but its small, blue, magnitude 7.8 disk is best seen with a telescope on the night before. The autumnal equinox occurs on the 22nd at 2:19 P.M. EDT.

○ FULL MOON	7th day	2:09 P.M.
● NEW MOON	21st day	3:54 P.M.
◑ LAST QUARTER	14th day	6:33 A.M.
◐ FIRST QUARTER	29th day	7:54 P.M.

All times are given in Eastern Daylight Time.

GET THESE PAGES WITH TIMES SET TO YOUR ZIP CODE VIA ALMANAC.COM/2025.

DAY OF YEAR	DAY OF MONTH	DAY OF WEEK	☼ RISES	RISE KEY	☼ SETS	SET KEY	LENGTH OF DAY	SUN FAST	SUN DECLINATION		HIGH TIDE TIMES BOSTON		☾ RISES	RISE KEY	☾ SETS	SET KEY	☾ ASTRON. PLACE	☾ AGE
			H. M.		H. M.		H. M.	M.	°	'			H. M.		H. M.			
244	1	M.	6:10	B	**7:18**	D	13 08	16	8 N.	00	6½	**6¾**	**3:45**	E	—	-	OPH	9
245	2	Tu.	6:11	B	**7:16**	D	13 05	16	7 N.	38	7½	**7¾**	**4:36**	E	12:03	A	SAG	10
246	3	W.	6:12	B	**7:14**	D	13 02	17	7 N.	16	8½	**8½**	**5:18**	E	1:04	A	SAG	11
247	4	Th.	6:13	C	**7:13**	D	13 00	17	6 N.	53	9¼	**9½**	**5:53**	E	2:13	B	SAG	12
248	5	Fr.	6:14	C	**7:11**	D	12 57	17	6 N.	31	10	**10¼**	**6:22**	E	3:25	B	CAP	13
249	6	Sa.	6:15	C	**7:09**	D	12 54	18	6 N.	09	10¾	**11**	**6:47**	E	4:40	C	CAP	14
250	7	**E**	6:16	C	**7:07**	D	12 51	18	5 N.	46	11½	**11¾**	**7:10**	D	5:55	D	AQU	15
251	8	M.	6:17	C	**7:06**	D	12 49	18	5 N.	24	12¼	—	**7:32**	C	7:11	D	PSC	16
252	9	Tu.	6:18	C	**7:04**	D	12 46	19	5 N.	01	12½	**1**	**7:55**	C	8:27	E	PSC	17
253	10	W.	6:19	C	**7:02**	D	12 43	19	4 N.	38	1½	**1¾**	**8:20**	B	9:45	E	PSC	18
254	11	Th.	6:20	C	**7:00**	D	12 40	19	4 N.	16	2¼	**2½**	**8:51**	B	11:05	E	ARI	19
255	12	Fr.	6:21	C	**6:59**	C	12 38	20	3 N.	53	3	**3¼**	**9:29**	A	**12:26**	E	ARI	20
256	13	Sa.	6:22	C	**6:57**	C	12 35	20	3 N.	30	4	**4¼**	**10:17**	A	**1:43**	E	TAU	21
257	14	**E**	6:23	C	**6:55**	C	12 32	20	3 N.	07	5	**5¼**	**11:16**	A	**2:52**	E	TAU	22
258	15	M.	6:24	C	**6:53**	C	12 29	21	2 N.	44	6	**6¼**	—	-	**3:48**	E	AUR	23
259	16	Tu.	6:25	C	**6:52**	C	12 27	21	2 N.	20	7¼	**7½**	12:24	B	**4:33**	E	GEM	24
260	17	W.	6:27	C	**6:50**	C	12 23	21	1 N.	57	8¼	**8½**	1:37	B	**5:07**	E	CAN	25
261	18	Th.	6:28	C	**6:48**	C	12 20	22	1 N.	34	9½	**9¾**	2:50	B	**5:34**	E	CAN	26
262	19	Fr.	6:29	C	**6:46**	C	12 17	22	1 N.	11	10¼	**10½**	4:00	C	**5:57**	D	LEO	27
263	20	Sa.	6:30	C	**6:44**	C	12 14	23	0 N.	47	11	**11¼**	5:08	C	**6:17**	D	LEO	28
264	21	**E**	6:31	C	**6:43**	C	12 12	23	0 N.	24	11¾	—	6:13	D	**6:35**	C	LEO	0
265	22	M.	6:32	C	**6:41**	C	12 09	23	0 N.	01	12	**12¼**	7:17	E	**6:53**	C	VIR	1
266	23	Tu.	6:33	C	**6:39**	C	12 06	24	0 s.	22	12¾	**1**	8:20	E	**7:13**	B	VIR	2
267	24	W.	6:34	C	**6:37**	C	12 03	24	0 s.	45	1¼	**1½**	9:24	E	**7:34**	B	VIR	3
268	25	Th.	6:35	C	**6:36**	C	12 01	24	1 s.	08	2	**2**	10:29	E	**7:59**	B	LIB	4
269	26	Fr.	6:36	C	**6:34**	C	11 58	25	1 s.	32	2¾	**2¾**	11:33	E	**8:30**	A	LIB	5
270	27	Sa.	6:37	C	**6:32**	C	11 55	25	1 s.	55	3¼	**3½**	**12:36**	E	**9:07**	A	SCO	6
271	28	**E**	6:38	C	**6:30**	C	11 52	25	2 s.	18	4¼	**4¼**	**1:35**	E	**9:54**	A	OPH	7
272	29	M.	6:39	C	**6:29**	C	11 50	26	2 s.	42	5	**5¼**	**2:28**	E	**10:49**	A	SAG	8
273	30	Tu.	6:40	C	**6:27**	C	11 47	26	3 s.	05	6	**6**	**3:13**	E	**11:53**	B	SAG	9

 To use this page, see p. 116; for Key Letters, see p. 238. LIGHT = A.M. BOLD = P.M.

The goldenrod is yellow, / The corn is turning brown,
The trees in apple orchards / With fruit are bending down.
–**Helen Hunt Jackson**

DAY OF MONTH	DAY OF WEEK	DATES, FEASTS, FASTS, ASPECTS, TIDE HEIGHTS, AND WEATHER	
1	M.	LABOR DAY • ☾ RUNS LOW • Alta. and Sask. entered Canadian Confederation, 1905	*Schools*
2	Tu.	Baseball player Albert Goodwill Spalding born, 1850 • Tides { 7.8 9.1	*begin,*
3	W.	*Thunder in September indicates a good crop of grain and fruit for next year.* • Tides { 7.9 9.4	*to*
4	Th.	☌♇☾ • Hunter Ewen blew up 910 balloons in 1 hour, setting record, 2015 • { 8.3 9.8	*students'*
5	Fr.	112°F, Centreville, Ala., 1925 • Cartoonist Cathy Guisewite born, 1950 • { 8.8 10.3	*chagrin!*
6	Sa.	⛢ STAT. • Educator Catharine Beecher born, 1800 • Tides { 9.4 10.7	*Raindrops*
7	E	13th S. af. P. • FULL CORN ○ • ECLIPSE ☾ • ☾ AT ☊	*sound*
8	M.	☾ ON EQ. • ☌♄☾ • ☌♆☾ • Deadly hurricane hit Galveston, Tex., 1900	*their*
9	Tu.	Cranberry bog harvest begins, Cape Cod, Mass. • California statehood, 1850 • { 11.1 11.1	*pitter-*
10	W.	☾ AT PERIG. • American Forestry Association organized, 1875 • { 11.1 11.3	*patters,*
11	Th.	PATRIOT DAY • Actor John Ritter died, 2003 • Tides { 10.8 11.3	*Nature*
12	Fr.	☌⛢☾ • Olympic track-and-field champion Jesse Owens born, 1913 • { 10.3 11.3	*paints*
13	Sa.	☿ IN SUP. ☌ • *Too little and too much spoils everything.* • Tides { 9.8 11.0	*leaves*
14	E	14th S. af. P. • ☾ RIDES HIGH • Elizabeth Ann Seton canonized, 1975	*when*
15	M.	Holy Cross[T] • Landscape architect André Le Nôtre died, 1700 • { 8.9 10.3	*chlorophyll*
16	Tu.	☌♃☾ • Businessman James C. Penney born, 1875 • B. B. King, musician, born, 1925	*scatters.*
17	W.	Ember Day • Boston (Mass.) founded (New Style date), 1630 • Tides { 8.8 10.1	*Quick as a*
18	Th.	Cosmonaut Arnaldo Tamayo Méndez 1st Latin American in space, 1980 • Tides { 9.1 10.2	*fox comes*
19	Fr.	Ember Day • ☌♀☾ • Frogs' eggs fell from sky, Berlin, Conn., 2003 • { 9.4 10.3	*the fall*
20	Sa.	Ember Day • ☾ AT ☋ • Pathologist Ernest Goodpasture died, 1960 • { 9.7 10.3	*equinox,*
21	E	15th S. af. P. • NEW ● • ECLIPSE ☉ • ☾ ON EQ. • ♄ AT ☍ • { 9.9 —	
22	M.	St. Matthew[T] • Rosh Hashanah begins at sundown • Harvest Home • AUTUMNAL EQUINOX • ☌☿☾	
23	Tu.	♆ AT ☍ • Musician Bruce Springsteen born, 1949 • { 10.0 10.1	*break*
24	W.	☌♂☾ • Sun/Moon appeared blue/pink/purple in northeastern U.S. due to Canadian fires, 1950	*out*
25	Th.	Gordon Cates kissed 10 monocled cobras and one king cobra consecutively, setting record, 1999	*wool*
26	Fr.	☾ AT APO. • Woodchucks hibernate now. • Tides { 9.0 9.6	*socks,*
27	Sa.	St. Vincent de Paul • Stockton & Darlington Railway, 1st steam-powered passenger railway, began operation, England, 1825	
28	E	16th S. af. P. • Canadian prime minister Pierre Trudeau died, 2000 • { 8.3 9.1	*fill up*
29	M.	St. Michael • ☾ RUNS LOW • 1st Canadian football game under lights, Athletic Park, Vancouver, B.C., 1930	*the*
30	Tu.	St. Gregory the Illuminator • *A happy heart is better than a full purse.* • { 7.8 8.9	*wood box.*

Farmer's Calendar

You know what to do about squirrels, right?

From the picnic table where I steep the day in strong coffee, my daughter and I study a circus of squirrels picking the last mulberries that droop over the coop. Poppop demonstrates the crier's bark that he uses to scare them off. It's not pretty, and it doesn't work. He encourages us to repel the rodents with a ragged scarf of hardware cloth on each trunk, but we are contortionists in our high defense of critter mischief: the calories that they shake into the chookie run, the purples that they plop onto the coop roof, the spectacle of their acrobatics alone. And, the surgeries that Louisa performs on discarded fruit: Pakistan mulberries in the gurney of her small hand, a 'Celeste' fig in the waiting room of her lap. She posits that a fig is an inside-out mulberry, and in a way she's not far off: The technical term is "multiple fruit." She tells us what she knows about fig wasps, how they burrow inside, get trapped, digested by the—*Poppop!* Huffing at a berry stain on the seat of his trousers, he tumbles over a bushel basket, lies there laughing. The ruckus scatters the animals with a delicious irony that pairs quite well with these sticky fig and mulberry muffins.

OCTOBER

SKY WATCH: Each morning at 6:15 A.M., Venus blazes in the east, each day steadily lower and dimmer all month long, while Jupiter gets continually higher. But observers will mostly focus on the evening, when Saturn—having risen before nightfall—will be halfway up the southern sky by midnight. On the Pisces/Aquarius border, the Ringed Planet is surrounded by only dim stars, so its solitary brightness highlights its location, which is just below the Moon on the 6th. Viewable through a telescope, the brightest "star" nearly touching Saturn's rings is its giant moon, Titan, the only celestial body besides Earth with a thick atmosphere consisting of mostly nitrogen. The waning crescent Moon meets Venus on the 19th.

○ FULL MOON	6th day 11:47 P.M.	● NEW MOON	21st day 8:25 A.M.
☽ LAST QUARTER	13th day 2:13 P.M.	☾ FIRST QUARTER	29th day 12:21 P.M.

All times are given in Eastern Daylight Time.

GET THESE PAGES WITH TIMES SET TO YOUR ZIP CODE VIA ALMANAC.COM/2025.

DAY OF YEAR	DAY OF MONTH	DAY OF WEEK	☀ RISES H.M.	RISE KEY	☀ SETS H.M.	SET KEY	LENGTH OF DAY H.M.	SUN FAST M.	SUN DECLINATION ° ′	HIGH TIDE TIMES BOSTON		☽ RISES H.M.	RISE KEY	☽ SETS H.M.	SET KEY	☽ ASTRON. PLACE	☽ AGE
274	1	W.	6:42	C	6:25	C	11 43	26	3 s. 28	6¾	7	3:50	E	—	-	SAG	10
275	2	Th.	6:43	C	6:23	C	11 40	27	3 s. 51	7¾	8	4:21	E	1:03	B	CAP	11
276	3	Fr.	6:44	C	6:22	C	11 38	27	4 s. 15	8¾	9	4:47	E	2:15	C	CAP	12
277	4	Sa.	6:45	C	6:20	C	11 35	27	4 s. 38	9½	9¾	5:10	D	3:29	C	AQU	13
278	5	E	6:46	D	6:18	C	11 32	28	5 s. 01	10¼	10½	5:33	C	4:44	D	AQU	14
279	6	M.	6:47	D	6:17	C	11 30	28	5 s. 24	11	11½	5:55	C	6:01	E	PSC	15
280	7	Tu.	6:48	D	6:15	C	11 27	28	5 s. 47	11¾	—	6:20	B	7:20	E	PSC	16
281	8	W.	6:49	D	6:13	C	11 24	28	6 s. 10	12¼	12½	6:49	B	8:41	E	ARI	17
282	9	Th.	6:50	D	6:12	C	11 22	29	6 s. 32	1	1¼	7:25	B	10:05	E	ARI	18
283	10	Fr.	6:52	D	6:10	C	11 18	29	6 s. 55	2	2	8:11	A	11:27	E	TAU	19
284	11	Sa.	6:53	D	6:08	C	11 15	29	7 s. 18	2¾	3	9:08	A	12:41	E	TAU	20
285	12	E	6:54	D	6:07	B	11 13	29	7 s. 40	3¾	4	10:15	A	1:44	E	AUR	21
286	13	M.	6:55	D	6:05	B	11 10	30	8 s. 02	4¾	5	11:27	B	2:33	E	GEM	22
287	14	Tu.	6:56	D	6:03	B	11 07	30	8 s. 25	6	6¼	—	-	3:10	E	CAN	23
288	15	W.	6:57	D	6:02	B	11 05	30	8 s. 47	7	7¼	12:41	B	3:39	E	CAN	24
289	16	Th.	6:59	D	6:00	B	11 01	30	9 s. 09	8	8½	1:52	C	4:03	E	LEO	25
290	17	Fr.	7:00	D	5:59	B	10 59	31	9 s. 31	9	9¼	2:59	C	4:23	D	LEO	26
291	18	Sa.	7:01	D	5:57	B	10 56	31	9 s. 53	10	10¼	4:04	D	4:41	D	LEO	27
292	19	E	7:02	D	5:55	B	10 53	31	10 s. 14	10½	11	5:08	D	4:59	C	VIR	28
293	20	M.	7:03	D	5:54	B	10 51	31	10 s. 36	11¼	11¾	6:11	E	5:18	C	VIR	29
294	21	Tu.	7:04	D	5:52	B	10 48	31	10 s. 57	11¾	—	7:14	E	5:39	B	VIR	0
295	22	W.	7:06	D	5:51	B	10 45	31	11 s. 18	12¼	12½	8:18	E	6:03	B	VIR	1
296	23	Th.	7:07	D	5:49	B	10 42	32	11 s. 39	1	1	9:22	E	6:31	A	LIB	2
297	24	Fr.	7:08	D	5:48	B	10 40	32	12 s. 00	1½	1½	10:26	E	7:06	A	SCO	3
298	25	Sa.	7:09	D	5:47	B	10 38	32	12 s. 21	2¼	2¼	11:26	E	7:49	A	SCO	4
299	26	E	7:10	D	5:45	B	10 35	32	12 s. 41	3	3	12:21	E	8:41	A	OPH	5
300	27	M.	7:12	D	5:44	B	10 32	32	13 s. 01	3¾	3¾	1:08	E	9:41	A	SAG	6
301	28	Tu.	7:13	D	5:42	B	10 29	32	13 s. 21	4½	4½	1:47	E	10:47	B	SAG	7
302	29	W.	7:14	D	5:41	B	10 27	32	13 s. 41	5¼	5½	2:19	E	11:56	B	CAP	8
303	30	Th.	7:15	D	5:40	B	10 25	32	14 s. 01	6¼	6½	2:47	E	—	-	CAP	9
304	31	Fr.	7:17	D	5:38	B	10 21	32	14 s. 20	7¼	7½	3:10	E	1:07	C	AQU	10

CALENDAR

Awake, ye mortals, raise your eyes / To yon eternal starry spheres. Look on these glories of the skies!
–Louis de Leon

DAY OF MONTH	DAY OF WEEK	DATES, FEASTS, FASTS, ASPECTS, TIDE HEIGHTS, AND WEATHER	
1	W.	Yom Kippur begins at sundown • ☌♇☾ • *A fault confessed is half redressed.* • {7.9 9.1	*On*
2	Th.	*Peanuts* cartoon debuted, 1950 • Movie *The Martian* premiered in U.S., 2015 • {8.2 9.4	*Yom Kippur,*
3	Fr.	Watch for banded woolly bear caterpillars now. • Writer Thomas Wolfe born, 1900 • {8.7 9.8	*a time*
4	Sa.	St. Francis of Assisi • MLB owner Joan Whitney Payson died, 1975 • Tides {9.4 10.3	*for*
5	**E**	**17th S. af. P.** • ☾ ON EQ. • ☾ AT ☊ • ☌♄☾ • {10.1 10.7	*reflection,*
6	M.	Sukkoth begins at sundown • FULL HARVEST ○ • ☌♆☾ • {10.8 11.0	*showers*
7	Tu.	Writer Edgar Allan Poe died, 1849 • Archbishop Desmond Tutu born, 1931 • {11.4 —	*meet*
8	W.	☾ AT PERIG. • 8-lb. 9-oz. brook trout caught, Waterdog Lake, Lake City, Colo., 2022	*sunshine*
9	Th.	Pepper X publicly announced as world's hottest pepper, 2023 • Tides {11.0 12.0	*for a*
10	Fr.	☌⛢☾ • Little brown bats hibernate now. • Tides {10.7 11.8	*rainbow*
11	Sa.	☾ RIDES HIGH • *Oct. 11–12:* Auroras seen in several U.S. states, 2021 • {10.2 11.5	*connection.*
12	**E**	**18th S. af. P.** • NATIONAL FARMER'S DAY • Tides {9.7 11.0	*Daylight*
13	M.	COLUMBUS DAY, OBSERVED • INDIGENOUS PEOPLES' DAY • THANKSGIVING DAY (CANADA) • ☌♃☾	
14	Tu.	♇ STAT. • Major hail damage, southern Okla., 1925 • Tides {8.9 10.0	*wanes*
15	W.	Hurricane Hazel reached southern Ont., 1954 • Tides {8.9 9.8	*but never*
16	Th.	Cape Breton Island re-annexed to N.S., 1820 • Actress Angela Lansbury born, 1925	*goes*
17	Fr.	St. Ignatius of Antioch • Almost-pure sine wave (Pc3 wave) caused by solar wind hit Earth's magnetosphere, 2023	*out,*
18	Sa.	St. Luke • ☾ ON EQ. • ☾ AT ☋ • St. Luke's little summer. • {9.6 9.7	*that's*
19	**E**	**19th S. af. P.** • ☌♀☾ • Poet Edna St. Vincent Millay died, 1950	*what*
20	M.	1st use of cork-centered baseball in World Series, Chicago, Ill., 1910 • Musician Tom Petty born, 1950	*Diwali*
21	Tu.	NEW ● • ☌☿♂ • *A new Moon with sharp horns threatens windy weather.* • {10.1 —	*is all*
22	W.	Dr. George Stanley's single maple leaf flag design approved by Cdn. Parliament nat'l flag committee, 1964	*about.*
23	Th.	St. James of Jerusalem • ☾ AT APO. • ☌☿☾ • ☌♂☾ • {9.3 10.1	*Here's*
24	Fr.	Dirty rain (from dust in Kans./Nebr.) fell, Minneapolis-St. Paul, Minn., 2022 • Tides {9.0 9.9	*a chilly,*
25	Sa.	Poet Geoffrey Chaucer died, 1400 • Composer Johann Strauss II born, 1825 • {8.8 9.7	*scary*
26	**E**	**20th S. af. P.** • ☾ RUNS LOW • Erie Canal opened, N.Y., 1825 • {8.5 9.5	*scene:*
27	M.	Timber rattlesnakes move to winter dens. • 2,019 flower bulbs planted by individual in 1 hr., setting record, Bradford, UK, 2018	
28	Tu.	Sts. Simon & Jude • National First Responders Day (U.S.) • Tides {8.1 9.1	*Goblins*
29	W.	☌♇☾ • ☿ GR. ELONG. (24° EAST) • 1st U.S. sale of ballpoint pen, Gimbels dept. store, N.Y.C., 1945	*in*
30	Th.	Entertainer Steve Allen died, 2000 • *Wise fear begets care.* • Tides {8.2 9.2	*flannels on*
31	Fr.	All Hallows' Eve • Reformation Day • Tides {8.7 9.4	*Halloween!*

Farmer's Calendar

What do you mean, "we"?!

We've kept the gardens up pretty late again, haven't we? There's a kind of late that turns our mind into its to-do listing. Don't forget to lop the 'San Marzano' vines at the stem base. Compost the tops, let the roots rot. Check. And we have to coil the trellis wire better this year, or future us will be right to look back and cuss a few blankety-blanks in our direction. For slowing erosion, improving tilth, restoring nutrients, let's go overboard with cover crops. Is there anything better to feed the microbiota? Anything more to the liking of our two-jake flock of turkey? What say we sow some of the radish oil drillers to break up the rows that we tried our best not to trample all season? Next year, we'll body up the walkways with more wood chips. Oat for its surefire winterkill—we will plant that plot early come spring. Strawberries sound good. Which were those small juicy ones from Gretchen's garden? Not the 'Cavendish', but the 'Earliglow'. Winter rye for a vernal green-up—we'll tractor the chickens here come what may of late April. Okay, you can stay up and work on the list some more. Me and the gardens, we're off to bed. G'night now.

NOVEMBER

SKY WATCH: On the 1st, brilliant Venus is low in the east, next to Virgo's main star, blue Spica. The morning star is gone after midmonth, with Mercury taking its place in November's final days. The Moon's closest approach of 2025 is on the 5th, at a distance of 221,725 miles. On the 15th, Jupiter rises before 9:00 P.M. to begin its optimum viewing season. Uranus reaches opposition on the 21st; below the Pleiades star cluster in Taurus at midnight, the Green Planet appears very dim to the naked eye even from pristine rural sites. Binoculars will make for easier viewing of Uranus's brightest appearance since the 1990s. Saturn stands to the left of the Moon on the 28th and to its lower right on the 29th.

○ **FULL MOON** 5th day 8:19 A.M. ● **NEW MOON** 20th day 1:47 A.M.
◐ **LAST QUARTER** 12th day 12:28 A.M. ◑ **FIRST QUARTER** 28th day 1:59 A.M.

After 2:00 A.M. on November 2, Eastern Standard Time is given.

GET THESE PAGES WITH TIMES SET TO YOUR ZIP CODE VIA ALMANAC.COM/2025.

DAY OF YEAR	DAY OF MONTH	DAY OF WEEK	☀ RISES H.M.	RISE KEY	☀ SETS H.M.	SET KEY	LENGTH OF DAY H.M.	SUN FAST M.	SUN DECLINATION ° '	HIGH TIDE TIMES BOSTON		☾ RISES H.M.	RISE KEY	☾ SETS H.M.	SET KEY	☾ ASTRON. PLACE	☾ AGE
305	1	Sa.	7:18	D	5:37	B	10 19	32	14 s. 39	8	8¼	3:33	D	2:19	D	AQU	11
306	2	E	6:19	D	4:36	B	10 17	32	14 s. 58	7¾	8¼	2:55	C	2:33	D	PSC	12
307	3	M.	6:20	D	4:35	B	10 15	32	15 s. 17	8¾	9¼	3:18	C	3:49	E	PSC	13
308	4	Tu.	6:22	D	4:33	B	10 11	32	15 s. 35	9½	10	3:45	B	5:09	E	PSC	14
309	5	W.	6:23	E	4:32	B	10 09	32	15 s. 54	10¼	10¾	4:18	B	6:33	E	ARI	15
310	6	Th.	6:24	E	4:31	B	10 07	32	16 s. 11	11	11¾	5:00	A	7:58	E	ARI	16
311	7	Fr.	6:25	E	4:30	B	10 05	32	16 s. 29	12	—	5:54	A	9:19	E	TAU	17
312	8	Sa.	6:27	E	4:29	B	10 02	32	16 s. 46	12½	12¾	6:59	A	10:30	E	TAU	18
313	9	E	6:28	E	4:28	B	10 00	32	17 s. 04	1½	1¾	8:13	B	11:26	E	GEM	19
314	10	M.	6:29	E	4:27	B	9 58	32	17 s. 20	2½	2¾	9:29	B	12:09	E	GEM	20
315	11	Tu.	6:30	E	4:26	B	9 56	32	17 s. 37	3½	3¾	10:42	C	12:41	E	CAN	21
316	12	W.	6:32	E	4:25	B	9 53	32	17 s. 53	4½	4¾	11:51	C	1:07	E	LEO	22
317	13	Th.	6:33	E	4:24	B	9 51	31	18 s. 09	5¾	6	—	-	1:28	D	LEO	23
318	14	Fr.	6:34	E	4:23	B	9 49	31	18 s. 24	6¾	7	12:57	D	1:48	D	LEO	24
319	15	Sa.	6:35	E	4:22	B	9 47	31	18 s. 40	7½	8	2:01	D	2:06	C	VIR	25
320	16	E	6:37	E	4:21	B	9 44	31	18 s. 55	8¼	8¾	3:04	E	2:24	C	VIR	26
321	17	M.	6:38	E	4:20	B	9 42	31	19 s. 09	9	9½	4:06	E	2:44	B	VIR	27
322	18	Tu.	6:39	E	4:19	B	9 40	31	19 s. 23	9¾	10¼	5:09	E	3:07	B	VIR	28
323	19	W.	6:40	E	4:19	B	9 39	30	19 s. 37	10¼	11	6:14	E	3:34	A	LIB	29
324	20	Th.	6:41	E	4:18	B	9 37	30	19 s. 51	11	11½	7:17	E	4:07	A	LIB	0
325	21	Fr.	6:43	E	4:17	B	9 34	30	20 s. 04	11½	—	8:19	E	4:48	A	SCO	1
326	22	Sa.	6:44	E	4:17	A	9 33	30	20 s. 17	12¼	12¼	9:16	E	5:37	A	OPH	2
327	23	E	6:45	E	4:16	A	9 31	29	20 s. 29	12¾	12¾	10:05	E	6:34	A	SAG	3
328	24	M.	6:46	E	4:15	A	9 29	29	20 s. 41	1½	1½	10:46	E	7:38	B	SAG	4
329	25	Tu.	6:47	E	4:15	A	9 28	29	20 s. 53	2¼	2¼	11:20	E	8:45	B	SAG	5
330	26	W.	6:48	E	4:14	A	9 26	28	21 s. 04	3	3	11:48	E	9:53	C	CAP	6
331	27	Th.	6:50	E	4:14	A	9 24	28	21 s. 15	3¾	4	12:12	E	11:02	C	CAP	7
332	28	Fr.	6:51	E	4:14	A	9 23	28	21 s. 25	4¾	4¾	12:34	D	—	-	AQU	8
333	29	Sa.	6:52	E	4:13	A	9 21	27	21 s. 35	5½	5¾	12:55	D	12:13	D	AQU	9
334	30	E	6:53	E	4:13	A	9 20	27	21 s. 45	6½	6¾	1:17	D	1:25	E	PSC	10

To use this page, see p. 116; for Key Letters, see p. 238. LIGHT = A.M. **BOLD** = P.M.

CALENDAR

NOVEMBER

For the year of peace and plenty / And for blessings without end,
Let the voices of the people / In Thanksgiving praises blend.
–George Carlton Rhoderick Jr.

DAY OF MONTH	DAY OF WEEK	DATES, FEASTS, FASTS, ASPECTS, TIDE HEIGHTS, AND WEATHER	
1	Sa.	All Saints' • Sadie Hawkins Day • ☾ at ☊ • Tides {9.3 / 9.7	*Clock hands*
2	E	21st S. af. P. • DST ends, 2:00 A.M. • ☾ on Eq. • ☌♄☾ • ☌♆☾	*spin,*
3	M.	All Souls' • 1st major auto show in U.S., Madison Sq. Garden, N.Y.C., 1900 • {10.7 / 10.4	*let's sleep in!*
4	Tu.	Election Day • Artist Guido Reni born, 1575 • Tides {11.4 / 10.7	*Snowfalls*
5	W.	Full Beaver ○ • ☾ at perig. • Franklin D. Roosevelt elected to 3rd term as U.S. president, 1940	*begin*
6	Th.	☌⛢☾ • 1st national Canadian Thanksgiving as annual event after Confederation, 1879	*and*
7	Fr.	*If horses stretch out their necks and sniff the air, rain will ensue.* • Tides {12.2 / —	*frost*
8	Sa.	☾ rides high • Game show host Alex Trebek died, 2020 • Tides {10.4 / 12.0	*nips*
9	E	22nd S. af. P. • ☿ stat. • Great Northeast Blackout, 1965 • {10.0 / 11.5	*your*
10	M.	☌♃☾ • Continental Marines (later, U.S. Marine Corps) established, 1775 • {9.6 / 10.9	*skin.*
11	Tu.	St. Martin of Tours • Veterans Day • ♃ stat. • Tides {9.3 / 10.3	*Veterans*
12	W.	Indian Summer (aka Second Summer) • ☌☿♂ • Suffragette Elizabeth C. Stanton born, 1815	*deserve*
13	Th.	World Kindness Day • Writer Robert Louis Stevenson born, 1850 • {9.1 / 9.4	*thanks*
14	Fr.	☾ at ☋ • Last use of manned maneuvering unit (MMU) in space, 1984 • {9.2 / 9.2	*from*
15	Sa.	☾ on Eq. • Arthur Dorrington 1st Black to sign professional hockey contract, 1950 • {9.4 / 9.1	*us all*
16	E	23rd S. af. P. • UNESCO established, 1945 • Tides {9.6 / 9.1	*and maybe*
17	M.	St. Hugh of Lincoln • 1st time U.S. Congress met in Capitol Bldg., D.C., 1800 • {9.8 / 9.0	*some*
18	Tu.	St. Hilda of Whitby • *New dishes beget new appetites.* • Tides {9.9 / 9.0	*help*
19	W.	☾ at apo. • ☌♀☾ • Frederick Blaisdell granted 1st U.S. patent for paper pencil, 1895	*when*
20	Th.	New ● • ☌☿☾ • ☿ in inf. ☌ • Tides {10.0 / 8.8	*shovelin'*
21	Fr.	☌♂☾ • ⛢ at ☍ • W. Berger (76 yrs., 128 days) oldest to summit tallest mtns. on 7 continents, 2013	
22	Sa.	☾ runs low • *First weigh, then venture.* • Tides {8.7 / 9.9	*calls!*
23	E	24th S. af. P. • Quarterback Doug Flutie completed "Hail Mary" pass in Boston College win over Miami, 1984	
24	M.	☌☿♀ • Tribal leader/activist Lucy Covington born, 1910 • Tides {8.5 / 9.7	*Annual*
25	Tu.	☌♇☾ • Robert S. Ledley granted patent for CT scanner, 1975 • Tides {8.4 / 9.5	*feasts now*
26	W.	Movie *Casablanca* premiered, 1942 • Tides {8.4 / 9.4	*are fixed,*
27	Th.	Thanksgiving Day • Martial artist/actor Bruce Lee born, 1940 • {8.5 / 9.3	*amidst*
28	Fr.	☾ at ☊ • ♄ stat. • *WSM Barn Dance* (later, *Grand Ole Opry*) debuted on radio, 1925	*a*
29	Sa.	☾ on Eq. • ☌♄☾ • ☌♆☾ • ☿ stat. • {9.2 / 9.3	*bone-chilling*
30	E	1st S. of Advent • Writer Oscar Wilde died, 1900 • {9.8 / 9.5	*wintry mix.*

Farmer's Calendar

Pop, this one looks like a bear paw!

Long drawn to treetops that rattle every which way on windy days, my daughter leads me on a saunter among the yellow stalks of time. The mammoth sunflowers have been ransacked by squirrels and jays. Most of the corn is hinged at the waist, fallen over. The scarecrow is so roughed up, it's practically a comedy. She starts tracking prints pressed into the top inch of soil: deer, turkey, and Bram, our Bernese Mountain Dog.

I'm thinking ahead to next year's crop, but mostly I'm taking a break from my labor. It's all leaves and aches around here. I swear that you could tell the time of year by which chore-based muscles are doing the throbbing. Over time, we've retired the fancy power tools—mulching mowers and leaf blowers—for a rake and a tarp. The stand of 100-year grandfather oak lets out a cackle. There are weeks of leaves still up in the limbs. Most will go where they please. The rest get dragged to the leaf mold pile or the chicken run, but there's still a gnaw to hauling at such scale. Next year, we ought to bribe the wind to blow in one convenient direction for a change.

SKY WATCH: From the 1st to the 15th, Saturn is highest and best seen around early evening; after midmonth, it sets by midnight. Brilliant Jupiter is below the Moon on the 6th and above it on the 7th. The year's best meteor shower occurs on the 13th and 14th. The Moon will not interfere with these Geminids, which produce a meteor a minute for observers watching any wide expanse of rural sky before 1:00 A.M. On the 31st, Jupiter is at its biggest and brightest of the year. It has no opposition in 2025—a rare occurrence—but the gas giant is now nearing its closest approach to Earth in 13 months, on January 9, 2026. Winter begins with the solstice on the 21st at 10:03 A.M. EST.

○ **FULL MOON** 4th day 6:14 P.M.   ● **NEW MOON** 19th day 8:43 P.M.
◐ **LAST QUARTER** 11th day 3:52 P.M.   ◑ **FIRST QUARTER** 27th day 2:10 P.M.

All times are given in Eastern Standard Time.

GET THESE PAGES WITH TIMES SET TO YOUR ZIP CODE VIA ALMANAC.COM/2025.

DAY OF YEAR	DAY OF MONTH	DAY OF WEEK	☼ RISES H. M.	RISE KEY	☼ SETS H. M.	SET KEY	LENGTH OF DAY H. M.	SUN FAST M.	SUN DECLINATION ° '	HIGH TIDE TIMES BOSTON		☾ RISES H. M.	RISE KEY	☾ SETS H. M.	SET KEY	☾ ASTRON. PLACE	☾ AGE
335	1	M.	6:54	E	4:12	A	9 18	27	21 s. 54	7¼	7¾	1:41	B	2:40	E	PSC	11
336	2	Tu.	6:55	E	4:12	A	9 17	26	22 s. 03	8	8¾	2:10	B	3:59	E	ARI	12
337	3	W.	6:56	E	4:12	A	9 16	26	22 s. 11	9	9¾	2:47	B	5:23	E	ARI	13
338	4	Th.	6:57	E	4:12	A	9 15	25	22 s. 19	9¾	10½	3:35	A	6:47	E	TAU	14
339	5	Fr.	6:58	E	4:12	A	9 14	25	22 s. 27	10¾	11½	4:36	A	8:05	E	TAU	15
340	6	Sa.	6:59	E	4:12	A	9 13	25	22 s. 34	11½	—	5:48	B	9:10	E	AUR	16
341	7	E	7:00	E	4:11	A	9 11	24	22 s. 41	12¼	12½	7:07	B	10:01	E	GEM	17
342	8	M.	7:01	E	4:11	A	9 10	24	22 s. 47	1¼	1½	8:24	C	10:39	E	CAN	18
343	9	Tu.	7:02	E	4:11	A	9 09	23	22 s. 53	2¼	2¼	9:38	C	11:08	E	CAN	19
344	10	W.	7:03	E	4:12	A	9 09	23	22 s. 58	3¼	3¼	10:47	D	11:32	D	LEO	20
345	11	Th.	7:03	E	4:12	A	9 09	22	23 s. 03	4	4¼	11:52	D	11:52	D	LEO	21
346	12	Fr.	7:04	E	4:12	A	9 08	22	23 s. 07	5	5¼	—	-	12:11	C	VIR	22
347	13	Sa.	7:05	E	4:12	A	9 07	21	23 s. 11	6	6¼	12:56	E	12:29	C	VIR	23
348	14	E	7:06	E	4:12	A	9 06	21	23 s. 15	6¾	7¼	1:58	E	12:49	B	VIR	24
349	15	M.	7:06	E	4:12	A	9 06	20	23 s. 18	7¾	8¼	3:01	E	1:11	B	VIR	25
350	16	Tu.	7:07	E	4:13	A	9 06	20	23 s. 20	8½	9	4:05	E	1:36	B	LIB	26
351	17	W.	7:08	E	4:13	A	9 05	19	23 s. 22	9¼	9¾	5:09	E	2:07	A	LIB	27
352	18	Th.	7:08	E	4:13	A	9 05	19	23 s. 24	9¾	10½	6:12	E	2:46	A	SCO	28
353	19	Fr.	7:09	E	4:14	A	9 05	18	23 s. 25	10½	11¼	7:10	E	3:33	A	OPH	0
354	20	Sa.	7:10	E	4:14	A	9 04	18	23 s. 26	11¼	11¾	8:02	E	4:28	A	SAG	1
355	21	E	7:10	E	4:14	A	9 04	18	23 s. 26	11¾	—	8:46	E	5:31	B	SAG	2
356	22	M.	7:11	E	4:15	A	9 04	17	23 s. 26	12½	12½	9:22	E	6:37	B	SAG	3
357	23	Tu.	7:11	E	4:16	A	9 05	17	23 s. 25	1¼	1¼	9:51	E	7:46	B	CAP	4
358	24	W.	7:11	E	4:16	A	9 05	16	23 s. 24	1¾	1¾	10:16	E	8:54	C	CAP	5
359	25	Th.	7:12	E	4:17	A	9 05	16	23 s. 22	2½	2¾	10:38	D	10:02	D	AQU	6
360	26	Fr.	7:12	E	4:17	A	9 05	15	23 s. 20	3¼	3½	10:59	D	11:11	D	AQU	7
361	27	Sa.	7:13	E	4:18	A	9 05	15	23 s. 17	4	4¼	11:20	C	—	-	PSC	8
362	28	E	7:13	E	4:19	A	9 06	14	23 s. 14	5	5¼	11:42	C	12:23	E	PSC	9
363	29	M.	7:13	E	4:20	A	9 07	14	23 s. 10	5¾	6¼	12:07	B	1:37	E	PSC	10
364	30	Tu.	7:13	E	4:21	A	9 08	13	23 s. 06	6¾	7¼	12:39	B	2:56	E	ARI	11
365	31	W.	7:13	E	4:22	A	9 09	13	23 s. 02	7¾	8½	1:20	A	4:17	E	ARI	12

DECEMBER

He seems as 'twere to prompt our merriest days,
And bid the dance and joke be long and loud.
–**Barry Cornwall, of winter**

DAY OF MONTH	DAY OF WEEK	DATES, FEASTS, FASTS, ASPECTS, TIDE HEIGHTS, AND WEATHER	
1	M.	St. Andrew[T] • Electronic engineer/video game pioneer Gerald "Jerry" Lawson born, 1940	*All the*
2	Tu.	St. Viviana • Babe Ruth's bat used to hit 1st Yankee Stadium home run sold for $1,265,000, in 2004	*cars*
3	W.	☌♅☾ • G. Gershwin presented "Concerto in F," 1st jazz concerto for piano and orchestra, at Carnegie Hall, N.Y.C., 1925	
4	Th.	FULL COLD ○ • ☾ AT PERIG. • Astronaut Roberta L. Bondar born, 1945 • {12.0 10.2	*are*
5	Fr.	☾ RIDES HIGH • Montgomery Bus Boycott began, Ala., 1955 • Tides {12.2 10.2	*going*
6	Sa.	St. Nicholas • U.S. Naval Observatory established (as Depot of Charts and Instruments), 1830	*slow*
7	**E**	2nd S. of Advent • NAT'L PEARL HARBOR REMEMBRANCE DAY • ☌♃☾ • ☿ GR. ELONG. (21° WEST)	*but*
8	M.	*Knowledge in youth is wisdom in age.* • Tides {9.9 11.4	*can't*
9	Tu.	1st U.S. stamp (10-cent Special Delivery) to depict bicycle issued, 1902 • Tides {9.7 10.8	*get far*
10	W.	St. Eulalia • ♆ STAT. • Mathematician Ada Lovelace born, 1815 • {9.5 10.2	*in blowing*
11	Th.	☾ AT ☋ • End of overnight tornado outbreak, southern U.S./Ohio Valley, 2021 • {9.3 9.5	*snow!*
12	Fr.	OUR LADY OF GUADALUPE • ☾ ON EQ. • Singer Dionne Warwick born, 1940	*Windchill*
13	Sa.	St. Lucia • Actor Dick Van Dyke born, 1925 • Tides {9.1 8.6	*grating,*
14	**E**	**3rd S. of Advent** • Chanukah begins at sundown • Halcyon Days begin.	*not*
15	M.	Beware the Pogonip. • 1st rendezvous of two manned spacecraft, *Gemini 6A* and *Gemini 7*, 1965	*abating.*
16	Tu.	Writer Jane Austen born, 1775 • Tides {9.4 8.4	*Plunging temps*
17	W.	Ember Day • ☾ AT APO. • Aztec Calendar Stone rediscovered, Mexico City, Mexico, 1790	*getting*
18	Th.	☌☿☾ • Ratification of 13th Amendment, prohibiting enslavement in the U.S., announced, 1865	*coldest*
19	Fr.	Ember Day • NEW ● • ☾ RUNS LOW • ☌♀☾ • {9.9 8.5	*right*
20	Sa.	Ember Day • ☌♂☾ • Surgeon Ambroise Paré died, 1590 • {10.0 8.6	*around the*
21	**E**	**4th S. of Advent** • WINTER SOLSTICE • Tides {10.0 —	*winter solstice.*
22	M.	St. Thomas[T] • ☌♇☾ • Edward Johnson employed the 1st electric Christmas tree lights, 1882	
23	Tu.	Pianist Victor Borge died, 2000 • Tides {8.7 10.0	*Holiday*
24	W.	Family moved into world's 1st fully solar-heated home, Dover, Mass., 1948 • Tides {8.8 9.9	*season now*
25	Th.	**Christmas** • ☾ AT ☊ • *Cheerful company shortens the miles.* • {8.9 9.7	*freezin'*
26	Fr.	St. Stephen • BOXING DAY (CANADA) • FIRST DAY OF KWANZAA • ☾ ON EQ. • ☌♄☾	*for*
27	Sa.	St. John • ☌♆☾ • ALH 84001 Mars meteorite found in Antarctica, 1984	*most . . .*
28	**E**	**1st S. af. Ch.** • –42.1°C (–44°F), Edmonton, Alta., 2021 • {9.7 9.1	*warm up*
29	M.	Holy Innocents[T] • Inventor Charles Goodyear born, 1800 • Texas statehood, 1845	*with a '26*
30	Tu.	*It takes three cloudy days to bring a heavy snow.* • Tides {10.5 9.1	*New Year's*
31	W.	St. Sylvester • Make Up Your Mind Day • ☌♅☾ • {10.9 9.2	*toast!*

Farmer's Calendar

Last offer: three buttercreams for two pizzelles.

Last year I set to keep the laundry from piling sky-high on the chair. Ha! Let's bring our resolutions down to Earth: • Ring an old friend, ask for their best recipe. Ask for their mother's, their grandmother's. • Give loved ones a single, elevated ingredient. Homemade extracts or toasted sugar. Brown a large block of butter for Dyane's ambitious baking schedule, then get out of the way. • Try not to guilt everyone over the generosity of your recent gifts, when it comes to horse-trading cookies later in the month. • But then again, do whatever it takes to get your hands on some extra buttercreams. • Pass out the leftover Halloween candy to the neighborhood kids to use on gingerbread houses. • Toss the hens some of the good mealworms. • Tell a knock-knock joke at dinner, a soldier's joke at dessert. • Turn your dignity over to Victorian parlor games. It's not a party until you get people playing "Are You There, Moriarty?" (Remember to have enough newspaper and blindfolds on hand.) • Sing your lover a song, especially since you can't sing. • Give yourself whole. Everything to everyone.

HOLIDAYS AND OBSERVANCES

2025 HOLIDAYS
FEDERAL HOLIDAYS ARE LISTED IN BOLD.

JAN. 1: New Year's Day

JAN. 7: Orthodox Christmas (Julian)

JAN. 20: Martin Luther King Jr.'s Birthday, observed
Inauguration Day *(D.C. metro federal employees only)*

FEB. 1: First day of Black History Month

FEB. 2: Groundhog Day

FEB. 12: Abraham Lincoln's Birthday

FEB. 14: Valentine's Day

FEB. 15: Susan B. Anthony's Birthday *(Fla.)*

FEB. 17: Presidents' Day

FEB. 22: George Washington's Birthday

MAR. 2: Texas Independence Day

MAR. 4: Mardi Gras *(Baldwin & Mobile counties, Ala.; La.)*
Town Meeting Day *(Vt.)*

MAR. 8: International Women's Day

MAR. 9: Daylight Saving Time begins

MAR. 17: St. Patrick's Day
Evacuation Day *(Suffolk Co., Mass.)*

MAR. 31: César Chávez Day
Seward's Day *(Alaska)*

APR. 2: Pascua Florida Day

APR. 21: Patriots Day *(Maine, Mass.)*
San Jacinto Day *(Tex.)*

APR. 22: Earth Day

APR. 23: Holocaust Remembrance Day begins at sundown

APR. 25: National Arbor Day

MAY 1: First day of Asian American, Native Hawaiian, and Pacific Islander Heritage Month

MAY 5: Cinco de Mayo

MAY 8: Truman Day *(Mo.)*

MAY 11: Mother's Day

MAY 17: Armed Forces Day

MAY 19: Victoria Day *(Canada)*

MAY 22: National Maritime Day

MAY 26: Memorial Day, observed

JUNE 1: First day of Pride Month

JUNE 5: World Environment Day

JUNE 6: D-Day

JUNE 11: King Kamehameha I Day *(Hawaii)*

JUNE 14: Flag Day

JUNE 15: Father's Day

JUNE 17: Bunker Hill Day *(Suffolk Co., Mass.)*

JUNE 19: Juneteenth National Independence Day

JUNE 20: West Virginia Day

JULY 1: Canada Day

JULY 4: Independence Day

JULY 20: International Moon Day

JULY 24: Pioneer Day *(Utah)*

JULY 26: National Day of the Cowboy

AUG. 1: Colorado Day

AUG. 4: Civic Holiday *(parts of Canada)*

AUG. 16: Bennington Battle Day *(Vt.)*

AUG. 19: National Aviation Day

AUG. 26: Women's Equality Day

SEPT. 1: Labor Day

SEPT. 7: Grandparents Day

SEPT. 9: Admission Day *(Calif.)*

SEPT. 11: Patriot Day

SEPT. 15: First day of National Hispanic/Latinx Heritage Month

SEPT. 17: Constitution Day

SEPT. 21: International Day of Peace

SEPT. 30: National Day for Truth and Reconciliation *(Canada)*

OCT. 6: Child Health Day

OCT. 9: Leif Eriksson Day

OCT. 12: National Farmer's Day

OCT. 13: Columbus Day, observed
Indigenous Peoples' Day *(parts of U.S.)*
Thanksgiving Day *(Canada)*

OCT. 18: Alaska Day

OCT. 24: United Nations Day

OCT. 31: Halloween
Nevada Day

NOV. 2: Daylight Saving Time ends

NOV. 4: Election Day
    Will Rogers Day *(Okla.)*
NOV. 11: **Veterans Day**
    Remembrance Day *(Canada)*
NOV. 19: Discovery of Puerto Rico Day
NOV. 27: **Thanksgiving Day**
NOV. 28: Acadian Day *(La.)*

DEC. 7: National Pearl Harbor
    Remembrance Day
DEC. 15: Bill of Rights Day
DEC. 17: Wright Brothers Day
DEC. 25: **Christmas Day**
DEC. 26: Boxing Day *(Canada)*
    First day of Kwanzaa

Movable Religious Observances

FEB. 16: Septuagesima Sunday
FEB. 28: Ramadan begins at sundown
MAR. 3: Orthodox Lent begins
MAR. 4: Shrove Tuesday
MAR. 5: Ash Wednesday
APR. 12: Passover begins at sundown
APR. 13: Palm Sunday
APR. 18: Good Friday
APR. 20: Easter
    Orthodox Easter
MAY 25: Rogation Sunday

MAY 29: Ascension Day
JUNE 8: Whitsunday–Pentecost
    Orthodox Pentecost
JUNE 15: Trinity Sunday
JUNE 22: Corpus Christi
SEPT. 22: Rosh Hashanah begins at
    sundown
OCT. 1: Yom Kippur begins at sundown
NOV. 30: First Sunday of Advent
DEC. 14: Chanukah begins at sundown

CHRONOLOGICAL CYCLES

Dominical Letter **E**
Epact **30**
Golden Number (Lunar Cycle) **12**
Roman Indiction **3**
Solar Cycle (Julian Calendar) **18**
Year of Julian Period **6738**

-Beth Krommes

ERAS

ERA	YEAR	BEGINS
Byzantine	7534	September 14
Jewish (A.M.)*	5786	September 22
Chinese (Lunar) [Year of the Snake]	4723	January 29
Roman (A.U.C.)	2778	January 14
Nabonassar	2774	April 23
Japanese	2685	January 1
Grecian (Seleucidae)	2337	September 14 (or October 14)
Indian (Saka)	1947	March 22
Diocletian	1742	September 11
Islamic (Hegira)*	1447	June 26
Bahá'í*	182	March 19

*Year begins at sundown.

GLOSSARY OF ALMANAC ODDITIES

Many readers have expressed puzzlement over the rather obscure entries that appear on our **Right-Hand Calendar Pages, 121–147.** These "oddities" have long been fixtures in the Almanac, and we are pleased to provide some definitions. Once explained, they may not seem so odd after all!

EMBER DAYS: These are the Wednesdays, Fridays, and Saturdays that occur in succession following (1) the First Sunday in Lent; (2) Whitsunday–Pentecost; (3) the Feast of the Holy Cross, September 14; and (4) the Feast of St. Lucia, December 13. The word *ember* is perhaps a corruption of the Latin *quatuor tempora,* "four times." The four periods are observed by some Christian denominations for prayer, fasting, and the ordination of clergy.

Folklore has it that the weather on each of the 3 days foretells the weather for the next 3 months; that is, in September, the first Ember Day, Wednesday, forecasts the weather for October; Friday predicts November; and Saturday foretells December.

DISTAFF DAY (JANUARY 7): This was the day after Epiphany, when women were expected to return to their spinning following the Christmas holiday. A distaff is the staff that women used for holding the flax or wool in spinning. Hence, the term "distaff" refers to women's work or the maternal side of the family.

PLOUGH MONDAY (JANUARY): Traditionally, the first Monday after Epiphany was called Plough Monday because it was the day when men returned to their plough, or daily work, following the Christmas holiday. (Every few years, Plough Monday and Distaff Day fall on the same day.) It was customary at this time for farm laborers to draw a plough through the village, soliciting money for a "plough light,"

–Beth Krommes

which was kept burning in the parish church all year. This traditional verse captures the spirit of it:

Yule is come and Yule is gone,
and we have feasted well;
so Jack must to his flail again
and Jenny to her wheel.

THREE CHILLY SAINTS (MAY): Mamertus, Pancras, and Gervais were three early Christian saints whose feast days, on May 11, 12, and 13, respectively, are traditionally cold; thus they have come to be known as the Three Chilly Saints. An old French saying translates to "St. Mamertus, St. Pancras, and St. Gervais do not pass without a frost."

MIDSUMMER DAY (JUNE 24): To the farmer, this day is the midpoint of the growing season, halfway between planting and harvest. The Anglican Church considered it a "Quarter Day," one of the four major divisions of the liturgical year. It also marks the feast day of St. John the Baptist. (Midsummer Eve is an occasion for festivity and celebrates fertility.)

CORNSCATEOUS AIR (JULY): First used by early almanac makers, this term signifies warm, damp air. Although it signals ideal climatic conditions for growing corn, warm, damp air poses a danger to those affected by asthma and other respiratory problems.

DOG DAYS (JULY 3–AUGUST 11): These 40 days are traditionally the year's hottest and unhealthiest. They once coincided with the year's heliacal (at sunrise) rising of the Dog Star, Sirius. Ancient folks thought that the "combined heat" of Sirius and the Sun caused summer's swelter.

LAMMAS DAY (AUGUST 1): Derived from the Old English *hlaf maesse,* meaning "loaf mass," Lammas Day marked the beginning of the harvest. Traditionally, loaves of bread were baked from the first-ripened grain and brought to the churches to be consecrated. In Scotland, Lammastide fairs became famous as the time when trial marriages could be made. These marriages could end after a year with no strings attached.

CAT NIGHTS COMMENCE (AUGUST 17): This term harks back to the days when people believed in witches. An Irish legend says that a witch could turn into a cat and regain herself eight times, but on the ninth time (August 17), she couldn't change back and thus began her final life permanently as a cat. Hence the saying "A cat has nine lives."

HARVEST HOME (SEPTEMBER): In Britain and other parts of Europe, this marked the conclusion of the harvest and a period of festivals for feasting and thanksgiving. It was also a time to hold elections, pay workers, and collect rents. These festivals usually took place around the autumnal equinox. Certain groups in the United States, e.g., the Pennsylvania Dutch, have kept the tradition alive.

ST. LUKE'S LITTLE SUMMER (OCTOBER): This is a period of warm weather that occurs on or near St. Luke's feast day (usually October 18).

INDIAN SUMMER (NOVEMBER): A period of warm weather following a cold spell or a hard frost, Indian summer, also called Second Summer, can occur between St. Martin's Day (November 11) and November 20. Although there are differing dates for its occurrence, the Almanac has adhered to the saying "If All Saints' [November 1] brings out winter, St. Martin's brings out Indian summer." The term may have come from early North American indigenous peoples, some of whom believed that the condition was caused by a warm wind sent from the court of their southwestern god, Cautantowwit.

HALCYON DAYS (DECEMBER): This period of about 2 weeks of calm weather often follows the blustery winds at autumn's end. Ancient Greeks and Romans experienced this weather at about the time of the winter solstice (around December 21), when the halcyon, or kingfisher—having charmed the wind and waves so that waters were especially calm at this time—was thought to brood in a nest floating on the sea.

BEWARE THE POGONIP (DECEMBER): The word *pogonip* refers to frozen fog and was coined by North American indigenous peoples to describe the frozen fogs of fine ice needles that occur in the mountain valleys of the western United States and Canada. According to tradition, breathing the fog is injurious to the lungs. ∎

–Beth Krommes

Stop the Germs
That make you sick

Pure copper kills bad germs, science has proved.

Now thousands of people use CopperZaps made of pure copper against germs that cause illness.

"I haven't been sick once!" reported Michelle, a longtime CopperZap user.

Each CopperZap® is specially shaped by skilled workers so it can reach cold and flu viruses where they first get in your nose. Pure copper can kill them *before* they make you sick.

Based on the strong scientific evidence, inventor Doug Cornell developed a pure copper probe with a tip and handle shaped just right.

When he felt a tickle in his nose

New research: Copper kills bad germs in seconds.

"I haven't had a cold or flu since," Bronny reported.

Hundreds of studies confirm copper kills viruses, bacteria, and fungus. These germs start to die instantly if copper touches them.

That's why ancient Greeks and others used copper to purify water and heal wounds. They didn't know about germs. Now we do.

"I haven't had a cold in 6 years!" exclaimed Julie. "It works!"

Scientists discovered that copper's high conductance disrupts the electrical balance in a germ cell and destroys the germ in seconds.

The EPA and NIH vouch for the power of copper. On their advice, several hospitals have now started using copper fixtures to kill germs like MRSA and save lives.

like a cold about to start, he rubbed it gently in his nose for 30 seconds.

"It worked!" he exclaimed. "The cold never happened." That was 2012. He hasn't had a single cold since!

"I used to get 2-3 bad colds or flu each year. Now I use my CopperZap right away at any sign I am about to get sick or have a sore throat."

After his initial success, he asked relatives and friends to try it. They all said it worked, so he patented it and put it on the market.

Soon hundreds of people had tried it. Over 99% said it worked if they used it right away at the first sign of bad germs, like a tickle in the nose or a scratchy throat.

It works on more than just colds. A man who used it for congestion said, "Best sleep I've had in years!"

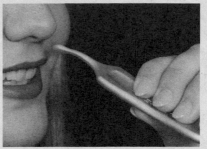

SPILLING THE TEA

BY FAYE WOLFE

PEACE, HAPPINESS, AND JOY ARE POSSIBLE DURING THE TIME I DRINK MY TEA.

–THICH NHAT HANH, VIETNAMESE ZEN MASTER (1926–2022)

Next to water, tea is the most widely consumed drink in the world—3.7 billion cups daily in one recent year. There are basic reasons for this. Tea quenches our thirst. We like the taste. It warms us up on a cold day and refreshes us on a scorcher. We brew a cup of Irish breakfast to get going in the A.M. and a mug of soothing chamomile before bed. Just the act of making a "cuppa" can be restorative. This is especially true in the UK, according to anthropologist Kate Fox: "Whenever the English feel awkward or uncomfortable in a social situation (that is, almost all the time), they make tea."

Tea has been around for two millennia or so; in 2016, archaeologists discovered tea in a Chinese emperor's tomb dating from 141 B.C., well past its "best by" date. One of the world's oldest and most popular drinks, tea is also one of the best for your health.

A DRINK A DAY

A translated ancient Chinese proverb posits that "drinking a daily cup of tea will surely starve the apothecary." In fact, tea was probably first imbibed as a medicine. Lu Yu, the Chinese author of *Ch'a Ching,* or "The Classic of Tea," promoted its healthfulness in the 8th century. In 1657, Garraway's Coffee House in London became the first business to sell tea in England, advertising that it "maketh the Body active and lusty . . . helpeth the Headach . . . removeth the Obstructions of the Spleen" and was "good against Lipitude Distillations." Quaint language aside ("lippitude" refers to bleary eyes), Garraway's was onto something. We know today that the caffeine in tea can alleviate a headache and may speed up the action of a pain reliever.

Caffeine is just one component of tea that can be beneficial. Catechins—a type of polyphenols, or plant chemicals with antioxidant properties—are also being studied for their preventative and curative powers. Here's a sampling of some of the more promising findings.

■ A 2020 meta-analysis of an array of studies found that drinking two to three cups of black or green tea a day was associated with a lower risk of death from cardiovascular disease and a lower risk of cardiac events and stroke. Other studies have suggested related cardiovascular benefits, such as the potential to lower cholesterol and blood pressure.

■ A 2021 review of research into green tea found that it has potential as a flu-fighter and may ward off the common cold.

■ According to a 2022 article in *Molecules,* the catechins in green and black tea may have prophylactic and therapeutic effects on Parkinson's disease and Alzheimer's and other forms of dementia.

■ A study published in 2023 showed that drinking tea may lower the risk of osteoporosis and hip fractures. This is encouraging news, given that osteoporosis affects millions and is difficult to treat.

HERBAL REME-TEAS?

When Agatha Christie's Hercule Poirot sipped a tisane to stimulate the "little gray cells," he knew what he was doing. Mint tea may foster brain health, particularly in relation to cognitive decline. Rooibos tea may improve blood pressure and boost good cholesterol while lowering bad cholesterol. Other findings indicate that drinking rooibos may promote higher bone mineral density in women—and it doesn't contain caffeine, which may be detrimental to bone health. In addition to relieving headaches, ginger tea also counters nausea and can help soothe the

TALKING TEA

Just what are we talking about when we say "tea"? You may remember when tea was just that stuff in dunkable little bags on a string with a tag. But during the past 30 years, the varieties of tea for sale have burgeoned.

You can sort by color: black, green, purple, red, white, yellow. Or by blend: Darjeeling; bergamot-flavor Earl Grey; smoky, bacon-y Lapsang souchong—to name but a few.

A key subgroup in the taxonomy of teas is made up of the "true" or "traditional" teas derived from *Camellia sinensis,* a cousin of the beautiful flowering plant. Depending on how its leaves are processed (oxidized, withered, fermented, flame-fired, steamed, crushed), these become black, green, or oolong tea. Matcha, green tea in powdered form, is used in the venerable Japanese tea ceremony. Black tea—mixed with milk, sugar, and spices—is the main ingredient in chai and in boba, or bubble, tea, from South Korea, which is served with milk, sugar, and tapioca pearls. When fermented with bacteria and yeast, black tea becomes kombucha.

Then, of course, there is also the array of teas from other plants, including rooibos (aka red or red bush tea), maté, and such classic herbal infusions as chamomile, ginger, hibiscus, lavender, and mint. Some classify the latter as tisanes.

Whatever "tea" means to you, chances are that you partake of it in some form. Worldwide, black tea is the most popular brew. In the United States, an average of more than four out of every five consumers drink true teas, with Millennials the biggest consumers. The Turks, Irish, and Brits outdrink Americans by a wide margin; Canadians drink about twice as much as their southern neighbors.

research suggests that drinking really hot tea (at least 158°F) in quantity may lead to esophageal cancer. In deciding how piping hot to make your tea, it might be better to cool it.

While both hot and cold tea pack an antioxidant punch, it turns out that the type of cold tea may matter, too. Homemade iced tea (brewed with hot water, then chilled) tends to be richer in antioxidants than store-bought, and iced tea from the supermarket may also have other ingredients, such as high-fructose corn syrup, which, from a nutritional perspective, aren't so . . . hot.

SIP AND SEE

A plethora of promising research notwithstanding, tea has not yet emerged as a panacea. There are still a lot of tea leaves floating around this pot that need to be read. For instance, tea's potential to help prevent cancer has been the subject of more than 3,000 studies, according to the Tea Association of the USA, but thus far the results have been inconclusive. In fact, many of the claims about tea on the Internet should be taken with a grain of salt. And, as is true with so many of the substances that we hope will bring us a long, healthy life, tea is probably best consumed in moderation. This being said, a cup or two a day might just keep the doctor away. ■

As **Faye Wolfe** writes her blog at Fayeswolfe.wordpress.com, she's fueled by cups of tea.

aches and pains of osteoarthritis. For people who struggle to get a good night's sleep (also a key ingredient of wellness), herbal teas have the edge over true teas, being caffeine-free.

SOME LIKE IT HOT

A nd some like it cold, as most Americans prefer iced tea. From a health standpoint, is hot tea better than iced tea?

One study measured the waistlines and body mass indexes (BMI) of drinkers of hot tea, iced tea, and no tea. The hot tea drinkers had trimmer waists and lower BMIs than nondrinkers, while the reverse was true for iced tea drinkers. (Sugar intake was not a factor.) As both of these measures are "bio-markers" for heart disease, these results would seem to give hot tea an edge. But bear in mind that some scientific

SNUG AS A BUG IN A HUG

BY TIM GOODWIN
ILLUSTRATIONS BY TIM ROBINSON

WE WRAP OUR ARMS AROUND OTHERS TO SAY HELLO
or good-bye. We embrace during times of joy
and sorrow. Hugging is a universal language with many
meanings—including "thank you" and "I'm sorry."
Hugging is such a fascinating cultural phenomenon
that scientific studies have determined just
how important a hug can be to our well-being.

Hugs for Health

There are no rules as to how long a hug should last. It comes down to what the situation calls for. On average, a hug lasts about 3 seconds. If you want to enjoy additional health benefits, hang on for a little longer: In 2003, researchers at the University of North Carolina found that a group of adults who received a hug lasting at least 20 seconds from a supportive partner prior to a public speaking event showed an increased level of oxytocin, which has been linked to reducing blood pressure and cortisol—the stress hormone.

SQUEEZE TO PLEASE

If there is a sweet spot for the amount of time that a hug should last, researchers in the UK may have found it by conducting a pair of studies in 2021 to determine the ideal length and preferred style of a hug. Participants hugged for 1-, 5-, and 10-second intervals. The results indicated that embraces that last between 5 and 10 seconds are the most enjoyable. When it came to hugging styles, the crisscross arm method (each hugger has one arm low and one high) was used 64.5 percent of the time when there was a mix of genders and with 82 percent frequency if both participants were male. The neck–waist contact style (one hugger around the neck, the other around the waist) was found to be used more often between two females—48 percent of the time.   *(continued)*

The Feeling of a Hug

For some, receiving a hug is not a pleasant experience, as the physical touch of others can cause undue stress. While in high school, Temple Grandin, now a professor of animal science at Colorado State University and autism advocate, developed a squeeze device or "hug machine." Somewhat ironically, Grandin created the machine—which simulates the pressure of a hug without any physical touching—before she herself was diagnosed with autism. To use the device, a person lies down between two padded side boards that apply gentle pressure. It's widely employed in schools and other settings to help to soothe people with autism.

HOLY HUGGER

Affectionately known by her followers as the Hugging Saint, Sri Mātā Amritānandamayī Devi is an Indian spiritual leader and humanitarian. Also known as "Amma," she hosts free programs around the world to inspire others to follow a path of selfless service, sharing her wisdom and inspiration. At the end of each program, Amma embraces all participants. It is said that she has "hugged" more than 34 million people worldwide and has been known to offer her soothing squeeze for more than 22 hours without interruption.

X's and O's

The origin of why "O" represents hugs—as in XOXO—is unclear, but some believe that in a bird's-eye view, an "O" resembles two pairs of arms coming together to complete a hug.

Hug Day

When the calendar turns to January 21, prepare yourself for a few extra hugs. Started in 1986 by Kevin Zaborney in Caro, Michigan, National Hugging Day was created to promote "the values and benefits directly related to love and kindness through the power of consensual hugging."

Do Bugs and Animals Hug?

They sure do—but not necessarily in the same way that humans use the embrace.

In one example, spider monkeys are known to hug during reunions after spending the day apart to hunt or feed. Many bugs "hug" other insects—but usually when they are preparing to consume the hug recipient for a meal.

NOW, THAT'S A LONG EMBRACE!

In the Italian village of Valdaro, archaeologists unearthed the skeletons of a man and woman buried together face-to-face, with their arms and legs entwined. The "Lovers of Valdaro" were discovered in 2007, but their story is much older: Experts have estimated that the pair—thought to be no more than 20 years old at the time of death—lived some 6,000 years ago.

Guinness World Records has numerous categories when it comes to hugging. Here are a few:

■ *Largest group hug:* 10,554 people embraced at the Rideau Canal in Ottawa, Ontario, on May 7, 2010.

■ *Longest group hug:* Stephen Rattigan, Brian Cawley, Nicky Kearney, and Robert Tuomey huddled together in Castlebar, Ireland, and remained locked in a group hug for 30 hours and 1 minute on May 4–5, 2019.

■ *Most couples hugging:* 5,730 pairs gathered in Bergamo, Italy, on July 3, 2016, to establish the world record. ■

Thanks to his doting young daughters, Almanac associate editor **Tim Goodwin** has become a grateful expert on hugging.

TUNE IN TO THE MOON

How to garden in harmony with our nearest celestial neighbor

● BY JANE HAWLEY STEVENS ●

MY FIRST employment after earning a horticulture degree from the University of Wisconsin involved creating an herb garden. From this fortuitous beginning, I started specializing in herbs for cooking and home remedies. I saw that plants healed my baby's repeated earaches better than antibiotics from the doctor. From there, I committed to organic practices, and my company that grows and sells herbal products was born.

I am an Aries—inclined to start projects. When I began growing, I planted seeds aggressively. I skipped over the weeding as I continued weeks of spring planting.

When I first opened up *The Old Farmer's Almanac* over 35 years ago, I thought that its advice about gardening according to the Moon's cycles was just folklore, yet I tried it. I found that the rhythms helped me to sort, schedule, and complete my tasks, while tuning me in to the greater forces of the elements. It gave me natural guidelines—like inserting necessary weeding days into every week. If I had but 1 hour to work in the garden, instead of wasting time wondering what chore to conquer, I referred to the "Best Days" chart in the Almanac—and soon I was focused on a fitting task.

HARVESTING MOON ENERGY

People who live near an ocean know that a full Moon pulls tides higher. Landlocked Midwesterners like me can not see this phenomenon, but the same thing is happening to water below the ground's surface.

This ebb and flow is a natural result of the magnetic pull of the monthly alignment of the Sun, Earth, and

The Sun's immense power over Earth and its creatures is scientific fact; in many people's eyes, to endow the Moon with equal power is to embrace fairy tales and ghost stories.

—Ferris Jabr, American writer (b. 1987)

Moon and is the basis for planting according to the Moon's phases. If the Moon moves the water table—and humans are 60 percent water and plants 80 percent to 90 percent so—it stands to reason that we, too, are influenced by the Moon, the only natural "satellite" in Earth's orbit.

Each Moon phase provides a distinctive energy. Now that I live according to this rhythm, I feel the difference between full Moon and new Moon energy. For example, starting 2 days before the full Moon, I can't fall asleep easily and I wake up more frequently. Maybe this happens to you, too.

NEW MOON

Let's start at the begin-ning, the first day of the cycle: The new Moon phase occurs when the Moon and Sun are on the same side of Earth. In this orientation, we face the Moon's dark half, where the Sun's light does not reach the surface directly. A new Moon is up during the day, basically rising and setting with the Sun. It can not usu-

---

LUNAR CYCLE TO-DO LIST

NEW MOON TO FIRST QUARTER

■ Ready your seeds, planting time begins!
■ Plant seeds for plants that produce their seeds outside their fruit: arugula, basil, broccoli, cabbage, grains, lettuce, radicchio, spinach, and most herbs. (Cucumbers like this phase even though they are an exception to the rule.)
■ Turn the soil between the new and full Moons, when there is less moisture in the soil and it is thus less dense and easier to move.
■ Prune for rejuvenation.

FIRST QUARTER TO FULL MOON

■ Keep on planting! The sweet spot is about 3 days before and until the full Moon.
■ Plant aboveground annuals with seeds inside their fruit: beans, melons, peas, peppers, squashes, and tomatoes.

FULL MOON TO LAST QUARTER

■ This is the time for planting root crops: beets, biennials, bulbs, carrots, onions, perennials, potatoes.
■ This is a good time for transplanting, due to active root growth.
■ For maximum vitamins, minerals, and herbal constituents, harvest now for storage.
■ Take advantage of the increased energy rising from the earth below to harvest apples and other fruit when their natural goodness is peaking.
■ Make herbal extracts.

LAST QUARTER TO NEW MOON

■ Weed and cultivate for weed suppression.
■ Inventory and order seeds.
■ Design your gardens.
■ Harvest for drying.
■ Prune for decreased growth.
■ Mow lawns to slow growth.

ally be seen with the naked eye because of the Sun's glare and the fact that we are facing the Moon's dark side. Watch the sky 3 days before the new Moon to see this crescent get narrower, rise about 50 minutes later each day, and, on the day of the new Moon, disappear.

New Moon energy is inquisitive and fresh, like a newborn baby. The lunar gravity pulls water up, however minutely, and helps seeds to swell and burst. This factor, plus the increasing moonlight, creates balanced root and leaf growth—which is especially beneficial for plants that produce their seeds outside their fruit.

FIRST QUARTER

At this time, the gravitational pull is less but the moonlight is strong, creating vigorous leaf growth. As the days pass, the first quarter Moon will become visible as a D-shape glowing orb in our sky, rising at noon and setting at midnight. This makes for great nighttime moongazing!

FULL MOON

At the full Moon, the water table is, for a moment, at its height: This is when the Moon's energy is pumping at capacity through all living things. Then, it begins to recede. As the Moon wanes, energy is drawn down into the earth, putting it into a plant's roots.

LAST QUARTER

This is a time of rest, endings, and introspection. Take a moment to dream. Relax in a way that will allow answers to find you. Refrain from planting seeds during the week before the new Moon; instead, wait until a couple of days after it. ■

Jane Hawley Stevens is the author of *The Celestial Garden* (Chelsea Green Publishing, 2023) and (along with her husband, David Garison Stevens) co-owner of Four Elements Organic Herbals, a 130-acre organic farm in the Baraboo Bluffs area of Wisconsin, where they grow herbs used for well-being.

MINERAL-RICH SPRING TONIC

Boost your immune system with this natural tonic. It is best to dig roots in the early spring or fall, when they are storing all of their best qualities and are at peak potency. Use one, two, or all three types of roots. Collect them away from roadways; if the plants look healthy, they are likely not in an area that has been sprayed with dangerous pesticides.

burdock, dandelion, and yellow dock (any amount; adjust your water level to the amount of roots in your pan)
water, as needed
molasses, as needed

■ Clean, chop, and rinse roots.

■ Put into a pot and cover with water twice as deep as the top of roots.

■ Simmer until half of the water evaporates. Let sit for at least 2 hours, up to overnight.

■ Strain and measure your decoction. (A decoction is an extract of roots, seeds, or bark that has been simmered.)

■ Add the same volume of molasses as your decoction. Stir, bottle, label, and refrigerate.

Take 1 tablespoon daily.

●

I found [smelt] best when cooked in Indian Stile, which is by [roasting] a number of them together on a wooden spit without any previous preparation whatever. They are so fat that they require no additional sauce, and I think them Superior to any fish I ever tasted, even more [delicate] and [luscious] than the white fish of the Lakes which have heretofore formed my Standard of excellence among the fishes.

—from the journals of explorers Capt. Meriwether Lewis and William Clark, February 25, 1806

SOMETHING

Cool to catch and tasty, too, the Osmeridae family have been the life of many a party.

BY CAROL CONNARE

Nothing says "rites of spring" like a night spent wading in a freezing-cold river dip-netting for silvery fish so small that you can palm several at once. This is the lure of the smelt run: the promise of buckets overflowing with lip-smacking fish, free for the catching, all you can eat!—but don't forget your headlamp and woolens!

Widely distributed in coastal waters in the Northern Hemisphere, smelt are, for the most part, anadromous like salmon: Born in fresh water, they spend part of their life in the ocean before being triggered by warming seasonal temperatures to return to fresh water to spawn. Smelt run in large schools along coastlines, and, during spring migrations, they spawn in freshwater tributaries, where they serve as fare for birds, other fish, and mammals—including people.

Slightly sweet with a hint of umami, smelt are as fun to eat as they are delicious. Traditionally dusted lightly with flour and pan- or deep-fried, smelt melt in your mouth after an initial crunch. Held by the tail, they are the ideal finger food—no utensils required, the original fish stick! They're also packed with vitamin B_{12}, selenium, and omega-3, which means that they boost heart health, immunity, and cognitive function. *(continued)*

SMELT

FISHY

ON THE RUN

■ **"SALVATION FISH":** To the Stó:lō First Nations people who lived along British Columbia's Fraser River, the spring return of eulachon smelt meant a renewed food supply just as reserves were running low, earning them this nickname.

■ **"GREASE TRAILS":** Because—unlike other fish oils—eulachon lipids are solid at room temperature, they could be easily transported and bartered by First Nations peoples.

TO CATCH A SMELT

There are three main ways to fish for smelt: dip-netting—using a handheld net to scoop spawners on their way upriver; employing a seine or dragnet held by two or more people and dragged along the shoreline or at the mouth of a tributary; and by hooking them, usually under the ice. During ice fishing, where legal, anglers drop a battery-powered bulb through a hole in the ice to attract zooplankton—a smelt's favorite snack—and then snag the smelt as they arrive to feed.

Such trading routes became known as "grease trails" due to the residue that was sometimes left behind by the oil.

■ **ESCAPEES:** In 1912, over 16 million smelt eggs from Maine were stocked in Crystal Lake, Michigan, as food for Atlantic salmon being raised there. However, the new fish soon made their way into Lake Michigan and then the rest of the Great Lakes, where—as nonnatives without any significant predators—they multiplied so prolifically that they outpaced their food supply.

■ **"SMELTMANIA":** In the 1930s and '40s, Great Lakes smelt-dipping was so popular that it became known by this name. Thousands of visitors arrived at rivers and shorelines, eventually starting the traditions of beach bonfires and late-night smelt-fry parties.

■ **"SMESTLING":** Some communities held parades and dances and crowned smelt royalty. At the 1939 and '40 Marinette, Wisconsin, Smelt Carnivals, men wrestled in a slimy, smelt-filled ring, trying to shove the

HOW SMELT FELT

Sometimes the schools were several feet in diameter, moving in undulating fashion through the current, never following the exact same route for more than a few seconds. The trick was to locate the school by the feel of the fish hitting the steel rim of the net and then rapidly stroking downstream to intercept as many as possible. On a good dip, as many as 50 pounds of fish could be intercepted, requiring more strength than I had to bring them to the surface.

–Donald Stradley, on smelt-fishing with his father in the 1940s from a wooden float anchored to the riverbank on the Sandy River, a tributary of the Columbia River near Portland, Oregon

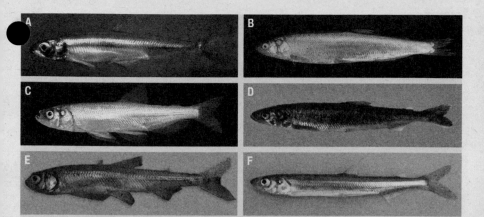

SMELT SCHOOL

Six types of smelt are found in North America, all having some manner of cucumber-like odor (hence their family name, Osmeridae, from the Greek *osme*, meaning "smell" or "odor").

COMMON NAME	SCIENTIFIC NAME	NORTH AMERICAN RANGE	KNOWN FOR . . .
A. Delta	*Hypomesus transpacificus*	Sacramento–San Joaquin River delta, CA	Smallest smelt
B. Eulachon (OO-le-kon), aka oolichan	*Thaleichthys pacificus*	Monterey Bay, CA, to Bristol Bay, AK	So fatty that they can be set alight, hence their nickname "candlefish"
C. Longfin	*Spirinchus thaleichthys*	San Francisco, CA, estuary to the Gulf of Alaska	Oily, soft, easily spoiled, unpleasant taste
D. Pacific rainbow	*Osmerus dentex*	West Coast	Live longer, mature later, and grow more slowly than other species
E. Pond	*H. olidus*	Copper River to Kobuk River, AK, to Peel River, YK, to Mackenzie River delta, NWT	Some are exclusively freshwater and remain landlocked for life
F. Rainbow	*O. mordax*	Newfoundland to PA; NWT to Vancouver Island	Have antifreeze protein and glycerol that enable survival in very cold temps; anadromous or landlocked

Photos, clockwise from top left: Wikimedia; Oregon Department of Fish & Wildlife; Springer Link; CT.gov; Alaska Department of Fish & Game; California Department of Fish & Wildlife

●

"BASKETS FULL OF SHINING FISH"

The smelt run in greatest number at night, and from 9:00 P.M. until midnight,
all of Marinette is festive. The Interstate Bridge is closed to traffic,
every foot is crowded with poles, flashlights, machines for lifting the seines,
and baskets full of shining fish. The riverbank is a blaze of light from bonfires. . . .
Barkers yell their wares, fireworks light the whole sky, and beer flows freely.
The festival reaches a climax with the crowning of the Smelt Queen.
—from *Wisconsin: A Guide to the Badger State* (Duell, Sloan, and Pearce, 1941)

fish onto their opponent's face.

■ **BULLDOZERS:** "So many smelt would run that beaches along the Great Lakes in the 1940s were cleaned with bulldozers to clear the dead smelt," Eric Dregni wrote in *Let's Go Fishing!: Fish Tales from the North Woods* (University of Minnesota Press, 2016).

■ **"SMELTANIA":** On Boyne City, Michigan's Lake Charlevoix, this pop-up village of ice shanties was the centerpiece of an on-and-off smelt-fishing festival of the same name

DOES "SMELT" MEAN "SMELT"?

The origin of the name "smelt" dates back centuries to numerous European areas—and all related monikers were used to describe fish. In Old English, "smelt" described small, salmonlike, saltwater fish. In Dutch, circa 1600, the same word identified sand eels. In Middle English, "smolt" described silvery young salmon. Other explanations for the name referenced the way in which the fish melted in your mouth when eaten.

that was started in the 1930s and has recently been revived.

■ **SINK OR SWIM:** Throughout the past century or so, the Great Lakes smelt fishery has had its ups and downs—but always managed to float along. At first, the fish were prolific invaders because another nonnative arrival, the sea lamprey, had devastated smelts' primary predator, lake trout. Eventually, though, advances in lamprey control led to a resurgence of trout at about the same time that another newly introduced smelt foe, Pacific salmon, arrived on the scene. Together, these two species created increased predation on smelt. Although by 1990 the declining smelt harvest in Lake Superior had fallen to 42,000 pounds, today there is still a commercial fishery on Lake Erie that delivers to stores and restaurants, and thousands of people continue to ply lakeshore waters in search of this delicious harbinger of spring.

Carol Connare, editor of *The Old Farmer's Almanac,* ate plenty of smelt every spring as a kid growing up in New Hampshire.

PAN-FRIED SMELT

Smelt can be eaten whole, including fins, bones, and tail, or you may remove the meat from the bones before eating.

vegetable or olive oil for frying

1 cup all-purpose flour

2 teaspoons garlic powder

1 teaspoon salt, plus more for seasoning

1 pound fresh smelt, rinsed

freshly ground black pepper, to taste

chopped fresh herbs, such as parsley, thyme, or rosemary, for garnish

1 lemon, sliced into wedges, for serving

mayonnaise or tartar sauce, for serving

Add oil to reach ½ inch up the side of a large pan. Heat to 350°F or until a pinch of flour dropped into it begins to bubble and lightly brown.

In a wide, shallow bowl, mix together flour, garlic powder, and 1 teaspoon salt. Dredge smelt in flour mixture and gently slide one at a time into the hot oil. Cook for 2 minutes on each side, being sure to not overcrowd the pan.

Remove smelt from oil and drain on a wire rack. Season with salt and pepper while hot. Sprinkle herbs over fish and serve hot with lemon wedges and mayonnaise or tartar sauce. ■

FAIRY BUTTER:
NOT A FLEETING FANCY

BY SARAH PERREAULT

C enturies before butter boards were popping up on social media, North American colonists were making a picture-worthy buttery concoction with minimal ingredients. "Fairy butter" was served beside gingerbread, scones, and other baked treats. Pale yellow and delicately sweet, the spread was a favorite of U.S. First Lady Dolley Madison (1768–1849), who often served it at afternoon tea at the White House.

One of the first known published recipes for fairy butter appeared in the 1747 cookbook *The Art of Cookery Made Plain and Easy* by Hannah Glasse. Perhaps the most popular cookbook in English-speaking regions (in today's terms, a "best-seller"), Glasse's collection of recipes dominated the kitchens of the Thirteen Colonies. This recipe called for four simple ingredients: hard-boiled egg yolks, loaf sugar, orange blossom water, and fresh butter. (Some early recipes used rose water.) After these components had been mixed completely, the resulting butter was pushed through a fine strainer onto a plate—for a spread almost too pretty to eat.

No one is certain how the culinary creation got its name, but there is a common theory that a fungus among us inspired it. Belief in fairies and other mythological creatures dates back to the Middle Ages (c. 500–1500 A.D.), and tales of little gossamer-winged sprites were still circulating when fairy butter

Photo: Samantha Jones/Vaughan Communications

"DO YOU BELIEVE
IN FAIRIES? SAY QUICK
THAT YOU BELIEVE!
IF YOU BELIEVE,
CLAP YOUR HANDS!"
–Sir James M. Barrie,
Scottish novelist and
playwright (1860–1937),
in *Peter Pan*

gained popularity in the 1700s. Some claimed that mischievous fairies stole freshly made butter from homesteads and hid it deep in the forest for future feasts. The butter was thought to be undetectable among jelly fungi *Tremella aurantia* and *T. mesenterica*—bright, yellowish-orange, gelatinous, fairy butter–lookalikes that grow in damp, dark areas such as on stumps and rotting wood, which are known to be favorite fairy dwelling places. Still, while fairy butter fungi is edible, it is said to have little flavor. We recommend eating its dairy namesake instead. ■

Sarah Perreault, food editor of *The Old Farmer's Almanac,* has been known to carry fairy dairy to her Aunt Geri's.

FAIRY BUTTER

2 hard-boiled egg yolks
1 tablespoon orange blossom or rose water
2 teaspoons superfine sugar
½ cup (1 stick) butter, softened

■ Using a fork or mortar and pestle, mash together egg yolks and flower water. Add sugar and combine until smooth. Add butter and combine until smooth. Place in the refrigerator for 1 hour to slightly firm up. Using a wooden spoon, push butter through a fine strainer or ricer into a small serving bowl or onto a plate.

■ If not using immediately, store in an airtight container in the refrigerator for up to 3 days.

Makes ½ cup.

(continued from page 77)

RED, WHITE, AND BLUEBERRY CHEESECAKE BARS

CRUST:
1½ cups graham cracker crumbs
½ cup (1 stick) unsalted butter, melted
¼ cup sugar

CHEESECAKE:
16 ounces (2 packages) cream cheese, softened
1 cup sugar
2 eggs
¼ cup all-purpose flour
1 teaspoon vanilla extract
1 cup fresh blueberries
1 cup fresh strawberries, hulled and sliced
½ cup fresh raspberries
½ cup fresh blackberries

GLAZE:
½ cup red currant jelly or seedless strawberry jam

■ *For crust:* Preheat oven to 325°F. Line a 13x9-inch baking dish with parchment paper, leaving an overhang on the sides for easy removal.

In a bowl, combine crumbs, butter, and sugar. Mix until crumbs are evenly coated with butter.

■ Press mixture firmly into bottom of the prepared dish. Use a spoon or the bottom of a glass to help compact it.

■ *For cheesecake:* Using a stand or hand mixer, beat together cream cheese and sugar until smooth. Add eggs, one at a time, beating well after each addition. Add flour and vanilla and mix until well combined and smooth.

■ Pour mixture over prepared crust, spreading evenly. Scatter berries evenly over the top. Bake for 35 to 40 minutes, or until edges are set and center is slightly jiggly.

■ Remove from oven and let cool to room temperature. Refrigerate for at least 2 hours, or until cheesecake is fully chilled.

■ *For glaze:* In a saucepan, warm jelly over low heat until it becomes liquid and smooth. Brush glaze over the top of chilled cheesecake.

■ Carefully lift cheesecake out of the baking dish and cut into squares.
Makes 24 bars.

–Shelby Trusty, Indianapolis, Indiana

MAPLE-ROASTED BUTTERNUT SQUASH PUDDING CAKES

CAKES:
2½ cups peeled, cubed butternut squash
1 tablespoon plus ¼ cup maple syrup
1 teaspoon olive oil
1 cup evaporated milk
⅓ cup sugar
2 teaspoons cornstarch
½ teaspoon pumpkin pie spice
2 eggs

TOPPING:
1 cup fresh or frozen cranberries
¼ cup chopped, pitted dates
3 tablespoons maple syrup
1 tablespoon brown sugar
⅓ cup chopped pecans

■ *For cakes:* Preheat oven to 350°F. Butter or grease sides and bottoms of eight 4-ounce ramekins or custard cups. Set ramekins into a 13x9-inch baking dish. Get out a baking sheet.

■ In a bowl, combine squash, 1 tablespoon maple syrup, and olive oil. Toss to coat, then spread squash onto baking sheet. Roast squash, turning once, for 18 minutes, or until golden.

■ Transfer squash to a blender or food processor along with ¼ cup maple syrup, evaporated milk, sugar, cornstarch, and pumpkin pie spice. Process until smooth, scraping down the sides as necessary. Add eggs, whirl just until blended; divide into ramekins. Pour enough hot water into baking dish to come 1 inch up the sides of ramekins.

■ Bake for 25 to 30 minutes, or until cakes are just set and tops are golden. Remove ramekins from water and let cool slightly or come to room temperature before serving. Top each with the cranberry topping.

■ *For topping:* In a pan over medium heat, bring cranberries, dates, maple syrup, and brown sugar to a slight boil. Stir often until cranberries start to pop. Remove from heat and stir in pecans.

Makes 8 servings.

–Margee Berry, White Salmon, Washington

NEW YEAR'S DAY SAUERKRAUT

5 slices bacon, chopped
1 medium onion, chopped
2 tablespoons (¼ stick) butter
1 medium potato, peeled and shredded
2 small Granny Smith apples, peeled, cored, and chopped
1 clove garlic, chopped
2 tablespoons brown sugar
½ teaspoon celery salt
½ teaspoon freshly ground black pepper
16 ounces sauerkraut, drained
½ to 1 cup chicken stock
fresh chopped parsley, for garnish

■ In a large pan over medium heat, cook bacon until just turning brown. Add onions and continue to cook for 3 minutes. Add butter, potatoes, and apples. Cook for 10 minutes. Add garlic, brown sugar, celery salt, and pepper. Reduce heat to medium-low. Stir in sauerkraut. Add ½ cup of chicken stock, bring to a simmer, cover, and cook for 10 minutes. Add more stock if sauerkraut gets dry. Uncover, stir well, remove from heat, and allow to cool.

Serve garnished with parsley.

Makes 6 servings.

–Donna Cianciola, Nottingham, Maryland

MOM'S CHRISTMAS CARAMEL CORN

8 cups popped popcorn
1 cup salted peanuts
¾ cup brown sugar
⅓ cup butter
3 tablespoons corn syrup
¼ teaspoon baking soda
¼ teaspoon vanilla extract

■ Preheat oven to 275°F.

■ Line a large, rimmed baking sheet with parchment paper and set aside. Grease a 13x9-inch baking dish.

■ Pour popcorn and peanuts into prepared baking dish.

■ In a saucepan over medium heat, combine brown sugar, butter, and corn syrup. Cook until mixture reaches 255°F on a candy thermometer. Remove from heat and stir in baking soda and vanilla.

■ Pour caramel mixture over popcorn and peanuts. Stir gently to coat.

■ Bake for 15 minutes, stir, then bake for 5 minutes more.

■ Remove from oven and turn out onto prepared baking sheet. Cool completely, then break into clusters and store in a container with a tight lid.

Makes about 9 cups.

–Patti Wilson, Port Hope, Ontario ■

THE TROUBLE WITH SPACE RUBBLE

Meet Bennu, our solar system's most dangerous asteroid.

BY CAROL CONNARE

In astronomical parlance, Bennu is a near-Earth object—or NEO for short. Discovered on September 11, 1999, the rare, carbonaceous asteroid first took shape 4.5 billion years ago, when our solar system was formed, and is potentially capable of holding the essence of life itself. Researchers' initial revelry gave way to grave concern when it was also discovered that Bennu could collide with Earth on September 24, 2182.

In 2004, NASA's OSIRIS-REx Asteroid Sample Return Mission to Bennu was proposed to potentially unlock the secrets of life's origins—and to avert a catastrophe. After the plan had gone through 7 years of revisions and rejections, Dante Lauretta, principal investigator of the mission and director of the Arizona Astrobiology Center at the University of Arizona, was finally charged with sending a spacecraft to the riskiest near-Earth asteroid.

"TOUCH AND GO"

After having been launched in 2016, the OSIRIS-REx spacecraft started sending back photos of Bennu 2 years later when it arrived in its orbit around the rock. It landed on the asteroid briefly

This mosaic of Bennu was created using observations made by NASA's OSIRIS-REx spacecraft, which was in close proximity to the asteroid for over 2 years.

Photo: NASA/Wikipedia

in October 2020 to retrieve material—a pogo-sticking maneuver called a "touch and go." The spacecraft spent several months mapping the surface of Bennu before leaving its orbit in May 2021 to finally deliver the sample back to Earth on September 24, 2023.

"There was a sense of achievement and wonder among the team, knowing that we had successfully collected a piece of an asteroid and brought it back to Earth," says Lauretta. "This was the culmination of years of hard work, planning, and anticipation."

WILL IT HIT US?

Bennu's orbit poses the risk of a collision with our planet in the 22nd century. The OSIRIS-REx mission studied the Yarkovsky effect (a consequence of radiation warming that can cause an object's orbit to drift) and found that multiple outcomes from Bennu's gradual inward drift are still plausible.

The orbit is well understood until the year 2135, but in September of that year, Bennu passes between Earth and the Moon. Due to gravitational interactions during this encounter, Bennu's subsequent trajectory isn't certain. In most scenarios, Bennu misses our planet and continues on its journey around the Sun. In other models, Bennu enters a trajectory to strike Earth, with the most likely impact occurring on September 24, 2182. The cumulative probability of any Earth impact through the year 2300 is small—1 in 1,750—but large enough to put Bennu at the top of the list of potentially hazardous space "neighbors."

HITTING (PAY) DIRT

The curation and study of the Bennu sample is performed in a specialized glovebox under a flow of nitrogen to keep it from being exposed to Earth's atmosphere, preserving its pristine state for scientific analysis. The sample shows evidence of high-carbon content and water, which together could mean that the building blocks of life on Earth may be found in the rock. The sample may also contain valuable

NAME THAT MISSION!

The first letters of the exploration's five primary scientific objectives make up the name OSIRIS-REx:

■ **Origins** (Where did the building blocks of life come from?)

■ **Spectral Interpretation** (How well do telescopic data inform us about asteroid properties?)

■ **Resource Identification** (Do near-Earth asteroids contain economically valuable materials?)

■ **Security** (What risk do asteroids like Bennu pose to humanity?)

■ **Regolith Explorer** (What can we learn from directly probing Bennu's surface layer of rocks and dust?)

KEEP AN EYE ON THE SKY

Check in on Earth's planetary neighbors:

■ The Planetary Defense Coordination Office (PDCO) manages NASA's ongoing mission of finding, tracking, and better understanding asteroids and comets that could pose an impact hazard to Earth. Science.nasa.gov/ planetary-defense

■ Managed for NASA at the Jet Propulsion Laboratory, the Center for Near-Earth Object Studies (CNEOS) characterizes the orbits of all known NEOs, predicts their close approaches with Earth, and makes comprehensive impact hazard assessments in support of the PDCO. JPL.nasa.gov/ asteroid-watch

■ The International Asteroid Warning Network (IAWN) is a group of organizations around the world involved in detecting, tracking, and characterizing NEOs. IAWN.net

Bennu: 1,640 feet

Empire State Building: 1,453 feet

or rare materials such as platinum-group elements, water, or other organic compounds that have scientific, industrial, or economic value.

SPACE WASTE

With a diameter of about 500 meters, Bennu has the mass of an aircraft carrier and is wider than the Empire State Building is tall. As is likely typical for other NEOs, Bennu is not solid but instead an accumulation of debris from previous impacts between larger bodies—in other words, a pile of space waste loosely held together by a weak gravitational field and perhaps a bit of "stickiness" among its rocks. Basically, then, Bennu—much like Ryugu, a similar asteroid visited by the Japanese-led Hayabusa2 mission in 2019—is a pile of space rubble in the shape of a spinning top.

A GREATER CRATER

In the unlikely event that Bennu winds up on a collision course with Earth, it would slam into our planet at a velocity of 12 kilometers (7.5 miles) per second,

Photo illustration: NASA Goddard Space Flight Center

releasing three times more energy than all nuclear weapon detonations in history. The enormity of such an event is difficult to grasp, but Earth has weathered roughly 40,000 impacts of similar magnitude over the past 4 billion years. This collision would leave a scar, in the form of a crater several kilometers wide and 500 meters (547 yards) deep.

FOLLOW THE SUN

It is much more probable that Bennu will bypass Earth. As its orbit contracts, there is a small chance of a later collision with Venus or Mercury. The most likely outcome is that Bennu will continue to spiral inward on its orbit until it at last falls into the Sun. (This is similar to what happens to an artificial satellite when its orbit decreases until it hits the top of our atmosphere.) While Bennu is not a direct threat to Earth in the next 100 years, studying it will contribute to our ability to predict and potentially mitigate the impact hazards posed by other NEOs.

SAVE THE DATE: 2029

OSIRIS-REx is now on its way to visit another near-Earth asteroid, Apophis. When it was first discovered in 2004, Apophis was also believed to be on a collision course with Earth, so it was named for the demon serpent who personifies evil and chaos in ancient Greek mythology. Apophis was determined not to pose an imminent threat once its orbit of the Sun was tracked with optical and radar telescopes.

Knowing the future trajectory of Apophis, NASA scientists have redirected OSIRIS-REx and renamed it OSIRIS-APEX (APophis EXplorer). The spacecraft will encounter Apophis during the asteroid's 2029 Earth flyby before entering orbit around it soon thereafter to provide a close-up look at the asteroid. Thrusters will be fired in an attempt to dislodge dust and small rocks on and below Apophis's surface for later study. ■

Carol Connare is the editor of *The Old Farmer's Almanac.*

NAME THAT ASTEROID!

The name "Bennu" was selected from entries by more than 8,000 students from dozens of countries around the world who entered a 2013 "Name That Asteroid!" contest. Third-grader Michael Puzio from North Carolina proposed the name in reference to the Egyptian mythological bird Bennu, which was associated with the Sun and rebirth and often depicted as a heron. To Puzio, the OSIRIS-REx spacecraft, with its extended sample retrieval arm, resembled the Egyptian deity.

●

> Canada exports two things to the
> United States: hockey players and cold fronts.
> And Canada imports two things from the
> United States: baseball players and acid rain.
>
> *–Pierre Trudeau (1919–2000), Canadian*
> *prime minister, in comments prior to the 1982 MLB*
> *All-Star Game, held in Montreal*

BASEBALL'S

THE SURPRISING CANADIAN ORIGINS OF AMERICA'S FAVORITE GAME

BY TIM GOODWIN

Baseball may be the "national pastime" of the United States, but the game has deep roots in Canadian soil. From the earliest first-hand account of a game of "base ball" played in Ontario in the 1830s to the Canadian teams and players who have been leaving their marks on the sport ever since, there is a rich history to share.

Baseball morphed from stick-and-ball games—with names like "rounders" and "stool ball"—played in mid–18th century England. Early mentions of "base ball" were found in the diary of William Bray, a prominent lawyer and antiquarian in Surrey, England, who noted having played the game with others as a teenager in the southeastern part of that country in 1755. English writer Jane Austen also referenced "base ball" in her novel *Northanger Abbey* (posthumously published in 1817, but actually written in 1798–99). Today's version can trace a distinct lineage back to the bat-and-ball games brought by settlers to North America, but its evolution after arriving in the New World is more a curveball than a heater down the middle of the plate. *(continued)*

Photo: Matt Krohn/Getty Images

TRUE NORTH

"GOOD, HONEST CALF SKIN"

When Dr. Adam Ford, an Ontario native living in Denver, Colorado, sent a letter to the editor of *Sporting Life* in 1886, he detailed "a base ball match" that he had witnessed on June 4, 1838, in Beachville, Ontario. Granted, this was almost half a century after the fact, but Ford's description depicted what is believed to have been the first-ever documented game—and it occurred in Canada.

"The game was played in a nice, smooth pasture field just [in] back of Enoch Burdick's shops," Ford wrote. "The ball was made of double and twisted woolen yarn, a little smaller than the regulation ball of today and covered with good, honest calf skin, sewed with waxed ends."

Ford went on to describe five bases—called "byes"—that were set up in a configuration resembling an irregular pentagon. The thrower (pitcher) and catcher stood 18 yards apart, and the baselines were 21 yards long, except for the stretch from home to first bye, which was only 6 yards. A fielder could record an out if he caught the batted ball after one bounce—which would count as a hit nowadays unless the batter were thrown out at first base. Games were from 5 to 9 innings long and played to a score of 18 or 21.

"The number of men on each side was a matter of agreement when the match was made," Ford continued. "I have frequently seen games played with 7 men on each side and never saw more than 12. They all fielded."

Although this was not exactly the game of baseball as we know it today, outside of a few quirks, it sounds very similar.

Photo: YouTube

OL' RELIABLE

Any guess as to the location of the oldest baseball park in operation? If you said London, Ontario, then you are correct. Labatt Memorial Park, with a seating capacity of 5,200, opened in 1877 and is currently home to the London Majors of the Intercounty Baseball League—the top-level baseball league in Canada. In 1994, Labatt Memorial Park was named a historic site by the city of London.

THE BIG SHOW

The Montreal Expos, Canada's first Major League Baseball team, debuted in 1969. The Expos called Montreal home for more than 30 years, but financial troubles forced the franchise to be relocated to Washington, D.C., for the 2005 season and be renamed the Washington Nationals.

The Toronto Blue Jays joined the American League in 1977 and remain the only MLB team in Canada, having won back-to-back World Series titles in 1992 and 1993.

LEAGUES OF THEIR OWN

The Vancouver Canadians, an affiliate of the Blue Jays, are the only remaining minor league team to call Canada home. Many Major League organizations once used Canadian locations—from Ontario to British Columbia—for their minor league teams. Canada is still home to a number of independent leagues and teams, including the aforementioned semiprofessional Intercounty Baseball League and the summer collegiate Western Canadian Baseball League, as well as three teams in the independent professional Frontier League. *(continued)*

CALLS TO THE HALLS

In the storied history of Major League Baseball (the National League was founded in 1876; the American, 1901), just two Canadians have been inducted into the National Baseball Hall of Fame, in Cooperstown, New York: Fergie Jenkins and Larry Walker.

Jenkins, a Chatham, Ontario, native, was elected in 1991 after a 19-year pitching career that included 284 wins; six consecutive seasons with at least 20 wins; 3,192 strikeouts; and the 1971 National League Cy Young Award—the first Canadian to win the pitching honor (Eric Gagne in 2003 was the second and only other).

Walker, from Maple Ridge, British Columbia, began his career with the Montreal Expos and won the 1997 National League MVP title with a .366 batting average, 49 home runs, and 130 runs batted in. Over his 17-year career, Walker amassed 2,160 hits, 383 home runs, a .313 career batting average, and seven Gold Glove awards—given annually to the best fielder in the American and National Leagues at each position.

Canada also has its own institution to recognize baseball talent. The Canadian Baseball Hall of Fame and Museum opened in Toronto in 1982—and closed in 1991. The hall was then moved to St. Marys, Ontario, where it re-opened in 1998 and is now home to more than 150 inductees "who have left their mark on Canadian baseball."

FERGIE JENKINS

LARRY WALKER

Photos, from left: Marquee Sports Network; Facebook

WHEN THE BABE "WENT YARD," CANADA-STYLE

After a professional stint that spanned some 22 years, George Herman "Babe" Ruth retired in 1935 with 714 career home runs, an MLB record that stood for almost four decades. His first professional round-tripper, though, had been slugged during his one partial minor league season with the Providence Grays in a game against the Toronto Maple Leafs in the latter's Hanlan's Point Stadium on September 5, 1914.

BREAKING THE BARRIER

Jackie Robinson broke the Major League Baseball color barrier in 1947 when he joined the Brooklyn Dodgers; his only minor league season had been played the year before with the Montreal Royals, the Dodgers' AAA affiliate. Robinson not only led the Royals to the International League championship, but also hit .349 with 113 runs scored and 40 stolen bases. He and his wife Rachel would be forever grateful for the gracious treatment afforded them by Montrealers.

HAND IN GLOVE

In 1885, Toronto native Arthur Irwin needed a way to keep playing despite two broken fingers on his left hand. So, at a time when gloves were worn only by catchers and first basemen, Irwin employed a large buckskin driving glove that he had outfitted with padding, a fastener on the back, and the third and fourth fingers sewn together to serve the purpose. Some historians credit Irwin with popularizing the use of a glove by fielders.

Although baseball may never be as popular as hockey in Canada, enthusiasm for what is sometimes termed America's "national pastime" proves to have had a long history not solely south of the border. ∎

Tim Goodwin, the Almanac's associate editor, reached his baseball playing peak at the age of 10 when he made the local all-star team.

HOW TO BE
COOL
WHEN YOU'RE
NOT

SOME LIKE IT HOT, BUT IF
THIS IS NOT YOU, TRY THESE TRICKS
WHEN THE MERCURY CLIMBS.

BY PATRICIA SULLIVAN

> *Our South is the abode of heat—and the source of what's good for it: . . . those precious and cooling summer fruit, small blue fig and great big watermelon; parties moved out to the porch and yard, where the moonlight, in patterns of leaf and flower, descends along with the possible breezes to our skin and clothes, and music sounds sweet when it is played outdoors or steals out through a window to us.*
>
> –EUDORA WELTY, AMERICAN WRITER (1909-2001)

In her essay "The Abode of Summer," novelist and short story writer Eudora Welty praises the "kaleidoscope of pleasures in the duress of heat." She extols china pitchers of tea and lemonade, ceiling fans wheeling on porches, and cotton nightgowns. Welty lived most of her life in Jackson, Mississippi, without air-conditioning; she consented to installing a window unit in her parlor only near the end of her life.

In a dangerously warming world beset by record-setting heat waves, we can look to Welty for inspiration. Scientists have since confirmed much of what she knew about coping with the heat, uncovering the data behind time-tested practices and refining methods for staying cool—without air-conditioning.

WET YOUR WHISTLE

The best thing that you can do for your body in hot weather is to drink lots and lots of water: The U.S. Army advises soldiers to "form a drinking habit," while the CDC recommends downing 1 cup of water every 15 to 20 minutes (24–32 ounces per hour) when you are working in the heat. Avoid energy drinks, which contain too much caffeine and sugar, and anything alcoholic.

Even a hot drink can cool you down (in dry heat) because it will make you sweat and you'll then feel cooler as the sweat evaporates. However, studies show that you'll drink much more if your water temperature is 72 degrees or less. If dairy-based beverages appeal to you, you'll be glad to hear that a study of

THE BEST THING THAT YOU CAN DO FOR YOUR BODY IN HOT WEATHER IS TO DRINK LOTS AND LOTS OF WATER.

drinking buttermilk showed that it hydrates as well as water. Coconut water replenishes important electrolytes—not to mention helps you to feel like you're on a tropical beach.

MINT CONDITION

Although the way in which menthol tricks our nerve endings into perceiving cold wasn't fully understood until 2022—when Duke University scientists used a cryogenic electron microscope to figure it out—we've long noted the chemically induced cool sensation that we get when we taste or touch something minty. So, let menthol activate your cold-sensing ion channels by having a peppermint iced tea or showering with mint-infused gel.

RELIEF BY THE SLICE

Why do we say "cool as a cucumber"? Because cukes are 96 percent water, a higher percentage than that of any other fruit or vegetable, according to Brigita DiMenna of Great Lakes Greenhouses, which grows more than 58.8 million cucumbers a year in Leamington, Ontario. DiMenna's 8-year-old daughter likes hers chilled with a sprinkle of salt. Besides its cooling properties, *Cucumis sativus* wins praise for its antioxidant, antidiabetic, and purifying effects on the body. Other cooling foods with high water content are melons, strawberries, and tomatoes.

FASHION FLO-WARD

We understand that in the heat it's best to wear loose-fitting cotton or linen clothing that's light in color because such shades reflect sunlight rather than absorb it, as darker hues do. However, in attempting to shed a little more light on the subject, researchers from Harvard and Tel Aviv Universities who studied the black robes of the Sinai Desert's bedouins made an interesting discovery: "The amount of heat gained by a bedouin exposed to the hot desert is the same whether he wears a black robe or a white robe. The additional heat absorbed by the black robe was lost before it reached the skin." Thus, if your clothes are sufficiently billowy, color may not matter.

HOMEMADE "AC"

In 1881, as President James Garfield lay dying from an assassin's bullet, naval engineers cooled his White House bedroom with an ingenious precursor to the air-conditioner by

IF YOUR CLOTHES ARE SUFFICIENTLY BILLOWY, COLOR MAY NOT MATTER.

Illustration: AI-generated/Adobe Firefly AI

rigging up a fan to blow air through cloths saturated with ice water.

Make your own simple Garfield AC by placing frozen water bottles in front of an electric fan. If you add 3 tablespoons of salt to each 1-liter bottle—leaving space in each bottle for expansion—before freezing it, the ice will start colder and melt faster, cooling the room a little more quickly. In dry climates, try hanging damp cloths or curtains over your open windows to cool the breeze.

A COOL BREATHE

Its efficacy is yet to be confirmed in a lab, but an ancient yogic breathing technique, *sitali pranayama,* translates as "cooling breath." Curl the sides of your tongue up and inhale slowly as if through a straw. Relax the tongue, close your mouth, exhale through the nose, and repeat. If you're among the 20 percent of people who can't roll their tongues (tongue-rolling ability is influenced by genes), just draw your breath into your mouth through closed teeth.

NAP HAPPILY

The rise of remote work is an opportunity to revive the siesta. Australian Aboriginal peoples are among those who long have napped to avoid the heat. A 2023 study found that indigenous Australians are less likely to die from the heat than non-indigenous people and posited that the *arvo* (afternoon) nap may be among the smart cultural practices that protect them.

Sleep experts say that 20-minute naps in which you don't enter deep sleep are the most refreshing. One small Swiss sleep study found that nappers got to sleep faster and slept better when swaying in a hammock. So, when the temperature rises, hop in a hammock to maximize the air flow around your body and doze!

Eudora Welty advised: "Find the shade of the biggest tree; in it your hammock is dreaming already, like a boat on the stream." ∎

Writer and editor **Patricia Sullivan** stays cool in the shade of her garden in Wilbraham, Massachusetts.

CAT CURIOSITIES EXPLAINED

Find out what's behind your tabby's blepping, kneading, and hiding—not to mention catnip craziness.

by Heidi Stonehill

PUZZLED ABOUT THE WHYS of furry feline ways? Some behaviors may seem baffling to us humans even though they make purr-fect sense to our kitty counterparts. Here we shed light on a few of the mysteries surrounding *Felis catus*.

(continued)

CAT, GOT YOUR TONGUE?

Have you ever seen a cat stick out the very tip of its tongue for a few seconds, almost like it forgot that it was there? This is called blepping.

Although it often provides quite an adorable photo op, the sight of a blep may also indicate that Kitty needs a little TLC.

Blepping can occur because . . .

■ Busy Kitty was startled or distracted while performing a task, such as grooming or eating.

■ Dental Kitty might have a gap between its front teeth where its wayward tongue creeps out at times.

■ Smart Kitty has discovered that people like the look and does it on purpose in exchange for kind words, petting, or a treat.

■ Happy and Sleepy Kitties are simply relaxed and content.

■ Flat-Face Kitty may be a member of the exotic shorthair, Himalayan, Persian, or other such breed, whose facial construction tends to promote this behavior because there is less space in their mouth for tucking in their tongue (a condition called brachycephaly).

Kitty Concerns: If a cat starts to blep frequently after not having done it before, this may mean that it is stressed or sick, perhaps experiencing mouth pain, nausea, or shortness of breath. Check for other symptoms, such as drooling, bad breath, or reduced appetite, and then contact your vet if necessary.

THE NEED TO KNEAD

Does your cat like to "make biscuits"? Although Fluffy may not be inclined to bake delectable tuna-flavor

SCENT GLANDS IN FLUFFY'S PAW PADS RELEASE PHEROMONES WHEN IT KNEADS.

Photo: SilviaJansen/Getty Images

KITTY CORNER

Have you ever seen a cat grimacing, with its mouth slightly open and its upper lip curled in toward the tops of its teeth? If so, you may be witnessing the flehmen response. This completely normal behavior is how a kitty "tastes" the air and gathers information about other felines or interesting things going on in the environment. The cat will use its tongue to direct inhaled air to the roof of its mouth, which contains a special structure called the vomeronasal, or Jacobson's, organ that allows it to detect chemical messages known as pheromones. Combined with a cat's normal olfactory sensors, this capability makes Mittens one super-"scents-itive" kitty!

treats in the kitchen, it may rhythmically open and close its paws, alternating one with another, often while pushing against a soft surface such as a blanket or your lap. (You might even hear it belt out a chorus of loud purrs at the same time.)

This two- to four-paw action is called kneading because it looks like your cat is kneading dough.

Fluffy may knead for a number of different reasons:

■ While nursing as a young kitten, it may have kneaded Momma cat to stimulate her flow of milk.

■ Kneading behavior continued as an adult may be a way of saying "We are bonded" or "I feel safe and loved!" If Fluffy is just relaxing on a blanket or cushion while kneading, and possibly sucking on the material, it may just be relaxed and fondly remembering its kittenhood.

■ Scent glands in Fluffy's paw pads (called "interdigital" glands) release pheromones when it kneads. In fact, there are nine sets of scent glands along a cat's body, including several on the head and around the tail. The scents imparted by these can aid in conveying various kitty communications, such as by serving to identify and mark ownership, define territory, strengthen friendly bonds, and reinforce familiarity. Scents left on Fluffy's favorite items (or people), for example, may tell other felines that these are already claimed.

■ A cat may also knead

KITTY CORNER

■ The *maneki-neko,* or beckoning cat, is a Japanese figurine traditionally believed to bring good luck. It typically features a raised paw that beckons.

■ British and Irish sailors believed that black or polydactyl cats (with extra toes) brought them luck.

AFTER A CATNIP SESSION, A FELINE MAY NOT BE RECEPTIVE TO THE HERB AGAIN FOR ANOTHER HOUR OR SO.

when getting ready for a nap. This may be a throwback to when its ancestors softened a patch of grass in preparation for curling up to sleep.

■ A female cat may knead when going into heat, indicating that she is ready to entertain suitors. Also, a pregnant cat may knead when she is going into labor.

Kitty Concerns: Kneading may often just mean that Fluffy is feeling content, safe, relaxed, and comfortable. However, frequent kneading can be an indicator of stress, pain, or compulsive behavior (Siamese and Birman cats are

more susceptible to this tendency). If your cat's health is in doubt, consult your vet.

CRAZY FOR CATNIP

Even an older, couch-potato cat can get frisky if it is partial to catnip. A member of the mint family, catnip *(Nepeta cataria)* is a strong herb that contains a compound called "nepetalactone." When inhaled through a feline nose, this binds to receptors that stimulate signals to the cat's brain, often resulting in behavior such as sniffing, licking, chewing, cheek-rubbing, rolling,

running, and/or meowing for up to 10 minutes or more—though it can make some cats more mellow instead. (Lions, tigers, bobcats, and certain other wild cats react to catnip, too!) After a catnip session, a feline may not be receptive to the herb again for another hour or so.

Only about two-thirds of cats have catnip receptors, which they develop by 6 months of age. So, don't be surprised if you toss a new catnip mouse to a pampered feline for the first time and its reaction is, "Yeah, so . . . ?"

Kitty Concerns: Catnip

...n sometimes make a cat a little too hyperactive or even aggressive. If such is the case, limit its playtime with this herb. Also, consuming too many fresh or dried catnip leaves may cause gastrointestinal upset in a cat. Usually, it knows when enough is enough, but with a new catnipper you might start by offering just a pinch for its culinary pleasure to see if this serves the purpose.

KITTY CORNER
Although it's often said that cats have nine lives, this purported number varies among different cultures. In certain Spanish-speaking regions, for example, the number is seven; in some Turkish and Arabic traditions, six.

FEARFUL FELINES

"Spirit cats" shy away from people and may rarely be seen in the home, especially by visitors. Often, though, they get along well with other cats, and sometimes they may even come to trust and bond with one or two people. They blossom best in quiet homes and those without young children.

Spirit cat behavior may evolve if a young kitten is not exposed to friendly humans and/or does not become used to being touched or gently handled; when an adult cat has its way of life suddenly changed, such as by being brought to a shelter or rehomed; or for any number of other reasons. Many spirit cats may never become comfortable with pats or other expressions of adoration. Given lots of time, love, and patience, however, some spirit cats may become lovebugs with their owners.

Kitty Concerns: To build their confidence and earn their trust, give these cats a safe haven for tending to their needs. Let *them* approach *you* when ready. Bonding with a spirit cat may take weeks to months (or even years!), but it can be very rewarding: Let your shy kitty know that you are with it in "spirit," and it may in turn make your spirits soar. ∎

A senior editor of *The Old Farmer's Almanac,* **Heidi Stonehill** strives to keep up with her inventive cat.

KITTY CORNER
Cats have 473 taste buds (compared to approximately 9,000 in young adult humans). They can not detect sweet tastes because they lack a receptor normally associated with this ability. If your kitty-cat loves to eat sweet treats, it likely is relishing the fat content instead.

ROLLING WITH THE TIDES

... IN A SEA OF PHILOSOPHY, MYTH, AND LORE

MUCH HAS BEEN SAID ABOUT THE NATURE
OF WATERS; BUT THE MOST WONDERFUL
CIRCUMSTANCE IS THE ALTERNATE FLOWING
AND EBBING OF THE TIDES, WHICH EXISTS,
INDEED, UNDER VARIOUS FORMS, BUT IS
CAUSED BY THE SUN AND THE MOON.

–Pliny the Elder, Roman writer (23-79 A.D.)

BY TIM GOODWIN

FOR CENTURIES, ocean tides were a mystery. Until the gravitational connections between the Moon and the Sun and their effects on Earth's oceans were proven, mankind used Earth's motion, mythical gods, underwater creatures, and magical gems to explain the tides' cyclical rise and fall.

DEEP THINKERS' DETERMINATIONS

Pytheas, a Greek geographer and astronomer (c. 350–285 B.C.), was one of the first to theorize about the Moon's effect on the ocean. He believed that high and low tides were related to "the fullness and faintness of the Moon," speculating that specific Moon phases impacted the tides. He based his conclusions on his observations of large swells during spring tides, which occur at full and new Moons when the gravitational pull on the ocean is greater.

Babylonian astronomer Seleucus of Seleucia (190–150 B.C.) noted the inconsistency of the two daily tides in the Arabian Sea: Their height changed from one tide to the next based on the position of the Moon.

Posidonius, a Greek astronomer (c. 135–51 B.C.), shared Pytheas's thinking that the Moon influenced the tides, but with a twist: He believed that heat from the Moon caused the ocean to swell. Like-minded Abū Ma'shar, a Persian-born astrologer (787–886 A.D.), theorized that the Moon's light warmed the ocean's water, causing it to expand.

Even in the late 16th century, speculation about the rise and fall of the tides continued to be wide-ranging. Johannes Kepler, a German astronomer (1571–1630), believed that gravity played a part. Italian astronomer Galileo Galilei (1564–1642) proclaimed that both the daily rotation of Earth on its axis and its annual orbit around the Sun turned the tides. He believed that different parts of Earth moved at different speeds and caused the ocean to react accordingly.

French philosopher René Descartes (1596–1650) advanced the theory that the tides were in direct relation to the Moon, but he believed that the Moon created the tides by pressure.

Roughly 100 years later, English

physicist Sir Isaac Newton (1643–1727) used his law of gravity to explain that tides were the result of the attractions between the Sun and Moon and oceans. This theory laid the groundwork for future astronomers and scientists to further solidify the connections.

SIR ISAAC NEWTON

LARGER-THAN-LIFE IDEAS

Ancient legends—found in cultures around the world—relied more on imaginative storytelling to illustrate the mystery of the tides.

According to Thai mythology, a giant sea dragon living in an undersea castle caused the tides by swishing its tail back and forth. This same dragon was said to cause tsunamis when it came to the surface and typhoons when it took flight.

Two shiny jewels—the manju and the kanju—were possessed by the sea god Ryo-Wo, aka the Dragon King, in Japanese mythology. When Ryo-Wo raised the manju, the tide would come in; when he raised the kanju, the tide would go out.

Chinese lore pitted two groups of gods against each other; the changing tides were the result of the battle that raged back and forth.

The Yolngu and the Anindilyakwa (aboriginal Australian peoples) believed that high tides filled the full Moon with water as it rose at dusk. As the tides dropped, the Moon released the water until it was high in the sky at dawn and would begin to fill again.

In Greek mythology, the sea monster Charybdis was said to create tides by sucking down the dark waters and then spitting them back up three times a day in the Strait of Messina (between Sicily and Italy), wreaking havoc on passing ships.

CHARYBDIS

THE HEART OF MAN IS VERY MUCH LIKE THE SEA: IT HAS ITS STORMS, ITS TIDES, AND, IN ITS DEPTHS, IT HAS ITS PEARLS, TOO.

–Vincent van Gogh, Dutch painter (1853–90)

According to Tlingit and First Nation legend, Raven and his people were hungry. The tide had not receded, and food at the edge of the Big Water was scarce. A spirit told him of an old woman in a cave at the end of the world who held the tide line across her lap. Raven knew that he must trick her into letting go of the tide line to help feed his people. He did just that, but soon creatures in the Big Water began to die. Raven returned to the cave and came to an agreement with the old woman, who would pull up the tide line but then every so often release it so that Raven's people could gather food.

THOR

In Scandinavian folklore, people believed that the Norse god Thor moved the tides simply by inhaling and exhaling.

HIGH AND LOW LORE

Rather than explain the tides, some observers throughout the centuries have pondered their symbolism.

The flow (rising/high) of the tide has long been thought to be a symbol of prosperity and good luck. The ebb (falling/low) was believed to foretell future failure and weakness.

ARISTOTLE

Greek philosopher Aristotle (384–322 B.C.) believed that death could occur only during the ebb of the tide, as the draining of one's spirit coincided with the water's receding. This theory continued to be held well into the Middle Ages among the people of Wales and Portugal, as well as medical practitioners in England and France.

Concurrently in the Middle Ages, many people in France's Brittany region were convinced that births occurred only with the rising tide. Some further maintained that boys were born when the tide came in, while girls entered the world as the tide went out.

The cyclical nature of the ocean's movements spawned many theories and beliefs, but one thing is certain: its relationship with the Sun and the Moon is a powerful connection to behold. ∎

Tim Goodwin, the Almanac's associate editor, has made longtime annual visits to coastal Maine that have left him both appreciative of and awash in tidal comings-and-goings. For whatever reason, he is generally known to go with the flow.

HOW WE PREDICT THE WEATHER

We derive our weather forecasts from a secret formula that was devised by the founder of this Almanac, Robert B. Thomas, in 1792. Thomas believed that weather on Earth was influenced by sunspots, which are magnetic storms on the surface of the Sun.

Over the years, we have refined and enhanced this formula with state-of-the-art technology and modern scientific calculations. We employ three scientific disciplines to make our long-range predictions: solar science, the study of sunspots and other solar activity; climatology, the study of prevailing weather patterns; and meteorology, the study of the atmosphere. We predict weather trends and events by comparing solar patterns and historical weather conditions with current solar activity.

Our forecasts emphasize temperature and precipitation deviations from averages, or normals. These are based on 30-year statistical averages prepared by government meteorological agencies and updated every 10 years. Our forecasts are based on the tabulations that span the period 1991 through 2020.

The borders of the 16 weather regions of the contiguous states **(page 205)** are based primarily on climatology and the movement of weather systems. For example, while the average weather in Richmond, Virginia, and Boston, Massachusetts, is very different (although both are in Region 2), both areas tend to be affected by the same storms and high-pressure centers and have weather deviations from normal that are similar.

We believe that nothing in the universe happens haphazardly and that there is a cause-and-effect pattern to all phenomena. However, although neither we nor any other forecasters have as yet gained sufficient insight into the mysteries of the universe to predict the weather with total accuracy, our results are almost always very close to our traditional claim of 80%.

WEATHER PHOBIAS

FEAR OF	PHOBIA
Clouds	Nephophobia
Cold	Cheimatophobia Frigophobia Psychrophobia
Dampness, moisture	Hygrophobia
Daylight, sunshine	Heliophobia Phengophobia
Extreme cold, frost, ice	Cryophobia Pagophobia
Floods	Antlophobia
Fog	Homichlophobia Nebulaphobia
Heat	Thermophobia
Hurricanes, tornadoes	Lilapsophobia
Lightning, thunder	Astraphobia Brontophobia Keraunophobia
Northern lights, southern lights	Auroraphobia
Rain	Ombrophobia Pluviophobia
Snow	Chionophobia
Thunder	Ceraunophobia Tonitrophobia
Wind	Ancraophobia Anemophobia

WEATHER

HOW ACCURATE WAS OUR FORECAST LAST WINTER?

Our overall accuracy rate in forecasting the direction of precipitation departure for a representative city in each region was 83.3%, as we were correct in 15 of the 18 regions. One of our most anomalous precipitation forecasts—for the Atlantic Corridor—worked out very well, as much of the area from Boston to Washington, D.C., recorded 125 to 150 percent of normal precipitation. The Pacific Northwest ended up a little wetter than we had forecast, while Hawaii saw a drier winter than we had anticipated.

Our warmer-than-normal temperature forecast also proved accurate along the East Coast and Gulf Coast. Elsewhere, while the polar vortex did make a visit to much of the country in mid-January, warmth dominated the weather throughout the winter from coast to coast. Overall, our accuracy rate in forecasting the direction of temperature departure for a representative city in each region was 44.4%. This makes our total accuracy rate for last winter 64%, slightly below our traditional average rate of 80%.

Our forecast for above-normal snowfall was correct in portions of the Intermountain West, the mountains of California, and an area from the central Plains into the Tennessee Valley, but getting above-normal snowfall in many other places across the Lower 48 proved difficult due to the lack of consistent cold air. Despite the abundance of precipitation in the Northeast, the constant warmth meant a lot more rain than snow, which itself led to below-normal snowfall. Our snowy forecast for southern Alaska, though, was indeed on target, as Anchorage had one of its snowiest winters on record and Juneau saw its snowiest January ever—with more than 76 inches of snow in that month alone.

The table below shows how the actual average precipitation differed from our forecast for November through March for one city in each region. On average, the actual winter precipitation differed from our forecasts by 0.44 in.

REGION/ CITY	Nov.-Mar. Monthly Precip. Change vs. Normal (in.) PREDICTED	ACTUAL	REGION/ CITY	Nov.-Mar. Monthly Precip. Change vs. Normal (in.) PREDICTED	ACTUAL
1. Burlington, VT	0.2	0.9	10. Topeka, KS	0.5	0.2
2. Boston, MA	1.3	1.3	11. San Antonio, TX	0.7	0.2
3. Harrisburg, PA	1.0	0.8	12. Denver, CO	0.34	0.2
4. Raleigh, NC	0.5	0.4	13. Salt Lake City, UT	0.3	0.4
5. Orlando, FL	0.1	0.5	14. Tucson, AZ	0.42	0.45
6. Syracuse, NY	0.4	0.5	15. Seattle, WA	–1.3	0.2
7. Pittsburgh, PA	1.2	0.1	16. San Diego, CA	0.75	0.8
8. New Orleans, LA	1.8	2.2	17. Nome, AK	–0.11	0.1
9. Duluth, MN	0.5	0.1	18. Kahului, HI	0.8	–0.6

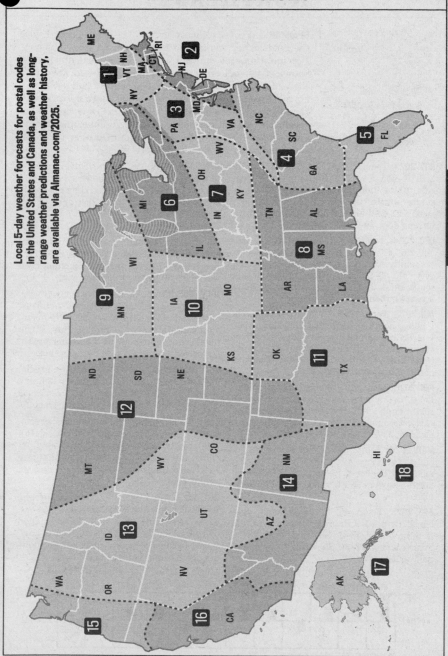

Local 5-day weather forecasts for postal codes in the United States and Canada, as well as long-range weather predictions and weather history, are available via Almanac.com/2025.

WEATHER

Caribou

Burlington Augusta

Concord

Albany

SUMMARY: Winter temperatures will be above normal, with the coldest periods in mid-December and late February. Precipitation and snowfall will be below normal, with the snowiest periods in early December, mid-February, and early March. **April** and **May** will be warmer and drier than normal. **Summer** temperatures will be above normal, with rainfall above normal in the north and below normal in the south. The hottest periods will be in mid-June, mid- to late July, and mid-August. **September** and **October** temperatures and rainfall will be below normal.

NOV. 2024: Temp. 44° (5° above avg.); precip. 2" (1" below avg.). 1–9 Showers; mild, then cold. 10–14 Rain and snow showers north, sunny south; turning mild. 15–20 Rainy, warm. 21–28 Flurries north, sunny south; turning cool. 29–30 Showers, mild.

DEC. 2024: Temp. 32° (2° above avg.); precip. 2.5" (1" below avg.). 1–5 Snow showers; chilly, then mild. 6–14 Snowy periods, very cold. 15–20 Rain and snow north, rainy south; mild. 21–31 Sunny, then snow showers; mild, then colder.

JAN. 2025: Temp. 27.5° (4° above avg. north, 1° above south); precip. 2" (1.5" below avg.). 1–14 Rain and snow north; showers, then sunny south; warm. 15–20 Snow showers, then sunny; chilly. 21–31 Snow showers north, sunny south; chilly.

FEB. 2025: Temp. 21° (2° below avg.); precip. 1.5" (1" below avg.). 1–8 Flurries north, sunny south; chilly. 9–14 Snowstorm, then sunny; chilly, then mild. 15–24 Snow showers, turning cold. 25–28 Snow showers, mild.

MAR. 2025: Temp. 36° (2° above avg.); precip. 4" (1" above avg.). 1–8 Snowy periods; mild, then cold. 9–12 Rainy, cool. 13–18 Sunny north, showers south; mild. 19–31 Showers, mild.

APR. 2025: Temp. 48° (3° above avg.); precip. 3" (avg.). 1–9 Rainy periods, warm. 10–12 Sunny, cool. 13–22 Showery, cool. 23–26 Sunny, warm. 27–30 Showers; chilly north, mild south.

MAY 2025: Temp. 58° (1° above avg.); precip. 2" (1.5" below avg.). 1–12 Showers, cool. 13–17 Sunny, warm. 18–23 Isolated showers north, sunny south; cool. 24–31 Scattered showers, mild.

JUNE 2025: Temp. 64° (2° below avg.); precip. 3" (1" below avg.). 1–14 Scattered showers, cool. 15–20 Isolated t-storms, hot. 21–27 Scattered t-storms, then sunny; cool, then warm. 28–30 Isolated showers, cool.

JULY 2025: Temp. 72° (2° above avg.); precip. 6" (2" above avg.). 1–4 Scattered t-storms; cool north, warm south. 5–8 Showers north, sunny south; warm. 9–16 T-storms; warm north, hot south. 17–21 T-storms north, sunny south; warm. 22–31 T-storms, hot.

AUG. 2025: Temp. 69° (2° above avg.); precip. 3.2" (avg. north, 1.5" below south). 1–13 Rainy periods, cool. 14–18 Sunny, hot. 19–26 Scattered t-storms, warm. 27–31 Sunny, warm.

SEPT. 2025: Temp. 59° (2° below avg.); precip. 3.5" (1" above avg. north, 1" below south). 1–5 Isolated showers, cool. 6–19 Rainy periods, cool. 20–24 Showers north, sunny south; cool, then warm. 25–30 Showers, then sunny; cool.

OCT. 2025: Temp. 46° (3° below avg.); precip. 2.5" (1.5" below avg.). 1–6 Scattered showers, cool. 7–10 Sunny, cool. 11–17 Showers, then sunny; mild, then cold. 18–19 Rainy, cool. 20–28 Isolated showers, chilly. 29–31 Showers north, sunny south; cool.

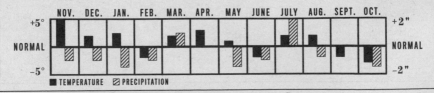

WEATHER

ATLANTIC CORRIDOR

SUMMARY: Winter temperatures will be above normal, with precipitation slightly below normal. Snowfall will be below normal in the north and above normal in the south. The coldest periods will be in mid-December, early and late January, and late February, with the most snow arriving in late December and late February. **April** and **May** will be warmer and wetter than normal. **Summer** will be warmer and drier than normal, with the hottest periods in mid-June and from mid-July into early August. Watch for a tropical storm in the far south in mid-July. **September** and **October** will be cooler than normal in the north and warmer than normal in the south, with below-normal precipitation.

NOV. 2024: Temp. 52° (5° above avg.); precip. 2.5" (0.5" below avg.). 1–7 Rainy periods, mild. 8–17 Sunny; cool, then warm. 18–19 Rain, warm. 20–28 Sunny; mild, then cool. 29–30 Showers, mild.

DEC. 2024: Temp. 43° (2° above avg.); precip. 1.5" (2" below avg.). 1–6 Sunny, then rain; warm. 7–10 Showers north, sunny south; mild. 11–16 Snow north, showers south, then sunny; cold, then mild. 17–18 Rain, warm. 19–27 Sunny; warm, then chilly. 28–31 Snow, heavy south; cold.

JAN. 2025: Temp. 37° (avg.); precip. 2" (1.5" below avg.). 1–3 Flurries north, sunny south; cold. 4–16 Rainy periods, mild. 17–22 Sunny, chilly. 23–31 Sunny north, snow showers south; cold.

FEB. 2025: Temp. 33° (2° below avg.); precip. 1.5" (1.5" below avg.). 1–3 Sunny north, snow south; chilly. 4–10 Sunny, then snow north, rain south; chilly. 11–18 Sunny, then flurries north, showers south; milder. 19–24 Flurries north, snowy south; very cold. 25–28 Showers, mild.

MAR. 2025: Temp. 45.5° (avg. north, 3° above south); precip. 6.5" (2.5" above avg.). 1–7 Showers, then rain to snow; mild, then colder. 8–9 Sunny, mild. 10–18 Rainy periods, mild. 19–20 Sunny, mild. 21–28 Rainy periods, cool. 29–31 Sunny, warm.

APR. 2025: Temp. 56.5° (2° above avg. north, 5° above south); precip. 4.5" (1" above avg.). 1–9 Rain, heavy at times; warm. 10–16 Sunny,

warm. 17–25 Rainy periods; cool north, mild south. 26–30 Sunny, then showers; warm.

MAY 2025: Temp. 66° (3° above avg.); precip. 3" (0.5" below avg.). 1–7 Showers, warm. 8–10 Sunny, mild. 11–18 T-storms, then sunny; warm. 19–22 Sunny, mild. 23–31 Scattered t-storms; warm, then cool.

JUNE 2025: Temp. 71° (1° below avg.); precip. 2" (2" below avg.). 1–13 Scattered t-storms, cool. 14–21 Sunny; cool, then hot. 22–30 Scattered t-storms, cool.

JULY 2025: Temp. 80° (3° above avg.); precip. 4" (avg.). 1–6 Isolated t-storms, mild. 7–14 Scattered t-storms, hot. 15–17 T-storms north, tropical storm threat south; cooler. 18–22 Sunny, then heavy rain north; warm. 23–31 Isolated t-storms, hot.

AUG. 2025: Temp. 79° (4° above avg.); precip. 2" (2" below avg.). 1–8 Scattered t-storms; warm north, hot south. 9–15 Showers, cooler. 16–26 Sunny; warm, then hot. 27–31 Sunny; warm north, hot south.

SEPT. 2025: Temp. 70.5° (avg. north, 3° above south); precip. 3" (1" below avg.). 1–13 Isolated t-storms, warm. 14–16 Sunny, hot. 17–27 Scattered showers; cool, then warm. 28–30 Sunny, cooler.

OCT. 2025: Temp. 55° (2° below avg.); precip. 4" (avg.). 1–8 Scattered showers, then sunny; turning cool. 9–12 Rainy, warm. 13–18 Sunny, then heavy rain; cool. 19–31 Scattered showers, cool.

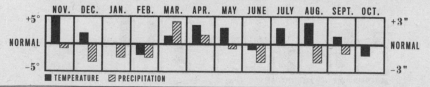

	NOV.	DEC.	JAN.	FEB.	MAR.	APR.	MAY	JUNE	JULY	AUG.	SEPT.	OCT.	
+5°													+3"
NORMAL													NORMAL
−5°													−3"

■ TEMPERATURE ◨ PRECIPITATION

APPALACHIANS

Elmira
Scranton
Harrisburg
Frederick
Roanoke
Asheville

WEATHER

SUMMARY: Winter will be slightly warmer than normal, with below-normal precipitation. Snowfall will be near normal in the north and above normal in the south. The coldest periods will occur from mid-January into early February and in late February, while the most snow will arrive in late December, late February, and early March. **April** and **May** will be warmer than normal, with above-normal rainfall. **Summer** will be warmer than normal, with below-normal rainfall. The hottest periods will be in early to mid-July and from late July into early August. **September** and **October** will be cooler and drier than normal.

NOV. 2024: Temp. 46° (2° above avg.); precip. 3" (1" below avg. north, 1" above south). 1–5 Rainy, mild. 6–15 Showers north, sunny south; cool, then warm. 16–19 Rainy, warm. 20–28 Sunny, cool. 29–30 Showers, mild.

DEC. 2024: Temp. 40° (2° above avg.); precip. 2" (1.5" below avg.). 1–10 Scattered showers; warm, then chilly. 11–14 Snow showers, cold. 15–20 Rainy, warm. 21–27 Sunny north, showers south; mild. 28–31 Snowy periods, heavy south; chilly.

JAN. 2025: Temp. 30° (1° below avg.); precip. 2.5" (1" below avg.). 1–11 Rainy, warm. 12–16 Sunny north, showers south; mild. 17–22 Flurries north, sunny south; cold. 23–24 Snowy, cold. 25–29 Sunny, cold. 30–31 Snowy, cold.

FEB. 2025: Temp. 27° (3° below avg.); precip. 1" (1.5" below avg.). 1–9 Snow showers north, snow then sunny south; cold. 10–12 Sunny, cold. 13–18 Flurries north, showers south; warm. 19–27 Flurries north, sunny then heavy snow south; very cold. 28 Showers, mild.

MAR. 2025: Temp. 41° (1° above avg.); precip. 5" (2" above avg.). 1–3 Showers, mild. 4–7 Snowy north, flurries south; cold. 8–18 Rain and snow north, rain south; mild. 19–23 Sunny, then rain; mild. 24–31 Isolated showers, warm.

APR. 2025: Temp. 52° (1° above avg.); precip. 4.5" (avg. north, 1" above south). 1–7 Rain, heavy at times; warm. 8–17 Isolated show-

ers north, sunny south; cold, then warm. 18–30 Showers, turning sunny south; cold, then warm.

MAY 2025: Temp. 62° (1° above avg.); precip. 4.5" (0.5" above avg.). 1–6 Rainy north, sunny south; chilly, then warm. 7–18 Rainy periods, mild. 19–24 Sunny, then showers; mild. 25–31 Showers north, sunny south; mild.

JUNE 2025: Temp. 67° (2° below avg.); precip. 3.5" (1" below avg.). 1–8 Isolated showers north, sunny south; cool. 9–13 Scattered t-storms, cool. 14–20 Sunny, t-storms north; warm north, cool south. 21–30 Scattered t-storms, warm.

JULY 2025: Temp. 77° (3° above avg.); precip. 2.5" (1" below avg.). 1–16 Scattered t-storms, hot. 17–19 Sunny, cooler. 20–22 T-storms, warm. 23–27 Sunny, hot. 28–31 T-storms, hot.

AUG. 2025: Temp. 75° (3° above avg.); precip. 1.5" (2" below avg.). 1–11 T-storms; hot then turning cool. 12–17 Sunny north, t-storms south; warm. 18–22 Sunny, hot north; t-storms, cool south. 23–31 Isolated t-storms north, sunny south; warm.

SEPT. 2025: Temp. 65° (avg.); precip. 3" (2" below avg. north, avg. south). 1–9 Sunny, warm. 10–19 T-storms, isolated north; warm. 20–30 Sunny north, t-storms south; cool.

OCT. 2025: Temp. 53° (1° below avg.); precip. 2.5" (1" below avg.). 1–9 Showers north, sunny south; cool. 10–24 Scattered showers, cool. 25–31 Sunny; cool, then turning warm.

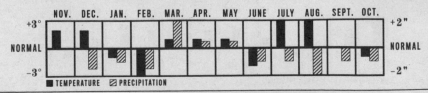

| | NOV. | DEC. | JAN. | FEB. | MAR. | APR. | MAY | JUNE | JULY | AUG. | SEPT. | OCT. |

+3° / NORMAL / –3° +2" / NORMAL / –2"

■ TEMPERATURE ▨ PRECIPITATION

SOUTHEAST

SUMMARY: Winter will be cooler than normal in the east and warmer than normal in the west, with the coldest periods in late November, late January, and late February. Precipitation and snowfall will be above normal, with the best chances for snow in late January and early and late February. **April** and **May** will be warmer than normal, with average rainfall. **Summer** will be warmer than normal, with the hottest periods in early and late June, early and late July, and early to mid-August. Rainfall will be below normal. Watch for a tropical storm in mid-July. **September** and **October** will be warmer than normal, with below-normal precipitation.

NOV. 2024: Temp. 57° (1° above avg.); precip. 3.8" (1.5" above avg. east, avg. west). 1–2 Sunny, warm. 3–6 Rainy, turning cool. 7–14 Sunny; cool, then turning warm. 15–19 Showers, warm. 20–28 Sunny, chilly. 29–30 Rainy, mild.

DEC. 2024: Temp. 49.5° (1° below avg. east, 2° above west); precip. 2" (2" below avg.). 1–9 Sunny, then showers; warm. 10–14 Sunny, cool. 15–18 Showers, warm. 19–31 Isolated showers, cool.

JAN. 2025: Temp. 46° (1° below avg.); precip. 5" (0.5" above avg.). 1–11 Rainy periods; cool, then warm. 12–14 Sunny, mild. 15–22 Rainy, mild. 23–31 Snow showers north, isolated showers south; very cold.

FEB. 2025: Temp. 45° (2° below avg.); precip. 3.5" (1.5" above avg. east, 0.5" above west). 1–3 Snowy north, rain south; cold. 4–9 Sunny, then showers; cold, then mild. 10–18 Showers north, sunny south; turning warm. 19–26 Snow, heavy north; very cold. 27–28 Showers, warmer.

MAR. 2025: Temp. 57° (1° above avg.); precip. 7.5" (3" above avg.). 1–6 Rain, heavy at times; warm, then chilly. 7–9 Sunny, cool. 10–23 Rainy periods, mild. 24–31 Isolated showers, warm.

APR. 2025: Temp. 65.5° (avg. east, 3° above west); precip. 2.5" (1" below avg.). 1–7 Rainy periods, warm. 8–11 Sunny, cool. 12–18 Sunny,

warm. 19–30 Isolated t-storms; cool, then warm.

MAY 2025: Temp. 74.5° (1° above avg. east, 4° above west); precip. 5" (1" above avg.). 1–3 Showers, cool. 4–6 Sunny, warmer. 7–18 T-storms, mild. 19–29 Sunny; mild, then hot. 30–31 T-storms, warm.

JUNE 2025: Temp. 80° (1° above avg.); precip. 3.5" (2" below avg. east, avg. west). 1–9 Sunny, turning hot. 10–19 T-storms, heavy west; cool. 20–30 Isolated t-storms, turning hot.

JULY 2025: Temp. 86° (3° above avg.); precip. 2.5" (2" below avg.). 1–10 Isolated t-storms, hot. 11–14 Sunny, warm. 15–19 Showers, tropical storm threat south; cool. 20–31 Isolated t-storms, turning hot.

AUG. 2025: Temp. 84° (2° above avg. east, 4° above west); precip. 2.5" (2" below avg.). 1–15 Isolated t-storms, hot. 16–23 Sunny, cooler. 24–31 Scattered t-storms, warm.

SEPT. 2025: Temp. 78° (3° above avg.); precip. 4" (1" below avg.). 1–6 Sunny west, isolated showers east; warm. 7–19 Scattered t-storms, hot. 20–25 T-storms, cooler. 26–30 Showers north, sunny south; cool.

OCT. 2025: Temp. 64° (1° below avg.); precip. 1.5" (1.5" below avg.). 1–7 Sunny; warm, then turning cool. 8–10 Sunny, warmer. 11–23 Showers; warm, then cooler. 24–26 Sunny, mild. 27–31 Showers, then sunny; cool.

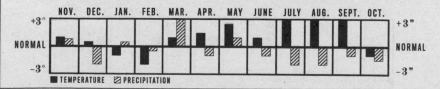

WEATHER

FLORIDA

SUMMARY: Winter will be cooler than usual and coldest in the late parts of the months of November, December, January, and February. Rainfall will be above normal. **April** and **May** will be warmer and wetter than usual in the north and cooler and drier in the south. **Summer** will be warmer and drier than normal in the north and cooler and wetter in the south. Temps will be hottest in early July and mid-August. Watch for tropical storms in mid-July and late August. **September** and **October** will be warmer and drier than normal.

NOV. 2024: Temp. 68° (1° below avg.); precip. 3.5" (1" above avg.). 1–6 Showers, warm. 7–14 Sunny, cool. 15–20 Showers, warm. 21–26 Showers, then sunny; turning cold. 27–30 Rainy, milder.

DEC. 2024: Temp. 64° (1° below avg.); precip. 1.5" (1" below avg.). 1–7 Sunny, warm. 8–9 Showers, cooler. 10–14 Sunny, cool. 15–23 Isolated showers, warm. 24–31 Sunny, cold.

JAN. 2025: Temp. 61° (avg.); precip. 2.0" (0.5" below avg.). 1–4 Sunny, warm. 5–7 Showers north, sunny south; warm. 8–15 Sunny, warm. 16–24 Rainy, then sunny; cool. 25–31 Isolated showers, very cold.

FEB. 2025: Temp. 59° (3° below avg.); precip. 2.5" (1" below avg. north, 1" above south). 1–12 Rainy periods, cool. 13–16 Sunny, milder. 17–23 Sunny, then heavy rain; turning cold. 24–28 Sunny; very cold, then turning warmer.

MAR. 2025: Temp. 71° (3° above avg.); precip. 4.5" (2" above avg.). 1–6 Heavy rain north, showers south; warm. 7–19 Isolated showers, then sunny; warm. 20–31 Rainy periods, warm.

APR. 2025: Temp. 73.5° (2° above avg. north, 1° below south); precip. 2.5" (avg.). 1–11 Showers, then sunny; turning cool. 12–13 Rainy, cool. 14–18 Sunny; warm north, mild south. 19–24 Showers north, sunny south; cool. 25–30 Isolated showers north, sunny south; warm.

MAY 2025: Temp. 79.5° (3° above avg. north, avg. south); precip. 4.2" (1.5" above avg.

north, 2" below south). 1–2 Rain, heavy at times; cooler. 3–7 Sunny; warm north, cool south. 8–19 Rain north, showers south; warm. 20–31 Sunny; cool, then warm.

JUNE 2025: Temp. 83° (avg.); precip. 4" (3" below avg.). 1–6 Isolated t-storms, cool. 7–10 Sunny, warm. 11–19 Scattered t-storms, warm. 20–30 Sunny north, isolated t-storms south; warm.

JULY 2025: Temp. 85° (2° above avg. north, avg. south); precip. 7" (2" below avg. north, 2" above south). 1–10 Sunny north, t-storms south; hot. 11–15 Scattered t-storms, warm. 16–18 Tropical storm threat. 19–31 Sunny north, t-storms south; warm.

AUG. 2025: Temp. 83° (1° above avg. north, 1° below south); precip. 8" (2" below avg. north, 2" above south). 1–8 Scattered t-storms, warm. 9–12 Sunny north, t-storms south; warm. 13–17 T-storms; hot north, warm south. 18–24 Isolated t-storms, warm. 25–26 Tropical storm threat. 27–31 T-storms, warm.

SEPT. 2025: Temp. 82° (1° above avg.); precip. 4.5" (3" below avg.). 1–11 Scattered t-storms, warm. 12–21 Sunny, then t-storms; hot. 22–30 Sunny north, scattered t-storms south; turning cooler.

OCT. 2025: Temp. 76° (avg.); precip. 2.5" (2" below avg.). 1–8 Sunny north, t-storms south; mild. 9–14 Sunny, warm. 15–20 Isolated showers, turning cooler. 21–24 Showers north, sunny south; warm. 25–31 Sunny; warm then cooler.

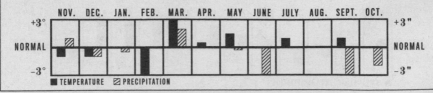

LOWER LAKES

SUMMARY: Winter will be warmer than normal in the east and colder than normal in the west, with the coldest periods in early and late November, in early December, from late January into early February, and from late February into early March. Precipitation and snowfall will be below normal, with the most snow in late December, from late January into early February, and from late February into early March. **April** and **May** will be warmer than normal, with rainfall above normal in the east and below normal in the west. **Summer** will be warmer than normal, on average, with the hottest periods in early to mid-July. Rainfall will be above normal. **September** and **October** will be cooler and drier than normal.

WEATHER

NOV. 2024: Temp. 42° (1° above avg.); precip. 2.5" (avg.). 1–8 Periods of rain, then snow showers; cold. 9–11 Sunny, milder. 12–19 Rainy periods, warm. 20–28 Snow showers, heavy lake snows east, then sunny; cold. 29–30 Showers, milder.

DEC. 2024: Temp. 38° (4° above avg.); precip. 3.5" (0.5" above avg.). 1–5 Sunny, then showers; warm. 6–13 Snowy east, sunny west; cold. 14–25 Rainy periods, then sunny; warm. 26–31 Snowy, chilly.

JAN. 2025: Temp. 27° (1° below avg.); precip. 1.5" (1.5" below avg.). 1–10 Showers, mild. 11–14 Sunny, chilly. 15–22 Lake snows east, snow showers west; cold. 23–31 Snowy, very cold.

FEB. 2025: Temp. 24° (4° below avg.); precip. 1.5" (0.5" below avg.). 1–10 Snowy periods, very cold. 11–16 Showers, warmer. 17–25 Snowy periods, turning very cold. 26–28 Snow showers, chilly.

MAR. 2025: Temp. 37.5° (1° above avg. east, 2° below west); precip. 4" (1" above avg.). 1–7 Snowy periods, very cold. 8–17 Rain and snow east, rainy west; mild. 18–20 Sunny; mild east, cold west. 21–31 Showers, mild.

APR. 2025: Temp. 49.5° (2° above avg. east, 1° below west); precip. 3" (1" below avg.). 1–9 Rain, mild east; rain and snow, cold west. 10–15 Sunny, warmer. 16–23 Showers; mild east, cold west. 24–30 Sunny, warmer.

MAY 2025: Temp. 60° (1° above avg.); precip.

5" (2" above avg. east, avg. west). 1–7 Sunny, then showers; mild east, cool west. 8–12 Scattered t-storms, cool. 13–20 Sunny, warm. 21–31 T-storms, locally heavy rain; warm, then cool.

JUNE 2025: Temp. 65° (2° below avg.); precip. 2.5" (1.5" below avg.). 1–13 Isolated t-storms, cool. 14–20 Sunny, warm. 21–30 Showers, cool east; isolated t-storms, turning warm west.

JULY 2025: Temp. 75° (3° above avg.); precip. 4.5" (2" above avg. east, avg. west). 1–15 Scattered t-storms, turning hot. 16–19 Sunny, cooler. 20–31 Scattered t-storms, warm.

AUG. 2025: Temp. 74° (4° above avg.); precip. 5.5" (avg. east, 3" above west). 1–14 Scattered t-storms, some heavy west; cool, turning warm. 15–26 Sunny, then t-storms; warm. 27–31 Sunny east, t-storms west; warm.

SEPT. 2025: Temp. 62° (avg.); precip. 2.5" (0.5" below avg.). 1–10 Showers; warm, then cool. 11–19 Rainy east, isolated showers west; very warm, turning cool. 20–24 Sunny, turning warm. 25–30 Showers east, sunny west; cool.

OCT. 2025: Temp. 51° (2° below avg.); precip. 2" (1" below avg.). 1–6 Scattered showers; warm, then cooler. 7–11 Showers, warm. 12–16 Sunny, cool. 17–21 Heavy rain east, showers west; chilly. 22–25 Sunny, cool. 26–31 Isolated showers, turning warm.

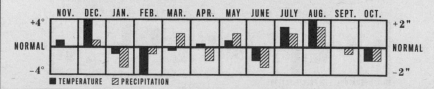

OHIO VALLEY

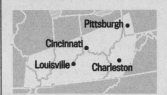

SUMMARY: Winter will be colder than normal, with the coldest periods in late November, from late January into early February, and in late February. Precipitation will be below normal, with snowfall below normal in the far east and above normal elsewhere. The snowiest periods will be in late December, from late January into early February, in late February, and in mid-March. **April** and **May** temperatures and precipitation will be above normal in the east and below normal in the west. **Summer** will be warmer than normal, with rainfall above average. The hottest periods will be in mid-June, early to mid-July, and early August. **September** and **October** will be cooler and drier than normal.

NOV. 2024: Temp. 46.5° (3° above avg. east, avg. west); precip. 3.5" (avg. east, 1" above west). 1–3 Rainy, mild. 4–9 Rain and snow showers east, sunny west; chilly. 10–21 Sunny, then rainy; warm. 22–26 Snow showers, cold. 27–30 Isolated showers, mild.

DEC. 2024: Temp. 41° (2° above avg.); precip. 2.5" (0.5" below avg.). 1–6 Sunny, then showers; turning warm. 7–13 Showers then sunny east, sunny west; cold, then warmer. 14–19 Rainy, warm. 20–26 Sunny, chilly. 27–31 Snowy, colder.

JAN. 2025: Temp. 32° (2° below avg.); precip. 2.5" (1" below avg.). 1–7 Sunny, then rainy; turning warm. 8–15 Isolated showers, mild. 16–21 Rain and snow showers, then sunny; turning cold. 22–31 Periods of snow, very cold.

FEB. 2025: Temp. 31° (4° below avg.); precip. 2.7" (avg. east, 1.5" below west). 1–10 Snowy periods, very cold. 11–17 Scattered showers, mild. 18–26 Snowy periods, very cold. 27–28 Showers, milder.

MAR. 2025: Temp. 44° (1° below avg.); precip. 4.5" (1" above avg. east, 1" below west). 1–7 Rain to snow east, showers west; turning cold. 8–14 Sunny, then snow east, rainy west; chilly. 15–28 Rainy periods, mild. 29–31 Sunny, mild.

APR. 2025: Temp. 54.5° (avg. east, 3° below west); precip. 3" (avg. east, 2" below west). 1–9 Showers, turning chilly. 10–18 Sunny; cool, then turning warm. 19–23 Showers, chilly. 24–30 Sunny, mild.

MAY 2025: Temp. 66° (2° above avg.); precip. 5" (1" above avg.). 1–3 Sunny, cool. 4–6 Heavy rain north, showers south; warm. 7–18 Some t-storms; cool, then turning warm. 19–22 Sunny, mild. 23–31 Some t-storms, warm.

JUNE 2025: Temp. 70° (2° below avg.); precip. 3.5" (1" below avg.). 1–6 T-storms, then sunny; cool. 7–15 Showers, then sunny; cool. 16–22 Isolated t-storms, turning hot. 23–30 Sunny north, t-storms south; warm.

JULY 2025: Temp. 79° (3° above avg.); precip. 5.5" (3" above avg. east, avg. west). 1–3 Heavy rain east, sunny west; warm. 4–13 Sunny, hot. 14–19 T-storms, then sunny; cooler. 20–31 Scattered t-storms, warm.

AUG. 2025: Temp. 78° (4° above avg.); precip. 4" (2" above avg. east, 1" below west). 1–6 Isolated t-storms, then sunny; hot. 7–11 Scattered showers, warm. 12–16 Showers east, sunny west; warm. 17–28 Sunny, then showery; warm. 29–31 Sunny, warm.

SEPT. 2025: Temp. 68° (1° above avg. east, 1° below west); precip. 2" (1" below avg.). 1–6 Showers, then sunny; warm. 7–13 Showers, then sunny; warm east, cool west. 14–18 Showers, warm. 19–24 Sunny, cool. 25–30 Showers, then sunny; cool.

OCT. 2025: Temp. 56° (2° below avg.); precip. 2" (0.5" below avg.). 1–7 Isolated showers, then sunny; warm then cooler. 8–11 Scattered showers, warm. 12–16 Sunny, cool. 17–26 Rainy, then sunny; cool. 27–31 Isolated showers, warmer.

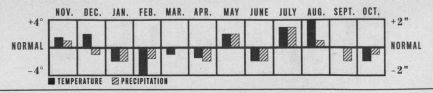

DEEP SOUTH

SUMMARY: Winter will be warmer than normal, with the coldest periods in early and late November, from late January into early February, and in late February. Precipitation will be above normal, with the greatest threats of snow in the north from late January into early February and in late February. **April** and **May** will be warmer and wetter than normal. **Summer** will be hotter and drier than normal, with the hottest periods from late June into early July and from late July through late August. Watch for a tropical storm in mid-July and a hurricane in late August. **September** and **October** will be warmer than normal, with rainfall below normal in the north and near normal in the south.

NOV. 2024: Temp. 53° (1° below avg.); precip. 5" (0.5" above avg.). 1–4 Rainy periods, turning cold. 5–13 Sunny; cold, then turning warm. 14–21 Rainy periods, mild. 22–26 Sunny, cold. 27–30 Showers, mild.

DEC. 2024: Temp. 52° (2° above avg.); precip. 4.5" (1" above avg. north, 2" below south). 1–7 Sunny, then rainy; warm. 8–12 Sunny, colder. 13–18 Periods of rain, mild. 19–31 Showers north, sunny south; mild.

JAN. 2025: Temp. 49° (2° above avg.); precip. 4.5" (1" below avg.). 1–15 Showers, heavy south; warm. 16–21 Sunny north, isolated showers south; mild. 22–31 Snowy periods north, showers south; cold.

FEB. 2025: Temp. 46° (2° below avg.); precip. 4.5" (2" below avg. north, avg. south). 1–7 Snow north, rain south, then sunny; cold. 8–16 Isolated showers; cold, then turning warm. 17–22 Sunny, mild. 23–25 Snow north, showers south; cold. 26–28 Showers, warmer.

MAR. 2025: Temp. 58° (avg. north, 2° above south); precip. 9" (3" above avg.). 1–6 Scattered showers, turning cool. 7–13 Sunny, then heavy rain; mild. 14–27 Rainy periods, heavy south; mild. 28–31 Sunny north, showers south; warm.

APR. 2025: Temp. 64° (avg.); precip. 6.8" (avg. north, 2.5" above south). 1–7 Rain, heavy south; turning cold. 8–17 Sunny, warmer. 18–26 Scattered t-storms; cool, then turning warm. 27–30 Sunny, warm.

MAY 2025: Temp. 74° (2° above avg.); precip. 6" (1" above avg.). 1–4 Sunny, cool. 5–15 Scattered t-storms, some heavy; warm. 16–23 Isolated t-storms, warm. 24–31 Sunny, warm.

JUNE 2025: Temp. 81° (2° above avg.); precip. 4" (1.5" below avg.). 1–9 Sunny; warm, hot south. 10–17 Scattered t-storms, warm. 18–26 Isolated t-storms north, sunny south; hot. 27–30 Sunny, hot.

JULY 2025: Temp. 85° (3° above avg.); precip. 4" (1" below avg.). 1–7 Sunny, hot. 8–12 Sunny north, t-storms south; warm. 13–16 T-storms north, tropical storm threat south; warm. 17–21 T-storms, hot. 22–26 Sunny, hot. 27–31 Isolated t-storms, hot.

AUG. 2025: Temp. 85° (4° above avg.); precip. 3" (2" below avg.). 1–7 Sunny north, isolated t-storms south; hot. 8–28 Isolated t-storms, hot. 29–31 Sunny north, hurricane threat south; hot.

SEPT. 2025: Temp. 79° (2° above avg.); precip. 3.5" (1" below avg.). 1–8 Sunny, hot. 9–15 Isolated t-storms, warm. 16–24 Heavy t-storms; cool north, warm south. 25–30 Sunny, cool.

OCT. 2025: Temp. 65° (1° below avg.); precip. 2.5" (2" below avg. north, 1" above south). 1–9 Sunny; warm, then cooler. 10–15 T-storms, then sunny; turning warm. 16–22 Scattered showers, heavy south; cool. 23–31 Sunny, warm.

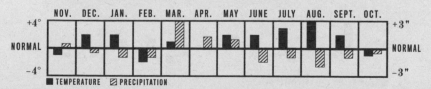

WEATHER

UPPER MIDWEST

International Falls
Marquette
Duluth
Minneapolis
Green Bay

SUMMARY: Winter will be not so cold as usual and coldest in early November, early and late January, late February, and early March. Precipitation and snowfall will be below normal, although snowiest in late November, late December, mid- and late January, early February, and mid-March. **April** and **May** will be warmer than usual and drier in the north, wetter in the south. **Summer** will be warmer and drier than usual and hottest in mid-June, early and late July, and mid- to late August. **September** and **October** will be cooler and drier than normal.

NOV. 2024: Temp. 30° (avg.); precip. 2" (0.5" above avg. east, 0.5" below west). 1–8 Snow showers, frigid. 9–14 Sunny, mild. 15–20 Some rain and snow, mainly E; chilly. 21–26 Sun, some snow E; cold. 27–30 Sunny, mild.

DEC. 2024: Temp. 25° (6° above avg.); precip. 0.5" (0.5" below avg.). 1–4 Snowy north, sunny south; cold, then milder. 5–14 Flurries, then sunny; mild. 15–18 Rain and snow showers E, sunny W; mild. 19–25 Sunny, warm. 26–31 Sunny, then snowy; turning cold.

JAN. 2025: Temp. 12° (1° below avg.); precip. 1" (avg.). 1–2 Sunny, frigid. 3–7 Flurries, cold. 8–10 Rainy east, a shower west; mild. 11–15 Snow east, sunny west; cold. 16–18 Snow showers, chilly. 19–25 Flurries, turning frigid. 26–31 Periods of snow, not as cold.

FEB. 2025: Temp. 9° (3° below avg.); precip. 0.5" (0.5" below avg.). 1–5 Snowy periods mainly north and west, chilly. 6–11 Snow east, sunny west; very cold. 12–16 Flurries, cold. 17–28 A little snow at times, bitterly cold.

MAR. 2025: Temp. 27° (1° below avg.); precip. 0.5" (1" below avg.). 1–7 Flurries E, snow W; very cold. 8–14 Sunny, cold. 15–20 Snow east, flurries and sun west; chilly. 21–26 Sunny, mild. 27–31 Sunny, then snow west; mild.

APR. 2025: Temp. 44° (3° above avg.); precip. 1" (1" below avg.). 1–9 A mix of rain and snow, chilly east; sunny, mild west. 10–15 Sunny, turning very warm. 16–19 A bit of rain and snow east, sunny west; chilly. 20–30 Drizzle east, sunny west; very warm, then chilly.

MAY 2025: Temp. 57° (3° above avg.); precip. 4" (1" below avg. north, 2" above south). 1–11 A couple of showers at times; chilly, then mild. 12–21 Sunny; very warm east, hot west. 22–26 Rain, turning cool. 27–31 Rain southeast, isolated showers northwest; cool.

JUNE 2025: Temp. 64° (2° below avg. east, 2° above west); precip. 2.5" (2" below avg.). 1–4 Drizzle; cool east, mild west. 5–11 Sunny, lonely t-storm; cool east, mild west. 12–18 Isolated rains, then sunny; very warm. 19–23 T-storms, cooler. 24–30 Sunny, warm.

JULY 2025: Temp. 71° (2° above avg.); precip. 3.5" (1" above avg. east, 1" below west). 1–3 Sunny, warm. 4–6 T-storms, warm. 7–13 Rain, cool. 14–16 Sunny, cool. 17–23 Showers E, sunny W; cool, then warm. 24–27 Sunny, then t-storms; warm. 28–31 Sunny, warm.

AUG. 2025: Temp. 68° (2° above avg.); precip. 4" (0.5" above avg.). 1–7 Sunny, then isolated t-storms; turning cool. 8–14 Rain and t-storms, some heavy; warm, then cool. 15–21 Intervals of t-storms; warm, then cool. 22–25 Sunny east, t-storms west; warm. 26–31 T-storms east, sunny west; seasonal temps.

SEPT. 2025: Temp. 57° (2° below avg.); precip. 3.5" (0.5" above avg.). 1–4 Rainy periods E, sunny W; seasonal temps. 5–7 Rain, cool. 8–19 Drizzle E, intervals of t-storms W; cool. 20–27 Rain and snow N, sunny S; warm, then cold. 28–30 Sunny, turning warm.

OCT. 2025: Temp. 45° (2° below avg.); precip. 1.5" (1" below avg.). 1–6 Rain and snow N, sunny S; warm, then chilly. 7–13 Rainy; turning warm, then chilly. 14–22 Rain and snow, then sunny; cold. 23–27 Sunny, warm. 28–31 Sunny, then rain and snow; turning chilly.

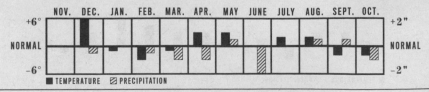

| | NOV. | DEC. | JAN. | FEB. | MAR. | APR. | MAY | JUNE | JULY | AUG. | SEPT. | OCT. |

+6°
NORMAL
-6°

+2"
NORMAL
-2"

■ TEMPERATURE ⊟ PRECIPITATION

HEARTLAND

SUMMARY: Winter will be warmer than normal, with precipitation and snowfall below normal. The coldest and snowiest periods will occur in late January and early and late February. **April** and **May** will be warm, with precipitation below normal. **Summer** will feature waves of heat with temperatures well above normal and precipitation below normal. The hottest period will be from late June into early July. Fall will start with above-normal temperatures in **September** before turning near-normal in **October.** Precipitation will be below normal, on average.

NOV. 2024: Temp. 44° (1° above avg.); precip. 1" (1" below avg.). 1–5 Rain E, drizzle W; cold. 6–12 Sunny, turning very warm. 13–15 Heavy rain, embedded t-storms; not as warm. 16–18 Sunny, chill in the air. 19–22 A bit of rain and snow, cold. 23–30 Sunny, turning warm.

DEC. 2024: Temp. 40° (5° above avg.); precip. 0.5" (1" below avg.). 1–2 Sunny, chilly. 3–5 Rain and snow, turning warm. 6–13 Sunny, turning cold. 14–18 Rain, heavy east; very warm. 19–24 Rain east, sunny west; warm. 25–31 Flurries, then rain and snow; not as warm.

JAN. 2025: Temp. 32° (2° above avg.); precip. 1" (1" above avg. east, 1" below west). 1–3 Flurries N, sunny S; chilly. 4–7 Sunny, turning warm. 8–14 Intervals of rain and snow, warm. 15–19 Sunny, warm. 20–24 Snowy, cold. 25–31 Snowy; cold, turning warm.

FEB. 2025: Temp. 29° (3° below avg.); precip. 1.5" (0.5" below avg.). 1–5 Some snow, then sun; turning cold. 6–11 Snow showers, then sun; very cold. 12–21 Flurries, cool. 22–28 Sun, then some snow; turning bitterly cold.

MAR. 2025: Temp. 45° (1° above avg.); precip. 3.5" (1" above avg.). 1–5 Sunny, then snow west, rain east; cool. 6–12 Rain east, sunny west; warmer. 13–17 Sunny north, a bit of rain south; turning cold. 18–23 Sunny, then t-storms; mild. 24–31 Rainy intervals, warm.

APR. 2025: Temp. 56° (3° above avg. north, 1° below south); precip. 1" (2.5" below avg.). 1–7 Rain, a bit of snow east; turning very cold. 8–15 A few t-storms, then sunny; turning warm. 16–24 Sunny, isolated t-storms east; warm. 25–30 Sunny, very warm.

MAY 2025: Temp. 66° (2° above avg.); precip. 4" (1" below avg.). 1–8 Sunny, then isolated t-storms; warm. 9–11 T-storms, some heavy; cooler. 12–18 A few t-storms east, sunny west; warm. 19–31 T-storms, some heavy north, isolated south; very warm.

JUNE 2025: Temp. 76° (1° above avg. north, 4° above south); precip. 4" (1" below avg.). 1–7 Sun, some storms N; mild. 8–16 T-storms, cool. 17–24 Sun, then t-storms E; warm. 25–30 A few t-storms N, sunny S; turning hot.

JULY 2025: Temp. 83° (5° above avg.); precip. 2.5" (1.5" below avg.). 1–6 Sunny, a few t-storms east; hot. 7–10 Sunny east, a few t-storms west; not as hot. 11–17 A few t-storms west, then east; very warm. 18–23 T-storms, then sunny. 24–31 Intervals of t-storms, warm.

AUG. 2025: Temp. 79° (4° above avg.); precip. 4" (2" above avg. north, 1" below south). 1–5 Sunny, then isolated t-storms; warm. 6–10 Rain and t-storms, warm. 11–22 Sunny, warm. 23–29 Intervals of t-storms, warm. 30–31 Sunny, very warm.

SEPT. 2025: Temp. 69° (1° above avg.); precip. 1.5" (2" below avg.). 1–4 Sunny east, a little rain west; turning cool. 5–10 A few t-storms, turning chilly. 11–17 Sunny, then some drizzle; warmer. 18–26 Sunny, intervals of cold. 27–30 Sunny, turning warm.

OCT. 2025: Temp. 57° (avg.); precip. 3" (avg.). 1–6 Sunny; very warm, turning chilly. 7–10 Rain and t-storms, warm. 11–15 Sunny, warm. 16–21 Intervals of rain and t-storms, some heavy; warm, then cold. 22–31 Sunny; cold, then very warm.

WEATHER

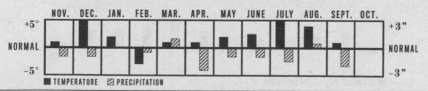

TEXAS–OKLAHOMA

Oklahoma City
Dallas
San Antonio
Houston

SUMMARY: Winter will be warmer than normal, with the coldest periods in late January and early and late February. Precipitation will be below normal, with the best chances for snow in early and late February. **April** and **May** will be warm, with below-normal rainfall. **Summer** will be very warm and dry, with the hottest periods in late June, early and late July, and early to mid-August. Watch for a tropical storm in mid-July, as well as a hurricane in early August and tropical storm in late August. **September** and **October** will be warmer and drier than normal.

NOV. 2024: Temp. 56° (avg. north, 2° below south); precip. 2" (1" below avg.). 1–9 Isolated showers, then sunny; chilly. 10–14 Rainy periods, warm. 15–17 Sunny north, showers south; cool. 18–24 Sunny; warm, then chilly. 25–30 Sunny, warm north; a few showers, cool south.

DEC. 2024: Temp. 54° (3° above avg.); precip. 3" (0.5" above avg.). 1–4 Sunny, warm. 5–8 Rainy periods, turning cold. 9–13 Sunny; cold, then warm. 14–22 Rainy periods, mild. 23–26 Sunny, then a few showers; chilly. 27–31 Sunny, turning mild.

JAN. 2025: Temp. 52° (1° above avg. north, 3° above south); precip. 2.5" (1" above avg. east, 1" below west). 1–9 Sunny, warm. 10–15 Rainy periods, some heavy east; turning chilly. 16–20 Sunny, chilly. 21–31 Showers, cold.

FEB. 2025: Temp. 49° (2° below avg.); precip. 0.5" (1" below avg.). 1–5 Periods of rain and snow north, rainy periods south; very cold. 6–11 A few showers; mild, then turning very cold. 12–21 Sunny, mild. 22–28 A few showers, mixed with snow north; frigid.

MAR. 2025: Temp. 61.5° (avg. north, 3° above south); precip. 1.5" (1" below avg.). 1–5 Sunny, then a few showers; cool north, warm south. 6–8 Sunny, warm. 9–12 Sunny, cool north; scattered showers, warm south. 13–22 Rainy periods, cool. 23–31 Sunny, turning warm.

APR. 2025: Temp. 66° (1° below avg.); precip. 2.5" (0.5" below avg.). 1–4 Sunny, cool. 5–7 Rainy periods, chilly. 8–16 Sunny, mild. 17–19 T-storms, turning cool. 20–22 Sunny, cool. 23–30 Scattered t-storms, turning warm.

MAY 2025: Temp. 77° (3° above avg.); precip. 5" (avg.). 1–5 Isolated t-storms, turning warm. 6–14 T-storms, some heavy; cool. 15–19 Sunny, turning hot. 20–22 T-storms OK, sunny TX; warm. 23–31 Sunny, hot.

JUNE 2025: Temp. 85° (5° above avg.); precip. 1" (2.5" below avg.). 1–9 A few t-storms, then sunny; turning hot. 10–15 Isolated t-storms, warm. 16–30 Sunny, hot.

JULY 2025: Temp. 86° (4° above avg.); precip. 1.5" (1.5" below avg.). 1–12 Sunny, hot. 13–16 Tropical storm threat. 17–21 Sunny, then a few t-storms; warm. 22–31 Sunny, then scattered t-storms; hot.

AUG. 2025: Temp. 85.5° (5° above avg. north, 2° above south); precip. 3" (2" below avg. north, 3" above south). 1–4 Hurricane threat. 5–14 Sunny, then isolated t-storms; hot. 15–17 Sunny, hot. 18–28 Isolated t-storms, warm. 29–31 Tropical storm threat.

SEPT. 2025: Temp. 80° (3° above avg.); precip. 2.5" (1" below avg.). 1–2 Showers, warm. 3–17 Sunny, then a few t-storms; hot. 18–22 Rainy; cool north, warm south. 23–30 Sunny, cool.

OCT. 2025: Temp. 68° (avg.); precip. 1" (2.5" below avg.). 1–6 Sunny, warm. 7–17 Sunny, then rainy periods; turning cool. 18–22 Showers, chilly. 23–31 Sunny, turning warm.

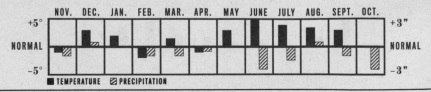

WEATHER

HIGH PLAINS

SUMMARY: Winter will be warmer than normal in the north and colder than normal in the south, with the coldest periods in early and mid-January and early and late February. Precipitation will be near normal, with near- to above-normal snowfall. The snowiest periods will be in mid-November, mid- and late January, and late February. **April** and **May** will be warm, with conditions drier than normal in the north but wetter in the south. **Summer** will be warm, with the hottest periods in mid- to late June, early and late July, and late August. Rainfall will be below normal. **September** and **October** will be warm, with the north wetter than normal and the south drier.

WEATHER

NOV. 2024: Temp. 38° (3° above avg. north, 1° below south); precip. 0.5" (0.5" below avg.). 1–4 Periods of rain and snow, cold. 5–11 Sunny, turning warm. 12–14 Snowy periods, cold. 15–21 Sunny, then flurries; chilly. 22–27 Sunny, turning warm. 28–30 A few snow showers, warm.

DEC. 2024: Temp. 33° (6° above avg. north, 2° above south); precip. 0.4" (0.1" below avg.). 1–2 Sunny, warm. 3–6 A few snow showers, turning chilly. 7–9 Flurries; warm, turning cold. 10–14 Sunny, warm. 15–26 Sunny, warm N; snowy periods, turning cold S. 27–31 Snowy periods N, sunny S; turning cold.

JAN. 2025: Temp. 27° (1° below avg.); precip. 0.7" (0.2" above avg.). 1–4 Snowy, very cold. 5–9 Sunny, warm. 10–17 Snowy, then sunny; cold, then warm. 18–24 Flurries, frigid. 25–31 Sunny, then snowy periods; warm, then cold.

FEB. 2025: Temp. 23° (4° below avg.); precip. 0.7" (0.2" above avg.). 1–3 Flurries; mild north, cold south. 4–10 Snow showers, cold. 11–20 Rain and snow showers, then sunny; mild. 21–28 Snowy periods, quite cold.

MAR. 2025: Temp. 39.25° (1.25° above avg. north, .75° below south); precip. 1.3" (0.3" above avg.). 1–8 A few snow showers, cold. 9–14 Rain and snow showers; mild north, cold south. 15–27 Periods of rain and snow, chilly. 28–31 Showers, chilly.

APR. 2025: Temp. 52° (6° above avg. north, avg. south); precip. 1.2" (1" below avg. north, 0.5" above south). 1–5 Rain and snow showers, chilly. 6–15 Sunny, turning very warm. 16–26 Sunny, warm north; rainy periods, cool south. 27–30 Showers, warm.

MAY 2025: Temp. 60° (2° above avg.); precip. 2.5" (avg.). 1–3 A few showers, cool. 4–16 Sunny north, a few t-storms south; turning warm. 17–25 Scattered t-storms, turning cool. 26–31 A few showers, cool north; sunny, turning hot south.

JUNE 2025: Temp. 71° (3° above avg.); precip. 2" (0.5" below avg.). 1–8 Sun, then t-storms; warm. 9–14 Some t-storms, warm. 15–23 Sun; warm N, hot S. 24–30 T-storms, hot.

JULY 2025: Temp. 76° (3° above avg.); precip. 1" (1" below avg.). 1–6 Sunny north, scattered t-storms south; hot. 7–14 A few t-storms, warm. 15–18 Scattered t-storms, hot. 19–31 Sunny, then isolated t-storms; very warm.

AUG. 2025: Temp. 71.5° (1° below avg. north, 2° above south); precip. 2" (1" above avg. north, 1" below south). 1–9 T-storms; cool north, warm south. 10–14 A few t-storms north, sunny south; turning cooler. 15–25 Isolated t-storms; warm north, hot south. 26–31 Sunny, hot.

SEPT. 2025: Temp. 65° (2° above avg.); precip. 0.9" (0.6" below avg.). 1–3 Showers, cool. 4–13 Isolated showers; cool, turning warm. 14–18 A few showers, cool. 19–30 Sunny, very warm.

OCT. 2025: Temp. 51° (2° above avg.); precip. 1" (1" above avg. north, 1" below south). 1–7 Sunny, warm. 8–10 Rainy north, sunny south; chilly. 11–13 Sunny, warm. 14–20 A few rain and snow showers, chilly. 21–31 Sunny, warm.

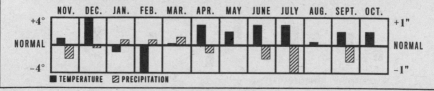

INTERMOUNTAIN

SUMMARY: Winter will be warmer than normal, with the coldest periods in late November and late January. Precipitation and snowfall will be above normal, with the snowiest periods in mid-November, early and late January, and mid-March. **April** and **May** will be warm with above-normal precipitation. **Summer** will be cooler than normal in the north and hotter than normal across the south, with the hottest periods in mid-July and early August. Rainfall will be below normal. **September** and **October** will be warm with below-normal rainfall.

NOV. 2024: Temp. 39° (2° below avg.); precip. 0.5" (0.5" below avg.). 1–8 Sunny, cold. 9–12 Periods of rain and snow, chilly. 13–19 Sunny, then snowy periods; cold. 20–23 Sunny, very cold. 24–30 Snow showers north, sunny south; turning mild.

DEC. 2024: Temp. 35° (4° above avg. north, avg. south); precip. 1" (0.5" below avg.). 1–8 A few rain and snow showers, mild north; sunny, chilly south. 9–18 Periods of rain and snow, mild. 19–23 Sunny, cold. 24–31 A few rain and snow showers; mild, then turning cold.

JAN. 2025: Temp. 34.5° (2° below avg. north, 3° above south); precip. 2.5" (1" above avg.). 1–6 Snowy, cold north; rain and snow, mild south. 7–11 Rain and snow showers, mild. 12–18 Sunny; cold north, mild south. 19–22 Flurries, frigid north; snowstorm, cold south. 23–31 Rain and snow showers, turning mild.

FEB. 2025: Temp. 38° (3° above avg.); precip. 3.5" (1.5" above avg.). 1–6 Sunny, cold. 7–16 Periods of rain and snow, mild. 17–21 Sunny, then a few showers; warm. 22–28 Periods of rain and snow, turning chilly.

MAR. 2025: Temp. 42° (2° below avg.); precip. 2" (0.5" above avg.). 1–11 Periods of rain and snow, chilly. 12–20 Snowy periods, cold. 21–26 Sunny north, periods of snow and rain south; cold. 27–31 A few rain and snow showers north, sunny south; chilly.

APR. 2025: Temp. 54° (4° above avg.); precip. 0.5" (0.5" below avg.). 1–3 Showers north, sunny south; chilly. 4–13 Sunny, turning

warm. 14–20 A few showers, then sunny; mild. 21–30 Scattered showers, warm.

MAY 2025: Temp. 55° (3° below avg.); precip. 2" (1" above avg.). 1–9 Showers, cool. 10–13 Sunny, warm. 14–22 Rainy periods north, isolated showers south; chilly. 23–31 Showers, then sunny; cool.

JUNE 2025: Temp. 67° (2° below avg. north, 3° above south); precip. 0.5" (0.2" below avg. north, 0.2" above south). 1–2 Sunny, warm. 3–8 A few showers north, sunny south; cool. 9–12 Sunny, warm. 13–19 Isolated showers, cool north; sunny, warm south. 20–30 Sunny, cool north; scattered t-storms, warm south.

JULY 2025: Temp. 76° (2° above avg.); precip. 0.2" (0.3" below avg.). 1–6 Some t-storms, warm. 7–16 Sunny, turning hot. 17–26 Sunny N, some t-storms S; hot. 27–31 Sunny, warm.

AUG. 2025: Temp. 72° (3° below avg. north, 1° above south); precip. 1" (avg.). 1–9 Sunny north, isolated t-storms south; hot. 10–15 A few t-storms north, sunny south; cool. 16–18 Sunny north, a few t-storms south; warm. 19–31 Isolated t-storms; cool north, warm south.

SEPT. 2025: Temp. 67° (3° above avg.); precip. 0.5" (0.5" below avg.). 1–6 Rainy, turning cool. 7–10 Sunny, warm. 11–14 A few showers, cool. 15–30 Sunny, turning very warm.

OCT. 2025: Temp. 52° (avg.); precip. 1" (avg.). 1–9 Sunny, then rainy periods; turning cool. 10–20 Sunny, then showers; chilly. 21–24 Sunny, chilly. 25–31 A few showers north, sunny south; turning very warm.

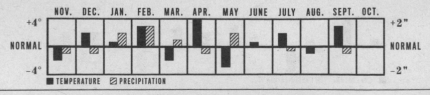

DESERT SOUTHWEST

SUMMARY: Winter will be colder than normal, with above-normal precipitation. The coldest periods will be in mid-November, mid- to late December, and early February. Snowfall will be above normal in most areas that normally receive snow, with the snowiest periods in mid-December and early February. **April** and **May**

will be cooler than normal, with above-normal rainfall. **Summer** will be hotter and drier than normal, with the hottest periods in mid-June and mid- to late July. **September** and **October** will be cooler than normal in the east and warmer than normal in the west. Rainfall will be below normal.

NOV. 2024: Temp. 54° (3° below avg.); precip. 0.2" (0.3" below avg.). 1–11 A few showers, then sunny; cool. 12–17 Isolated showers, cold. 18–30 Sunny; chilly, turning warm.

DEC. 2024: Temp. 48° (avg.); precip. 0.2" (0.3" below avg.). 1–4 Sunny, mild. 5–7 A few showers east, sunny west; cool. 8–12 Sunny, mild. 13–20 A few rain and snow showers, cold. 21–31 Sunny; cold, then mild.

JAN. 2025: Temp. 52° (3° above avg.); precip. 1" (0.5" above avg.). 1–13 Rainy periods, warm. 14–20 A few showers east, sunny west; chilly. 21–31 Showers, then sunny; warm.

FEB. 2025: Temp. 53° (1° above avg.); precip. 1" (0.5" above avg.). 1–4 Snowy periods east, sunny west; cold. 5–13 Rainy periods, mild. 14–23 Sunny, turning warm. 24–28 Sunny, mild east; a few showers, chilly west.

MAR. 2025: Temp. 57° (3° below avg.); precip. 0.5" (avg.). 1–10 Rainy periods, then sunny; cool. 11–16 Isolated showers, then sunny; cool. 17–24 A few rain and snow showers east, isolated showers west; chilly. 25–31 Sunny, turning warmer.

APR. 2025: Temp. 64.5° (3° below avg. east, avg. west); precip. 0.6" (0.1" above avg.). 1–3 Sunny, warm. 4–6 Showers east, sunny west; chilly. 7–13 Sunny; mild east, turning hot west. 14–20 Isolated showers, cool. 21–24 Sunny east, showers west; cool. 25–30 A few showers east, sunny west; turning warm.

MAY 2025: Temp. 70° (4° below avg.); precip. 0.6" (0.1" above avg.). 1–9 Isolated showers, cool. 10–16 Sunny, warm. 17–26 Isolated showers, then sunny; cool. 27–31 Sunny, turning hot.

JUNE 2025: Temp. 87.5° (4° above avg. east, 1° above west); precip. 0.3" (0.4" below avg. east, 0.1" above west). 1–10 Sunny; hot east, warm west. 11–21 Isolated t-storms, hot. 22–30 Sunny, hot east; isolated t-storms, warm west.

JULY 2025: Temp. 92° (4° above avg.); precip. 0.5" (1" below avg.). 1–12 Isolated t-storms, then sunny; warm. 13–18 A few t-storms, hot. 19–25 Sunny, hot. 26–31 Isolated t-storms, hot.

AUG. 2025: Temp. 87° (avg.); precip. 1.5" (0.5" above avg. east, 0.5" below west). 1–7 Scattered t-storms, cool east; sunny, hot west. 8–13 Sunny, warm. 14–27 Isolated t-storms east, sunny west; warm. 28–31 A few t-storms; warm east, hot west.

SEPT. 2025: Temp. 82° (2° above avg.); precip. 0.7" (avg. east, 0.5" below west). 1–7 Isolated t-storms, warm. 8–16 Sunny, hot. 17–20 A few t-storms; cool east, hot west. 21–30 Sunny, very warm.

OCT. 2025: Temp. 67.5° (3° below avg. east, avg. west); precip. 0.5" (0.5" below avg.). 1–6 Sunny, warm. 7–12 Isolated showers, chilly. 13–21 Sunny, then a few showers; cool. 22–31 Sunny; cool, turning warm.

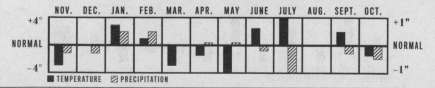

WEATHER

PACIFIC NORTHWEST

SUMMARY: Winter will be colder than normal in the north and warmer in the south, with the coldest periods in early and late January and early March. Precipitation and snowfall will be above average in the north and below average in the south. The snowiest periods will be in late December, early January, and early February. **April** and **May** will be warmer and drier than normal. **Summer** will be cooler and drier than usual. The hottest period will be in mid-July. **September** and **October** will be warmer and wetter than normal.

NOV. 2024: Temp. 49° (1° below avg. north, 3° above south); precip. 5.5" (0.5" below avg.). 1–11 Sunny, then rainy; chilly north, warm south. 12–19 Sunny, then periods of rain; chilly. 20–23 Sunny; chilly north, warm south. 24–30 Rainy periods, some heavy; quite mild.

DEC. 2024: Temp. 47° (3° above avg.); precip. 7.3" (2.5" above avg. north, 2" below south). 1–9 Rainy periods, mild north; sunny, chilly south. 10–14 Rainy, mild. 15–22 Showers, then sunny; mild. 23–29 Rainy periods, mild. 30–31 Snowy north, showers south; cold.

JAN. 2025: Temp. 41° (3° below avg.); precip. 6.5" (0.5" above avg.). 1–6 Snowy periods north, rainy south; quite cold. 7–10 Rainy, mild. 11–18 Sunny, then a few showers; cold. 19–25 Sunny, then periods of rain and snow; frigid. 26–31 Showers, mild.

FEB. 2025: Temp. 46° (avg. north, 4° above south); precip. 3.5" (1" below avg.). 1–6 Sunny; cold north, mild south. 7–13 Periods of rain and snow, cold north; rainy periods, warm south. 14–21 Rainy periods, quite mild. 22–28 Sunny, then showers; mild.

MAR. 2025: Temp. 45° (2° below avg.); precip. 4" (1" below avg. north, 1" above south). 1–14 Occasional rain, cold. 15–19 Scattered showers, cool. 20–31 Sunny, then showers; chilly.

APR. 2025: Temp. 54° (3° above avg.); precip. 3" (0.5" below avg.). 1–3 Showers, cool. 4–6 Sunny, warm. 7–10 Showers, then sunny; warm. 11–16 Rainy periods, then sunny; turning cool. 17–30 Isolated show-

ers; warm, then cool.

MAY 2025: Temp. 54° (2° below avg.); precip. 1.5" (0.5" below avg.). 1–6 Showers, then sunny; cool. 7–13 Isolated showers, then sunny; mild. 14–20 Rainy periods, chilly. 21–31 Sunny, then showers; cool.

JUNE 2025: Temp. 60° (2° below avg. north, avg. south); precip. 1.5" (avg.). 1–7 A few showers, warm. 8–14 Isolated showers, then sunny; warm. 15–19 Rainy periods; cool north, warm south. 20–30 Sunny, then a few showers; cool.

JULY 2025: Temp. 65° (1° below avg.); precip. 0.2" (0.3" below avg.). 1–9 Isolated t-storms, cool. 10–15 Sunny, turning hot. 16–31 Sunny; warm, turning cool.

AUG. 2025: Temp. 65° (2° below avg.); precip. 1" (0.2" above avg. north, 0.2" below south). 1–9 Sunny; warm, turning cool. 10–18 Isolated t-storms, then sunny; cool. 19–26 Showers north, sunny south; cool. 27–31 Isolated t-storms, warm.

SEPT. 2025: Temp. 63° (1° above avg.); precip. 1" (0.5" below avg.). 1–4 Sunny, warm. 5–7 Showers, cool. 8–10 Sunny, warm. 11–14 Rainy periods, cool. 15–23 Sunny, then isolated showers; turning warm. 24–30 Sunny, very warm.

OCT. 2025: Temp. 57° (2° above avg.); precip. 4.5" (1" above avg.). 1–6 Sunny, then showers; turning cool. 7–16 Sunny, cool. 17–20 Showers, cool. 21–31 Sunny, then rainy periods; quite warm.

PACIFIC SOUTHWEST

SUMMARY: Winter will be warmer and wetter than normal, with above-normal mountain snows. The coldest temperatures will occur in mid-December and mid- to late January. The stormiest periods will be in mid-December, early January, and mid- and late February. **April** and **May** will be cooler than normal. Rainfall will be below normal in the north and above normal in the south. **Summer** will be hotter and drier than normal, with the hottest periods in late June and mid- to late July. **September** and **October** will be warmer in the north and drier than normal.

San Francisco · Fresno · Los Angeles · San Diego

NOV. 2024: Temp. 61° (2° above avg.); precip. 0.5" (0.5" below avg.). 1–8 Sunny, turning warm. 9–14 Showers, then sunny; turning chilly. 15–19 A few showers, warm. 20–30 Sunny, warm.

DEC. 2024: Temp. 57° (2° above avg.); precip. 1" (1" below avg.). 1–11 Sunny; cool, turning warm. 12–21 Rainy periods, then sunny; turning chilly. 22–31 Rainy periods north, sunny south; warm.

JAN. 2025: Temp. 59° (3° above avg.); precip. 4" (1" above avg.). 1–11 Rainy periods, some heavy; warm. 12–19 Sunny, chilly. 20–23 Sunny, cool north; rainy, warm south. 24–31 Sunny, warm.

FEB. 2025: Temp. 56° (3° above avg.); precip. 5" (2" above avg.). 1–5 Sunny, mild. 6–15 Rainy periods, warm. 16–23 Showers north, sunny south; warm. 24–28 Rainy periods, turning chilly.

MAR. 2025: Temp. 57° (1° below avg.); precip. 1.5" (1" below avg.). 1–4 A few showers, warm. 5–10 Isolated showers, chilly north; sunny, warm south. 11–19 Scattered showers, chilly. 20–31 Sunny, then showers; cool.

APR. 2025: Temp. 62° (1° above avg.); precip. 0.7" (1" below avg. north, 0.5" above south). 1–12 Sunny, warm. 13–20 A few showers, chilly. 21–25 Sunny, warm north; showers, cool south. 26–30 Sunny, warm.

MAY 2025: Temp. 61° (3° below avg.); precip. 0.2" (0.3" below avg.). 1–6 A few showers, chilly. 7–14 Sunny; cool coast, warm inland. 15–31 Sunny inland; A.M. sprinkles, P.M. sun coast; cool.

JUNE 2025: Temp. 69° (avg.); precip. 0" (0.1" below avg.). 1–8 Sunny, cool. 9–19 Sunny inland; A.M. clouds, P.M. sun coast; cool. 20–23 Sunny, hot. 24–30 Isolated sprinkles; cool north, warm south.

JULY 2025: Temp. 74° (2° above avg.); precip. 0" (avg.). 1–14 Sunny, turning hot inland; A.M. clouds, P.M. sun, warm coast. 15–26 Sunny, hot. 27–31 Sunny, warm.

AUG. 2025: Temp. 71° (1° below avg.); precip. 0" (avg.). 1–6 Isolated sprinkles, cool north; sunny, hot south. 7–24 Sunny inland; A.M. clouds, P.M. sun coast; warm. 25–31 Sunny; hot inland, cool coast.

SEPT. 2025: Temp. 72.5° (3° above avg. north, 2° below south); precip. 0.1" (avg.). 1–9 Sunny, cool. 10–21 Isolated showers; warm, turning cool. 22–30 Sunny; hot north, cool south.

OCT. 2025: Temp. 67° (1° above avg.); precip. 0.2" (0.3" below avg.). 1–7 Isolated showers north, sunny south; cool. 8–17 Sunny, turning warm. 18–21 A few showers, cool. 22–31 Sunny, warm.

+3° / NORMAL / -3°   NOV. DEC. JAN. FEB. MAR. APR. MAY JUNE JULY AUG. SEPT. OCT.   +2" / NORMAL / -2"

■ TEMPERATURE ▨ PRECIPITATION

WEATHER

SUMMARY: Winter will be not so cold as usual and coldest in December and early January. Precipitation will be below normal. The south and west will see more snow than usual and the north and east, less. It will be snowiest in late November, December, and early and late January. **April** and **May** will be warmer than normal, with above-normal precipitation. **Summer** will be cooler than normal, with precipitation below normal in the north and above normal in the south. The hottest periods will be in mid-June, mid- and late July, and early August. **September** and **October** will be milder than normal, with precipitation below normal in the north and near normal in the south.

KEY: north (N), central (C), south (S), panhandle (P), elsewhere (EW).

NOV. 2024: Temp. 11° N, 48° S (7° above avg.); precip. 0.3" N, 6.5" S (0.1" below avg. N, 1.5" above S). 1–11 Periods of rain and snow, warm. 12–17 Clear, cold N; rain and snow, warm S. 18–27 Snowy periods N+C, rain and snow showers S; mild. 28–30 Snow showers, cold.

DEC. 2024: Temp. –9° N, 28° S (4° below avg.); precip. 0.2" N, 5" S (avg.). 1–4 Snowstorm P, flurries EW; very cold. 5–8 Flurries, mild N; clear, cold EW. 9–11 Snowstorm P, snowy EW; very cold. 12–18 Sunny, frigid N; snowy, cold EW. 19–23 Snowy, cold. 24–27 Snowstorm P, clear EW; bitter cold. 28–31 Sunny N, snowy C+S, clear P; turning milder.

JAN. 2025: Temp. –11° N, 34° S (1° below avg. N, 5° above S); precip. 0.2" N, 3.5" S (avg. N, 1.5" below S). 1–5 Clear, frigid. 6–11 Clear, very cold N; snowy, then mild S. 12–16 Snow showers, quite mild. 17–23 Flurries; cold P, mild EW. 24–27 Snowstorm C+S; clear, cold EW. 28–31 Rainy P, snow showers EW; mild.

FEB. 2025: Temp. 0° N, 42° S (11° above avg.); precip. 0.2" N, 3" S (avg. N, 1" below S). 1–11 Clear, very mild. 12–20 Snowy; cold, then mild. 21–28 Clear, then snow and rain; mild.

MAR. 2025: Temp. –6° N, 39° S (5° above avg.); precip. 0.3" N, 4.8" S (0.2" below avg.). 1–8 Snow showers; mild, then cold. 9–16 Flurries N+C, rain and snow showers S; mild. 17–25 Clear, cold N; rain and snow showers, mild C+S. 26–31 A few showers P, clear EW; mild.

APR. 2025: Temp. 8° N, 45° S (4° above avg.); precip. 0.4" N, 2.7" S (0.3" below avg.). 1–5 Sunny, cold N; rain and snow showers, mild EW. 6–14 Rainy periods P, flurries EW; turning mild. 15–21 Rain and snow showers, warm. 22–30 Sunny, cold N; showers, warm EW.

MAY 2025: Temp. 24.5° N, 49° EW (2° above avg.); precip. 1.1" N, 3.5" S (0.5" above avg.). 1–10 Flurries, chilly N; a few showers, mild EW. 11–20 Flurries N, isolated showers EW; turning warm. 21–24 Sunny N, rainy EW; warm. 25–31 Rainy periods N+C, sunny EW; mild.

JUNE 2025: Temp. 35° N, 54.5° EW (1° below avg.); precip. 1.7" N, 4.5" S (1° above avg.). 1–8 A few showers, cool. 9–19 Sunny, warm N; scattered showers, turning warm EW. 20–30 A few rainy periods, cool.

JULY 2025: Temp. 41.5° N, 56.5° EW (1° below avg.); precip. 0.7" N, 6" S (0.5" below avg. N, 1.5" above S). 1–9 Sunny, then showers; cool. 10–16 Rainy, cool P; sunny, warm EW. 17–26 Rainy periods S, a few showers EW; cool. 27–31 A few showers, turning warm.

AUG. 2025: Temp. 39.5° N, 55° EW (2° below avg.); precip. 0.5" N, 4.8" S (0.7" below avg.). 1–5 A few showers, quite warm. 6–13 Sunny N, isolated showers C, rainy periods S; cool. 14–20 Showers N, isolated showers EW; cool. 21–31 Showers, turning chilly.

SEPT. 2025: Temp. 36.5° N, 57° EW (2° above avg.); precip. 0.6" N, 9.5" S (0.5" below avg. N, 2" above S). 1–2 Rain P, sun EW; cool. 3–11 Showers, mild. 12–18 Sun N+C, rain S; cool. 19–30 Snowy, cold N; rainy periods, mild S.

OCT. 2025: Temp. 25° N, 48° S (5° above avg.); precip. 0.3" N, 5" S (0.2" below avg. N, 2" below S). 1–4 Periods of rain and snow, cold. 5–14 Flurries N, rainy periods C+S; turning warm. 15–20 Sunny N+C, a few showers S; warm. 21–31 Scattered rain and snow showers, mild.

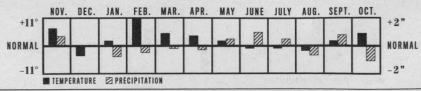

HAWAII

SUMMARY: Winter will be warmer than usual and coolest in early and late November, mid-January, and mid-February. Skies will be drier than usual in the east and wetter in central and western areas. It will be stormiest in early November, early January, and early to mid-March. **April** and **May** will be warmer in the east and wetter than usual. **Summer** will be warmer than normal in the east, cooler in the west, and hottest in early to mid-August. Rainfall will be above normal. **September** and **October** will be cooler than normal and hottest in mid- to late September. Skies will be wetter in the east and west and drier in central areas. Watch for a tropical storm in late September.

KEY: east (E), central (C), west (W). Note: Temperature and precipitation are substantially based upon topography. The detailed forecast focuses on the Honolulu–Waikiki area and provides general trends elsewhere.

WEATHER

NOV. 2024: Temp. 76.5° (1° below avg.); precip. 3.8" (6" above avg. E, 1" below C&W). 1–11 Heavy rains E, showers C+W; cool. 12–20 Showers E, sunny C&W; warm, turning cool. 21–30 Scattered showers E&W, sunny C; cool.

DEC. 2024: Temp. 76° (1° above avg.); precip. 1.3" (6" below avg. E, avg. C&W). 1–10 Scattered showers, warm. 11–14 Showers E, sunny C&W; warm. 15–24 Rainy periods, mild. 25–31 Sunny, then showers; mild.

JAN. 2025: Temp. 73° (avg.); precip. 3.5" (5" below avg. E, 4" above C&W). 1–4 Rain, heavy C&W; warm. 5-19 Isolated showers; warm, turning chilly. 20–31 Sunny E, showers C&W; mild.

FEB. 2025: Temp. 73.3° (1° above avg. E, 0.5° below W); precip. 0.7" (4" below avg. E, avg. C&W). 1–8 Showers, warm. 9–12 Sunny, cool. 13–20 Sunny E, scattered showers C&W; warm. 21–28 Rainy E&W, sunny C; mild.

MAR. 2025: Temp. 75° (1° above avg.); precip. 4" (8" above avg. E, 1" below C&W). 1–5 Scattered showers, warm. 6–13 Stormy with heavy rains E, showers C&W; mild. 14–27 Rainy periods, heavy W; warm. 28–31 Showers W, sunny C&W; warm.

APR. 2025: Temp. 76.5° (2° above avg. E, avg. W); precip. 1.2" (0.5" above avg.). 1–13 Rainy periods E&W, isolated showers C; turning cool. 14–16 Showers; warm E, mild C&W. 17–30 Showers E&W, sunny C; warm.

MAY 2025: Temp. 78.5° (3° above avg. E, avg. W); precip. 2.4" (avg. E&C, 5" above W). 1–8 Showers E&W, sunny C; warm. 9–11 Rain, heavy W; sunny C; warm. 12–19 Daily showers, warm. 20–23 Showers, heavy W; warm. 24–31 Scattered showers, warm.

JUNE 2025: Temp. 80° (2° above avg. E, 1° below W); precip. 2.1" (2" above avg. E&W, 1" above C). 1–8 Showers, isolated C; warm E&C, mild W. 9–18 Scattered showers E&W, sunny C; warm, mild W. 19–24 Showers east, sunny C&W; warm. 25–30 Showers; warm E, mild C&W.

JULY 2025: Temp. 81° (avg.); precip. 0.3" (0.2" below avg.). 1–11 Showers E&W, sunny C; warm E&C, mild W. 12–31 Showers, isolated C&W; warm.

AUG. 2025: Temp. 80.5° (1° below avg.); precip. 0.2" (0.4" below avg.). 1–16 Scattered showers E&W, sunny C; hot. 17–31 Showers, isolated C&W; warm.

SEPT. 2025: Temp. 81° (0.5° below avg.); precip. 3.3" (4" above avg. E&W, 0.5° below C). 1–8 Scattered showers, warm. 9–11 Rain, heavy W; mild. 12–14 Heavy rain E, sunny C&W; warm. 15–22 Isolated showers E, sunny C&W; hot. 23–25 Tropical storm threat. 26–30 Showers, warm.

OCT. 2025: Temp. 79° (1° below avg.); precip. 1" (1" below avg.). 1–5 Showers, warm. 6–16 Showers E&W, sunny C; warm. 17–24 Daily showers, mild. 25–31 Sunny, mild.

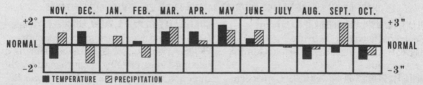

SECRETS OF THE ZODIAC

The Man of the Signs

Ancient astrologers believed that each astrological sign influenced a specific part of the body. The first sign of the zodiac—Aries—was attributed to the head, with the rest of the signs moving down the body, ending with Pisces at the feet.

♈ Aries, head	ARI	*Mar. 21–Apr. 20*
♉ Taurus, neck	TAU	*Apr. 21–May 20*
♊ Gemini, arms	GEM	*May 21–June 20*
♋ Cancer, breast	CAN	*June 21–July 22*
♌ Leo, heart	LEO	*July 23–Aug. 22*
♍ Virgo, belly	VIR	*Aug. 23–Sept. 22*
♎ Libra, reins	LIB	*Sept. 23–Oct. 22*
♏ Scorpio, secrets	SCO	*Oct. 23–Nov. 22*
♐ Sagittarius, thighs	SAG	*Nov. 23–Dec. 21*
♑ Capricorn, knees	CAP	*Dec. 22–Jan. 19*
♒ Aquarius, legs	AQU	*Jan. 20–Feb. 19*
♓ Pisces, feet	PSC	*Feb. 20–Mar. 20*

ASTROLOGY VS. ASTRONOMY

Astrology is a tool we use to plan events according to the placements of the Sun, the Moon, and the planets in the 12 signs of the zodiac. In astrology, the planetary movements do not cause events; rather, they explain the path, or "flow," that events tend to follow. *The Moon's astrological place is given on the next page.* **Astronomy** is the study of the actual placement of the known planets and constellations. The Moon's astronomical place is given in the **Left-Hand Calendar Pages, 120–146.** *(The placement of the planets in the signs of the zodiac is not the same astrologically and astronomically.)*

The dates in the **Best Days** table, **pages 226–227,** are based on the astrological passage of the Moon.

WHEN MERCURY IS RETROGRADE

Sometimes the other planets appear to be traveling backward through the zodiac; this is an illusion. We call this illusion *retrograde motion.*

According to astrology, Mercury's retrograde periods can cause our plans to go awry. However, intuition is high during these periods and coincidences can be extraordinary.

When Mercury is retrograde, stay flexible, allow more time for travel, and don't sign contracts. Review projects and plans but wait until Mercury is direct again to make final decisions.

In 2025, Mercury will be retrograde during March 14–April 6, July 17–August 10, and November 9–29.

–Celeste Longacre

GARDENING BY THE MOON'S SIGN

USE CHART ON NEXT PAGE TO FIND THE BEST DATES FOR THE FOLLOWING GARDEN TASKS . . .

PLANT, TRANSPLANT, AND GRAFT: Cancer, Scorpio, Pisces, or Taurus
HARVEST: Aries, Leo, Sagittarius, Gemini, or Aquarius
BUILD/FIX FENCES OR GARDEN BEDS: Capricorn

CONTROL INSECT PESTS, PLOW, AND WEED: Aries, Gemini, Leo, Sagittarius, or Aquarius
PRUNE: Aries, Leo, or Sagittarius. During a waxing Moon, pruning encourages growth; during a waning Moon, it discourages it.

SETTING EGGS BY THE MOON'S SIGN

Chicks take about 21 days to hatch. Those born under a waxing Moon in Cancer, Scorpio, or Pisces are healthier and mature faster. To ensure that chicks are born during these times, "set eggs" (place eggs in an incubator or under a hen) 21 days before the desired hatching dates.

EXAMPLE:
The Moon is new on March 29 and full on April 12 (EDT). Between these dates, the Moon is in the sign of Cancer on April 4 and 5. To have chicks born on April 4, count back 21 days; set eggs on March 14.

Below are the best days to set eggs in 2025, using only the fruitful dates between the new and full Moons and counting back 21 days:

JAN.: 10, 11, 18, 19   APR.: 10, 11, 20, 21   JULY: 10–12   OCT.: 1, 2, 10, 11
FEB.: 6, 7, 14–16   MAY: 8, 9, 17, 18   AUG.: 7, 8, 16, 17   NOV.: 7, 8
MAR.: 14, 15   JUNE: 4, 5, 13–15   SEPT.: 3–5, 13, 14, 30 DEC.: 4, 5, 12, 13, 31

The Moon's Astrological Place, 2024–25

	NOV.	DEC.	JAN.	FEB.	MAR.	APR.	MAY	JUNE	JULY	AUG.	SEPT.	OCT.	NOV.	DEC.
1	SCO	SAG	AQU	PSC	ARI	TAU	CAN	LEO	VIR	SCO	SAG	CAP	PSC	ARI
2	SCO	SAG	AQU	ARI	ARI	GEM	CAN	VIR	LIB	SCO	CAP	AQU	ARI	TAU
3	SAG	CAP	PSC	ARI	TAU	GEM	LEO	VIR	LIB	SAG	CAP	AQU	ARI	TAU
4	SAG	CAP	PSC	TAU	TAU	CAN	LEO	LIB	SCO	SAG	AQU	PSC	TAU	GEM
5	CAP	AQU	PSC	TAU	GEM	CAN	LEO	LIB	SCO	CAP	AQU	PSC	TAU	GEM
6	CAP	AQU	ARI	GEM	GEM	LEO	VIR	LIB	SCO	CAP	PSC	ARI	GEM	CAN
7	CAP	PSC	ARI	GEM	CAN	LEO	VIR	SCO	SAG	CAP	PSC	ARI	GEM	CAN
8	AQU	PSC	TAU	CAN	CAN	VIR	LIB	SCO	SAG	AQU	PSC	TAU	CAN	LEO
9	AQU	ARI	TAU	CAN	CAN	VIR	LIB	SAG	CAP	AQU	ARI	TAU	CAN	LEO
10	PSC	ARI	GEM	LEO	LEO	VIR	LIB	SAG	CAP	PSC	ARI	GEM	CAN	VIR
11	PSC	TAU	GEM	LEO	LEO	LIB	SCO	SAG	AQU	PSC	TAU	GEM	LEO	VIR
12	ARI	TAU	CAN	LEO	VIR	LIB	SCO	CAP	AQU	ARI	TAU	CAN	LEO	LIB
13	ARI	TAU	CAN	VIR	VIR	SCO	SAG	CAP	AQU	ARI	GEM	CAN	VIR	LIB
14	TAU	GEM	LEO	VIR	VIR	SCO	SAG	AQU	PSC	TAU	GEM	LEO	VIR	LIB
15	TAU	GEM	LEO	LIB	LIB	SCO	SAG	AQU	PSC	TAU	CAN	LEO	LIB	SCO
16	GEM	CAN	VIR	LIB	LIB	SAG	CAP	AQU	ARI	GEM	CAN	LEO	LIB	SCO
17	GEM	CAN	VIR	LIB	SCO	SAG	CAP	PSC	ARI	GEM	LEO	VIR	LIB	SAG
18	CAN	LEO	VIR	SCO	SCO	CAP	AQU	PSC	TAU	GEM	LEO	VIR	SCO	SAG
19	CAN	LEO	LIB	SCO	SCO	CAP	AQU	ARI	TAU	CAN	VIR	LIB	SCO	SAG
20	LEO	VIR	LIB	SAG	SAG	CAP	PSC	ARI	GEM	CAN	VIR	LIB	SAG	CAP
21	LEO	VIR	SCO	SAG	SAG	AQU	PSC	TAU	GEM	LEO	VIR	SCO	SAG	CAP
22	LEO	VIR	SCO	SAG	CAP	AQU	ARI	TAU	CAN	LEO	LIB	SCO	SAG	AQU
23	VIR	LIB	SCO	CAP	CAP	PSC	ARI	GEM	CAN	VIR	LIB	SCO	CAP	AQU
24	VIR	LIB	SAG	CAP	AQU	PSC	ARI	GEM	LEO	VIR	SCO	SAG	CAP	AQU
25	LIB	SCO	SAG	AQU	AQU	ARI	TAU	CAN	LEO	LIB	SCO	SAG	AQU	PSC
26	LIB	SCO	CAP	AQU	AQU	ARI	TAU	CAN	LEO	LIB	SCO	CAP	AQU	PSC
27	LIB	SCO	CAP	PSC	PSC	TAU	GEM	LEO	VIR	LIB	SAG	CAP	AQU	ARI
28	SCO	SAG	CAP	PSC	PSC	TAU	GEM	LEO	VIR	SCO	SAG	CAP	PSC	ARI
29	SCO	SAG	AQU	—	ARI	GEM	CAN	VIR	LIB	SCO	CAP	AQU	PSC	TAU
30	SAG	CAP	AQU	—	ARI	GEM	CAN	VIR	LIB	SAG	CAP	AQU	ARI	TAU
31	—	CAP	PSC	—	TAU	—	LEO	—	SCO	SAG	—	PSC	—	GEM

BEST DAYS FOR 2025

This chart is based on the Moon's sign and shows the best days each month for certain activities. –*Celeste Longacre*

	JAN.	FEB.	MAR.	APR.	MAY	JUNE	JULY	AUG.	SEPT.	OCT.	NOV.	DEC.
Quit smoking	19, 24	15, 20	15, 20	16, 21	13, 16	14, 19	16, 24	12, 16	8, 17	6, 27	10, 15	8, 17
Bake	12, 13	8, 9	7–9	4, 5	1, 2, 29, 30	25, 26	22, 23	19, 20	15, 16	12, 13	8–10	6, 7
Brew	21–23	18, 19	17–19	13–15	11, 12	7, 8	4–6, 31	1, 2, 28, 29	24–26	21–23	18, 19	15, 16
Dry fruit, vegetables, or meat	24, 25	20–22	20, 21	16, 17	13–15	19, 20	16, 17	12, 13	17, 18	14–16	11, 12	8, 9
Make jams or jellies	3–5, 31	1, 27, 28	27, 28	23, 24	20, 21	17, 18	14, 15	10, 11	6–8	4, 5, 31	1, 28, 29	25, 26
Can, pickle, or make sauerkraut	21–23	18, 19	17–19	13–15	20, 21	17, 18	14, 15	19, 20	15, 16	12, 13	18, 19	15, 16
Begin diet to lose weight	19, 24	15, 20	15, 20	16, 21	13, 16	14, 19	16, 24	12, 16	8, 17	6, 27	10, 15	8, 17
Begin diet to gain weight	6, 11	2, 6	1, 5	6, 11	6, 11	4, 9	2, 7	3, 25	3, 25	23, 29	2, 30	3, 27
Cut hair to encourage growth	8, 9	5, 6	3, 4	1, 11, 12	8–10	4–6	2, 3, 29, 30	25–27	22, 23	4, 5, 31	4, 28, 29	2, 3, 29, 30
Cut hair to discourage growth	19, 20	15–17	15, 16	23, 24	25, 26	21, 22	18, 19	14, 15	11, 12	19, 20	15–17	12–14
Perm hair	1, 2, 29, 30	25, 26	24–26	21, 22	18, 19	14–16	11–13	8, 9	4, 5	2, 3, 29, 30	25–27	22–24
Color hair	8, 9	4, 5	3, 4, 31	1, 27, 28	25, 26	21, 22	18, 19	14, 15	11, 12	8, 9	4, 5	2, 3, 29, 30
Straighten hair	24, 25	20–22	20, 21	16, 17	13–15	9–11	7, 8	3, 4, 30, 31	1, 27, 28	24, 25	20–22	17–19
Have dental care	16–18	13, 14	12–14	8–10	6, 7	2, 3, 29, 30	1, 27, 28	23, 24	19–21	17, 18	13, 14	10, 11
Start projects	30	28	30	28	27	26	25	24	22	22	21	20
End projects	28	26	28	26	25	24	23	22	20	20	19	18
Demolish	21–23	18, 19	17–19	13–15	11, 12	7, 8	4–6, 31	1, 2, 28, 29	24–26	21–23	18, 19	15, 16
Lay shingles	14, 15	10–12	10, 11	6, 7	3–5, 31	1, 27, 28	24–26	21, 22	17, 18	14–16	11, 12	8, 9
Paint	8, 9	4, 5	3, 4	1, 27, 28	25, 26	21, 22	18, 19	14, 15	11, 12	8, 9	4, 5	2, 3, 29, 30
Wash windows	6, 7	2, 3	1, 2, 29, 30	25, 26	22–24	19, 20	16, 17	12, 13	9, 10	6, 7	2, 3, 30	1, 27, 28
Wash floors	3–5, 31	1, 27, 28	27, 28	23, 24	20, 21	17, 18	14, 15	10, 11	6–8	4, 5, 31	1, 28, 29	25, 26
Go camping	24, 25	20–22	20, 21	16, 17	13–15	9–11	7, 8	3, 4, 30, 31	1, 27, 28	24, 25	20–22	17–19

See what to do when via Almanac.com/2025.

	JAN.	FEB.	MAR.	APR.	MAY	JUNE	JULY	AUG.	SEPT.	OCT.	NOV.	DEC.
Entertain	14, 15	10–12	10, 11	6, 7	3–5, 31	1, 27, 28	24–26	21, 22	17, 18	14–16	11, 12	8, 9
Travel for pleasure	14, 15	10–12	10, 11	6, 7	3–5, 31	1, 27, 28	24–26	21, 22	17, 18	14–16	11, 12	8, 9
Get married	19, 20	15–17	15, 16	11, 12	8–10	4–6	2, 3, 29, 30	25–27	22, 23	19, 20	15–17	12–14
Ask for a loan	21–23	18, 19	17–19	14, 15	20, 21	21, 22	18, 19	14, 15	11, 12	8, 9	18, 19	15, 16
Buy a home	8, 9	4, 5	3, 4, 31	1, 28	6, 7, 11	7, 8	4, 5	1, 2, 28, 29	24–26	22, 23	4, 28, 29	2, 3, 29, 30
Move (house/household)	10, 11	6, 7	5, 6	2, 3, 29, 30	27, 28	23, 24	20, 21	16–18	13, 14	10, 11	6, 7	4, 5
Advertise to sell	8, 9	4, 5	3, 4	1, 28	3–5	7, 8	4–6	1, 2, 28, 29	24–26	21–23	4, 28, 29	2, 3, 29, 30
Mow to promote growth	3–5	8, 9	7–9	4, 5	1, 2, 29, 30	7, 8	4–6	1, 2, 28, 29	24–26	4, 5	1, 28, 29	25, 26
Mow to slow growth	21–23	18, 19	17–19	13–15	25, 26	21, 22	18, 19	19, 20	15, 16	12, 13	8–10	6, 7
Plant aboveground crops	3–5, 31	8, 9	7–9	4, 5	1, 2, 29, 30	7, 8	4–6	1, 2, 28, 29	24–26	4, 5	1, 28, 29	25, 26
Plant belowground crops	21–23	18, 19	17–19	13–15	20, 21	17, 18	22, 23	19, 20	15, 16	12, 13	8–10	6, 7
Destroy pests and weeds	6, 7	2, 3	1, 2, 29, 30	25, 26	23, 24	19, 20	16, 17	12, 13	9, 10	6, 7	2, 3, 30	1, 27, 28
Graft or pollinate	12, 13	8, 9	7–9	4, 5	1, 2, 29, 30	25, 26	22, 23	19, 20	15, 16	12, 13	8–10	6, 7
Prune to encourage growth	6, 7	2, 3	1, 2, 29, 30	6, 7	3–5	9–11	7, 8	3, 4, 30, 31	1, 27, 28	6, 24, 25	20–22, 30	1, 27, 28
Prune to discourage growth	24, 25	20–22	20, 21	16, 17	13–15	19, 20	16, 17	12, 13	9, 10	14–16	11, 12	17, 18
Pick fruit	16–18	13, 14	12–14	8–10	6, 7	2, 3, 29, 30	1, 27, 28	23, 24	19–21	17, 18	13, 14	10, 11
Harvest aboveground crops	8, 9	4, 5	3, 4	8–10	6, 7	2, 3, 29, 30	1, 27, 28	23, 24	2, 3, 29, 30	1, 26–28	4, 5, 23, 24	2, 3, 29, 30
Harvest belowground crops	16–18	13, 14	22, 23	23, 24	16, 17, 25	21, 22	18, 19	14, 15	11, 12	17, 18	13, 14	10, 11
Cut hay	6, 7	2, 3	1, 2, 29, 30	25, 26	22–24	19, 20	16, 17	12, 13	9, 10	6, 7	2, 3, 30	1, 27, 28
Begin logging, set posts, pour concrete	26–28	23, 24	22, 23	18–20	16, 17	12, 13	9, 10	5–7	2, 3, 29, 30	1, 26–28	23, 24	20, 21
Purchase animals	12, 13	8, 9	7–9	4, 5	1, 2, 29, 30	25, 26	22, 23	19, 20	15, 16	12, 13	8–10	6, 7
Breed animals	21–23	18, 19	17–19	13–15	11, 12	7, 8	4–6, 31	1, 2, 28, 29	24–26	21–23	18, 19	15, 16
Wean	19, 24	15, 20	15, 20	16, 21	13, 16	14, 19	16, 24	12, 16	8, 17	6, 27	10, 15	8, 17
Castrate animals	1, 2, 29, 30	25, 26	24–26	21, 22	18, 19	14–16	11–13	8, 9	4, 5	2, 3, 29, 30	25–27	22–24
Slaughter livestock	21–23	18, 19	17–19	13–15	11, 12	7, 8	4–6, 31	1, 2, 28, 29	24–26	21–23	18, 19	15, 16

BEST FISHING DAYS AND TIMES

The best times to fish are when the fish are naturally most active. The Sun, Moon, tides, and weather all influence fish activity. For example, fish tend to feed more at sunrise and sunset, and also during a full Moon (when tides are higher than average). However, most of us go fishing simply when we can get the time off. But there are best times, according to fishing lore:

▣ One hour before and one hour after high tides, and one hour before and one hour after low tides. The times of high tides for Boston are given on **pages 120–146**; also see **pages 236–237**. (Inland, the times for high tides correspond with the times when the Moon is due south. Low tides are halfway between high tides.)

GET TIDE TIMES AND HEIGHTS NEAREST TO YOUR LOCATION VIA ALMANAC.COM/2025.

▣ During the "morning rise" (after sunup for a spell) and the "evening rise" (just before sundown and the hour or so after).

▣ During the rise and set of the Moon.

▣ Just before the arrival of a storm, although the falling barometric pressure will eventually slow down their feeding. Angling can also be good when the pressure is either steady or on the rise 1 to 2 days after a storm. High pressure accompanying clear weather can bring on sluggishness and reduced activity.

▣ When there is a hatch of flies—caddis flies or mayflies, commonly.

▣ When the breeze is from a westerly quarter, rather than from the north or east.

▣ When the water is still or slightly rippled, rather than during a wind.

THE BEST FISHING DAYS FOR 2025, WHEN THE MOON IS BETWEEN NEW AND FULL

January 1–13, 29–31
February 1–12, 27, 28
March 1–14, 29–31
April 1–12, 27–30
May 1–12, 26–31
June 1–11, 25–30
July 1–10, 24–31
August 1–9, 23–31
September 1–7, 21–30
October 1–6, 21–31
November 1–5, 20–30
December 1–4, 19–31

Dates based on Eastern Time.

HOW TO ESTIMATE THE WEIGHT OF A FISH

Measure the fish from the tip of its nose to the tip of its tail. Then measure its girth at the thickest portion of its midsection.

The weight of a fat-bodied fish (bass, salmon) = (length x girth x girth)/800

The weight of a slender fish (trout, northern pike) = (length x girth x girth)/900

EXAMPLE: If a trout is 20 inches long and has a 12-inch girth, its estimated weight is (20 x 12 x 12)/900 = 2,880/900 = 3.2 pounds

SALMON

TROUT

CATFISH

GESTATION AND MATING TABLES

	PROPER AGE OR WEIGHT FOR FIRST MATING	PERIOD OF FERTILITY (YRS.)	NUMBER OF FEMALES FOR ONE MALE	PERIOD OF GESTATION (DAYS) AVERAGE	RANGE
CATTLE: Cow	15–18 mos.[1]	10–14		283	279–290[2] 262–300[3]
Bull	1 yr., well matured	10–12	50[4] / thousands[5]		
GOAT: Doe	10 mos. or 85–90 lbs.	6		150	145–155
Buck	well matured	5	30		
HORSE: Mare	3 yrs.	10–12		336	310–370
Stallion	3 yrs.	12–15	40–45[4] / record 252[5]		
PIG: Sow	5–6 mos. or 250 lbs.	6		115	110–120
Boar	250–300 lbs.	6	50[6] / 35–40[7]		
RABBIT: Doe	6 mos.	5–6		31	30–32
Buck	6 mos.	5–6	30		
SHEEP: Ewe	1 yr. or 90 lbs.	6		147 / 151[8]	142–154
Ram	12–14 mos., well matured	7	50–75[6] / 35–40[7]		
CAT: Queen	12 mos.	6		63	60–68
Tom	12 mos.	6	6–8		
DOG: Bitch	16–18 mos.	8		63	58–67
Male	12–16 mos.	8	8–10		

[1]Holstein and beef: 750 lbs.; Jersey: 500 lbs. [2]Beef; 8–10 days shorter for Angus. [3]Dairy. [4]Natural. [5]Artificial. [6]Hand-mated. [7]Pasture. [8]For fine wool breeds.

INCUBATION PERIOD OF POULTRY (DAYS)

Chicken	21
Duck	26–32
Goose	30–34
Guinea	26–28
Turkey	28

AVERAGE LIFE SPAN OF ANIMALS IN CAPTIVITY (YEARS)

Cat (domestic)	14	Goose (domestic)	20
Chicken (domestic)	8	Horse	22
Dog (domestic)	13	Pig	12
Duck (domestic)	10	Rabbit	6
Goat (domestic)	14	Turkey (domestic)	10

	ESTRAL/ESTROUS CYCLE (INCLUDING HEAT PERIOD) AVERAGE	RANGE	LENGTH OF ESTRUS (HEAT) AVERAGE	RANGE	USUAL TIME OF OVULATION	WHEN CYCLE RECURS IF NOT BRED
Cow	21 days	18–24 days	18 hours	10–24 hours	10–12 hours after end of estrus	21 days
Doe goat	21 days	18–24 days	2–3 days	1–4 days	Near end of estrus	21 days
Mare	21 days	10–37 days	5–6 days	2–11 days	24–48 hours before end of estrus	21 days
Sow	21 days	18–24 days	2–3 days	1–5 days	30–36 hours after start of estrus	21 days
Ewe	16½ days	14–19 days	30 hours	24–32 hours	12–24 hours before end of estrus	16½ days
Queen cat		15–21 days	3–4 days, if mated	9–10 days, in absence of male	24–56 hours after coitus	Pseudo-pregnancy
Bitch	24 days	16–30 days	7 days	5–9 days	1–3 days after first acceptance	Pseudo-pregnancy

PLANTING BY THE MOON'S PHASE

ACCORDING TO THIS AGE-OLD PRACTICE, CYCLES OF THE MOON AFFECT PLANT GROWTH.

Plant annual flowers and vegetables that bear crops above ground during the light, or waxing, of the Moon: from the day the Moon is new to the day it is full.

Plant flowering bulbs, biennial and perennial flowers, and vegetables that bear crops below ground during the dark, or waning, of the Moon: from the day after it is full to the day before it is new again.

The Planting Dates columns give the safe periods for planting in areas that receive frost. (See **page 232** for frost dates in your area.) The Moon Favorable columns give the best planting days within the Planting Dates based on the Moon's phases for 2025. (See **pages 120–146** for the exact days of the new and full Moons.)

The dates listed in this table are meant as general guidelines only. For seed-sowing dates based on frost dates in your local area, go to **Almanac.com/2025.**

Aboveground crops are marked *.
(E) means early; (L) means late.

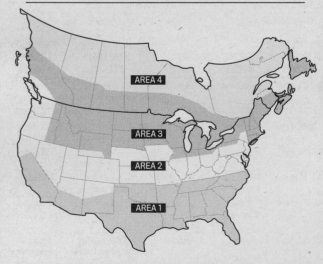

* Barley	
* Beans	(E)
	(L)
Beets	(E)
	(L)
* Broccoli plants	(E)
	(L)
* Brussels sprouts	
* Cabbage plants	
Carrots	(E)
	(L)
* Cauliflower plants	(E)
	(L)
* Celery plants	(E)
	(L)
* Collards	(E)
	(L)
* Corn, sweet	(E)
	(L)
* Cucumbers	
* Eggplant plants	
* Endive	(E)
	(L)
* Kale	(E)
	(L)
Leek plants	
* Lettuce	
* Muskmelons	
* Okra	
Onion sets	
* Parsley	
Parsnips	
* Peas	(E)
	(L)
* Pepper plants	
Potatoes	
* Pumpkins	
Radishes	(E)
	(L)
* Spinach	(E)
	(L)
* Squashes	
Sweet potatoes	
* Swiss chard	
* Tomato plants	
Turnips	(E)
	(L)
* Watermelons	
* Wheat, spring	
* Wheat, winter	

	AREA 1		AREA 2		AREA 3		AREA 4	
	PLANTING DATES	MOON FAVORABLE	PLANTING DATES	MOON FAVORABLE	PLANTING DATES	MOON FAVORABLE	PLANTING DATES	MOON FAVORABLE
	2/15-3/7	2/27-3/7	3/15-4/7	3/29-4/7	5/15-6/21	5/26-6/11	6/1-30	6/1-11, 6/25-30
	3/15-4/7	3/29-4/7	4/15-30	4/27-30	5/7-6/21	5/7-12, 5/26-6/11	5/30-6/15	5/30-6/11
	8/7-31	8/7-9, 8/23-31	7/1-21	7/1-10	6/15-7/15	6/25-7/10	–	–
	2/7-28	2/13-26	3/15-4/3	3/15-28	4/25-5/15	4/25-26, 5/13-15	5/25-6/10	5/25
	9/1-30	9/8-20	8/15-31	8/15-22	7/15-8/15	7/15-23, 8/10-15	6/15-7/8	6/15-24
	2/15-3/15	2/27-3/14	3/7-31	3/7-14, 3/29-31	5/15-31	5/26-31	6/1-25	6/1-11, 6/25
	9/7-30	9/7, 9/21-30	8/1-20	8/1-9	6/15-7/7	6/25-7/7	–	–
	2/11-3/20	2/11-12, 2/27-3/14	3/7-4/15	3/7-14, 3/29-4/12	5/15-31	5/26-31	6/1-25	6/1-11, 6/25
	2/11-3/20	2/11-12, 2/27-3/14	3/7-4/15	3/7-14, 3/29-4/12	5/15-31	5/26-31	6/1-25	6/1-11, 6/25
	2/15-3/7	2/15-26	3/7-31	3/15-28	5/15-31	5/15-25	5/25-6/10	5/25
	8/1-9/7	8/10-22	7/7-31	7/11-23	6/15-7/21	6/15-24, 7/11-21	6/15-7/8	6/15-24
	2/15-3/7	2/27-3/7	3/15-4/7	3/29-4/7	5/15-31	5/26-31	6/1-25	6/1-11, 6/25
	8/7-31	8/7-9, 8/23-31	7/1-8/7	7/1-10, 7/24-8/7	6/15-7/21	6/25-7/10	–	–
	2/15-28	2/27-28	3/7-31	3/7-14, 3/29-31	5/15-6/30	5/26-6/11, 6/25-30	6/1-30	6/1-11, 6/25-30
	9/15-30	9/21-30	8/15-9/7	8/23-9/7	7/15-8/15	7/24-8/9	–	–
	2/11-3/20	2/11-12, 2/27-3/14	3/7-4/7	3/7-14, 3/29-4/7	5/15-31	5/26-31	6/1-25	6/1-11, 6/25
	9/7-30	9/7, 9/21-30	8/15-31	8/23-31	7/1-8/7	7/1-10, 7/24-8/7	–	–
	3/15-31	3/29-31	4/1-17	4/1-12	5/10-6/15	5/10-12, 5/26-6/11	5/30-6/20	5/30-6/11
	8/7-31	8/7-9, 8/23-31	7/7-21	7/7-10	6/15-30	6/25-30	–	–
	3/7-4/15	3/7-14, 3/29-4/12	4/7-5/15	4/7-12, 4/27-5/12	5/7-6/20	5/7-12, 5/26-6/11	5/30-6/15	5/30-6/11
	3/7-4/15	3/7-14, 3/29-4/12	4/7-5/15	4/7-12, 4/27-5/12	6/1-30	6/1-11, 6/25-30	6/15-30	6/25-30
	2/15-3/20	2/27-3/14	4/7-5/15	4/7-12, 4/27-5/12	5/15-31	5/26-31	6/1-25	6/1-11, 6/25
	8/15-9/7	8/23-9/7	7/15-8/15	7/24-8/9	6/7-30	6/7-11, 6/25-30	–	–
	2/11-3/20	2/11-12, 2/27-3/14	3/7-4/7	3/7-14, 3/29-4/7	5/15-31	5/26-31	6/1-15	6/1-11
	9/7-30	9/7, 9/21-30	8/15-31	8/23-31	7/1-8/7	7/1-10, 7/24-8/7	6/25-7/15	6/25-7/10
	2/15-4/15	2/15-26, 3/15-28, 4/13-15	3/7-4/7	3/15-28	5/15-31	5/15-25	6/1-25	6/12-24
	2/15-3/7	2/27-3/7	3/1-31	3/1-14, 3/29-31	5/15-6/30	5/26-6/11, 6/25-30	6/1-30	6/1-11, 6/25-30
	3/15-4/7	3/29-4/7	4/15-5/7	4/27-5/7	5/15-6/30	5/26-6/11, 6/25-30	6/1-30	6/1-11, 6/25-30
	4/15-6/1	4/27-5/12, 5/26-6/1	5/25-6/15	5/26-6/11	6/15-7/10	6/25-7/10	6/15-7/7	6/25-7/7
	2/1-28	2/13-26	3/1-31	3/15-28	5/15-6/7	5/15-25	6/1-25	6/12-24
	2/20-3/15	2/27-3/14	3/1-31	3/1-14, 3/29-31	5/15-31	5/26-31	6/1-15	6/1-11
	1/15-2/4	1/15-28	3/7-31	3/15-28	4/1-30	4/13-26	5/10-31	5/13-25
	1/15-2/7	1/29-2/7	3/7-31	3/7-14, 3/29-31	4/15-5/7	4/27-5/7	5/15-31	5/26-31
	9/15-30	9/21-30	8/7-31	8/7-9, 8/23-31	7/15-31	7/24-31	7/10-25	7/10, 7/24-25
	3/1-20	3/1-14	4/1-30	4/1-12, 4/27-30	5/15-6/30	5/26-6/11, 6/25-30	6/1-30	6/1-11, 6/25-30
	2/10-28	2/13-26	4/1-30	4/13-26	5/1-31	5/13-25	6/1-25	6/12-24
	3/7-20	3/7-14	4/23-5/15	4/27-5/12	5/15-31	5/26-31	6/1-30	6/1-11, 6/25-30
	1/21-3/1	1/21-28, 2/13-26	3/7-31	3/15-28	4/15-30	4/15-26	5/15-6/5	5/15-25
	10/1-21	10/7-20	9/7-30	9/8-20	8/15-31	8/15-22	7/10-31	7/11-23
	2/7-3/15	2/7-12, 2/27-3/14	3/15-4/20	3/29-4/12	5/15-31	5/26-31	6/1-25	6/1-11, 6/25
	10/1-21	10/1-6, 10/21	8/1-9/15	8/1-9, 8/23-9/7	7/17-9/7	7/24-8/9, 8/23-9/7	7/20-8/5	7/24-8/5
	3/15-4/15	3/29-4/12	4/15-30	4/27-30	5/15-6/15	5/26-6/11	6/1-30	6/1-11, 6/25-30
	3/23-4/7	3/23-28	4/21-5/9	4/21-26	5/15-6/15	5/15-25, 6/12-15	6/1-30	6/12-24
	2/7-3/15	2/7-12, 2/27-3/14	3/15-4/15	3/29-4/12	5/1-31	5/1-12, 5/26-31	5/15-31	5/26-31
	3/7-21	3/7-14	4/7-30	4/7-12, 4/27-30	5/15-31	5/26-31	6/1-15	6/1-11
	1/20-2/15	1/20-28, 2/13-15	3/15-31	3/15-28	4/7-30	4/13-26	5/10-31	5/13-25
	9/1-10/15	9/8-20, 10/7-15	8/1-20	8/10-20	7/1-8/15	7/11-23, 8/10-15	–	–
	3/15-4/7	3/29-4/7	4/15-5/7	4/27-5/7	5/15-6/30	5/26-6/11, 6/25-30	6/1-30	6/1-11, 6/25-30
	2/15-28	2/27-28	3/1-20	3/1-14	4/7-30	4/7-12, 4/27-30	5/15-6/10	5/26-6/10
	10/15-12/7	10/21-11/5, 11/20-12/4	9/15-10/20	9/21-10/6	8/11-9/15	8/23-9/7	8/5-30	8/5-9, 8/23-30

FROSTS AND GROWING SEASONS

Dates given are normal averages (from 1991–2020) for a light freeze; local weather and topography may cause variations. The possibility of frost occurring after the spring dates and before the fall dates is 30 percent. The classification of freeze temperatures is usually based on their effect on plants. **Light freeze:** 29° to 32°F—tender plants killed. **Moderate freeze:** 25° to 28°F—widely destructive to most plants. **Severe freeze:** 24°F and colder—heavy damage to most plants.

–dates courtesy of National Centers for Environmental Information

STATE	CITY	GROWING SEASON (DAYS)	LAST SPRING FROST	FIRST FALL FROST	STATE	CITY	GROWING SEASON (DAYS)	LAST SPRING FROST	FIRST FALL FROST
AK	Juneau	171	Apr. 26	Oct. 15	NC	Fayetteville	212	Apr. 5	Nov. 4
AL	Mobile	269	Mar. 3	Nov. 28	ND	Bismarck	126	May 19	Sept. 23
AR	Pine Bluff	230	Mar. 22	Nov. 8	NE	Omaha	174	Apr. 23	Oct. 15
AZ	Phoenix	354*	Jan. 9	Dec. 30	NE	North Platte	131	May 16	Sept. 25
AZ	Tucson	309*	Feb. 2	Dec. 9	NH	Concord	136	May 15	Sept. 29
CA	Eureka	268	Mar. 4	Nov. 28	NJ	Newark	211	Apr. 6	Nov. 4
CA	Sacramento	281*	Feb. 17	Nov. 26	NM	Carlsbad	223	Mar. 27	Nov. 6
CO	Denver	154	May 4	Oct. 6	NM	Los Alamos	149	May 9	Oct. 6
CO	Grand Junction	159	May 3	Oct. 10	NV	Las Vegas	292*	Feb. 11	Dec. 1
CT	Hartford	165	Apr. 27	Oct. 10	NY	Albany	159	May 2	Oct. 9
DE	Wilmington	199	Apr. 13	Oct. 30	NY	Syracuse	158	May 5	Oct. 11
FL	Orlando	337*	Jan. 30	Jan. 3**	OH	Akron	174	Apr. 30	Oct. 22
FL	Tallahassee	238	Mar. 19	Nov. 13	OH	Cincinnati	179	Apr. 23	Oct. 20
GA	Athens	217	Mar. 31	Nov. 4	OK	Lawton	206	Apr. 7	Oct. 31
GA	Savannah	253	Mar. 12	Nov. 21	OK	Tulsa	207	Apr. 5	Oct. 30
IA	Atlantic	142	May 6	Sept. 26	OR	Pendleton	155	Apr. 30	Oct. 3
IA	Cedar Rapids	155	May 4	Oct. 7	OR	Portland	260	Mar. 6	Nov. 22
ID	Boise	166	Apr. 30	Oct. 14	PA	Franklin	160	May 9	Oct. 17
IL	Chicago	193	Apr. 17	Oct. 28	PA	Williamsport	167	May 1	Oct. 16
IL	Springfield	177	Apr. 20	Oct. 15	RI	Kingston	148	May 8	Oct. 4
IN	Indianapolis	172	Apr. 26	Oct. 16	SC	Charleston	305*	Feb. 17	Dec. 20
IN	South Bend	159	May 7	Oct. 14	SC	Columbia	235	Mar. 21	Nov. 12
KS	Topeka	182	Apr. 19	Oct. 19	SD	Rapid City	144	May 9	Oct. 1
KY	Lexington	185	Apr. 20	Oct. 23	TN	Memphis	229	Mar. 24	Nov. 9
LA	Monroe	238	Mar. 14	Nov. 8	TN	Nashville	206	Apr. 6	Oct. 30
LA	New Orleans	311*	Feb. 8	Dec. 17	TX	Amarillo	184	Apr. 20	Oct. 22
MA	Boston	208	Apr. 8	Nov. 3	TX	Denton	235	Mar. 21	Nov. 12
MA	Worcester	167	Apr. 29	Oct. 14	TX	San Antonio	267	Mar. 2	Nov. 25
MD	Baltimore	192	Apr. 16	Oct. 26	UT	Cedar City	119	May 31	Sept. 28
ME	Portland	160	May 1	Oct. 9	UT	Spanish Fork	162	May 2	Oct. 12
MI	Lansing	151	May 7	Oct. 6	VA	Norfolk	239	Mar. 23	Nov. 18
MI	Marquette	152	May 15	Oct. 15	VA	Richmond	204	Apr. 9	Oct. 31
MN	Duluth	129	May 19	Sept. 26	VT	Burlington	158	May 3	Oct. 9
MN	Willmar	149	May 4	Oct. 1	WA	Seattle	246	Mar. 12	Nov. 14
MO	Jefferson City	193	Apr. 14	Oct. 25	WA	Spokane	158	May 1	Oct. 7
MS	Columbia	243	Mar. 13	Nov. 12	WI	Green Bay	148	May 7	Oct. 3
MS	Tupelo	218	Mar. 30	Nov. 4	WI	Sparta	133	May 15	Sept. 26
MT	Fort Peck	135	May 13	Sept. 26	WV	Parkersburg	186	Apr. 20	Oct. 24
MT	Helena	132	May 15	Sept. 25	WY	Casper	105	June 1	Sept. 15

*In leap years, add 1 day **In following year

PHENOLOGY: NATURE'S CALENDAR

Study nature, love nature, stay close to nature. It will never fail you.
–FRANK LLOYD WRIGHT, AMERICAN ARCHITECT (1867–1959)

For centuries, farmers and gardeners have looked to events in nature to tell them when to plant vegetables and flowers and when to expect insects. Making such observations is called "phenology," the study of phenomena. Specifically, this refers to the life cycles of plants and animals as they correlate to weather and temperature, or nature's calendar.

VEGETABLES

- Plant peas when forsythias bloom.
- Plant potatoes when the first dandelion blooms.
- Plant beets, carrots, cole crops (broccoli, brussels sprouts, collards), lettuce, and spinach when lilacs are in first leaf or dandelions are in full bloom.
- Plant corn when oak leaves are the size of a squirrel's ear (about ½ inch in diameter). Or, plant corn when apple blossoms fade and fall.
- Plant bean, cucumber, and squash seeds when lilacs are in full bloom.
- Plant tomatoes when lilies-of-the-valley are in full bloom.
- Transplant eggplants and peppers when bearded irises bloom.
- Plant onions when red maples bloom.

FLOWERS

- Plant morning glories when maple trees have full-size leaves.
- Plant zinnias and marigolds when black locusts are in full bloom.
- Plant pansies, snapdragons, and other hardy annuals when aspens and chokecherries have leafed out.

INSECTS

- When purple lilacs bloom, grasshopper eggs hatch.
- When chicory blooms, beware of squash vine borers.
- When Canada thistles bloom, protect susceptible fruit; apple maggot flies are at peak.
- When foxglove flowers open, expect Mexican beetle larvae.
- When crabapple trees are in bud, eastern tent caterpillars are hatching.
- When morning glory vines begin to climb, Japanese beetles appear.
- When wild rocket blooms, cabbage root maggots appear.

If the signal plants are not growing in your area, notice other coincident events; record them and watch for them in ensuing seasons.

TABLE OF MEASURES

LINEAR

1 hand = 4 inches
1 foot = 12 inches
1 yard = 3 feet
1 rod = $5\frac{1}{2}$ yards
1 mile = 320 rods = 1,760 yards = 5,280 feet
1 international nautical mile = 6,076.1155 feet
1 knot = 1 nautical mile per hour
1 fathom = 2 yards = 6 feet
1 furlong = $\frac{1}{8}$ mile = 660 feet = 220 yards
1 league = 3 miles = 24 furlongs

SQUARE

1 square foot = 144 square inches
1 square yard = 9 square feet
1 square rod = $272\frac{1}{4}$ square feet
1 acre = 160 square rods = 43,560 square feet
1 square mile = 640 acres = 102,400 square rods

CUBIC

1 cubic foot = 1,728 cubic inches
1 cubic yard = 27 cubic feet
1 cord = 128 cubic feet
1 U.S. liquid gallon = 4 quarts = 231 cubic inches
1 imperial gallon = 1.20 U.S. gallons = 0.16 cubic foot
1 board foot = 144 cubic inches

DRY

2 pints = 1 quart
4 quarts = 1 gallon
2 gallons = 1 peck
4 pecks = 1 bushel

LIQUID

4 gills = 1 pint
63 gallons = 1 hogshead
2 hogsheads = 1 pipe or butt
2 pipes = 1 tun

KITCHEN

3 teaspoons = 1 tablespoon
16 tablespoons = 1 cup
1 cup = 8 ounces
2 cups = 1 pint
2 pints = 1 quart
4 quarts = 1 gallon

WEIGHT: AVOIRDUPOIS
(for general use)

1 ounce = 16 drams
1 pound = 16 ounces
1 short hundredweight = 100 pounds
1 short ton = 2,000 pounds
1 long ton = 2,240 pounds

METRIC CONVERSIONS

LINEAR

1 inch = 2.54 centimeters
1 centimeter = 0.39 inch
1 foot = 30.48 centimeters
1 yard = 0.914 meter
1 meter = 39.37 inches
1 mile = 1.61 kilometers
1 kilometer = 0.62 mile

SQUARE

1 square inch = 6.45 square centimeters
1 square foot = 0.09 square meter
1 square yard = 0.84 square meter
1 square meter = 10.76 square feet
1 square mile = 2.59 square kilometers
1 square kilometer = 0.386 square mile
1 acre = 0.40 hectare
1 hectare = 2.47 acres

CUBIC

1 cubic yard = 0.76 cubic meter
1 cubic meter = 1.31 cubic yards

WEIGHT

1 gram = 0.035 ounce
1 ounce = 28.349 grams
1 kilogram = 2.2 pounds
1 pound = 0.45 kilogram
1 short ton = 0.091 metric ton
1 metric ton = 1.10 short tons

KITCHEN

$\frac{1}{2}$ teaspoon = 2.46 mL
1 teaspoon = 4.93 mL
1 tablespoon = 14.79 mL
$\frac{1}{4}$ cup = 59.15 mL
$\frac{1}{3}$ cup = 78.86 mL
$\frac{1}{2}$ cup = 118.29 mL
$\frac{3}{4}$ cup = 177.44 mL
1 cup = 236.59 mL
1 U.S. fluid ounce = 30.0 mL
1 milliliter (mL) = 0.034 U.S. fluid ounce
1 U.S. liquid pint = 0.47 liter
1 U.S. liquid quart = 0.946 liter
1 liter = 2.1 U.S. liquid pints = 1.057 U.S. liquid quarts
1 U.S. liquid gallon = 3.78 liters

TO CONVERT CELSIUS AND FAHRENHEIT: $°C = (°F − 32)/1.8$; $°F = (°C × 1.8) + 32$

TIDAL GLOSSARY

APOGEAN TIDE: A monthly tide of decreased range that occurs when the Moon is at apogee (farthest from Earth).

CURRENT: Generally, a horizontal movement of water. Currents may be classified as tidal and nontidal. Tidal currents are caused by gravitational interactions between the Sun, Moon, and Earth and are part of the same general movement of the sea that is manifested in the vertical rise and fall, called tide. Nontidal currents include the permanent currents in the general circulatory systems of the sea as well as temporary currents arising from more pronounced meteorological variability.

DIURNAL TIDE: A tide with one high water and one low water in a tidal day of approximately 24 hours.

MEAN LOWER LOW WATER: The arithmetic mean of the lesser of a daily pair of low waters, observed over a specific 19-year cycle called the National Tidal Datum Epoch.

NEAP TIDE: A tide of decreased range that occurs twice a month, when the Moon is in quadrature (during its first and last quarters, when the Sun and the Moon are at right angles to each other relative to Earth).

PERIGEAN TIDE: A monthly tide of increased range that occurs when the Moon is at perigee (closest to Earth).

RED TIDE: Toxic algal blooms caused by several genera of dinoflagellates that usually turn the sea red or brown. These pose a serious threat to marine life and may be harmful to humans.

RIP CURRENT: A potentially dangerous, narrow, intense, surf-zone current flowing outward from shore.

SEMIDIURNAL TIDE: A tide with one high water and one low water every half-day. East Coast tides, for example, are semidiurnal, with two highs and two lows during a tidal day of approximately 24 hours.

SLACK WATER (SLACK): The state of a tidal current when its speed is near zero, especially the moment when a reversing current changes direction and its speed is zero.

SPRING TIDE: A tide of increased range that occurs at times of syzygy each month. Named not for the season of spring but from the German *springen* ("to leap up"), a spring tide also brings a lower low water.

STORM SURGE: The local change in the elevation of the ocean along a shore due to a storm, measured by subtracting the astronomic tidal elevation from the total elevation. It typically has a duration of a few hours and is potentially catastrophic, especially on low-lying coasts with gently sloping offshore topography.

SYZYGY: The nearly straight-line configuration that occurs twice a month, when the Sun and the Moon are in conjunction (on the same side of Earth, at the new Moon) and when they are in opposition (on opposite sides of Earth, at the full Moon). In both cases, the gravitational effects of the Sun and the Moon reinforce each other, and tidal range is increased.

TIDAL BORE: A tide-induced wave that propagates up a relatively shallow and sloping estuary or river with a steep wave front.

TSUNAMI: Sometimes mistakenly called a "tidal wave," a tsunami is a series of long-period waves caused by an underwater earthquake or volcanic eruption. In open ocean, the waves are small and travel at high speed; as they near shore, some may build to more than 30 feet high, becoming a threat to life and property.

VANISHING TIDE: A mixed tide of considerable inequality in the two highs and two lows, so that the lower high (or higher low) may appear to vanish. ∎

TIDE CORRECTIONS

Many factors affect tides, including the shoreline, time of the Moon's southing (crossing of the meridian), and the Moon's phase. The High Tide Times column on the **Left-Hand Calendar Pages, 120–146,** lists the times of high tide at Commonwealth Pier in Boston (MA) Harbor. The heights of some of these tides, reckoned from Mean Lower Low Water, are given on the **Right-Hand Calendar Pages, 121–147.** Use the table below to calculate the approximate times and heights of high tide at the places shown. Apply the time difference to the times of high tide at Boston and the height difference to the heights at Boston. A more detailed and accurate tide calculator for the United States and Canada can be found via **Almanac.com/2025.**

EXAMPLE:

The conversion of the times and heights of the tides at Boston to those at Cape Fear, North Carolina, is given below:

High tide at Boston	11:45 A.M.
Correction for Cape Fear	- 3 55
High tide at Cape Fear	7:50 A.M.

Tide height at Boston	11.6 ft.
Correction for Cape Fear	- 5.0 ft.
Tide height at Cape Fear	6.6 ft.

Estimations derived from this table are *not* meant to be used for navigation. *The Old Farmer's Almanac* accepts no responsibility for errors or any consequences ensuing from the use of this table.

TIDAL SITE	TIME (H. M.)	HEIGHT (FT.)	TIDAL SITE	TIME (H. M.)	HEIGHT (FT.)
CANADA			Cape Cod Canal		
Alberton, PE	*–5 45	–7.5	East Entrance	–0 01	–0.8
Charlottetown, PE	*–0 45	–3.5	West Entrance	–2 16	–5.9
Halifax, NS	–3 23	–4.5	Chatham Outer Coast	+0 30	–2.8
North Sydney, NS	–3 15	–6.5	Inside	+1 54	**0.4
Saint John, NB	+0 30	+15.0	Cohasset	+0 02	–0.07
St. John's, NL	–4 00	–6.5	Cotuit Highlands	+1 15	**0.3
Yarmouth, NS	–0 40	+3.0	Dennis Port	+1 01	**0.4
MAINE			Duxbury–Gurnet Point	+0 02	–0.3
Bar Harbor	–0 34	+0.9	Fall River	–3 03	–5.0
Belfast	–0 20	+0.4	Gloucester	–0 03	–0.8
Boothbay Harbor	–0 18	–0.8	Hingham	+0 07	0.0
Chebeague Island	–0 16	–0.6	Hull	+0 03	–0.2
Eastport	–0 28	+8.4	Hyannis Port	+1 01	**0.3
Kennebunkport	+0 04	–1.0	Magnolia–Manchester	–0 02	–0.7
Machias	–0 28	+2.8	Marblehead	–0 02	–0.4
Monhegan Island	–0 25	–0.8	Marion	–3 22	–5.4
Old Orchard Beach	0 00	–0.8	Monument Beach	–3 08	–5.4
Portland	–0 12	–0.6	Nahant	–0 01	–0.5
Rockland	–0 28	+0.1	Nantasket Beach	+0 04	–0.1
Stonington	–0 30	+0.1	Nantucket	+0 56	**0.3
York	–0 09	–1.0	Nauset Beach	+0 30	**0.6
NEW HAMPSHIRE			New Bedford	–3 24	–5.7
Hampton	+0 02	–1.3	Newburyport	+0 19	–1.8
Portsmouth	+0 11	–1.5	Oak Bluffs	+0 30	**0.2
Rye Beach	–0 09	–0.9	Onset–R.R. Bridge	–2 16	–5.9
MASSACHUSETTS			Plymouth	+0 05	0.0
Annisquam	–0 02	–1.1	Provincetown	+0 14	–0.4
Beverly Farms	0 00	–0.5	Revere Beach	–0 01	–0.3

TIDAL SITE	TIME (H. M.)	HEIGHT (FT.)	TIDAL SITE	TIME (H. M.)	HEIGHT (FT.)
Rockport	−0 08	−1.0	**PENNSYLVANIA**		
Salem	0 00	−0.5	Philadelphia	+2 40	−3.5
Scituate	−0 05	−0.7	**DELAWARE**		
Wareham	−3 09	−5.3	Cape Henlopen	−2 48	−5.3
Wellfleet	+0 12	+0.5	Rehoboth Beach	−3 37	−5.7
West Falmouth	−3 10	−5.4	Wilmington	+1 56	−3.8
Westport Harbor	−3 22	−6.4	**MARYLAND**		
Woods Hole			Annapolis	+6 23	−8.5
Little Harbor	−2 50	**0.2	Baltimore	+7 59	−8.3
Oceanographic			Cambridge	+5 05	−7.8
Institute	−3 07	**0.2	Havre de Grace	+11 21	−7.7
RHODE ISLAND			Point No Point	+2 28	−8.1
Bristol	−3 24	−5.3	Prince Frederick–		
Narragansett Pier	−3 42	−6.2	Plum Point	+4 25	−8.5
Newport	−3 34	−5.9	**VIRGINIA**		
Point Judith	−3 41	−6.3	Cape Charles	−2 20	−7.0
Providence	−3 20	−4.8	Hampton Roads	−2 02	−6.9
Sakonnet	−3 44	−5.6	Norfolk	−2 06	−6.6
Watch Hill	−2 50	−6.8	Virginia Beach	−4 00	−6.0
CONNECTICUT			Yorktown	−2 13	−7.0
Bridgeport	+0 01	−2.6	**NORTH CAROLINA**		
Madison	−0 22	−2.3	Cape Fear	−3 55	−5.0
New Haven	−0 11	−3.2	Cape Lookout	−4 28	−5.7
New London	−1 54	−6.7	Currituck	−4 10	−5.8
Norwalk	+0 01	−2.2	Hatteras		
Old Lyme–			Inlet	−4 03	−7.4
Highway Bridge	−0 30	−6.2	Kitty Hawk	−4 14	−6.2
Stamford	+0 01	−2.2	Ocean	−4 26	−6.0
Stonington	−2 27	−6.6	**SOUTH CAROLINA**		
NEW YORK			Charleston	−3 22	−4.3
Coney Island	−3 33	−4.9	Georgetown	−1 48	**0.36
Fire Island Light	−2 43	**0.1	Hilton Head	−3 22	−2.9
Long Beach	−3 11	−5.7	Myrtle Beach	−3 49	−4.4
Montauk Harbor	−2 19	−7.4	St. Helena–		
New York City–Battery	−2 43	−5.0	Harbor Entrance	−3 15	−3.4
Oyster Bay	+0 04	−1.8	**GEORGIA**		
Port Chester	−0 09	−2.2	Jekyll Island	−3 46	−2.9
Port Washington	−0 01	−2.1	St. Simon's Island	−2 50	−2.9
Sag Harbor	−0 55	−6.8	Savannah Beach		
Southampton–			River Entrance	−3 14	−5.5
Shinnecock Inlet	−4 20	**0.2	Tybee Light	−3 22	−2.7
Willets Point	0 00	−2.3	**FLORIDA**		
NEW JERSEY			Cape Canaveral	−3 59	−6.0
Asbury Park	−4 04	−5.3	Daytona Beach	−3 28	−5.3
Atlantic City	−3 56	−5.5	Fort Lauderdale	−2 50	−7.2
Bay Head–Sea Girt	−4 04	−5.3	Fort Pierce Inlet	−3 32	−6.9
Beach Haven	−1 43	**0.24	Jacksonville–		
Cape May	−3 28	−5.3	Railroad Bridge	−6 55	**0.1
Ocean City	−3 06	−5.9	Miami Harbor Entrance	−3 18	−7.0
Sandy Hook	−3 30	−5.0	St. Augustine	−2 55	−4.9
Seaside Park	−4 03	−5.4			

***VARIES WIDELY; ACCURATE ONLY TO WITHIN 1½ HOURS. CONSULT LOCAL TIDE TABLES FOR PRECISE TIMES AND HEIGHTS.**

****WHERE THE DIFFERENCE IN THE HEIGHT COLUMN IS SO MARKED, THE HEIGHT AT BOSTON SHOULD BE MULTIPLIED BY THIS RATIO.**

Astronomical data for Boston (42°22' N, 71°3' W) is given on **pages 104, 106, 108–109,** and **120–146.** Use the Key Letters shown on those pages with this table to find the number of minutes that you must add to or subtract from Boston time to get the correct time for your city. (Times are approximate.) For more information on the use of Key Letters, see **How to Use This Almanac, page 116.**

GET TIMES SIMPLY AND SPECIFICALLY: Download astronomical times calculated for your zip code and presented as Left-Hand Calendar Pages via **Almanac.com/2025.**

TIME ZONES CODES represent standard time. Atlantic is –1, Eastern is 0, Central is 1, Mountain is 2, Pacific is 3, Alaska is 4, and Hawaii-Aleutian is 5.

STATE	CITY	NORTH LATITUDE °	NORTH LATITUDE '	WEST LONGITUDE °	WEST LONGITUDE '	TIME ZONE CODE	A	B	C	D	E
AK	Anchorage	61	10	149	59	4	–46	+27	+71	+122	+171
AK	Cordova	60	33	145	45	4	–55	+13	+55	+103	+149
AK	Fairbanks	64	48	147	51	4	–127	+2	+61	+131	+205
AK	Juneau	58	18	134	25	4	–76	–23	+10	+49	+86
AK	Ketchikan	55	21	131	39	4	–62	–25	0	+29	+56
AK	Kodiak	57	47	152	24	4	0	+49	+82	+120	+154
AL	Birmingham	33	31	86	49	1	+30	+15	+3	–10	–20
AL	Decatur	34	36	86	59	1	+27	+14	+4	–7	–17
AL	Mobile	30	42	88	3	1	+42	+23	+8	–8	–22
AL	Montgomery	32	23	86	19	1	+31	+14	+1	–13	–25
AR	Fort Smith	35	23	94	25	1	+55	+43	+33	+22	+14
AR	Little Rock	34	45	92	17	1	+48	+35	+25	+13	+4
AR	Texarkana	33	26	94	3	1	+59	+44	+32	+18	+8
AZ	Flagstaff	35	12	111	39	2	+64	+52	+42	+31	+22
AZ	Phoenix	33	27	112	4	2	+71	+56	+44	+30	+20
AZ	Tucson	32	13	110	58	2	+70	+53	+40	+24	+12
AZ	Yuma	32	43	114	37	2	+83	+67	+54	+40	+28
CA	Bakersfield	35	23	119	1	3	+33	+21	+12	+1	–7
CA	Barstow	34	54	117	1	3	+27	+14	+4	–7	–16
CA	Fresno	36	44	119	47	3	+32	+22	+15	+6	0
CA	Los Angeles-Pasadena-Santa Monica	34	3	118	14	3	+34	+20	+9	–3	–13
CA	Palm Springs	33	49	116	32	3	+28	+13	+1	–12	–22
CA	Redding	40	35	122	24	3	+31	+27	+25	+22	+19
CA	Sacramento	38	35	121	30	3	+34	+27	+21	+15	+10
CA	San Diego	32	43	117	9	3	+33	+17	+4	–9	–21
CA	San Francisco-Oakland-San Jose	37	47	122	25	3	+40	+31	+25	+18	+12
CO	Craig	40	31	107	33	2	+32	+28	+25	+22	+20
CO	Denver-Boulder	39	44	104	59	2	+24	+19	+15	+11	+7
CO	Grand Junction	39	4	108	33	2	+40	+34	+29	+24	+20
CO	Pueblo	38	16	104	37	2	+27	+20	+14	+7	+2
CO	Trinidad	37	10	104	31	2	+30	+21	+13	+5	0
CT	Bridgeport	41	11	73	11	0	+12	+10	+8	+6	+4
CT	Hartford-New Britain	41	46	72	41	0	+8	+7	+6	+5	+4
CT	New Haven	41	18	72	56	0	+11	+8	+7	+5	+4
CT	New London	41	22	72	6	0	+7	+5	+4	+2	+1
CT	Norwalk-Stamford	41	7	73	22	0	+13	+10	+9	+7	+5
CT	Waterbury-Meriden	41	33	73	3	0	+10	+9	+7	+6	+5
DC	Washington	38	54	77	1	0	+35	+28	+23	+18	+13
DE	Wilmington	39	45	75	33	0	+26	+21	+18	+13	+10

STATE	CITY	NORTH LATITUDE °	'	WEST LONGITUDE °	'	TIME ZONE CODE	KEY LETTERS (MINUTES) A	B	C	D	E
FL	Fort Myers	26	38	81	52	0	+87	+63	+44	+21	+4
FL	Jacksonville	30	20	81	40	0	+77	+58	+43	+25	+11
FL	Miami	25	47	80	12	0	+88	+57	+37	+14	−3
FL	Orlando	28	32	81	22	0	+80	+59	+42	+22	+6
FL	Pensacola	30	25	87	13	1	+39	+20	+5	−12	−26
FL	St. Petersburg	27	46	82	39	0	+87	+65	+47	+26	+10
FL	Tallahassee	30	27	84	17	0	+87	+68	+53	+35	+22
FL	Tampa	27	57	82	27	0	+86	+64	+46	+25	+9
FL	West Palm Beach	26	43	80	3	0	+79	+55	+36	+14	−2
GA	Atlanta	33	45	84	24	0	+79	+65	+53	+40	+30
GA	Augusta	33	28	81	58	0	+70	+55	+44	+30	+19
GA	Macon	32	50	83	38	0	+79	+63	+50	+36	+24
GA	Savannah	32	5	81	6	0	+70	+54	+40	+25	+13
HI	Hilo	19	44	155	5	5	+94	+62	+37	+7	−15
HI	Honolulu	21	18	157	52	5	+102	+72	+48	+19	−1
HI	Lanai City	20	50	156	55	5	+99	+69	+44	+15	−6
HI	Lihue	21	59	159	23	5	+107	+77	+54	+26	+5
IA	Davenport	41	32	90	35	1	+20	+19	+17	+16	+15
IA	Des Moines	41	35	93	37	1	+32	+31	+30	+28	+27
IA	Dubuque	42	30	90	41	1	+17	+18	+18	+18	+18
IA	Waterloo	42	30	92	20	1	+24	+24	+24	+25	+25
ID	Boise	43	37	116	12	2	+55	+58	+60	+62	+64
ID	Lewiston	46	25	117	1	3	−12	−3	+2	+10	+17
ID	Pocatello	42	52	112	27	2	+43	+44	+45	+46	+46
IL	Cairo	37	0	89	11	1	+29	+20	+12	+4	−2
IL	Chicago–Oak Park	41	52	87	38	1	+7	+6	+6	+5	+4
IL	Danville	40	8	87	37	1	+13	+9	+6	+2	0
IL	Decatur	39	51	88	57	1	+19	+15	+11	+7	+4
IL	Peoria	40	42	89	36	1	+19	+16	+14	+11	+9
IL	Springfield	39	48	89	39	1	+22	+18	+14	+10	+6
IN	Fort Wayne	41	4	85	9	0	+60	+58	+56	+54	+52
IN	Gary	41	36	87	20	1	+7	+6	+4	+3	+2
IN	Indianapolis	39	46	86	10	0	+69	+64	+60	+56	+52
IN	Muncie	40	12	85	23	0	+64	+60	+57	+53	+50
IN	South Bend	41	41	86	15	0	+62	+61	+60	+59	+58
IN	Terre Haute	39	28	87	24	0	+74	+69	+65	+60	+56
KS	Fort Scott	37	50	94	42	1	+49	+41	+34	+27	+21
KS	Liberal	37	3	100	55	1	+76	+66	+59	+51	+44
KS	Oakley	39	8	100	51	1	+69	+63	+59	+53	+49
KS	Salina	38	50	97	37	1	+57	+51	+46	+40	+35
KS	Topeka	39	3	95	40	1	+49	+43	+38	+32	+28
KS	Wichita	37	42	97	20	1	+60	+51	+45	+37	+31
KY	Lexington–Frankfort	38	3	84	30	0	+67	+59	+53	+46	+41
KY	Louisville	38	15	85	46	0	+72	+64	+58	+52	+46
LA	Alexandria	31	18	92	27	1	+58	+40	+26	+9	−3
LA	Baton Rouge	30	27	91	11	1	+55	+36	+21	+3	−10
LA	Lake Charles	30	14	93	13	1	+64	+44	+29	+11	−2
LA	Monroe	32	30	92	7	1	+53	+37	+24	+9	−1
LA	New Orleans	29	57	90	4	1	+52	+32	+16	−1	−15
LA	Shreveport	32	31	93	45	1	+60	+44	+31	+16	+4
MA	Brockton	42	5	71	1	0	0	0	0	0	−1
MA	Fall River–New Bedford	41	42	71	9	0	+2	+1	0	0	−1
MA	Lawrence–Lowell	42	42	71	10	0	0	0	0	0	+1
MA	Pittsfield	42	27	73	15	0	+8	+8	+8	+8	+8
MA	Springfield–Holyoke	42	6	72	36	0	+6	+6	+6	+5	+5
MA	Worcester	42	16	71	48	0	+3	+2	+2	+2	+2

STATE	CITY	NORTH LATITUDE		WEST LONGITUDE		TIME ZONE CODE	KEY LETTERS (MINUTES)				
		°	'	°	'		A	B	C	D	E
MD	Baltimore	39	17	76	37	0	+32	+26	+22	+17	+13
MD	Hagerstown	39	39	77	43	0	+35	+30	+26	+22	+18
MD	Salisbury	38	22	75	36	0	+31	+23	+18	+11	+6
ME	Augusta	44	19	69	46	0	–12	–8	–5	–1	0
ME	Bangor	44	48	68	46	0	–18	–13	–9	–5	–1
ME	Eastport	44	54	67	0	0	–26	–20	–16	–11	–8
ME	Ellsworth	44	33	68	25	0	–18	–14	–10	–6	–3
ME	Portland	43	40	70	15	0	–8	–5	–3	–1	0
ME	Presque Isle	46	41	68	1	0	–29	–19	–12	–4	+2
MI	Cheboygan	45	39	84	29	0	+40	+47	+53	+59	+64
MI	Detroit-Dearborn	42	20	83	3	0	+47	+47	+47	+47	+47
MI	Flint	43	1	83	41	0	+47	+49	+50	+51	+52
MI	Ironwood	46	27	90	9	1	0	+9	+15	+23	+29
MI	Jackson	42	15	84	24	0	+53	+53	+53	+52	+52
MI	Kalamazoo	42	17	85	35	0	+58	+57	+57	+57	+57
MI	Lansing	42	44	84	33	0	+52	+53	+53	+54	+54
MI	St. Joseph	42	5	86	26	0	+61	+61	+60	+60	+59
MI	Traverse City	44	46	85	38	0	+49	+54	+57	+62	+65
MN	Albert Lea	43	39	93	22	1	+24	+26	+28	+31	+33
MN	Bemidji	47	28	94	53	1	+14	+26	+34	+44	+52
MN	Duluth	46	47	92	6	1	+6	+16	+23	+31	+38
MN	Minneapolis-St. Paul	44	59	93	16	1	+18	+24	+28	+33	+37
MN	Ortonville	45	19	96	27	1	+30	+36	+40	+46	+51
MO	Jefferson City	38	34	92	10	1	+36	+29	+24	+18	+13
MO	Joplin	37	6	94	30	1	+50	+41	+33	+25	+18
MO	Kansas City	39	1	94	20	1	+44	+37	+33	+27	+23
MO	Poplar Bluff	36	46	90	24	1	+35	+25	+17	+8	+1
MO	St. Joseph	39	46	94	50	1	+43	+38	+35	+30	+27
MO	St. Louis	38	37	90	12	1	+28	+21	+16	+10	+5
MO	Springfield	37	13	93	18	1	+45	+36	+29	+20	+14
MS	Biloxi	30	24	88	53	1	+46	+27	+11	–5	–19
MS	Jackson	32	18	90	11	1	+46	+30	+17	+1	–10
MS	Meridian	32	22	88	42	1	+40	+24	+11	–4	–15
MS	Tupelo	34	16	88	34	1	+35	+21	+10	–2	–11
MT	Billings	45	47	108	30	2	+16	+23	+29	+35	+40
MT	Butte	46	1	112	32	2	+31	+39	+45	+52	+57
MT	Glasgow	48	12	106	38	2	–1	+11	+21	+32	+42
MT	Great Falls	47	30	111	17	2	+20	+31	+39	+49	+58
MT	Helena	46	36	112	2	2	+27	+36	+43	+51	+57
MT	Miles City	46	25	105	51	2	+3	+11	+18	+26	+32
NC	Asheville	35	36	82	33	0	+67	+55	+46	+35	+27
NC	Charlotte	35	14	80	51	0	+61	+49	+39	+28	+19
NC	Durham	36	0	78	55	0	+51	+40	+31	+21	+13
NC	Greensboro	36	4	79	47	0	+54	+43	+35	+25	+17
NC	Raleigh	35	47	78	38	0	+51	+39	+30	+20	+12
NC	Wilmington	34	14	77	55	0	+52	+38	+27	+15	+5
ND	Bismarck	46	48	100	47	1	+41	+50	+58	+66	+73
ND	Fargo	46	53	96	47	1	+24	+34	+42	+50	+57
ND	Grand Forks	47	55	97	3	1	+21	+33	+43	+53	+62
ND	Minot	48	14	101	18	1	+36	+50	+59	+71	+81
ND	Williston	48	9	103	37	1	+46	+59	+69	+80	+90
NE	Grand Island	40	55	98	21	1	+53	+51	+49	+46	+44
NE	Lincoln	40	49	96	41	1	+47	+44	+42	+39	+37
NE	North Platte	41	8	100	46	1	+62	+60	+58	+56	+54
NE	Omaha	41	16	95	56	1	+43	+40	+39	+37	+36
NH	Berlin	44	28	71	11	0	–7	–3	0	+3	+7
NH	Keene	42	56	72	17	0	+2	+3	+4	+5	+6

STATE	CITY	NORTH LATITUDE °	NORTH LATITUDE ′	WEST LONGITUDE °	WEST LONGITUDE ′	TIME ZONE CODE	KEY LETTERS (MINUTES) A	B	C	D	E
NH	Manchester-Concord	42	59	71	28	0	0	0	+1	+2	+3
NH	Portsmouth	43	5	70	45	0	−4	−2	−1	0	0
NJ	Atlantic City	39	22	74	26	0	+23	+17	+13	+8	+4
NJ	Camden	39	57	75	7	0	+24	+19	+16	+12	+9
NJ	Cape May	38	56	74	56	0	+26	+20	+15	+9	+5
NJ	Newark-East Orange	40	44	74	10	0	+17	+14	+12	+9	+7
NJ	Paterson	40	55	74	10	0	+17	+14	+12	+9	+7
NJ	Trenton	40	13	74	46	0	+21	+17	+14	+11	+8
NM	Albuquerque	35	5	106	39	2	+45	+32	+22	+11	+2
NM	Gallup	35	32	108	45	2	+52	+40	+31	+20	+11
NM	Las Cruces	32	19	106	47	2	+53	+36	+23	+8	−3
NM	Roswell	33	24	104	32	2	+41	+26	+14	0	−10
NM	Santa Fe	35	41	105	56	2	+40	+28	+19	+9	0
NV	Carson City-Reno	39	10	119	46	3	+25	+19	+14	+9	+5
NV	Elko	40	50	115	46	3	+3	0	−1	−3	−5
NV	Las Vegas	36	10	115	9	3	+16	+4	−3	−13	−20
NY	Albany	42	39	73	45	0	+9	+10	+10	+11	+11
NY	Binghamton	42	6	75	55	0	+20	+19	+19	+18	+18
NY	Buffalo	42	53	78	52	0	+29	+30	+30	+31	+32
NY	New York	40	45	74	0	0	+17	+14	+11	+9	+6
NY	Ogdensburg	44	42	75	30	0	+8	+13	+17	+21	+25
NY	Syracuse	43	3	76	9	0	+17	+19	+20	+21	+22
OH	Akron	41	5	81	31	0	+46	+43	+41	+39	+37
OH	Canton	40	48	81	23	0	+46	+43	+41	+38	+36
OH	Cincinnati-Hamilton	39	6	84	31	0	+64	+58	+53	+48	+44
OH	Cleveland-Lakewood	41	30	81	42	0	+45	+43	+42	+40	+39
OH	Columbus	39	57	83	1	0	+55	+51	+47	+43	+40
OH	Dayton	39	45	84	10	0	+61	+56	+52	+48	+44
OH	Toledo	41	39	83	33	0	+52	+50	+49	+48	+47
OH	Youngstown	41	6	80	39	0	+42	+40	+38	+36	+34
OK	Oklahoma City	35	28	97	31	1	+67	+55	+46	+35	+26
OK	Tulsa	36	9	95	60	1	+59	+48	+40	+30	+22
OR	Eugene	44	3	123	6	3	+21	+24	+27	+30	+33
OR	Pendleton	45	40	118	47	3	−1	+4	+10	+16	+21
OR	Portland	45	31	122	41	3	+14	+20	+25	+31	+36
OR	Salem	44	57	123	1	3	+17	+23	+27	+31	+35
PA	Allentown-Bethlehem	40	36	75	28	0	+23	+20	+17	+14	+12
PA	Erie	42	7	80	5	0	+36	+36	+35	+35	+35
PA	Harrisburg	40	16	76	53	0	+30	+26	+23	+19	+16
PA	Lancaster	40	2	76	18	0	+28	+24	+20	+17	+13
PA	Philadelphia-Chester	39	57	75	9	0	+24	+19	+16	+12	+9
PA	Pittsburgh-McKeesport	40	26	80	0	0	+42	+38	+35	+32	+29
PA	Reading	40	20	75	56	0	+26	+22	+19	+16	+13
PA	Scranton-Wilkes-Barre	41	25	75	40	0	+21	+19	+18	+16	+15
PA	York	39	58	76	43	0	+30	+26	+22	+18	+15
RI	Providence	41	50	71	25	0	+3	+2	+1	0	0
SC	Charleston	32	47	79	56	0	+64	+48	+36	+21	+10
SC	Columbia	34	0	81	2	0	+65	+51	+40	+27	+17
SC	Spartanburg	34	56	81	57	0	+66	+53	+43	+32	+23
SD	Aberdeen	45	28	98	29	1	+37	+44	+49	+54	+59
SD	Pierre	44	22	100	21	1	+49	+53	+56	+60	+63
SD	Rapid City	44	5	103	14	2	+2	+5	+8	+11	+13
SD	Sioux Falls	43	33	96	44	1	+38	+40	+42	+44	+46
TN	Chattanooga	35	3	85	19	0	+79	+67	+57	+45	+36
TN	Knoxville	35	58	83	55	0	+71	+60	+51	+41	+33
TN	Memphis	35	9	90	3	1	+38	+26	+16	+5	−3
TN	Nashville	36	10	86	47	1	+22	+11	+3	−6	−14

STATE/PROVINCE	CITY	NORTH LATITUDE °	NORTH LATITUDE '	WEST LONGITUDE °	WEST LONGITUDE '	TIME ZONE CODE	KEY LETTERS (MINUTES) A	B	C	D	E
TX	Amarillo	35	12	101	50	1	+85	+73	+63	+52	+43
TX	Austin	30	16	97	45	1	+82	+62	+47	+29	+15
TX	Beaumont	30	5	94	6	1	+67	+48	+32	+14	0
TX	Brownsville	25	54	97	30	1	+91	+66	+46	+23	+5
TX	Corpus Christi	27	48	97	24	1	+86	+64	+46	+25	+9
TX	Dallas–Fort Worth	32	47	96	48	1	+71	+55	+43	+28	+17
TX	El Paso	31	45	106	29	2	+53	+35	+22	+6	−6
TX	Galveston	29	18	94	48	1	+72	+52	+35	+16	+1
TX	Houston	29	45	95	22	1	+73	+53	+37	+19	+5
TX	McAllen	26	12	98	14	1	+93	+69	+49	+26	+9
TX	San Antonio	29	25	98	30	1	+87	+66	+50	+31	+16
UT	Kanab	37	3	112	32	2	+62	+53	+46	+37	+30
UT	Moab	38	35	109	33	2	+46	+39	+33	+27	+22
UT	Ogden	41	13	111	58	2	+47	+45	+43	+41	+40
UT	Salt Lake City	40	45	111	53	2	+48	+45	+43	+40	+38
UT	Vernal	40	27	109	32	2	+40	+36	+33	+30	+28
VA	Charlottesville	38	2	78	30	0	+43	+35	+29	+22	+17
VA	Danville	36	36	79	23	0	+51	+41	+33	+24	+17
VA	Norfolk	36	51	76	17	0	+38	+28	+21	+12	+5
VA	Richmond	37	32	77	26	0	+41	+32	+25	+17	+11
VA	Roanoke	37	16	79	57	0	+51	+42	+35	+27	+21
VA	Winchester	39	11	78	10	0	+38	+33	+28	+23	+19
VT	Brattleboro	42	51	72	34	0	+4	+5	+5	+6	+7
VT	Burlington	44	29	73	13	0	0	+4	+8	+12	+15
VT	Rutland	43	37	72	58	0	+2	+5	+7	+9	+11
VT	St. Johnsbury	44	25	72	1	0	−4	0	+3	+7	+10
WA	Bellingham	48	45	122	29	3	0	+13	+24	+37	+47
WA	Seattle–Tacoma–Olympia	47	37	122	20	3	+3	+15	+24	+34	+42
WA	Spokane	47	40	117	24	3	−16	−4	+4	+14	+23
WA	Walla Walla	46	4	118	20	3	−5	+2	+8	+15	+21
WI	Eau Claire	44	49	91	30	1	+12	+17	+21	+25	+29
WI	Green Bay	44	31	88	0	1	0	+3	+7	+11	+14
WI	La Crosse	43	48	91	15	1	+15	+18	+20	+22	+25
WI	Madison	43	4	89	23	1	+10	+11	+12	+14	+15
WI	Milwaukee	43	2	87	54	1	+4	+6	+7	+8	+9
WI	Oshkosh	44	1	88	33	1	+3	+6	+9	+12	+15
WI	Wausau	44	58	89	38	1	+4	+9	+13	+18	+22
WV	Charleston	38	21	81	38	0	+55	+48	+42	+35	+30
WV	Parkersburg	39	16	81	34	0	+52	+46	+42	+36	+32
WY	Casper	42	51	106	19	2	+19	+19	+20	+21	+22
WY	Cheyenne	41	8	104	49	2	+19	+16	+14	+12	+11
WY	Sheridan	44	48	106	58	2	+14	+19	+23	+27	+31
CANADA											
AB	Calgary	51	5	114	5	2	+13	+35	+50	+68	+84
AB	Edmonton	53	34	113	25	2	−3	+26	+47	+72	+93
BC	Vancouver	49	13	123	6	3	0	+15	+26	+40	+52
MB	Winnipeg	49	53	97	10	1	+12	+30	+43	+58	+71
NB	Saint John	45	16	66	3	−1	+28	+34	+39	+44	+49
NS	Halifax	44	38	63	35	−1	+21	+26	+29	+33	+37
NS	Sydney	46	10	60	10	−1	+1	+9	+15	+23	+28
ON	Ottawa	45	25	75	43	0	+6	+13	+18	+23	+28
ON	Peterborough	44	18	78	19	0	+21	+25	+28	+32	+35
ON	Thunder Bay	48	27	89	12	0	+47	+61	+71	+83	+93
ON	Toronto	43	39	79	23	0	+28	+30	+32	+35	+37
QC	Montreal	45	28	73	39	0	−1	+4	+9	+15	+20
SK	Saskatoon	52	10	106	40	1	+37	+63	+80	+101	+119

(continued)

Classifieds

Advertisements and statements contained herein are the sole responsibility of the persons or entities that post the advertisement, and *The Old Farmer's Almanac* does not make any warranty as to the accuracy, completeness, truthfulness, or reliability of such advertisements.

Classifieds

PSYCHICS

REV. JACKSON, VOODOO HEALER. Guaranteed to remove Cross Conditions, Bad Luck, Sickness, Roots, Pain. **Call: 252-469-6420.**

2 FREE QUESTIONS
Powerful Love Specialist—Psychic Savannah
Need Answers? Worried? Depressed?
Confused? Reunites Lovers, Finds Soulmates,
Stops Breakups, Removes Negativity.
Never Fails! Guaranteed.
Call: 818-388-2277

PSYCHIC HEALER LYNN. Worried? Suffering? Solves all problems! Specializes: Love, Health, Finances. Call Today! **704-550-5975.**

FREE SAMPLE READING. Psychic Gina. Love and Relationship Specialist Reunites Lovers Fast! Never Fails! **Call: 512-554-3693 or 737-757-6877.**

PSYCHIC HEALER solves all problems! Reunites lovers, Restores nature, Removes bad luck, evil, roots. **Call: 770-862-6553.**

PSYCHIC DINA—Helps where others failed! Solves problems immediately. Reunites lovers. Removes evil, rootwork. **Call: 954-394-7127.**

SPIRITUALIST PROPHET HEALER Ms. Janie. Helps and give advice in all matters of life. **Call: 206-854-0889.**

Psychic Grace Taylor
FREE CONSULTATION!
World-renowned Love Expert.
Reunites lovers. Clears emotional
obstacles. Solves all problems. Love,
Relationships, Family, Career.
Answers ALL questions! **856-813-7753**

FREE READING! PSYCHIC SONYA
God-Gifted Indian Spiritualist
Chakra Healing—Love Cleansing
Solves impossible problems;
Love, Marriage, Finance, Career, Happiness,
Luck. Reunites Lovers. Guaranteed.
786-514-8062

FREE READING!
Problems? Unhappy? Separated from lover?
Bring them back! Control his/her mind.
Call enemies' name. Removes sickness
& bad luck! Immediate Solutions!
(Psychic Lisa) 407-300-3357

REAL ESTATE

CALIFORNIA REAL ESTATE

Fast, Fair, & Friendly!
Conejo Mike — Buy & Sell Property.

Mike John Hornick:
Real Estate Made Easy

www.conejomike.realtor
call or text 805-390-0843
email: MJHornick@aol.com

RE Broker License #01402970
Let Conejo Mike help with your
California Real Estate.

SPIRITUALISTS

ANN, GOD'S MESSENGER. Religious Holy Worker. Reunites lovers forever. Clears stumbling blocks. Stops rootwork! Solves problems. Never fails! 50 years' exp. Fayetteville, N.C. **Call: 910-864-3981.**

NATALIA, SPIRITUALIST—Heals broken hearts. Reunites lovers fast. Removes negativity. Get Answers! FREE CONSULTATION! **Call: 214-664-5168.**

**MASTER SPIRITUALIST
BROTHER DANIEL**
55 years' experience
Helping all matters of life.
Stop your searching!
Ends confusion, negativity.
I can and will solve your problems!
Love, Marriage, Family,
Divorce, Blockages,
Substance Abuse, Court Cases,
Sickness.
True Answers! Real Results!
Call: 772-971-2830

PAY AFTER LOVER RETURNS
Call: 310-269-9949
Scotty Gray
Reconnects energy flow.
And watch your love grow!

The Old Farmer's Almanac has no liability whatsoever for any third-party claims arising in connection with such advertisements or any products or services mentioned therein.

(continued)

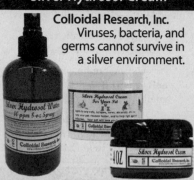

www.LuckShop.com

LUCKY 7 GAMBLERS GOOD LUCK NECKLACE

No. J4215 Only $16.95
(2 for $30.00)

This Necklace is good for any game or casino:
- Bingo
- River Boat Gambling
- Dice or Craps
- Lottery [All Games]
- Horses or Dogs
- Horses or Dogs
- Cards or Blackjack
- Slot Machines
- Any Las Vegas-style Numbers Game

RUB THE GENIE WISHING LAMP
for INSTANT MIRACLES!

GRANTS UP TO 7 WISHES:
Rub the Genie for... Instant Money Miracles; Removing Jinx and Bad Luck; Turning Back Evil and Enemies; Having Luck and Success; Health and Happiness; Win Court Case and Make Law Stay Away; and Improve & Make Love Stronger.

ORDER NOW! SUPPLIES ARE LIMITED!
PUT TO EVERY TEST — 100% GUARANTEED OR MONEY BACK
No. J4230...Only $16.95 (2 for $30.00)

Rev. Moses LUCKY HAND BAG

No. M4000   Only $19.95 each

Brings you fast luck and good fortune in ALL situations. Helps you Hit that Jackpot! At casino and gambling games, and get on a hot streak! Hit that Winning Number! Carry or place in a secret place in your car or home to be Lucky and keep the money rolling in.

TRIPLE STRENGTH OILS

Powerful Working Formula - Use When All Else has Failed!

X3024 - GAMBLERS - Win big and hit that jackpot to be rich.

X3036 - LOVE POTION - Draw, Hold, and Make your lover stay close.

X3048 - TURN BACK EVIL - Send all evil, enemies, and the devil running.

X3056 - WEALTHY WAY - Draw money, riches and power to you very quickly!

**$11.98 each
Any 2 for $20**
Comes with Directions

TRIPLE STRENGTH LUCKY MOJO COIN

No. J1005   Only $16.95 each
(2 for $30.00)

FREE! Xtra Strong Fast Luck Oil & Carrying Bag

Be Lucky in all games of chance. Brings Good Luck in Love, Wealth, Health and Provides strong Protection Against Evil & Enemies.

LUCKY RABBIT'S FOOT
- PERFUMED OIL -

No. P5100 $8.95 each   (2 for $15.00)

Use for FAST LUCK in everything: money, love, family or work problems.

Sweet-smelling oil comes with a LUCKY RABBIT'S FOOT attached.

Put some oil on you and your rabbit's foot and be RICHER, HAPPIER, LUCKIER than ever before.

LUCKY PENNY
(IN A BOTTLE)
GAMBLERS OIL

No. X1778   Only $7.98

Brings Fast Luck and winnings to you — for any gambling game. A lot of oldtimers swear by it.
GET IT NOW!

GOOD LUCK CRYSTAL

**No. J2311 Only $11.95
2 for $20.00**
Are you down, lonely, confused, jinxed? If so, get rid of bad luck & evil. **Carry or wear this Healing Necklace.**

SPELL BREAKER COLOGNE

- Breaks any evil spell or curse on you.
- Be protected from all harm.
- Feel cleansed, happy & healthy.

No. A1655 $8.95 each

TRIPLE STRENGTH (XXX) POWDERS
$7.98 each

P1357 - LUCKY GAMBLERS
Hit that Winning Number and Jackpot! Win & Get Rich Quick!

P1365 - MONEY DRAWING
For body or sprinkling to get some money, fast!

FREE!

FREE GIFT & CATALOG WITH EVERY ORDER!

CALL 312-332-1634
to place Credit/Debit Card orders

- Credit/Debit Card orders are shipped out the same day or next day.
- PREPAID CASH OR MONEY ORDER ACCEPTED
- NO C.O.D. ORDERS
- PREPAID CHECK – please include STREET ADDRESS & PHONE NUMBER on check or order will be delayed.
- ADD $4.95 for POSTAGE & HANDLING
- ADD $4.00 Extra ($8.95 Total) for RUSH SERVICE

CHURCH GOODS CO. ° DEPT. F-25
P.O. Box 718 • Glenview, Illinois 60025
www.LuckShop.com

For online orders, please enter code "F-25" to get above discounted Postage & Handling Rates

2024 ESSAY CONTEST WINNERS

"The Best Money I Ever Spent"

We received hundreds of amusing and moving anecdotes and stories. Thank you to all who submitted entries!

First Prize: $300

It was an uncomfortably warm day as I sat on near-empty bleachers watching my son race bicycles. A few rows behind me, a young family was also trying to watch their son through the dust. With them was another son who looked to be about 7. Bored. It was easy to overhear the escalating frustrations on both sides. Then I heard, "What are you going to do with that rock?" "I'm going to sell it." "Nobody's going to buy a rock that you just picked up under the bleachers!"

A few moments later, I heard a little voice ask, "Ma'am, would you like to buy a rock?" "How much?," I said. "A dollar," he replied. I reached into my purse and got a dollar for him. Then, behind me, I heard, "Where did you get that money?" "I sold the rock." "For a dollar?" Then I heard laughing, encouragement, praise. No more frustration. He had become their budding entrepreneur. That was the best money I ever spent.

–*Ruth Davis, Mogadore, Ohio*

Second Prize: $200

I was hauling a shipment of Rocky Mountain oysters to Laramie, Wyoming, on a Friday afternoon, and the last stop was at a small grocery store. As the lumpers were getting the truck unloaded, I wandered over to the Kum & Go to get a snack. A lady in the parking lot had a laundry basket full of puppies in the bed of an old Dodge truck. I hesitated momentarily but decided that my newborn son might enjoy some company when I was on the road, and $25 wasn't a bad deal for a good-looking retriever pup. Fast-forward 6 years or so: My son and his beloved pup, whom we had named Rusty, were playing out in the pasture when I heard a scuffle with a lot of barking and screaming. I ran out to find my son scared and in tears and Rusty scratched up and limping—but seemingly in good spirits. After a short investigation, I came to find out that a bobcat or small mountain lion had been stalking my boy and Rusty as they were playing. If I hadn't spent $25 so many years before on a great dog, my son might not be alive today.

–*Brenton Chinn, Fort Collins, Colorado*

Third Prize: $100

The best money I ever spent was the 35 cents that I plunked down in the Christmas season of 1963 to buy a gift that my family would consult throughout the year. I thereafter discovered, in perusing that 1964 *Old Farmer's Almanac,* that a total eclipse of the Moon would occur the evening of June 24. The problem was that when it was nearly at the end of its totality at 8:57 P.M., the eclipse would be half-lost in the glow of twilight. There would be only a thin sliver of time when the Moon would be high enough in the east and the sky dark enough in the west to enjoy the full event.

I invited a special young lady to view it with me from a vantage-point in a field with broad eastward exposure. Alas, as sunset approached, clouds gathered, and it started raining. I was, of course, extremely disappointed. But she smiled brightly and said, "It really means a lot that you wanted to share this with me. And I bet you're the only boy around who even knew that it was going to happen!" It made me really glad that I'd bought that 35-cent Almanac!

–Rand Peabody, Peabody, Massachusetts

Honorable Mention

The best money I ever spent was on hogs. For the past 10 years, I've invested in market hogs. In July of each year, I would show them at my local fair and sell them at the end of the fair week. Because I made this investment over and over again, I was able to accomplish many things. I was able to buy my first vehicle by myself, and I was able to pay for my college education without a loan. Not only did I earn money from raising market hogs, but also, from being part of a 4-H club, I learned valuable life lessons about responsibility, leadership (from my 4-H officer role), and money management. Therefore, the best money I've ever spent was on pigs—as funny as that may sound!

–Kylee Williams, Lebanon, Pennsylvania

Also Noted: J. Cramer, San Diego, California; A. DeMonte, Pleasantville, New York; F. Levy, Alexandria, Virginia; A. Lopez, San Antonio, Texas; T. Rumsy, Woodstock, New York. ■

ANNOUNCING THE 2025 ESSAY CONTEST TOPIC:
THE BEST GIFT I EVER GAVE
SEE CONTEST RULES ON PAGE 251.

MADDENING MIND-MANGLERS

A. OBLIQUE QUESTION
In an oblique-angled triangle, the product of the two sides is 186 and their difference is 3.5. The ratio of the shortest side to the base is 4:7. What are the lengths of the sides?
–From the 1825 Old Farmer's Almanac

B. MAN OVERBOARD!
When faced with a dangerous storm that might sink his ship, a sea captain found it necessary to throw half of his 30 passengers overboard in order to lighten the vessel. Fifteen of the passengers, like the captain, were lefthanders; the other 15 were righthanders. The passengers agreed that for the sake of fairness, they would form a line and allow the captain to throw every ninth person over the side, the line thus decreasing in length as each choice was made. If the captain wished to end up by saving all 15 of his fellow lefthanders, how would he place the passengers in line to begin his selections?
–From the 1836 Old Farmer's Almanac, adapted from a puzzle published in 1628

C. ALL-STAR QUESTION
I am a word of four letters, in which may be found a former ruler, a verb, an animal, a viscous liquid, a humanity, a conjunction, and a preposition. What words are we?

D. ROUNDABOUT
Two women travel by day in the same direction around and around an island 24 miles in circumference and camp at night. Woman A has a 1 mile head start and travels 1 mile in the first day, 3 miles in the second, and so on, increasing her rate by 2 miles each day. Woman B goes 5 miles each day. When will they camp together?

E. THE FOLLY OF HEIGHT
Match the following objects or places with their height or elevation:

____ **1.** Washington Monument		**a.** 5,725 ft.
____ **2.** Mt. Olympus, Greece		**b.** 1,776 ft.
____ **3.** Denali (Mt. McKinley), Alaska		**c.** 9,570 ft.
____ **4.** One World Trade Center, NYC tower		**d.** 6,288 ft.
____ **5.** Mt. Washington, New Hampshire		**e.** 555 ft.
____ **6.** Willis (formerly Sears) Tower, Chicago		**f.** 1,450 ft.
____ **7.** Mt. Rushmore, South Dakota		**g.** 29,032 ft.
____ **8.** Mt. Everest, Nepal		**h.** 20,310 ft.
____ **9.** Highest water drop, Victoria Falls, Zimbabwe		**i.** 354 ft.
____ **10.** Mt. Kilimanjaro, Tanzania		**j.** 19,341 ft.

Do you have a favorite puzzler for "Mad-dening Mind-Manglers" that you'd like to share? Send it to us at Mind-Manglers, The Old Farmer's Almanac, P.O. Box 520, Dublin, NH 03444, or via Almanac .com/Contact, Subject: Mind-Manglers.

ANSWERS TO MIND-MANGLERS

A. 3.5 multiplied by 3.5 equals 12.25. This divided by 4 is equal to 3.0625. This added to 186 is equal to 189.0625, the square root of which is 13.75. Then, 3.5 divided by 2 is equal to 1.75, which, subtracted from 13.75, is equal to 12— the shortest side. Then, 13.75 added to 1.75 (or, 3.5 added to 12) is equal to 15.5—the longer side. Thus, for the ratio between the shortest side and base to be 4:7, if the shortest side is 12, then the base must be 21. (Answered correctly by seven readers in 1825.) **B.** L-L-L-L-R-R-R-R-R-L-L-L-R-L-L-L-R-L-R-R-L-L-R-R-R-L-R-R-L-L-R. **C.** Star, tsar, sat, rat, tar, art, as, at. **D.** Never. **E.** 1. e. 2. c. 3. h. 4. b. 5. d. 6. f. 7. a. 8. g. 9. i. 10. j.

ANSWERS TO ANECDOTES & PLEASANTRIES

Quizzical: **1.** b. **2.** Juneau, AK; Dover, DE; Jefferson City, MO; Pierre, SD. *Cringe:* **1.** A "step farther." **2.** Because it is let out at night and taken in by day. **3.** A vile inn. **4.** A good appetite. **5.** Because you make his feet-yours. **6.** Make the pants and vest first. **7.** Why, that it ate the tiger, of course! **8.** No cow, because no cow has more than four legs. **9.** cares (caress). *Earworm:* "It's a Small World (After All)." *Food:* Bananas.

ESSAY AND RECIPE CONTEST RULES

ANECDOTES & PLEASANTRIES

A sampling from the thousands of letters, clippings, articles, and emails sent to us during the past year by our Almanac family in the United States and Canada.

ILLUSTRATIONS BY TIM ROBINSON

DOGGIE DISPATCHES OF THE YEAR

■ **GOING WITH THE FLOE:** Nanuq, a 1-year-old Australian shepherd, apparently "chilled out" a little too much and ended up getting "lost" while hunting on ice that detached and floated away. Later found 150 miles away along the Alaskan coast, the pooch appeared none the worse for wear except for a leg swollen from a "really big bite," according to his owner, which could have come from a wolverine, seal, small polar bear, or . . . who knows? *–N. S., Ketchikan, Alaska*

■ **MAXED-OUT MAYORS:** For the third time, voters in Idyllwild, Calfornia, have elected a golden retriever— Max III—to take the lead in their community. *–C. S., Hollywood, California*

■ **SLANTED STUDY:** Animal behavior researchers have reported in *Animal Cognition* that while dogs may tilt their heads for any number of reasons while looking at you, this is most likely because they are trying to better understand you. We observe that no one appears to have even tried to investigate this phenomenon in cats. *–B. W., Gadsden, Alabama*

QUIZZICAL QUERIES *(Answers on page 251.)*

1. "DODGING" THE ISSUE: Major League Baseball's Los Angeles (née Brooklyn) Dodgers were so named because . . .
a. Their owners were known to always be dodging bill collectors.
b. Fans were always dodging trolley cars around the team's home park, Ebbets Field.
c. The team was known for trying to use trick plays, or "dodges," on the field.
d. Brooklyn was home to many Dodge automobiles. *–C. B., Parsippany, New Jersey*

2. A CAPITAL IDEA: Which four U.S. state capitals can not be accessed via the Interstate Highway System? *–G. S., Calgary, Alberta*

Highway Hijinx

■ **"DON'T LET THIS HAPPEN AGAIN!":** Before running away after having been pulled over for doing 52 in a 30-mph zone, a DUI Colorado driver tried to switch places with his dog. According to a later report, "the dog did not face any charges and was let go with a warning." *–J. B., Fort Collins, Colorado*

■ **REACHING THEIR LIMIT:** We're told that a trooper recently pulled over a car because it was proceeding very slowly. Inside, he found four elderly ladies. "Was I doing anything wrong, officer?," asked the driver. "No, not really," replied the trooper, "but driving too slow is as dangerous as driving too fast—and you were going very slowly." "But the sign says '22'," the lady answered. "Oh, ma'am," the officer said, "that's the route sign, not the speed limit." By this time, he'd noticed that the other three women were sitting very stiff and still, each one staring straight ahead. "Ladies, are you all right?," he inquired. There was no answer, and no one even moved. He asked again, and finally the lady in the passenger seat said, "We just got off Route 119." *–Z. G., Berne, New York*

■ **A LOT OF BULL:** In Nebraska, a driver was stopped for carrying a giant half-longhorn, half-Watusi bull named Howdy Doody—weighing more than a ton—in the passenger seat of his "beefed up" 1996 Ford Crown Victoria. "It's a solid car," the owner reported, "so I just cut the top off and we were good to go." *–T. L., St. Joseph, Missouri*

(continued)

ODE TO A COW

When life seems one too many for you,
Go and look at a cow.
When the future's black and the
  outlook blue,
Go and look at a cow.
For she does nothing but eat her food,
And sleep in the meadows entirely nood,
Refusing to fret or worry or brood
Because she doesn't know how.

Whenever you're feeling bothered
  and sore,
Go and look at a cow.
When everything else is a fearful bore,
Go and look at a cow.
Observe her gentle and placid air.
Her nonchalance and savoir faire,
Her absolute freedom from every care,
Her imperturbable brow.

So when you're at the end of your wits,
Go and look at a cow.
Or when your nerves are frayed to bits,
And wrinkles furrow your brow;
She'll merely moo in her gentle way,
Switching her rudder as if to say:
"Bother tomorrow! Let's live today!"
Take the advice of a cow.

–from the London News-Chronicle, *in*
The 1936 Old Farmer's Almanac

Cringe Binge

(Answers on page 251.)

1. What relation is the doormat to the doorstep?

2. Why is a watchdog bigger by night than by day?

3. What sort of musical instrument resembles a bad hotel?

4. What is it that everyone wishes for and yet wishes to get rid of as soon as it is obtained?

5. Why, when you paint a man's portrait, may you be described as stepping into his shoes?

6. What is the best way to make a suit coat last?

7. Would you rather that a lion ate you or a tiger?

8. Which has the most legs, a cow or no cow?

9. What is a noun of a plural number,
Foe to peace and tranquil slumber,
That add to it the letter s,
And, wondrous metamorphosis,
Plural is plural now no more,
And sweet what bitter was before?

–from Puniana: or, Thoughts Wise and Otherwise, *by the Hon. Hugh Rowley, London, 1867*

EARWORM TRIGGER ALERT!

No, not a *real* earworm—we're talking about a song melody that you can't get out of your head. Researchers at Scotland's University of St Andrews not only derived a formula for rating such nemeses but also produced a ranking. Coming in—or going on and on and on and on—at #1 was "We Will Rock You" by Queen, who also scored #3 with "We Are the Champions" and #6 with "Bohemian Rhapsody." "Happy" by Pharrell Williams was #2. Other "winners" included "YMCA" (#5), "Never Gonna Give You Up" (#12), and "Beat It" (#16). Admirably holding up the honor of the traditional, James Lord Pierpont (1822–93) came in at #9 with "Jingle Bells." However, if you're a true believer in self-punishment, please turn to page 251 to learn the Almanac's pick for all-time #1 earworm, which we believe is far more dangerous than any of these. Remember: You have been warned. *–M. D., Marquette, Michigan*

"Food" for Thought—or Naught

■ **VICTORIOUS VICTUAL:** Can you guess the most popular grocery store food item in North America? *(Answer on page 251.)*

-R. S., Bethlehem, Pennsylvania

■ **DULLEST DUBIOUS DISTINCTION OF THE DECADE (YES, BEFORE THE 10 YEARS ARE EVEN UP!):** This recognition goes out to an obvious bread-lover in Vancouver, B.C., who had the half-baked idea of collecting (and mounting on homemade monthly calendars, no less) plastic bread bag clips with expiration dates for every day of the year—plus the rare, unicorn-like fastener for November 31! If you ask us, a pretty "crumby" accomplishment.

-P. R., Lethbridge, Alberta

■ **WHY DIDN'T WE THINK OF THIS?** Actually, why *would* we think of this? To generate some Halloween Night traffic at his out-of-the-way house, one Massachusetts homeowner successfully gave out rotisserie chickens that he had been able to get for $4.69 each—and *voilà*, a new tradition was born, er, hatched: Trickin'-or-Chicken!

-W. T., Pittsfield, Massachusetts

Send your contribution for *The 2026 Old Farmer's Almanac* by January 31, 2025, to "A & P," The Old Farmer's Almanac, P.O. Box 520, Dublin, NH 03444, or via Almanac.com/Contact.

THE GOLDEN RULE
(It's true in all faiths.)

BRAHMANISM:

This is the sum of duty: Do naught unto others which would cause you pain if done to you.

Mahabharata 5:1517

BUDDHISM:

Hurt not others in ways that you yourself would find hurtful.

Udana-Varga 5:18

CHRISTIANITY:

All things whatsoever ye would that men should do to you, do ye even so to them; for this is the law and the prophets.

Matthew 7:12

CONFUCIANISM:

Surely it is the maxim of loving-kindness: Do not unto others what you would not have them do unto you.

Analects 15:23

ISLAM:

No one of you is a believer until he desires for his brother that which he desires for himself.

Sunnah

JUDAISM:

What is hateful to you, do not to your fellow man. That is the entire Law; all the rest is commentary.

Talmud, Shabbat 31a

TAOISM:

Regard your neighbor's gain as your own gain and your neighbor's loss as your own loss.

T'ai Shang Kan Ying P'ien

ZOROASTRIANISM:

That nature alone is good which refrains from doing unto another whatsoever is not good for itself.

Dadistan-i-dinik 94:5
–courtesy of Elizabeth Pool

FAMOUS LAST WORDS

Waiting, are they? Waiting, are they? Well—let 'em wait.
(To an attending doctor who attempted to comfort him by saying, "General, I fear the angels are waiting for you.")
–Ethan Allen, American Revolutionary general, d. February 12, 1789

A dying man can do nothing easy.
–Benjamin Franklin, American statesman, d. April 17, 1790

Now I shall go to sleep. Good night.
–Lord George Byron, English writer, d. April 19, 1824

Is it the Fourth?
–Thomas Jefferson, 3rd U.S. president, d. July 4, 1826

Thomas Jefferson—still survives . . .
(Actually, Jefferson had died earlier that same day.)
–John Adams, 2nd U.S. president, d. July 4, 1826

Friends, applaud. The comedy is finished.
–Ludwig van Beethoven, German-Austrian composer, d. March 26, 1827

Moose . . . Indian . . .
–Henry David Thoreau, American writer, d. May 6, 1862

Go on, get out—last words are for fools who haven't said enough.
(To his housekeeper, who urged him to tell her his last words so she could write them down for posterity.)
–Karl Marx, German political philosopher, d. March 14, 1883

Is it not meningitis?
–Louisa M. Alcott, American writer, d. March 6, 1888

How were the receipts today at Madison Square Garden?
–P. T. Barnum, American entrepreneur, d. April 7, 1891

Turn up the lights, I don't want to go home in the dark.
–O. Henry (William Sydney Porter), American writer, d. June 5, 1910

Get my swan costume ready.
–Anna Pavlova, Russian ballerina, d. January 23, 1931

Is everybody happy? I want everybody to be happy. I know I'm happy.
–Ethel Barrymore, American actress, d. June 18, 1959

I'm bored with it all.
(Before slipping into a coma. He died 9 days later.)
–Winston Churchill, English statesman, d. January 24, 1965

You be good. You'll be in tomorrow. I love you.
–Alex, highly intelligent African Gray parrot, d. September 6, 2007

A Reference Compendium

REFERENCE

REFERENCE

PHASES OF THE MOON

New

Waxing Crescent

First Quarter

Waxing Gibbous

Full

Waning Gibbous

Last Quarter

Waning Crescent

New

W A X I N G

W A N I N G

WHEN WILL THE MOON RISE?

Use the following saying to remember the time of moonrise on a day when a Moon phase occurs. Keep in mind that the phase itself may happen earlier or later that day, depending on location.

The new Moon always rises near sunrise;

The first quarter, near noon;

The full Moon always rises near sunset;

The last quarter, near midnight.

Moonrise occurs about 50 minutes later each day.

FULL MOON NAMES

NAME	MONTH	VARIATIONS
Full Wolf Moon	JANUARY	Full Greetings Moon
Full Snow Moon	FEBRUARY	Full Hungry Moon
Full Worm Moon	MARCH	Full Eagle Moon Full Sore Eye Moon Full Sugar Moon Full Wind Strong Moon
Full Pink Moon	APRIL	Full Budding Moon Moon When the Geese Lay Eggs
Full Flower Moon	MAY	Full Frog Moon Full Planting Moon
Full Strawberry Moon	JUNE	Full Hoer Moon Full Hot Moon
Full Buck Moon	JULY	Full Raspberry Moon Full Salmon Moon
Full Sturgeon Moon	AUGUST	Full Black Cherries Moon Full Flying Up Moon
Full Harvest Moon*	SEPTEMBER	Full Corn Moon Full Yellow Leaf Moon
Full Hunter's Moon	OCTOBER	Full Falling Leaves Moon Full Migrating Moon
Full Beaver Moon	NOVEMBER	Full Frost Moon
Full Cold Moon	DECEMBER	Full Long Night Moon

*The Harvest Moon is always the full Moon closest to the autumnal equinox. If the Harvest Moon occurs in October, the September full Moon is usually called the Corn Moon.

THE ORIGIN OF FULL MOON NAMES

Historically, some Native Americans who lived in the area that is now the United States kept track of the seasons by giving a distinctive name to each recurring full Moon. (This name was applied to the entire lunar month in which it occurred.) The names were used by various tribes and/or by colonial Americans, who also brought their own traditions.

Meanings of Full Moon Names

JANUARY'S full Moon was called the **Wolf Moon** because wolves were more often heard at this time.

FEBRUARY'S full Moon was called the **Snow Moon** because it was a time of heavy snow. It was also called the **Hungry Moon** because hunting was difficult and hunger often resulted.

MARCH'S full Moon was called the **Worm Moon** because, as the weather warmed, wormlike insect larvae emerged from winter homes such as the bark of trees.

APRIL'S full Moon was called the **Pink Moon** because it heralded the appearance of the moss pink, or wild ground phlox—one of the first spring flowers.

MAY'S full Moon was called the **Flower Moon** because blossoms were abundant everywhere at this time.

JUNE'S full Moon was called the **Strawberry Moon** because it appeared when the strawberry harvest took place.

JULY'S full Moon was called the **Buck Moon**; it arrived when a male deer's antlers were in full growth mode.

AUGUST'S full Moon was called the **Sturgeon Moon** because this large fish, which is found in the Great Lakes and Lake Champlain, was caught easily at this time.

SEPTEMBER'S full Moon was called the **Corn Moon** because this was the time to harvest corn.

The **Harvest Moon** is the full Moon that occurs closest to the autumnal equinox. It can occur in either September or October. Around this time, the Moon rises only about 30 minutes later each night, providing extra light after sunset for harvesting.

OCTOBER'S full Moon was called the **Hunter's Moon** because this was the time to hunt in preparation for winter.

NOVEMBER'S full Moon was called the **Beaver Moon** because it was the time when beavers finished preparations for winter and retreated to their lodges.

DECEMBER'S full Moon was called the **Cold Moon.** It was also called the **Long Night Moon** because nights at this time of year were the longest.

REFERENCE

THE ORIGIN OF MONTH NAMES

JANUARY. For the Roman god Janus, protector of gates and doorways. Janus is depicted with two faces, one looking into the past, the other into the future.

FEBRUARY. From the Latin *februa,* "to cleanse." The Roman Februalia was a festival of purification and atonement that took place during this time of year.

MARCH. For the Roman god of war, Mars. This was the time of year to resume military campaigns that had been interrupted by winter.

APRIL. From the Latin *aperio,* "to open (bud)," because plants begin to grow now.

MAY. For the Roman goddess Maia, who oversaw the growth of plants. Also from the Latin *maiores,* "elders," who were celebrated now.

JUNE. For the Roman goddess Juno, patroness of marriage and the well-being of women. Also from the Latin *juvenis,* "young people."

JULY. To honor Roman dictator Julius Caesar (100 B.C.–44 B.C.). In 46 B.C., with the help of Sosigenes, he developed the Julian calendar.

AUGUST. To honor the first Roman emperor (and grandnephew of Julius Caesar), Augustus Caesar (63 B.C.–A.D. 14).

SEPTEMBER. From the Latin *septem,* "seven," because this was the seventh month of the early Roman calendar.

OCTOBER. From the Latin *octo,* "eight," because this was the eighth month of the early Roman calendar.

NOVEMBER. From the Latin *novem,* "nine," because this was the ninth month of the early Roman calendar.

DECEMBER. From the Latin *decem,* "ten," because this was the tenth month of the early Roman calendar.

Easter Dates (2025–28)

Christian churches that follow the Gregorian calendar celebrate Easter on the first Sunday after the paschal full Moon on or just after the vernal equinox.

YEAR	EASTER
2025	April 20
2026	April 5
2027	March 28
2028	April 16

The Julian calendar is used by some churches, including many Eastern Orthodox. The dates below are Julian calendar dates for Easter converted to Gregorian dates.

YEAR	EASTER
2025	April 20
2026	April 12
2027	May 2
2028	April 16

FRIGGATRISKAIDEKAPHOBIA TRIVIA

Here are a few facts about Friday the 13th:

In the 14 possible configurations for the annual calendar (see any perpetual calendar), the occurrence of Friday the 13th is this:

6 of 14 years have one Friday the 13th.
6 of 14 years have two Fridays the 13th.
2 of 14 years have three Fridays the 13th.

No year is without one Friday the 13th, and no year has more than three.

Months that have a Friday the 13th begin on a Sunday.

2025 has a Friday the 13th in June.

REFERENCE

THE ORIGIN OF DAY NAMES

The days of the week were named by ancient Romans with the Latin words for the Sun, the Moon, and the five known planets. These names have survived in European languages, but English names also reflect Anglo-Saxon and Norse influences.

ENGLISH	LATIN	FRENCH	ITALIAN	SPANISH	ANGLO-SAXON AND NORSE
SUNDAY	dies Solis (Sol's day)	dimanche	domenica	domingo	Sunnandaeg (Sun's day)
		from the Latin for "Lord's day"			
MONDAY	dies Lunae (Luna's day)	lundi	lunedì	lunes	Monandaeg (Moon's day)
TUESDAY	dies Martis (Mars's day)	mardi	martedì	martes	Tiwesdaeg (Tiw's day)
WEDNESDAY	dies Mercurii (Mercury's day)	mercredi	mercoledì	miércoles	Wodnesdaeg (Woden's day)
THURSDAY	dies Jovis (Jupiter's day)	jeudi	giovedì	jueves	Thursdaeg (Thor's day)
FRIDAY	dies Veneris (Venus's day)	vendredi	venerdì	viernes	Frigedaeg (Frigga's day)
SATURDAY	dies Saturni (Saturn's day)	samedi	sabato	sábado	Saeterndaeg (Saturn's day)
		from the Latin for "Sabbath"			

How to Find the Day of the Week for Any Given Date

To compute the day of the week for any given date as far back as the mid–18th century, proceed as follows:

Add the last two digits of the year to one-quarter of the last two digits (discard any remainder), the day of the month, and the month key from the key box below. Divide the sum by 7; the remainder is the day of the week (1 is Sunday, 2 is Monday, and so on). If there is no remainder, the day is Saturday. If you're searching for a weekday prior to 1900, add 2 to the sum before dividing; prior to 1800, add 4. The formula doesn't work for days prior to 1753. From 2000 through 2099, subtract 1 from the sum before dividing.

Example:

THE DAYTON FLOOD WAS ON MARCH 25, 1913.

Last two digits of year:	13
One-quarter of these two digits:	3
Given day of month:	25
Key number for March:	4
Sum:	45

45 ÷ 7 = 6, with a remainder of 3. The flood took place on Tuesday, the third day of the week.

KEY

JANUARY	1
LEAP YEAR	0
FEBRUARY	4
LEAP YEAR	3
MARCH	4
APRIL	0
MAY	2
JUNE	5
JULY	0
AUGUST	3
SEPTEMBER	6
OCTOBER	1
NOVEMBER	4
DECEMBER	6

REFERENCE

ANIMAL SIGNS OF THE CHINESE ZODIAC

The animal designations of the Chinese zodiac follow a 12-year cycle and are always used in the same sequence. The Chinese year of 354 days begins 3 to 7 weeks into the western 365-day year, so the animal designation changes at that time, rather than on January 1. This year, the Lunar New Year in China starts on January 29.

RAT

Ambitious and sincere, you can be generous with your money. Compatible with the dragon and the monkey. Your opposite is the horse.

1936	1948	1960
1972	1984	1996
2008	2020	2032

OX OR BUFFALO

A leader, you are bright, patient, and cheerful. Compatible with the snake and the rooster. Your opposite is the sheep.

1937	1949	1961
1973	1985	1997
2009	2021	2033

TIGER

Forthright and sensitive, you possess great courage. Compatible with the horse and the dog. Your opposite is the monkey.

1938	1950	1962
1974	1986	1998
2010	2022	2034

RABBIT OR HARE

Talented and affectionate, you are a seeker of tranquility. Compatible with the sheep and the pig. Your opposite is the rooster.

1939	1951	1963
1975	1987	1999
2011	2023	2035

DRAGON

Robust and passionate, your life is filled with complexity. Compatible with the monkey and the rat. Your opposite is the dog.

1940	1952	1964
1976	1988	2000
2012	2024	2036

SNAKE

Strong-willed and intense, you display great wisdom. Compatible with the rooster and the ox. Your opposite is the pig.

1929	1941	1953
1965	1977	1989
2001	2013	2025

HORSE

Physically attractive and popular, you like the company of others. Compatible with the tiger and the dog. Your opposite is the rat.

1930	1942	1954
1966	1978	1990
2002	2014	2026

GOAT OR SHEEP

Aesthetic and stylish, you enjoy being a private person. Compatible with the pig and the rabbit. Your opposite is the ox.

1931	1943	1955
1967	1979	1991
2003	2015	2027

MONKEY

Persuasive, skillful, and intelligent, you strive to excel. Compatible with the dragon and the rat. Your opposite is the tiger.

1932	1944	1956
1968	1980	1992
2004	2016	2028

ROOSTER OR COCK

Seeking wisdom and truth, you have a pioneering spirit. Compatible with the snake and the ox. Your opposite is the rabbit.

1933	1945	1957
1969	1981	1993
2005	2017	2029

DOG

Generous and loyal, you have the ability to work well with others. Compatible with the horse and the tiger. Your opposite is the dragon.

1934	1946	1958
1970	1982	1994
2006	2018	2030

PIG OR BOAR

Gallant and noble, your friends will remain at your side. Compatible with the rabbit and the sheep. Your opposite is the snake.

1935	1947	1959
1971	1983	1995
2007	2019	2031

REFERENCE

A Table Foretelling the Weather Through All the Lunations of Each Year, or Forever

This table is the result of many years of actual observation and shows what sort of weather will probably follow the Moon's entrance into any of its quarters. For example, the table shows that the week following January 6, 2025, will be fair and frosty if the wind is north or northeast or have rain or snow if the wind is south or southwest, because the Moon enters the first quarter at 6:56 P.M. EST. (See the **Left-Hand Calendar Pages, 120–146,** for Moon phases.)

EDITOR'S NOTE: Although the data in this table is taken into consideration in the year-long process of compiling the annual long-range weather forecasts for *The Old Farmer's Almanac,* we rely far more on our projections of solar activity.

TIME OF CHANGE	SUMMER	WINTER
Midnight to 2 A.M.	Fair	Hard frost, unless wind is south or west
2 A.M. to 4 A.M.	Cold, with frequent showers	Snow and stormy
4 A.M. to 6 A.M.	Rain	Rain
6 A.M. to 8 A.M.	Wind and rain	Stormy
8 A.M. to 10 A.M.	Changeable	Cold rain if wind is west; snow, if east
10 A.M. to noon	Frequent showers	Cold with high winds
Noon to 2 P.M.	Very rainy	Snow or rain
2 P.M. to 4 P.M.	Changeable	Fair and mild
4 P.M. to 6 P.M.	Fair	Fair
6 P.M. to 10 P.M.	Fair if wind is northwest; rain if wind is south or southwest	Fair and frosty if wind is north or northeast; rain or snow if wind is south or southwest
10 P.M. to midnight	Fair	Fair and frosty

This table was created more than 190 years ago by Dr. Herschell for the Boston Courier; *it first appeared in* The Old Farmer's Almanac *in 1834.*

SAFE ICE THICKNESS*

ICE THICKNESS	PERMISSIBLE LOAD	ICE THICKNESS	PERMISSIBLE LOAD
4 inches	Single person on foot	8–10 inches	Passenger car, small SUV
5 inches	Small group skating	10–12 inches	Light truck, compact SUV
5–7 inches	Snowmobile, small ATV	12–15 inches	Medium truck, mid-size SUV
7–8 inches	Multi-rider ATV, UTV	16 inches	Heavy truck, full-size SUV

Ice is never 100 percent safe. It forms on lakes and ponds unevenly, so while it may be 4 inches thick in one area, it could be much thinner a few feet away. Avoid ice that is cracked or near inlets or moving water.

*Solid, clear, blue/black pond and lake ice

The strength value of river ice is 15 percent less. Slush ice has only half the strength of blue ice.

HEAT INDEX °F (°C)

TEMP. °F (°C)	RELATIVE HUMIDITY (%)								
	40	45	50	55	60	65	70	75	80
100 (38)	109 (43)	114 (46)	118 (48)	124 (51)	129 (54)	136 (58)			
98 (37)	105 (41)	109 (43)	113 (45)	117 (47)	123 (51)	128 (53)	134 (57)		
96 (36)	101 (38)	104 (40)	108 (42)	112 (44)	116 (47)	121 (49)	126 (52)	132 (56)	
94 (34)	97 (36)	100 (38)	103 (39)	106 (41)	110 (43)	114 (46)	119 (48)	124 (51)	129 (54)
92 (33)	94 (34)	96 (36)	99 (37)	101 (38)	105 (41)	108 (42)	112 (44)	116 (47)	121 (49)
90 (32)	91 (33)	93 (34)	95 (35)	97 (36)	100 (38)	103 (39)	105 (41)	109 (43)	113 (45)
88 (31)	88 (31)	89 (32)	91 (33)	93 (34)	95 (35)	98 (37)	100 (38)	103 (39)	106 (41)
86 (30)	85 (29)	87 (31)	88 (31)	89 (32)	91 (33)	93 (34)	95 (35)	97 (36)	100 (38)
84 (29)	83 (28)	84 (29)	85 (29)	86 (30)	88 (31)	89 (32)	90 (32)	92 (33)	94 (34)
82 (28)	81 (27)	82 (28)	83 (28)	84 (29)	84 (29)	85 (29)	86 (30)	88 (31)	89 (32)
80 (27)	80 (27)	80 (27)	81 (27)	81 (27)	82 (28)	82 (28)	83 (28)	84 (29)	84 (29)

RISK LEVEL FOR HEAT DISORDERS: CAUTION   EXTREME CAUTION   DANGER

EXAMPLE: *When the temperature is 88°F (31°C) and the relative humidity is 60 percent, the heat index, or how hot it feels, is 95°F (35°C).*

THE UV INDEX FOR MEASURING ULTRAVIOLET RADIATION RISK

The U.S. National Weather Service's daily forecasts of ultraviolet levels use these numbers for various exposure levels:

UV INDEX NUMBER	EXPOSURE LEVEL	ACTIONS TO TAKE
0, 1, 2	Low	Wear UV-blocking sunglasses on bright days. In winter, reflection off snow can nearly double UV strength. If you burn easily, cover up and apply SPF 30+ sunscreen.
3, 4, 5	Moderate	Apply SPF 30+ sunscreen; wear a hat and sunglasses. Stay in shade when sun is strongest.
6, 7	High	Apply SPF 30+ sunscreen; wear a hat, sunglasses, and protective clothing; limit midday exposure.
8, 9, 10	Very High	Apply SPF 30+ sunscreen; wear a hat, sunglasses, and protective clothing; limit midday exposure. Seek shade. Unprotected skin will be damaged and can burn quickly.
11 or higher	Extreme	Apply SPF 30+ sunscreen; wear a hat, sunglasses, and protective clothing; avoid midday exposure; seek shade. Unprotected skin can burn in minutes.

85	90	95	100
135 (57)			
126 (52)	131 (55)		
117 (47)	122 (50)	127 (53)	132 (56)
110 (43)	113 (45)	117 (47)	121 (49)
102 (39)	105 (41)	108 (42)	112 (44)
96 (36)	98 (37)	100 (38)	103 (39)
90 (32)	91 (33)	93 (34)	95 (35)
85 (29)	86 (30)	86 (30)	87 (31)

HOW TO MEASURE HAIL

The **TORRO HAILSTORM INTENSITY SCALE** was introduced by Jonathan Webb of Oxford, England, in 1986 as a means of categorizing hailstorms. The name derives from the private and mostly British research body named the TORnado and storm Research Organisation.

INTENSITY/DESCRIPTION OF HAIL DAMAGE

H0   True hail of pea size causes no damage

H1   Leaves and flower petals are punctured and torn

H2   Leaves are stripped from trees and plants

H3   Panes of glass are broken; auto bodies are dented

H4   Some house windows are broken; small tree branches are broken off; birds are killed

H5   Many windows are smashed; small animals are injured; large tree branches are broken off

H6   Shingle roofs are breached; metal roofs are scored; wooden window frames are broken away

H7   Roofs are shattered to expose rafters; autos are seriously damaged

H8   Shingle and tile roofs are destroyed; small tree trunks are split; people are seriously injured

H9   Concrete roofs are broken; large tree trunks are split and knocked down; people are at risk of fatal injuries

H10   Brick houses are damaged; people are at risk of fatal injuries

What Are Cooling/Heating Degree Days?

In an attempt to measure the need for air-conditioning, each degree of a day's mean temperature that is above a base temperature, such as 65°F (U.S.) or 18°C (Canada), is considered one cooling degree day. If the daily mean temperature is 75°F, for example, that's 10 cooling degree days.

Similarly, to measure the need for heating fuel consumption, each degree of a day's mean temperature that is below 65°F (18°C) is considered one heating degree. For example, a day with a high of 60°F and low of 40°F results in a mean of 50°, or 15 degrees less than 65°. Hence, that day had 15 heating degree days.

HOW TO MEASURE WIND SPEED

The **BEAUFORT WIND FORCE SCALE** is a common way of estimating wind speed. It was developed in 1805 by Admiral Sir Francis Beaufort of the British Navy to measure wind at sea. We can also use it to measure wind on land.

Admiral Beaufort arranged the numbers 0 to 12 to indicate the strength of the wind from calm, force 0, to hurricane, force 12. Here's a scale adapted to land.

"Used Mostly at Sea but of Help to All Who Are Interested in the Weather"

BEAUFORT FORCE	DESCRIPTION	WHEN YOU SEE OR FEEL THIS EFFECT	WIND SPEED (mph)	(km/h)
0	CALM	Smoke goes straight up	less than 1	less than 2
1	LIGHT AIR	Wind direction is shown by smoke drift but not by wind vane	1–3	2–5
2	LIGHT BREEZE	Wind is felt on the face; leaves rustle; wind vanes move	4–7	6–11
3	GENTLE BREEZE	Leaves and small twigs move steadily; wind extends small flags straight out	8–12	12–19
4	MODERATE BREEZE	Wind raises dust and loose paper; small branches move	13–18	20–29
5	FRESH BREEZE	Small trees sway; waves form on lakes	19–24	30–39
6	STRONG BREEZE	Large branches move; wires whistle; umbrellas are difficult to use	25–31	40–50
7	NEAR GALE	Whole trees are in motion; walking against the wind is difficult	32–38	51–61
8	GALE	Twigs break from trees; walking against the wind is very difficult	39–46	62–74
9	STRONG GALE	Buildings suffer minimal damage; roof shingles are removed	47–54	75–87
10	STORM	Trees are uprooted	55–63	88–101
11	VIOLENT STORM	Widespread damage	64–72	102–116
12	HURRICANE	Widespread destruction	73+	117+

RETIRED ATLANTIC HURRICANE NAMES
These storms have been some of the most destructive and costly.

NAME	YEAR	NAME	YEAR	NAME	YEAR	NAME	YEAR
Gustav	2008	Ingrid	2013	Irma	2017	Eta	2020
Ike	2008	Erika	2015	Maria	2017	Iota	2020
Igor	2010	Joaquin	2015	Nate	2017	Laura	2020
Tomas	2010	Matthew	2016	Florence	2018	Ida	2021
Irene	2011	Otto	2016	Michael	2018	Fiona	2022
Sandy	2012	Harvey	2017	Dorian	2019	Ian	2022

REFERENCE

ATLANTIC TROPICAL (AND SUBTROPICAL) STORM NAMES FOR 2025			EASTERN NORTH-PACIFIC TROPICAL (AND SUBTROPICAL) STORM NAMES FOR 2025		
Andrea	Humberto	Olga	Alvin	Ivo	Raymond
Barry	Imelda	Pablo	Barbara	Juliette	Sonia
Chantal	Jerry	Rebekah	Cosme	Kiko	Tico
Dexter	Karen	Sebastien	Dalila	Lorena	Velma
Erin	Lorenzo	Tanya	Erick	Mario	Wallis
Fernand	Melissa	Van	Flossie	Narda	Xina
Gabrielle	Nestor	Wendy	Gil	Octave	York
			Henriette	Priscilla	Zelda

The lists above are used in rotation and recycled every 6 years, e.g., the 2025 list will be used again in 2031.

How to Measure Hurricane Strength

The **SAFFIR-SIMPSON HURRICANE WIND SCALE** assigns a rating from 1 to 5 based on a hurricane's intensity. It is used to give an estimate of the potential property damage from a hurricane landfall. Wind speed is the determining factor in the scale, as storm surge values are highly dependent on the slope of the continental shelf in the landfall region. Wind speeds are measured at a height of 33 feet (10 meters) using a 1-minute average.

CATEGORY ONE. Average wind: 74–95 mph. Significant damage to mobile homes. Some damage to roofing and siding of well-built frame homes. Large tree branches snap and shallow-rooted trees may topple. Power outages may last a few to several days.

CATEGORY TWO. Average wind: 96–110 mph. Mobile homes may be destroyed. Major roof and siding damage to frame homes. Many shallow-rooted trees snap or topple, blocking roads. Widespread power outages could last from several days to weeks. Potable water may be scarce.

CATEGORY THREE. Average wind: 111–129 mph. Most mobile homes destroyed.

Frame homes may sustain major roof damage. Many trees snap or topple, blocking numerous roads. Electricity and water may be unavailable for several days to weeks.

CATEGORY FOUR. Average wind: 130–156 mph. Mobile homes destroyed. Frame homes severely damaged or destroyed. Windborne debris may penetrate protected windows. Most trees snap or topple. Residential areas isolated by fallen trees and power poles. Most of the area uninhabitable for weeks to months.

CATEGORY FIVE. Average wind: 157+ mph. Most homes destroyed. Nearly all windows blown out of high-rises. Most of the area uninhabitable for weeks to months.

REFERENCE

HOW TO MEASURE A TORNADO

The original **FUJITA SCALE** (or F Scale) was developed by Dr. Theodore Fujita to classify tornadoes based on wind damage. All tornadoes, and other severe local windstorms, were assigned a number according to the most intense damage caused by the storm. An enhanced F (EF) scale was implemented in the United States on February 1, 2007. The EF scale uses 3-second gust estimates based on a more detailed system for assessing damage, taking into account different building materials.

F SCALE		EF SCALE (U.S.)
F0 · 40–72 mph (64–116 km/h)	LIGHT DAMAGE	EF0 · 65–85 mph (105–137 km/h)
F1 · 73–112 mph (117–180 km/h)	MODERATE DAMAGE	EF1 · 86–110 mph (138–178 km/h)
F2 · 113–157 mph (181–253 km/h)	CONSIDERABLE DAMAGE	EF2 · 111–135 mph (179–218 km/h)
F3 · 158–207 mph (254–332 km/h)	SEVERE DAMAGE	EF3 · 136–165 mph (219–266 km/h)
F4 · 208–260 mph (333–419 km/h)	DEVASTATING DAMAGE	EF4 · 166–200 mph (267–322 km/h)
F5 · 261–318 mph (420–512 km/h)	INCREDIBLE DAMAGE	EF5 · over 200 mph (over 322 km/h)

Wind/Barometer Table

BAROMETER (REDUCED TO SEA LEVEL)	WIND DIRECTION	CHARACTER OF WEATHER INDICATED
30.00 to 30.20, and steady	WESTERLY	Fair, with slight changes in temperature, for 1 to 2 days
30.00 to 30.20, and rising rapidly	WESTERLY	Fair, followed within 2 days by warmer and rain
30.00 to 30.20, and falling rapidly	SOUTH TO EAST	Warmer, and rain within 24 hours
30.20 or above, and falling rapidly	SOUTH TO EAST	Warmer, and rain within 36 hours
30.20 or above, and falling rapidly	WEST TO NORTH	Cold and clear, quickly followed by warmer and rain
30.20 or above, and steady	VARIABLE	No early change
30.00 or below, and falling slowly	SOUTH TO EAST	Rain within 18 hours that will continue a day or two
30.00 or below, and falling rapidly	SOUTHEAST TO NORTHEAST	Rain, with high wind, followed within 2 days by clearing, colder
30.00 or below, and rising	SOUTH TO WEST	Clearing and colder within 12 hours
29.80 or below, and falling rapidly	SOUTH TO EAST	Severe storm of wind and rain imminent; in winter, snow or cold wave within 24 hours
29.80 or below, and falling rapidly	EAST TO NORTH	Severe northeast gales and heavy rain or snow, followed in winter by cold wave
29.80 or below, and rising rapidly	GOING TO WEST	Clearing and colder

NOTE: *A barometer should be adjusted to show equivalent sea-level pressure for the altitude at which it is to be used. A change of 100 feet in elevation will cause a decrease of ¹/₁₀ inch in the reading.*

REFERENCE

WINDCHILL TABLE

As wind speed increases, your body loses heat more rapidly, making the air feel colder than it really is. The combination of cold temperature and high wind can create a cooling effect so severe that exposed flesh can freeze.

	Calm	35	30	25	20	15	10	5	0	-5	-10	-15	-20	-25	-30	-35
WIND SPEED (mph)	5	31	25	19	13	7	1	-5	-11	-16	-22	-28	-34	-40	-46	-52
	10	27	21	15	9	3	-4	-10	-16	-22	-28	-35	-41	-47	-53	-59
	15	25	19	13	6	0	-7	-13	-19	-26	-32	-39	-45	-51	-58	-64
	20	24	17	11	4	-2	-9	-15	-22	-29	-35	-42	-48	-55	-61	-68
	25	23	16	9	3	-4	-11	-17	-24	-31	-37	-44	-51	-58	-64	-71
	30	22	15	8	1	-5	-12	-19	-26	-33	-39	-46	-53	-60	-67	-73
	35	21	14	7	0	-7	-14	-21	-27	-34	-41	-48	-55	-62	-69	-76
	40	20	13	6	-1	-8	-15	-22	-29	-36	-43	-50	-57	-64	-71	-78
	45	19	12	5	-2	-9	-16	-23	-30	-37	-44	-51	-58	-65	-72	-79
	50	19	12	4	-3	-10	-17	-24	-31	-38	-45	-52	-60	-67	-74	-81
	55	18	11	4	-3	-11	-18	-25	-32	-39	-46	-54	-61	-68	-75	-82
	60	17	10	3	-4	-11	-19	-26	-33	-40	-48	-55	-62	-69	-76	-84

TEMPERATURE (°F)

FROSTBITE OCCURS IN　　30 MINUTES　　10 MINUTES　　5 MINUTES

EXAMPLE: *When the temperature is 15°F and the wind speed is 30 miles per hour, the windchill, or how cold it feels, is -5°F. See a Celsius version of this table via Almanac.com/2025.*
–courtesy of National Weather Service

HOW TO MEASURE EARTHQUAKES

In 1979, seismologists developed a measurement of earthquake size called **MOMENT MAGNITUDE**. It is more accurate than the previously used Richter scale, which is precise only for earthquakes of a certain size and at a certain distance from a seismometer. All earthquakes can now be compared on the same magnitude scale.

MAGNITUDE	DESCRIPTION	EFFECT
LESS THAN 3	MICRO	GENERALLY NOT FELT
3-3.9	MINOR	OFTEN FELT, LITTLE DAMAGE
4-4.9	LIGHT	SHAKING, SOME DAMAGE
5-5.9	MODERATE	SLIGHT TO MAJOR DAMAGE
6-6.9	STRONG	DESTRUCTIVE
7-7.9	MAJOR	SERIOUS DAMAGE
8 OR MORE	GREAT	SEVERE DAMAGE

REFERENCE

A GARDENER'S WORST PHOBIAS

NAME OF FEAR	OBJECT FEARED
Alliumphobia	Garlic
Anthophobia	Flowers
Apiphobia	Bees
Arachnophobia	Spiders
Botanophobia	Plants
Bufonophobia	Toads
Dendrophobia	Trees
Entomophobia	Insects
Lachanophobia	Vegetables
Mottephobia	Moths
Myrmecophobia	Ants
Ophidiophobia	Snakes
Ornithophobia	Birds
Ranidaphobia	Frogs
Rupophobia	Dirt
Scoleciphobia	Worms
Spheksophobia	Wasps

PLANTS FOR LAWNS

Choose varieties that suit your soil and your climate. All of these can withstand mowing and considerable foot traffic.

Ajuga or bugleweed (*Ajuga reptans*)
Corsican mint (*Mentha requienii*)
Dwarf cinquefoil (*Potentilla tabernaemontani*)
English pennyroyal (*Mentha pulegium*)
Green Irish moss (*Sagina subulata*)
Pearly everlasting (*Anaphalis margaritacea*)
Roman chamomile (*Chamaemelum nobile*)
Rupturewort (*Herniaria glabra*)
Speedwell (*Veronica officinalis*)
Stonecrop (*Sedum ternatum*)
Sweet violets (*Viola odorata* or *V. tricolor*)
Thyme (*Thymus serpyllum*)
White clover (*Trifolium repens*)
Wild strawberries (*Fragaria virginiana*)
Wintergreen or partridgeberry (*Mitchella repens*)

Lawn-Growing Tips

• Test your soil: The pH balance should be 6.2 to 6.7; less than 6.0 puts your lawn at risk for fungal diseases. If the pH is too low, correct it with liming, best done in the fall.

• The best time to apply fertilizer is just before a light rain.

• If you put lime and fertilizer on your lawn, spread half of it as you walk north to south, the other half as you walk east to west to cut down on missed areas.

• Any feeding of lawns in the fall should be done with a low-nitrogen, slow-acting fertilizer.

• In areas of your lawn where tree roots compete with the grass, apply some extra fertilizer to benefit both.

• Moss and sorrel in lawns usually means poor soil, poor aeration or drainage, or excessive acidity.

• Control weeds by promoting healthy lawn growth with natural fertilizers in spring and early fall.

• Raise the level of your lawn-mower blades during the hot summer days. Taller grass resists drought better than short.

• You can reduce mowing time by redesigning your lawn, reducing sharp corners and adding sweeping curves.

• During a drought, let the grass grow longer between mowings and reduce fertilizer.

• Water your lawn early in the morning or in the evening.

REFERENCE

Flowers and Herbs That Attract Butterflies

Allium...................... *Allium*
Aster.......... *Aster, Symphyotrichum*
Bee balm .... *Monarda*
Butterfly bush............. *Buddleia*
Catmint .... *Nepeta*
Clove pink .... *Dianthus*
Coreopsis................. *Coreopsis*
Cornflower .... *Centaurea*
Creeping thyme ..... *Thymus serpyllum*
Daylily................. *Hemerocallis*
Dill.............. *Anethum graveolens*
False indigo............... *Baptisia*
Fleabane.................. *Erigeron*
Floss flower............... *Ageratum*
Globe thistle .... *Echinops*
Goldenrod .... *Solidago*
Helen's flower .... *Helenium*
Hollyhock.... ............ *Alcea*
Honeysuckle .... *Lonicera*
Lavender ...... *Lavandula*
Lilac .... *Syringa*
Lupine...................... *Lupinus*

Lychnis.................... *Lychnis*
Mallow .... *Malva*
Mealycup sage .... *Salvia farinacea*
Milkweed.................. *Asclepias*
Mint........................ *Mentha*
Oregano......... *Origanum vulgare*
Pansy .... *Viola*
Parsley .... *Petroselinum crispum*
Phlox........................ *Phlox*
Privet .... *Ligustrum*
Purple coneflower . *Echinacea purpurea*
Rock cress................... *Arabis*
Sea holly................. *Eryngium*
Shasta daisy .... *Leucanthemum*
Snapdragon............... *Antirrhinum*
Stonecrop ...... *Hylotelephium, Sedum*
Sweet alyssum .... *Lobularia*
Sweet marjoram .. *Origanum majorana*
Sweet rocket............... *Hesperis*
Verbena .... *Verbena*
Zinnia .... *Zinnia*

FLOWERS* THAT ATTRACT HUMMINGBIRDS

Beard tongue .... *Penstemon*
Bee balm .... *Monarda*
Butterfly bush............. *Buddleia*
Catmint .... *Nepeta*
Clove pink .... *Dianthus*
Columbine .... *Aquilegia*
Coral bells .... *Heuchera*
Daylily................. *Hemerocallis*
Desert candle .... *Yucca*
Flag iris .... *Iris*
Flowering tobacco..... *Nicotiana alata*
Foxglove.................... *Digitalis*
Larkspur .... *Delphinium*
Lily .... *Lilium*
Lupine...................... *Lupinus*
Petunia..................... *Petunia*
Pincushion flower .... *Scabiosa*
Red-hot poker............. *Kniphofia*
Scarlet sage......... *Salvia splendens*

Soapwort .... *Saponaria*
Summer phlox .... *Phlox paniculata*
Trumpet honeysuckle........ *Lonicera sempervirens*
Verbena .... *Verbena*
Weigela..................... *Weigela*

*NOTE: *Choose varieties in red and orange shades, if available.*

REFERENCE

pH PREFERENCES OF TREES, SHRUBS, FLOWERS, AND VEGETABLES

An accurate soil test will indicate your soil pH and will specify the amount of lime or sulfur that is needed to bring it up or down to the appropriate level. A pH of 6.5 is just about right for most home gardens, since most plants thrive in the 6.0 to 7.0 (slightly acidic to neutral) range. Some plants (azaleas, blueberries) prefer more strongly acidic soil in the 4.0 to 6.0 range, while a few (asparagus, plums) do best in soil that is neutral to slightly alkaline. Acidic, or sour, soil (below 7.0) is counteracted by applying finely ground limestone, and alkaline, or sweet, soil (above 7.0) is treated with ground sulfur.

COMMON NAME	OPTIMUM pH RANGE	COMMON NAME	OPTIMUM pH RANGE	COMMON NAME	OPTIMUM pH RANGE
TREES AND SHRUBS		Bee balm	6.0–7.5	Snapdragon	5.5–7.0
Apple	5.0–6.5	Begonia	5.5–7.0	Sunflower	6.0–7.5
Azalea	4.5–6.0	Black-eyed Susan	5.5–7.0	Tulip	6.0–7.0
Beautybush	6.0–7.5	Bleeding heart	6.0–7.5	Zinnia	5.5–7.0
Birch	5.0–6.5	Canna	6.0–8.0		
Blackberry	5.0–6.0	Carnation	6.0–7.0	**VEGETABLES**	
Blueberry	4.0–5.0	Chrysanthemum	6.0–7.5	Asparagus	6.0–8.0
Boxwood	6.0–7.5	Clematis	5.5–7.0	Bean	6.0–7.5
Cherry, sour	6.0–7.0	Coleus	6.0–7.0	Beet	6.0–7.5
Crab apple	6.0–7.5	Coneflower, purple	5.0–7.5	Broccoli	6.0–7.0
Dogwood	5.0–7.0	Cosmos	5.0–8.0	Brussels sprout	6.0–7.5
Fir, balsam	5.0–6.0	Crocus	6.0–8.0	Cabbage	6.0–7.5
Hemlock	5.0–6.0	Daffodil	6.0–6.5	Carrot	5.5–7.0
Hydrangea, blue-flowered	4.5–5.5	Dahlia	6.0–7.5	Cauliflower	5.5–7.5
Hydrangea, pink-flowered	6.0–7.0	Daisy, Shasta	6.0–8.0	Celery	5.8–7.0
		Daylily	6.0–8.0	Chive	6.0–7.0
Juniper	5.0–6.0	Delphinium	6.0–7.5	Collard	6.5–7.5
Laurel, mountain	4.5–6.0	Foxglove	6.0–7.5	Corn	5.5–7.0
Lemon	6.0–7.5	Geranium	5.5–6.5	Cucumber	5.5–7.0
Lilac	6.0–7.0	Gladiolus	5.0–7.0	Eggplant	6.0–7.0
Maple, sugar	6.0–7.5	Hibiscus	6.0–8.0	Garlic	5.5–8.0
Oak, white	5.0–6.5	Hollyhock	6.0–8.0	Kale	6.0–7.5
Orange	6.0–7.5	Hyacinth	6.5–7.5	Leek	6.0–8.0
Peach	6.0–7.0	Iris, blue flag	5.0–7.5	Lettuce	6.0–7.0
Pear	6.0–7.5	Lily-of-the-valley	4.5–6.0	Okra	6.0–7.0
Pecan	6.4–8.0	Lupine	5.0–6.5	Onion	6.0–7.0
Plum	6.0–8.0	Marigold	5.5–7.5	Pea	6.0–7.5
Raspberry, red	5.5–7.0	Morning glory	6.0–7.5	Pepper, sweet	5.5–7.0
Rhododendron	4.5–6.0	Narcissus, trumpet	5.5–6.5	Potato	4.8–6.5
Willow	6.0–8.0	Nasturtium	5.5–7.5	Pumpkin	5.5–7.5
		Pansy	5.5–6.5	Radish	6.0–7.0
FLOWERS		Peony	6.0–7.5	Spinach	6.0–7.5
Alyssum	6.0–7.5	Petunia	6.0–7.5	Squash, crookneck	6.0–7.5
Aster, New England	6.0–8.0	Phlox, summer	6.0–8.0	Squash, Hubbard	5.5–7.0
Baby's breath	6.0–7.0	Poppy, oriental	6.0–7.5	Swiss chard	6.0–7.0
Bachelor's button	6.0–7.5	Rose, hybrid tea	5.5–7.0	Tomato	5.5–7.5
		Rose, rugosa	6.0–7.0	Watermelon	5.5–6.5

How to Rotate Crops

Crop rotation is the practice of planting annual vegetables with their botanical families. Each vegetable family rotates together; it is not necessary to grow every family or every plant in each family. The benefits of rotating crops include fewer pests and soil-borne diseases, improved soil nutrition, and better soil structure. Failure to rotate vegetable crops eventually results in plants that fail to thrive and decreased harvest.

Here's how crop rotation works: In a single-crop plot, legumes (pea family) are planted in year 1, nightshade plants (tomatoes, etc.) in year 2, and gourds in year 3. In year 4, the cycle begins again. Alternatively, these three crops could be planted in three separate plots in year 1 and moved to the next plot in ensuing years. Additional families can be added. A simple plot plan keeps track of what goes where.

PLANT FAMILIES AND MEMBERS

Plants in the same family are genetically related and thus share similar characteristics (e.g., leaf appearance, tendrils for climbing).

CARROT, aka **PARSLEY** (Apiaceae, aka Umbelliferae): caraway, carrot*, celeriac, celery, chervil, coriander, dill, fennel, lovage, parsley, parsnip

GOOSEFOOT, aka **CHARD** (Chenopodiaceae): beet*, orache, quinoa, spinach, Swiss chard

GOURD, aka **SQUASH** (Cucurbitaceae): cucumber, gourd, melon, pumpkin, squash (summer and winter), watermelon

GRASS (Poaceae, aka Gramineae): sweet corn

MALLOW (Malvaceae): okra

MINT (Lamiaceae, aka Labiatae): basil, Chinese artichoke, oregano, rosemary, sage, summer savory, sweet marjoram

MORNING GLORY (Convolvulaceae): sweet potato

MUSTARD (Brassicaceae, aka Cruciferae): arugula, bok choy, broccoli, brussels sprouts, cabbage, cauliflower, collard, kale, kohlrabi, komatsuna, mizuna, mustard greens, radish*, rutabaga, turnip

NIGHTSHADE (Solanaceae): eggplant, pepper, potato, tomatillo, tomato

ONION (Amaryllidaceae*): chives, garlic, leek, onion, shallot

PEA (Fabaceae, aka Leguminosae): bush, kidney, lima, pole, and soy beans; lentil; pea; peanut

SUNFLOWER (Asteraceae, aka Compositae): artichoke (globe and Jerusalem), calendula, chamomile, endive, escarole, lettuce, radicchio, salsify, sunflower, tarragon

*These can be planted among any family.

REFERENCE

SOWING VEGETABLE SEEDS

SOW OR PLANT IN COOL WEATHER	Beets, broccoli, brussels sprouts, cabbage, lettuce, onions, parsley, peas, radishes, spinach, Swiss chard, turnips
SOW OR PLANT IN WARM WEATHER	Beans, carrots, corn, cucumbers, eggplant, melons, okra, peppers, squashes, tomatoes
SOW OR PLANT FOR ONE CROP PER SEASON	Corn, eggplant, leeks, melons, peppers, potatoes, spinach (New Zealand), squashes, tomatoes
RESOW FOR ADDITIONAL CROPS	Beans, beets, cabbage, carrots, kohlrabi, lettuce, radishes, rutabagas, spinach, turnips

A Beginner's Vegetable Garden

The vegetables suggested below are common, easy-to-grow crops. Make 11 rows, 10 feet long, with at least 18 inches between them. Ideally, the rows should run north and south to take full advantage of the sun. This garden, planted as suggested, can feed a family of four for one summer, with a little extra for canning and freezing or giving away.

ROW
1. Zucchini (4 plants)
2. Tomatoes (5 plants, staked)
3. Peppers (6 plants)
4. Cabbage

ROW
5. Bush beans
6. Lettuce
7. Beets
8. Carrots
9. Swiss chard
10. Radishes
11. Marigolds (to discourage rabbits!)

SOIL FIXES

If you have **sandy** soil, amend with compost; humus; aged manure; sawdust with extra nitrogen; heavy, clay-rich soil.

If your soil contains a lot of **silt**, amend with coarse sand (not beach sand) or gravel and compost, or aged horse manure mixed with fresh straw.

If your soil is dense with **clay**, amend with coarse sand (not beach sand) and compost.

TO IMPROVE YOUR SOIL, ADD THE PROPER AMENDMENT(S) . . .

bark, ground: made from various tree barks; improves soil structure

compost: an excellent conditioner

leaf mold: decomposed leaves, which add nutrients and structure to soil

lime: raises the pH of acidic soil and helps to loosen clay soil.

manure: best if composted; never add fresh ("hot") manure; is a good conditioner

coarse sand (not beach sand): improves drainage in clay soil

topsoil: usually used with another amendment; replaces existing soil

REFERENCE

IMPORTANT TIMES TO . . .

	. . . FERTILIZE:	. . . WATER:
BEANS	After heavy bloom and set of pods	When flowers form and during pod-forming and picking
BEETS	At time of planting	Before soil gets bone-dry
BROCCOLI	3 weeks after transplanting	Continuously for 4 weeks after transplanting
BRUSSELS SPROUTS	3 weeks after transplanting	Continuously for 4 weeks after transplanting
CABBAGE	2 weeks after transplanting	Frequently in dry weather
CARROTS	5 to 6 weeks after sowing	Before soil gets bone-dry
CAULIFLOWER	3 to 4 weeks after transplanting	Frequently
CELERY	At time of transplanting, and after 2 months	Frequently
CORN	When 8 to 10 inches tall, and when first silk appears	When tassels form and when cobs swell
CUCUMBERS	1 week after bloom, and every 3 weeks thereafter	Frequently
LETTUCE	3 weeks after transplanting	Frequently
MELONS	1 week after bloom, and again 3 weeks later	Once a week
ONION SETS	At time of planting, and then every 2 weeks until bulbing begins	In early stage to get plants going
PARSNIPS	1 year before planting	Before soil gets bone-dry
PEAS	After heavy bloom and set of pods	When flowers form and during pod-forming and picking
PEPPERS	At time of planting, and after first fruit-set	Need a steady supply
POTATO TUBERS	At bloom time or time of second hilling	When the size of marbles
PUMPKINS	Just before vines start to run, when plants are about 1 foot tall	1 inch of water per week; water deeply, especially during fruit set
RADISHES	Before spring planting	Need plentiful, consistent moisture
SPINACH	When plants are one-third grown	Frequently
SQUASHES, SUMMER & WINTER	When first blooms appear	Frequently
TOMATOES	When fruit are 1 inch in diameter, and then every 2 weeks	For 3 to 4 weeks after transplanting and when flowers and fruit form

REFERENCE

HOW TO GROW HERBS

HERB	START SEEDS INDOORS (WEEKS BEFORE LAST SPRING FROST)	START SEEDS OUTDOORS (WEEKS BEFORE/AFTER LAST SPRING FROST)	HEIGHT/ SPREAD (INCHES)	SOIL	LIGHT**
BASIL*	6–8	Anytime after	12–24/12	Rich, moist	○
BORAGE*	Not recommended	Anytime after	12–36/12	Rich, well-draining, dry	○
CHERVIL	Not recommended	3–4 before	12–24/8	Rich, moist	◑
CHIVES	8–10	3–4 before	12–18/18	Rich, moist	○
CILANTRO/ CORIANDER	Not recommended	Anytime after	12–36/6	Light	○◑
DILL	Not recommended	4–5 before	36–48/12	Rich	○
FENNEL	4–6	Anytime after	48–80/18	Rich	○
LAVENDER, ENGLISH*	8–12	1–2 before	18–36/24	Moderately fertile, well-draining	○
LAVENDER, FRENCH	Not recommended	Not recommended	18–36/24	Moderately fertile, well-draining	○
LEMON BALM*	6–10	2–3 before	12–24/18	Rich, well-draining	○◑
LOVAGE*	6–8	2–3 before	36–72/36	Fertile, sandy	○◑
MINT	Not recommended	Not recommended	12–24/18	Rich, moist	◑
OREGANO*	6–10	Anytime after	12–24/18	Poor	○
PARSLEY*	10–12	3–4 before	18–24/6–8	Medium-rich	◑
ROSEMARY*	8–10	Anytime after	48–72/48	Not too acidic	○
SAGE	6–10	1–2 before	12–48/30	Well-draining	○
SORREL	6–10	2–3 after	20–48/12–14	Rich, organic	○
SUMMER SAVORY	4–6	Anytime after	4–15/6	Medium-rich	○
SWEET CICELY	6–8	2–3 after	36–72/36	Moderately fertile, well-draining	○◑
TARRAGON, FRENCH	Not recommended	Not recommended	24–36/12	Well-draining	○◑
THYME, COMMON*	6–10	2–3 before	2–12/7–12	Fertile, well-draining	○◑

*Recommend minimum soil temperature of 70°F to germinate

** ○ FULL SUN   ◑ PARTIAL SHADE

Annual
Annual, biennial
Annual, biennial
Perennial
Annual
Annual
Annual
Perennial
Tender perennial
Perennial
Perennial
Perennial
Tender perennial
Biennial
Tender perennial
Perennial
Perennial
Annual
Perennial
Perennial
Perennial

DRYING HERBS

Before drying, remove any dead or diseased leaves or stems. Wash under cool water, shake off excess water, and put on a towel to dry completely. Air-drying preserves an herb's essential oils; use for sturdy herbs. A microwave dries herbs more quickly, so mold is less likely to develop; use for moist, tender herbs.

HANGING METHOD: Gather four to six stems of fresh herbs in a bunch and tie with string, leaving a loop for hanging. Or, use a rubber band with a paper clip attached to it. Hang the herbs in a warm, well-ventilated area, out of direct sunlight, until dry. For herbs that have full seed heads, such as dill or coriander, use a paper bag. Punch holes in the bag for ventilation, label it, and put the herb bunch into the bag before you tie a string around the top of the bag. The average drying time is 1 to 3 weeks.

MICROWAVE METHOD: This is better for small quantities, such as a cup or two at a time. Arrange a single layer of herbs between two paper towels and put them in the microwave for 1 to 2 minutes on high power. Let the leaves cool. If they are not dry, reheat for 30 seconds and check again. Repeat as needed. Let cool. Do not overcook, or the herbs will lose their flavor.

STORING HERBS AND SPICES

FRESH HERBS: Dill and parsley will keep for about 2 weeks with stems immersed in a glass of water tented with a plastic bag. Most other fresh herbs (and greens) will keep for short periods unwashed and refrigerated in tightly sealed plastic bags with just enough moisture to prevent wilting. For longer storage, use moisture- and gas-permeable paper and cellophane. Plastic cuts off oxygen to the plants and promotes spoilage.

SPICES AND DRIED HERBS: Store in a cool, dry place.

COOKING WITH HERBS

A **BOUQUET GARNI** is usually made with bay leaves, thyme, and parsley tied with string or wrapped in cheesecloth. Use to flavor casseroles and soups. Remove after cooking.

FINES HERBES use equal amounts of fresh parsley, tarragon, chives, and chervil chopped fine. Commonly used in French cooking, they make a fine omelet or add zest to soups and sauces. Add to salads and butter sauces or sprinkle on noodles, soups, and stews.

HOW TO GROW BULBS

COMMON NAME	LATIN NAME	HARDINESS ZONE	SOIL	LIGHT*	SPACING (INCHES)
SPRING-PLANTED BULBS					
ALLIUM	*Allium*	3–10	Well-draining/moist	○	12
BEGONIA, TUBEROUS	*Begonia*	10–11	Well-draining/moist	◐●	12–15
BLAZING STAR/GAYFEATHER	*Liatris*	7–10	Well-draining	○	6
CALADIUM	*Caladium*	10–11	Well-draining/moist	◐●	8–12
CALLA LILY	*Zantedeschia*	8–10	Well-draining/moist	○◐	8–24
CANNA	*Canna*	8–11	Well-draining/moist	○	12–24
CYCLAMEN	*Cyclamen*	7–9	Well-draining/moist	◐	4
DAHLIA	*Dahlia*	9–11	Well-draining/fertile	○	12–36
DAYLILY	*Hemerocallis*	3–10	Adaptable to most soils	○◐	12–24
FREESIA	*Freesia*	9–11	Well-draining/moist/sandy	○◐	2–4
GARDEN GLOXINIA	*Incarvillea*	4–8	Well-draining/moist	○	12
GLADIOLUS	*Gladiolus*	4–11	Well-draining/fertile	○◐	4–9
IRIS	*Iris*	3–10	Well-draining/sandy	○	3–6
LILY, ASIATIC/ORIENTAL	*Lilium*	3–8	Well-draining	○◐	8–12
PEACOCK FLOWER	*Tigridia*	8–10	Well-draining	○	5–6
SHAMROCK/SORREL	*Oxalis*	5–9	Well-draining	○◐	4–6
WINDFLOWER	*Anemone*	3–9	Well-draining/moist	○◐	3–6
FALL-PLANTED BULBS					
BLUEBELL	*Hyacinthoides*	4–9	Well-draining/fertile	○◐	4
CHRISTMAS ROSE/HELLEBORE	*Helleborus*	4–8	Neutral–alkaline	○◐	18
CROCUS	*Crocus*	3–8	Well-draining/moist/fertile	○◐	4
DAFFODIL	*Narcissus*	3–10	Well-draining/moist/fertile	○◐	6
FRITILLARY	*Fritillaria*	3–9	Well-draining/sandy	○◐	3
GLORY OF THE SNOW	*Chionodoxa*	3–9	Well-draining/moist	○◐	3
GRAPE HYACINTH	*Muscari*	4–10	Well-draining/moist/fertile	○◐	3–4
IRIS, BEARDED	*Iris*	3–9	Well-draining	○◐	4
IRIS, SIBERIAN	*Iris*	4–9	Well-draining	○◐	4
ORNAMENTAL ONION	*Allium*	3–10	Well-draining/moist/fertile	○	12
SNOWDROP	*Galanthus*	3–9	Well-draining/moist/fertile	○◐	3
SNOWFLAKE	*Leucojum*	5–9	Well-draining/moist/sandy	○◐	4
SPRING STARFLOWER	*Ipheion uniflorum*	6–9	Well-draining loam	○◐	3–6
STAR OF BETHLEHEM	*Ornithogalum*	5–10	Well-draining/moist	○◐	2–5
STRIPED SQUILL	*Puschkinia scilloides*	3–9	Well-draining	○◐	6
TULIP	*Tulipa*	4–8	Well-draining/fertile	○◐	3–6
WINTER ACONITE	*Eranthis*	4–9	Well-draining/moist/fertile	○◐	3

REFERENCE

* ○ **FULL SUN**   ◑ **PARTIAL SHADE**   ● **FULL SHADE**

DEPTH (INCHES)	BLOOMING SEASON	HEIGHT (INCHES)	NOTES
3–4	Spring to summer	6–60	Usually pest-free; a great cut flower
1–2	Summer to fall	8–18	North of Zone 10, lift in fall
4	Summer to fall	8–20	An excellent flower for drying; north of Zone 7, plant in spring, lift in fall
2	Summer	8–24	North of Zone 10, plant in spring, lift in fall
1–4	Summer	24–36	Fragrant; north of Zone 8, plant in spring, lift in fall
Level	Summer	18–60	North of Zone 8, plant in spring, lift in fall
1–2	Spring to fall	3–12	Naturalizes well in warm areas; north of Zone 7, lift in fall
4–6	Late summer	12–60	North of Zone 9, lift in fall
2	Summer	12–36	Mulch in winter in Zones 3 to 6
2	Summer	12–24	Fragrant; can be grown outdoors in warm climates
3–4	Summer	6–20	Does well in woodland settings
3–6	Early summer to early fall	12–80	North of Zone 10, lift in fall
4	Spring to late summer	3–72	Divide and replant rhizomes every 2 to 5 years
4–6	Early summer	36	Fragrant; self-sows; requires excellent drainage
4	Summer	18–24	North of Zone 8, lift in fall
2	Summer	2–12	Plant in confined area to control
2	Early summer	3–18	North of Zone 6, lift in fall
3–4	Spring	8–20	Excellent for borders, rock gardens, and naturalizing
1–2	Spring	12	Hardy, but requires shelter from strong, cold winds
3	Early spring	5	Naturalizes well in grass
6	Early spring	14–24	Plant under shrubs or in a border
3	Midspring	6–30	Different species can be planted in rock gardens, woodland gardens, or borders
3	Spring	4–10	Self-sows easily; plant in rock gardens, raised beds, or under shrubs
2–3	Late winter to spring	6–12	Use as a border plant or in wildflower and rock gardens; self-sows easily
4	Early spring to early summer	3–48	Naturalizes well; a good cut flower
4	Early spring to midsummer	18–48	An excellent cut flower
3–4	Late spring to early summer	6–60	Usually pest-free; a great cut flower
3	Spring	6–12	Best when clustered and planted in an area that will not dry out in summer
4	Spring	6–18	Naturalizes well
3	Spring	4–6	Fragrant; naturalizes easily
4	Spring to summer	6–24	North of Zone 5, plant in spring, lift in fall
3	Spring	4–6	Naturalizes easily; makes an attractive edging
4–6	Early to late spring	8–30	Excellent for borders, rock gardens, and naturalizing
2–3	Late winter to spring	2–4	Self-sows and naturalizes easily

Substitutions for Common Ingredients

ITEM	QUANTITY	SUBSTITUTION
BAKING POWDER	1 teaspoon	¼ teaspoon baking soda plus ¼ teaspoon cornstarch plus ½ teaspoon cream of tartar
BUTTERMILK	1 cup	1 tablespoon lemon juice or vinegar plus milk to equal 1 cup; or 1 cup plain yogurt
CHOCOLATE, UNSWEETENED	1 ounce	3 tablespoons cocoa plus 1 tablespoon unsalted butter, shortening, or vegetable oil
CRACKER CRUMBS	¾ cup	1 cup dry bread crumbs; or 1 tablespoon quick-cooking oats (for thickening)
CREAM, HEAVY	1 cup	¾ cup milk plus ⅓ cup melted, unsalted butter (this will not whip)
CREAM, LIGHT	1 cup	⅞ cup milk plus 3 tablespoons melted, unsalted butter
CREAM, SOUR	1 cup	⅞ cup buttermilk or plain yogurt plus 3 tablespoons melted, unsalted butter
CREAM, WHIPPING	1 cup	⅔ cup well-chilled evaporated milk, whipped; or 1 cup nonfat dry milk powder whipped with 1 cup ice water
EGG	1 whole	2 yolks plus 1 tablespoon cold water; or 3 tablespoons vegetable oil plus 1 tablespoon water (for baking); or 2 to 3 tablespoons mayonnaise (for cakes)
EGG WHITE	1 white	2 teaspoons meringue powder plus 3 tablespoons water, combined
FLOUR, ALL-PURPOSE	1 cup	1 cup plus 3 tablespoons cake flour (not advised for cookies or quick breads); or 1 cup self-rising flour (omit baking powder and salt from recipe)
FLOUR, CAKE	1 cup	1 cup minus 3 tablespoons sifted all-purpose flour plus 3 tablespoons cornstarch
FLOUR, SELF-RISING	1 cup	1 cup all-purpose flour plus 1½ teaspoons baking powder plus ¼ teaspoon salt
HERBS, DRIED	1 teaspoon	1 tablespoon fresh, minced and packed
HONEY	1 cup	1¼ cups sugar plus ½ cup liquid called for in recipe (such as water or oil); or 1 cup pure maple syrup
KETCHUP	1 cup	1 cup tomato sauce plus ¼ cup sugar plus 3 tablespoons apple-cider vinegar plus ½ teaspoon salt plus pinch of ground cloves combined; or 1 cup chili sauce
LEMON JUICE	1 teaspoon	½ teaspoon vinegar
MAYONNAISE	1 cup	1 cup sour cream or plain yogurt; or 1 cup cottage cheese (puréed)
MILK, SKIM	1 cup	⅓ cup instant nonfat dry milk plus ¾ cup water

ITEM	QUANTITY	SUBSTITUTION
MILK, TO SOUR	1 cup	1 tablespoon vinegar or lemon juice plus milk to equal 1 cup. Stir and let stand 5 minutes.
MILK, WHOLE	1 cup	½ cup evaporated whole milk plus ½ cup water; or ¾ cup 2 percent milk plus ¼ cup half-and-half
MOLASSES	1 cup	1 cup honey or dark corn syrup
MUSTARD, DRY	1 teaspoon	1 tablespoon prepared mustard less 1 teaspoon liquid from recipe
OAT BRAN	1 cup	1 cup wheat bran or rice bran or wheat germ
OATS, OLD-FASHIONED	1 cup	1 cup steel-cut Irish or Scotch oats
QUINOA	1 cup	1 cup millet or couscous (whole wheat cooks faster) or bulgur
SUGAR, DARK-BROWN	1 cup	1 cup light-brown sugar, packed; or 1 cup granulated sugar plus 2 to 3 tablespoons molasses
SUGAR, GRANULATED	1 cup	1 cup firmly packed brown sugar; or 1¾ cups confectioners' sugar (makes baked goods less crisp); or 1 cup superfine sugar
SUGAR, LIGHT-BROWN	1 cup	1 cup granulated sugar plus 1 to 2 tablespoons molasses; or ½ cup dark-brown sugar plus ½ cup granulated sugar
SWEETENED CONDENSED MILK	1 can (14 oz.)	1 cup evaporated milk plus 1¼ cups granulated sugar. Combine and heat until sugar dissolves.
VANILLA BEAN	1-inch bean	1 teaspoon vanilla extract
VINEGAR, APPLE-CIDER	—	malt, white-wine, or rice vinegar
VINEGAR, BALSAMIC	1 tablespoon	1 tablespoon red- or white-wine vinegar plus ½ teaspoon sugar
VINEGAR, RED-WINE	—	white-wine, sherry, champagne, or balsamic vinegar
VINEGAR, RICE	—	apple-cider, champagne, or white-wine vinegar
VINEGAR, WHITE-WINE	—	apple-cider, champagne, fruit (raspberry), rice, or red-wine vinegar
YEAST	1 cake (⅗ oz.)	1 package (¼ ounce) or 1 scant tablespoon active dried yeast
YOGURT, PLAIN	1 cup	1 cup sour cream (thicker; less tart) or buttermilk (thinner; use in baking, dressings, sauces)

REFERENCE

Types of Fat

One way to minimize your total blood cholesterol is to manage the amount and types of fat in your diet. Aim for monounsaturated and polyunsaturated fats; avoid saturated and trans fats.

MONOUNSATURATED FAT lowers LDL (bad cholesterol) and may raise HDL (good cholesterol) or leave it unchanged; found in almonds, avocados, canola oil, cashews, olive oil, peanut oil, and peanuts.

POLYUNSATURATED FAT lowers LDL and may lower HDL; includes omega-3 and omega-6 fatty acids; found in corn oil, cottonseed oil, fish such as salmon and tuna, safflower oil, sesame seeds, soybeans, and sunflower oil.

SATURATED FAT raises both LDL and HDL; found in chocolate, cocoa butter, coconut oil, dairy products (milk, butter, cheese, ice cream), egg yolks, palm oil, and red meat.

TRANS FAT raises LDL and lowers HDL; a type of fat common in many processed foods, such as most margarines (especially stick), vegetable shortening, partially hydrogenated vegetable oil, many commercial fried foods (doughnuts, french fries), and commercial baked goods (cookies, crackers, cakes).

FREEZER STORAGE TIME
(freezer temperature 0°F or colder)

PRODUCT	MONTHS IN FREEZER
FRESH MEAT	
Beef	6 to 12
Lamb	6 to 9
Veal	6 to 9
Pork	4 to 6
Ground beef, veal, lamb, pork	3 to 4
Frankfurters	1 to 2
Sausage, fresh pork	1 to 2
Cold cuts	Not recommended
FRESH POULTRY	
Chicken, turkey (whole)	12
Chicken, turkey (pieces)	6 to 9
Cornish game hen, game birds	6 to 9
Giblets	3 to 4
COOKED POULTRY	
Breaded, fried	4
Pieces, plain	4
Pieces covered with broth, gravy	6
FRESH FISH AND SEAFOOD	
Clams, mussels, oysters, scallops, shrimp	3 to 6
Fatty fish (bluefish, mackerel, perch, salmon)	2 to 3
Lean fish (flounder, haddock, sole)	6
FRESH FRUIT (PREPARED FOR FREEZING)	
All except those listed next	10 to 12

PRODUCT	MONTHS IN FREEZER
Avocados, bananas, plantains	3
Lemons, limes, oranges	4 to 6
FRESH VEGETABLES (PREPARED FOR FREEZING)	
Beans, beets, bok choy, broccoli, brussels sprouts, cabbage, carrots, cauliflower, celery, corn, greens, kohlrabi, leeks, mushrooms, okra, onions, peas, peppers, soybeans, spinach, summer squashes	10 to 12
Asparagus, rutabagas, turnips	8 to 10
Artichokes, eggplant	6 to 8
Tomatoes (overripe or sliced)	2
Bamboo shoots, cucumbers, endive, lettuce, radishes, watercress	Not recommended
CHEESE (except those listed below)	6
Cottage cheese, cream cheese, feta, goat, fresh mozzarella, Neufchâtel, Parmesan, processed cheese (opened)	Not recommended
DAIRY PRODUCTS	
Margarine (not diet)	12
Butter	6 to 9
Cream, half-and-half	4
Milk	3
Ice cream	1 to 2

REFERENCE

WHEN TO REPLACE/CLEAN/RENEW COMMON HOUSEHOLD ITEMS

How long do commonly used food products stay viable or safe after opening or using? What are the recommended time frames for replacing or cleaning things—inside and outside the home? Here are some guidelines for items found around the house.

ITEM	STATUS	STORAGE	DURATION	TIPS
Baking soda	Open	Pantry, cupboard	6 months	Put a little in bowl, add lemon juice or vinegar. If it fizzes, it's still suitable for baking.
Butter	Open	Counter	1 to 2 days	Can turn rancid; refrigeration will extend life.
	Open	Refrigerator	1 to 2 months	
Jelly/jam	Open	Refrigerator	6 to 12 months	Replace if smell or color changes; mold may occur.
Mayonnaise	Open	Refrigerator	2 months	Throw away if discoloration or odor occurs.
Nut oils	Open	Pantry, cupboard	3 to 8 months	Store in a cool, dry place; refrigeration may extend life.
Olive/ vegetable oil	Open	Pantry, cupboard	3 to 5 months	Store in a cool, dry place; refrigeration may extend life.
Peanut butter	Open	Pantry, cupboard	2 to 3 months	Replace if rancid taste or smell occurs.
	Open	Refrigerator	6 to 9 months	
Red/white wine	Open	Refrigerator	2 to 5 days	Use a stopper for a tight seal.

ITEM	USE	STORAGE	REPLACE	TIPS
20-lb. propane tank	As needed	Outside	10 to 12 years	Can not be refilled past date on tank; recertified tanks good for additional 5 years.
Bleach	As needed	Laundry area	6 to 12 months	Will begin to break down after 6 months.
Fire extinguisher	As needed	Kitchen, other	12 years	Check gauge monthly to ensure factory-recommended pressure level.
Gasoline for equipment	As needed	Shed, detached garage	3 to 6 months	Store in tightly closed container, away from heat sources and light.
Smoke alarms	Ongoing	Bedrooms, hallways	10 years	Test monthly to ensure proper function.
Sponges	Daily	Kitchen	1 to 2 weeks	To clean between replacements, soak in 1:10 bleach/warm water solution for 1 minute, microwave damp (if nonmetallic) for 1 minute, or run through dishwasher cycle.
Toothbrushes	Daily	Bathroom	3 to 4 months	Replace more often if bristles fray or when user(s) have been sick.

ITEM	USE	LOCATION	CLEAN	TIPS
Bird feeders	Daily	Outdoors	Twice a month	To avoid bacteria buildup, wash with soap and boiling water or diluted bleach solution; rinse and dry completely.
Chimney	Heating season	Furnace, fireplace	Once a year	Professional inspection will show if chimney sweep or maintenance is needed.
Dryer vent hose	Daily, weekly	Dryer to outdoor vent	Once a year	Clean lint trap after each use; if clothes do not dry properly, check/clean vent hose.
Gutters	During storms	Roofline	Twice a year	Leaves will be more prevalent during fall, so clean out more often.

REFERENCE

PLASTICS

In your quest to go green, use this guide to use and sort plastic. The number, usually found with a triangle symbol on a container, indicates the type of resin used to produce the plastic. Visit **EARTH911.COM** for recycling information in your state.

NUMBER 1 · *PETE or PET (polyethylene terephthalate)*

PETE

IS USED IN . . . . microwavable food trays; salad dressing, soft drink, water, and juice bottles

STATUS . . . . hard to clean; absorbs bacteria and flavors; avoid reusing

IS RECYCLED TO MAKE. . . carpet, furniture, new containers, Polar fleece

NUMBER 2 · *HDPE (high-density polyethylene)*

HDPE

IS USED IN . . . . household cleaner and shampoo bottles, milk jugs, cutting boards

STATUS . . . . transmits no known chemicals into food

IS RECYCLED TO MAKE. . . detergent bottles, fencing, floor tiles, pens

NUMBER 3 · *V or PVC (vinyl)*

V

IS USED IN . . . . clear food packaging, window frames, blister packs for medicine and retail packaging

STATUS . . . . is believed to contain phalates that interfere with hormonal development; avoid reusing

IS RECYCLED TO MAKE. . . cables, mud flaps, paneling, roadway gutters

NUMBER 4 · *LDPE (low-density polyethylene)*

LDPE

IS USED IN . . . . bread and shopping bags, carpet, clothing, furniture

STATUS . . . . transmits no known chemicals into food

IS RECYCLED TO MAKE. . . envelopes, floor tiles, lumber, trash-can liners

NUMBER 5 · *PP (polypropylene)*

PP

IS USED IN . . . . food storage containers, medicine and syrup bottles, drinking straws, yogurt tubs

STATUS . . . . transmits no known chemicals into food

IS RECYCLED TO MAKE. . . battery cables, brooms, ice scrapers, rakes

NUMBER 6 · *PS (polystyrene)*

PS

IS USED IN . . . . disposable cups and plates, egg cartons, take-out containers

STATUS . . . . is believed to leach styrene, a possible human carcinogen, into food; avoid reusing

IS RECYCLED TO MAKE. . . foam packaging, insulation, light switchplates, rulers

NUMBER 7 · *Other (miscellaneous)*

OTHER

IS USED IN . . . . 3- and 5-gallon water jugs, nylon, some food containers

STATUS . . . . contains bisphenol A, which has been linked to heart disease and obesity; avoid reusing

IS RECYCLED TO MAKE. . . . custom-made products

REFERENCE

Practical Uses for Household Ingredients

Baking soda, lemon juice, salt, and vinegar are kitchen staples. Did you know that there are other uses for these common ingredients? Keep these items stocked to help with housekeeping and to reduce your need for multiple costly cleaners.

BAKING SODA

■ To soothe an insect bite/sting, apply a paste of baking soda and water.

■ Clean toothbrushes by soaking them in a mixture of 2 tablespoons of baking soda and 1 cup of warm water for 15 minutes and then allowing them to air-dry.

■ Remove gas and oil odors from clothing by allowing it to sit in a trash bag with baking soda for at least 24 hours prior to washing.

■ Remove coffee stains from mugs and tomato sauce stains from plastic containers by wiping them with a damp sponge dipped in baking soda paste.

■ To remove pesticides and/or dirt, wash fresh fruit and vegetables in a mixture of 2 teaspoons of baking soda and 2 cups of water.

LEMON

■ To keep insects away while painting outdoors, add a few drops of lemon juice to house paint.

■ Clean discolored kitchen utensils with a cloth dipped in lemon juice. Rinse with warm water.

■ Freshen the air in your house by simmering a pot of sliced lemons and water on the stovetop.

■ Dry out a poison ivy rash by applying lemon juice for about 15 minutes before rinsing off with cool water. Repeat as necessary.

■ Lighten hair color by rinsing with a mixture of 1 part lemon juice and 2 parts water.

SALT

■ Kill weeds in driveway cracks and between bricks and stones by pouring boiling salted water over them.

■ To relieve a sore throat, gargle with warm saltwater (¼ teaspoon salt to 1 cup water).

■ Sprinkle salt on carpets to dry muddy footprints. Allow it to sit for 15 minutes, then vacuum.

■ Rub a paste of salt and olive oil over watermarks on wood with a sponge until removed.

■ Revive kitchen sponges by soaking them in a saltwater solution (¼ cup salt per liter of water) overnight.

VINEGAR

■ To loosen a bumper sticker, cover it for up to 5 minutes with a paper towel saturated in white vinegar. Slowly peel the sticker off and remove any bumper residue with a clean cloth wet with white vinegar.

■ Run white vinegar through a brewing cycle to clean drip coffeemakers. Rinse thoroughly by running two brewing cycles with water before using.

■ Apply white vinegar to disinfect wooden cutting boards.

■ Clean tile grout by spraying it with diluted white vinegar. Leave for 10 minutes and then scrub.

■ To deter ants, spray a solution of equal parts white vinegar and water on kitchen surfaces.

SIGN LANGUAGE: WHAT'S THE TITLE?

Use the alphabet below to decode.

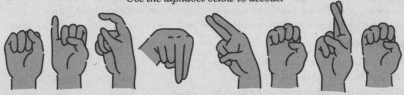

____ ____ ____ ____ ____ ____ ____ ____

Sign language is a way to communicate without using your voice. It involves using your hands, body posture, and facial expressions. Although sign language is used mostly by people who are deaf or can't hear well, it can be used by anyone. There are even animals that use sign language. A gorilla named Koko learned more than 1,000 signs! In North America, we use American Sign Language, but there are different versions across the world.

Using the alphabet below, spell your name.

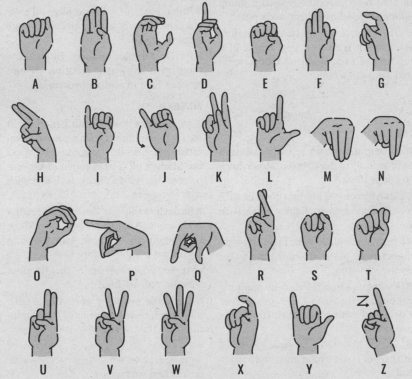

REFERENCE

Illustrations: Antonov Maxim/Shutterstock

Here are some common signs and phrases to get you started . . .

HELLO: Open your hand with all of your fingers pointing up and your thumb crossed in front of your palm. Touch the side of your forehead, then quickly move your hand away from your head.

NO: Open and close your index and middle finger over your thumb twice.

I LOVE YOU: With your palm facing out, hold up your thumb, index finger, and pinky.

GOOD-BYE: Open your palm, fold down your fingers, then open your palm again. Repeat once or twice.

FAMILY: Make an "F" sign with each hand, palms facing out, with thumbs touching. Move your hands away from each other, making a circle in front of you. End with the backs of your hands facing out.

LOVE: Make a fist with each hand and cross your arms over your chest.

PLEASE: Open your hand and rub your chest in a circular motion.

YES: Make an "S" sign and bend your wrist forward like you are nodding "yes."

SORRY: Make an "S" sign and rub your chest in a circular motion toward your shoulder.

THANK YOU: Open your hand and touch your chin with your fingertips. Move the hand away from you.

REFERENCE

TALKING ABOUT MY GENERATION

While we often refer to those born during a particular time span as being of a certain generation, we sometimes forget that each such period also saw the "arrival" of other interesting historical phenomena—which are thus of the same "generation." The sampling provided here is just a glimpse—to spur discussion and reflection.

GENERATION	DEFINING MOMENTS	ASTRONOMY	WEATHER	INVENTION
Greatest (b. 1901-27)	First flight—Wright Brothers, Kitty Hawk, N.C. (1903) World War I (1914-18) Spanish Flu (1918-19) Women's right to vote ratified (1920)	Halley's Comet (1910) Black holes predicted (1916) First liquid propellant rocket launch (1926)	Great Tri-State Tornado (MO, IL, IN; 1925) Mississippi River flood (1927)	Air-conditioning (1902) Neon light (1910) Band-Aid (1920) Traffic signal (1923) Television (1927)
Silent (b. 1928-45)	The Great Depression (1929-39) World War II (1939-45) United Nations established (1945)	Pluto found (1930) Space radio waves detected (1932) Dark matter discovered (1933)	Dust Bowl (1930s) Great New England Hurricane (1938)	Scotch transparent tape (1930) Nylon (1935) Microwave oven (1945) Atomic Bomb (1945)
Baby Boomers (b. 1946-64)	Korean War (1950-53) March on Washington/ MLK Jr. "I Have a Dream" speech (1963) John F. Kennedy assassination (1963)	NASA created (1958) First American in space (Shepard; 1961) *Mariner 2* Venus flyby (1962)	First tornado forecast (OK; 1948) First weather satellite, *TIROS I*, launched (1960)	Tupperware (1946) Product bar codes (1952) First working laser (1960) Zip codes (1963)
Gen X (b. 1965-80)	Vietnam War (1964-73) Woodstock (1969) Watergate scandal/Nixon resignation (1972-74) U.S. Bicentennial (1976)	Leonids (40 shooting stars per second, U.S. West; 1966) Moon landing (1969) Uranus's rings discovered (1977)	NOAA formed (1970) The Great Blizzard (U.S. Midwest; 1978)	First video game console, Magnavox Odyssey (1972) Magic (later Rubik's) Cube (1974) GPS (1978)
Millennial/ Gen Y (b. 1981-96)	First woman Supreme Court justice (O'Connor; 1981) Gulf War (1991) Oklahoma City bombing (1995)	*Challenger* explosion (1986) Northern lights (seen as far south as FL, TX; 1989) Hubble Telescope launch (1990)	Hurricane Andrew (FL, LA; 1992) Storm of the Century (U.S. East; 1993)	Apple Macintosh computer (1984) Disposable contact lenses (1987) World Wide Web (1989)
Gen Z (b. 1997-2010/12)	Y2K (1999/2000) September 11 attacks (2001) Great Recession (2007-09) First Black U.S. president elected (Obama; 2008)	*Columbia* explosion (2003) Pluto reclassified as dwarf planet (2006)	Hurricane Katrina (LA, MS; 2005) Super Tuesday tornado outbreak (U.S. South; 2008)	Camera phone (1997) YouTube (2005) iPhone (2007)

REFERENCE